Michael R. Heithaus

Director, School of Environment and Society
Associate Professor, Department of Biological Sciences
Florida International University
North Miami, Florida

Mike Heithaus joined the Florida International University Biology Department in 2003. He has served as Director of the Marine Sciences Program and is now Director of the School of Environment and Society, which brings together the natural and social sciences and humanities to develop solutions to today's environmental challenges. While earning his doctorate, he began the research that grew into the Shark Bay Ecosystem Project in Western Australia, with which he still works. Back in the U.S., he served as a Research Fellow with National Geographic, using remote imaging in his research and hosting a 13-part *Crittercam* television series on the National Geographic Channel. His current research centers on predator-prey interactions among vertebrates, such as tiger sharks, dolphins, dugongs, sea turtles, and cormorants.

Donna M. Ogle

Professor of Reading and Language
National-Louis University
Chicago, Illinois

Creator of the well-known KWL strategy, Donna Ogle has directed many staff development projects translating theory and research into school practice in middle and secondary schools throughout the United States. She is a past president of the International Reading Association and has served as a consultant on literacy projects worldwide. Her extensive international experience includes coordinating the Reading and Writing for Critical Thinking Project in Eastern Europe, developing an integrated curriculum for a USAID Afghan Education Project, and speaking and consulting on projects in several Latin American countries and in Asia. Her books include *Coming Together as Readers; Reading Comprehension: Strategies for Independent Learners; All Children Read;* and *Literacy for a Democratic Society.*

Teacher Advisory Board

Program Advisors/Reviewers

Program Advisors

Rose Pringle, Ph.D.
Associate Professor
School of Teaching and Learning
College of Education
University of Florida
Gainesville, FL

Carolyn Staudt, M.Ed.
Curriculum Designer for Technology
KidSolve, Inc. / The Concord Consortium
Concord, MA

Content Reviewers

Paul D. Asimow, Ph.D.
Associate Professor of Geology and Geochemistry
Division of Geological and Planetary Sciences
California Institute of Technology
Pasadena, CA

Nigel S. Atkinson, Ph.D.
Professor of Neurobiology
Section of Neurobiology
The University of Texas at Austin
Austin, TX

Laura K. Baumgartner, Ph.D.
Postdoctoral Researcher
Pace Laboratory
Molecular, Cellular, and Developmental Biology
University of Colorado
Boulder, CO

Sonal Blumenthal, Ph.D.
Science Education Consultant
Austin, TX

Eileen Cashman, Ph.D.
Professor
Department of Environmental Resources Engineering
Humboldt State University
Arcata, CA

Wesley N. Colley, Ph.D.
Senior Research Scientist
Center for Modeling, Simulation, and Analysis
The University of Alabama in Huntsville
Huntsville, AL

Joe W. Crim, Ph.D.
Professor Emeritus
Department of Cellular Biology
The University of Georgia
Athens, GA

Elizabeth A. De Stasio, Ph.D.
Raymond H. Herzog Professor of Science
Professor of Biology
Department of Biology
Lawrence University
Appleton, WI

John E. Hoover, Ph.D.
Professor
Department of Biology
Millersville University
Millersville, PA

Charles W. Johnson, Ph.D.
Chairman, Division of Natural Sciences, Mathematics and Physical Education
Associate Professor of Physics
South Georgia College
Douglas, GA

Ping H. Johnson, Ph.D.
Associate Professor
Department of Health, Physical Education and Sport Science
Kennesaw State University
Kennesaw, GA

Tatiana A. Krivosheev, Ph.D.
Associate Professor of Physics
Department of Natural Sciences
Clayton State University
Morrow, GA

Louise McCullough, M.D., Ph.D.
Associate Professor of Neurology and Neuroscience
Director of Stroke Research and Education
University of Connecticut Health Center &
The Stroke Center at Hartford Hospital
Farmington, CT

Mark Moldwin, Ph.D.
Professor of Space Sciences
Atmospheric, Oceanic and Space Sciences
University of Michigan
Ann Arbor, MI

Hilary Clement Olson, Ph.D.
Research Scientist Associate V
Institute for Geophysics, Jackson School of Geosciences
The University of Texas at Austin
Austin, TX

Russell S. Patrick, Ph.D.
Professor of Physics
Department of Biology, Chemistry, and Physics
Southern Polytechnic State University
Marietta, GA

James L. Pazun, Ph.D.
Professor and Chairman
Chemistry and Physics
Pfeiffer University
Misenheimer, NC

L. Jeanne Perry, Ph.D.
Director (Retired)
Protein Expression Technology Center
Institute for Genomics and Proteomics
University of California, Los Angeles
Los Angeles, CA

Kenneth H. Rubin, Ph.D.
Professor
Department of Geology and Geophysics
University of Hawaii
Honolulu, HI

Michael J. Ryan, Ph.D.
Clark Hubbs Regents Professor in Zoology
Section of Integrative Biology
University of Texas
Austin, TX

Brandon E. Schwab, Ph.D.
Associate Professor
Department of Geology
Humboldt State University
Arcata, CA

Miles R. Silman, Ph.D.
Associate Professor
Department of Biology
Wake Forest University
Winston-Salem, NC

Marllin L. Simon, Ph.D.
Associate Professor
Department of Physics
Auburn University
Auburn, AL

Matt A. Wood, Ph.D.
Professor
Department of Physics & Space Sciences
Florida Institute of Technology
Melbourne, FL

Adam D. Woods, Ph.D.
Associate Professor
Department of Geological Sciences
California State University, Fullerton
Fullerton, CA

Teacher Reviewers

Lamica Caldwell
Tavares Middle School
Tavares, FL

Brad Carreker
Foundation Academy
Winter Garden, FL

Lynda L. Garrett, M.Ed.
Gamble Rogers Middle School
St. Augustine, FL

Barbara A. Humphreys
New River Middle School
Fort Lauderdale, FL

Lisa J. Larson
Conway Middle School
Orlando, FL

Sabine R. Laser
St. Cloud Middle School
St. Cloud, FL

Stacy Loeak
Rodgers Middle School
Riverview, FL

Susan McKinney
Nova Middle School
Davie, FL

Mindy N. Pearson, M.Ed. & NBCT
Van Buren Middle School
Tampa, FL

Kathleen M. Poe
Fletcher Middle School
Jacksonville Beach, FL

Barbara Riley
Science Education Consultant
Merritt Island, FL

Kimberly Scarola, M.Ed.
Pembroke Pines Charter Middle School
Pembroke Pines, FL

Leyla Shaughnessy, M.Ed.
Jones High School
Orlando, FL

Nancy Sneed Stitt, M.S.
Science Instructional Coach
Pinellas Park High School
Largo, FL

Contents
in Brief

Plants use the sun's energy to produce food.

© Houghton Mifflin Harcourt Publishing Company • Image Credits: (tr) ©Oleg Shpak/Alamy; (bc) ©Dorling Kindersley/Getty Images

I want to learn how Burmese pythons ended up in Florida!

Contents

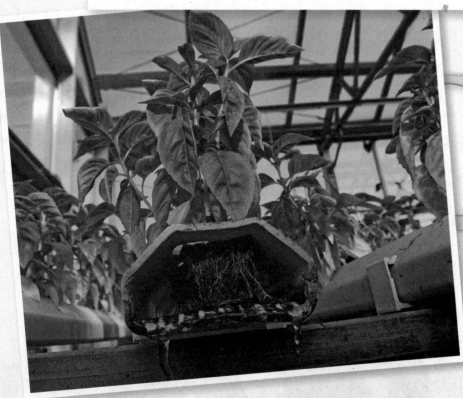

Modern agriculture allows us to grow plants anywhere. Plants can even grow without soil!

It's fascinating to see how cells work. We can watch a plant cell divide!

Assignments:

_____

_____

_____

_____

_____

Contents (continued)

My brain controls everything I do. It's my body's control center.

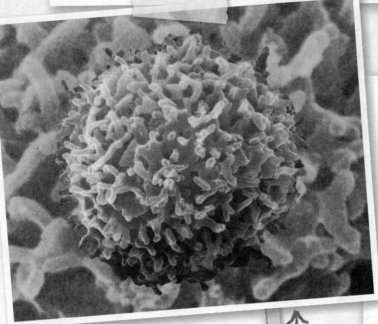

White blood cells patrol our bodies to keep out invaders.

Assignments:

Contents (continued)

This blue frog uses hemoglobins in its red blood cells to get oxygen from air. Human beings do the same thing!

© Houghton Mifflin Harcourt Publishing Company • Image Credits: ©www.lifeonwhite.eu/Alamy

Assignments:
_____
_____
_____
_____
_____
_____
_____
_____
_____
_____

During fertilization, male sperm fight to enter the female egg. It's a race to the finish line!

Contents (continued)

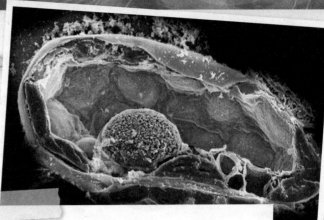

It's fascinating that some cells can make their own food!

Assignments:
_____
_____
_____
_____
_____
_____
_____

Power up
with *Science* *Fusion!*

Your program fuses...

Online Virtual Experiences

Inquiry-Based Labs and Activities

Active Reading and Writing

... to generate energy for today's science learner — you.

Active Reading and Writing

Be an active reader and make this book your own!

You can answer questions, ask questions, create graphs, make notes, write your own ideas, and highlight information right in your book.

By the end of the school year, your book will become a record of the knowledge and skills you learned in science.

Inquiry-Based Labs and Activities

ScienceFusion includes lots of exciting hands-on inquiry labs and activities, each one designed to bring science skills and concepts to life and get you involved.

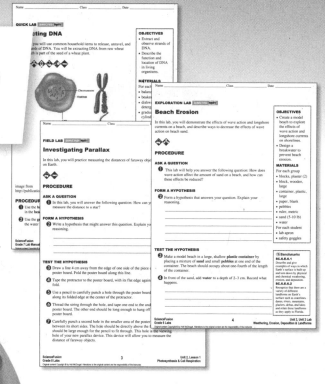

By asking questions, testing your ideas, organizing and analyzing data, drawing conclusions, and sharing what you learn...

You are the scientist!

Online Virtual Experiences

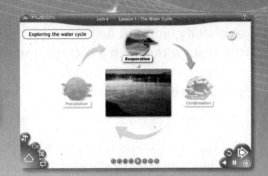

Explore cool labs, activities, interactive lessons, and videos in the virtual world—where science comes alive and you make it happen.

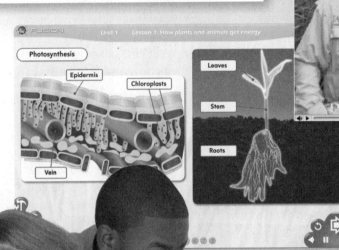

See your science lessons from a completely different point of view—a digital point of view.

Science Fusion!
is a new source of energy... just for YOU!

Sunshine State Standards

An Overview and What It Means to You

This book and this class are structured around the Next Generation Sunshine State Standards. As you read, experiment, and study, you will be learning what you need to know to take the tests with which educators measure your progress. You will also be continuing to build your science literacy, which makes you a more skillful person both in and out of school.

The test you'll take in eighth grade is intended to measure how well you learned scientific facts and procedures, and how well you can apply them to situations you might find in the real world. What you remember long after that test, called enduring understandings, will help you see, measure, interpret, and evaluate many more situations you encounter in life.

The Next Generation Sunshine State Standards grew out of 18 Big Ideas that describe major themes and overarching concepts in science. The Big Ideas and Benchmarks appear throughout your book. Look for them on the opening pages of each Unit and Lesson.

The next few pages address several questions, including:

- What are the standards underlying the instruction?
- Where is each Benchmark found in this book?
- What makes the Benchmarks relevant to you now?
- What kinds of questions will you be asked in the tests?

Notice the **Essential Question** on the Lesson opener. This question is a hint to the enduring understanding you may take away from this lesson, long after you've studied it and passed a test and perhaps forgotten some of the details.

Find the name and number of the **Big Ideas** for the unit on the Unit opener.

Find the **Benchmarks** for each lesson on the Lesson opener.

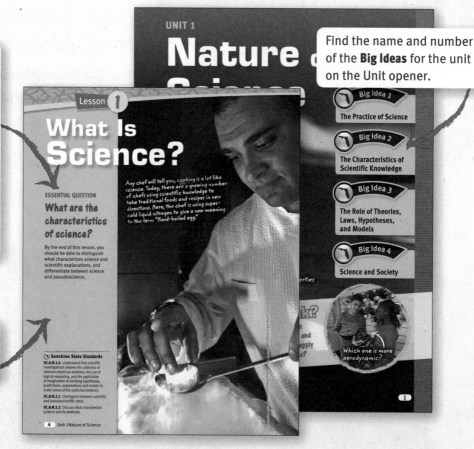

Big Idea 1 The Practice of Science

What It Means to You

You have done science without knowing it. If you've ever tried to understand something new to you by drawing on what you already knew, you have thought scientifically. Science is more than a collection of facts or the following of one method. It is an attempt to understand the natural world in a way agreed upon by all.

Benchmarks

SC.6.N.1.1 Define a problem from the sixth grade curriculum, use appropriate reference materials to support scientific understanding, plan and carry out scientific investigation of various types, such as systematic observations or experiments, identify variables, collect and organize data, interpret data in charts, tables, and graphics, analyze information, make predictions, and defend conclusions.
Where to Check It Out Unit 2, Lesson 2

SC.6.N.1.2 Explain why scientific investigations should be replicable.
Where to Check It Out Unit 1, Lesson 3

SC.6.N.1.3 Explain the difference between an experiment and other types of scientific investigation, and explain the relative benefits and limitations of each.
Where to Check It Out Unit 5, Lesson 1

SC.6.N.1.4 Discuss, compare, and negotiate methods used, results obtained, and explanations among groups of students conducting the same investigation.
Where to Check It Out Unit 1, Think Science

SC.6.N.1.5 Recognize that science involves creativity, not just in designing experiments, but also in creating explanations that fit evidence.
Where to Check It Out Unit 1, Lesson 1

SC.7.N.1.1 Define a problem from the seventh grade curriculum, use appropriate reference materials to support scientific understanding, plan and carry out scientific investigation of various types, such as systematic observations or experiments, identify variables, collect and organize data, interpret data in charts, tables, and graphics, analyze information, make predictions, and defend conclusions.
Where to Check It Out Unit 7, Lesson 1

SC.7.N.1.2 Differentiate replication (by others) from repetition (multiple trials).
Where to Check It Out Unit 1, Lesson 3

SC.7.N.1.3 Distinguish between an experiment (which must involve the identification and control of variables) and other forms of scientific investigation and explain that not all scientific knowledge is derived from experimentation.
Where to Check It Out Unit 5, Think Science

SC.7.N.1.4 Identify test variables (independent variables) and outcome variables (dependent variables) in an experiment.
Where to Check It Out Unit 7, Think Science

SC.7.N.1.5 Describe the methods used in the pursuit of a scientific explanation as seen in different fields of science such as biology, geology, and physics.
Where to Check It Out Unit 7, Lesson 1

SC.7.N.1.6 Explain that empirical evidence is the cumulative body of observations of a natural phenomenon on which scientific explanations are based.
Where to Check It Out Unit 1, Lesson 1

SC.7.N.1.7 Explain that scientific knowledge is the result of a great deal of debate and confirmation within the science community.
Where to Check It Out Unit 1, Lesson 2

SC.8.N.1.1 Define a problem from the curriculum using appropriate reference materials to support scientific understanding, plan and carry out scientific investigations of various types, such as systematic observations or experiments, identify variables, collect and organize data, interpret data in charts, tables, and graphics, analyze information, make predictions, and defend conclusions.
Where to Check It Out Unit 1, Lesson 3

SC.8.N.1.2 Design and conduct a study using repeated trials and replication.
Where to Check It Out Unit 1, Lesson 3

SC.8.N.1.3 Use phrases such as "results support" or "fail to support" in science, understanding that science does not offer conclusive "proof" of a knowledge claim.
Where to Check It Out Unit 1, Lesson 2

SC.8.N.1.4 Explain how hypotheses are valuable if they lead to further investigations, even if they turn out not to be supported by the data.
Where to Check It Out Unit 1, Lesson 3

SC.8.N.1.5 Analyze the methods used to develop a scientific explanation as seen in different fields of science.
Where to Check It Out Unit 1, Lessons 2, 3, & 4

SC.8.N.1.6 Understand that scientific investigations involve the collection of relevant empirical evidence, the use of logical reasoning, and the application of imagination in devising hypotheses, predictions, explanations and models to make sense of the collected evidence.
Where to Check It Out Unit 1, Lessons 1 & 4

Nature of Science

Big Idea 2 The Characteristics of Scientific Knowledge

What It Means to You

Scientific knowledge is different from other forms of thought because it is based on empirical evidence, or evidence gained by the senses. Scientists gather a lot of empirical evidence before they try to form explanations from it. What this means is that scientific knowledge can be tested and measured. It can change when new evidence arises. Scientific knowledge is more than one person's opinion.

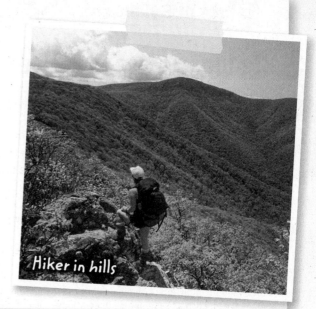

Hiker in hills

Benchmarks

SC.6.N.2.1 Distinguish science from other activities involving thought.
Where to Check It Out Unit 1, Lesson 1

SC.6.N.2.2 Explain that scientific knowledge is durable because it is open to change as new evidence or interpretations are encountered.
Where to Check It Out Unit 1, Lesson 2

SC.6.N.2.3 Recognize that scientists who make contributions to scientific knowledge come from all kinds of backgrounds and possess varied talents, interests, and goals.
Where to Check It Out Unit 3, People in Science

SC.7.N.2.1 Identify an instance from the history of science in which scientific knowledge has changed when new evidence or new interpretations are encountered.
Where to Check It Out Unit 1, Lesson 2

SC.8.N.2.1 Distinguish between scientific and pseudoscientific ideas.
Where to Check It Out Unit 1, Lesson 1

SC.8.N.2.2 Discuss what characterizes science and its methods.
Where to Check It Out Unit 1, Lesson 1

Sample Question Circle the correct answer.

1 Astrologers relate the locations of stars and planets to events in humans lives. Centuries ago, astrology was thought to be a science. Why do scientists today classify it as a pseudoscience?

A. Astrology came before the telescope.

B. The claims made by astrologers cannot be measured and tested accurately.

C. Stars and planets can't be distinguished from one another.

D. Scientists distrust anything from the past.

Big Idea 3 The Role of Theories, Laws, Hypotheses, and Models

What It Means to You

Learning science is like learning a language. Terms like *theory*, *model*, and *law*, while used loosely in everyday language, have specific meanings in science.

Benchmarks

SC.6.N.3.1 Recognize and explain that a scientific theory is a well-supported and widely accepted explanation of nature and is not simply a claim posed by an individual. Thus, the use of the term theory in science is very different than how it is used in everyday life.
Where to Check It Out Unit 1, Lesson 2

SC.6.N.3.2 Recognize and explain that a scientific law is a description of a specific relationship under given conditions in the natural world. Thus, scientific laws are different from societal laws.
Where to Check It Out Unit 9, Lesson 2

SC.6.N.3.3 Give several examples of scientific laws.
Where to Check It Out Unit 1, Lesson 4

SC.6.N.3.4 Identify the role of models in the context of the sixth grade science benchmarks.
Where to Check It Out Unit 1, Lesson 4

SC.7.N.3.1 Recognize and explain the difference between theories and laws and give several examples of scientific theories and the evidence that supports them.
Where to Check It Out Unit 1, Lesson 2

SC.7.N.3.2 Identify the benefits and limitations of the use of scientific models.
Where to Check It Out Unit 1, Lesson 4

SC.8.N.3.1 Select models useful in relating the results of their own investigations.
Where to Check It Out Unit 1, Lesson 4

SC.8.N.3.2 Explain why theories may be modified but are rarely discarded.
Where to Check It Out Unit 1, Lesson 2

Big Idea 4 Science and Society

What It Means to You

Science should be important to you, because it affects your life. Lawmakers base many decisions on how we live on science. The more scientifically literate you become, the better able you will be to understand these decisions and influence them. Science both affects and is affected by society.

Benchmarks

SC.8.N.4.1 Explain that science is one of the processes that can be used to inform decision making at the community, state, national, and international levels.
Where to Check It Out Unit 1, Lesson 5

SC.8.N.4.2 Explain how political, social, and economic concerns can affect science, and vice versa.
Where to Check It Out Unit 1, Lesson 5

Sample Question Circle the correct answer.

2 Which of the following best describes a way economics can affect science?

A. Limited funding may cause scientists to research one topic over another.

B. Legislators may make laws about the use of natural resources based on scientific findings.

C. A health crisis may cause scientists to drop some research to focus on finding a vaccine.

D. Health officials in a town may limit swimming in a lake based on pollution regulations.

Sunshine State Standards (continued)

Big Idea 14 Organization and Development of Living Organisms

What It Means to You

You're not as different from a plant as you might think. All living things share some characteristics. Like the tiniest bacteria, you also are composed of cells that perform the basic functions necessary for life. More complex organisms have specialized cells, which can form structures such as tissue and organs. Your body is made up of organ systems that work together to keep you alive.

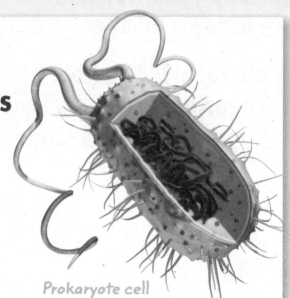

Prokaryote cell

Benchmarks

SC.6.L.14.1 Describe and identify patterns in the hierarchical organization of organisms from atoms to molecules and cells to tissues to organs to organ systems to organisms.
Where to Check It Out Unit 2, Lessons 2 & 4

SC.6.L.14.2 Investigate and explain the components of the scientific theory of cells (cell theory): all organisms are composed of cells (single-celled or multi-cellular), all cells come from pre-existing cells, and cells are the basic unit of life.
Where to Check It Out Unit 2, Lesson 1

SC.6.L.14.3 Recognize and explore how cells of all organisms undergo similar processes to maintain homeostasis, including extracting energy from food, getting rid of waste, and reproducing.
Where to Check It Out Unit 2, Lesson 5

SC.6.L.14.4 Compare and contrast the structure and function of major organelles of plant and animal cells, including cell wall, cell membrane, nucleus, cytoplasm, chloroplasts, mitochondria, and vacuoles.
Where to Check It Out Unit 2, Lesson 3

SC.6.L.14.5 Identify and investigate the general functions of the major systems of the human body (digestive, respiratory, circulatory, reproductive, excretory, immune, nervous, and musculoskeletal) and describe ways these systems interact with each other to maintain homeostasis.
Where to Check It Out Unit 3, Lessons 1, 2, 3, 4, 5, & 6

SC.6.L.14.6 Compare and contrast types of infectious agents that may infect the human body, including viruses, bacteria, fungi, and parasites.
Where to Check It Out Unit 4, Lesson 2

Sample Question Circle the correct answer.

3 Mariella is using a microscope to observe an organism from a sample of pond water. She observes that the cells of the organism have ribosomes, mitochondria, and lysosomes. She also observes that the cells do not have a cell wall. What type of organism is Mariella most likely to have found?

A. a plant

B. a fungus

C. an animal

D. a prokaryote

Big Idea 15 Diversity and Evolution of Living Organisms

What It Means to You

The cuttlefish is an amazing animal. It has a soft body with eight legs, like an octopus. What makes it really unique is the ability to change its appearance to hide from predators. It can look like a chunk of coral in a reef or blend in with a sandy ocean bottom. To scare a predator away, it may display bright colors along its skin. These abilities have been selected for by nature over time, through generations of genetic changes that have enabled the cuttlefish to stay alive. All living things, from earthworms to whales, have features that help them survive in their environments. Those organisms we see today have been the ones able to survive and reproduce. Much evidence shows that nature has guided the selection of species that can best survive in their particular environments.

Scientific illustration of a dinosaur

Benchmarks

SC.7.L.15.1 Recognize that fossil evidence is consistent with the scientific theory of evolution that living things evolved from earlier species.
Where to Check It Out Unit 5, Lessons 1 & 2

SC.7.L.15.2 Explore the scientific theory of evolution by recognizing and explaining ways in which genetic variation and environmental factors contribute to evolution by natural selection and diversity of organisms.
Where to Check It Out Unit 5, Lesson 1

SC.7.L.15.3 Explore the scientific theory of evolution by relating how the inability of a species to adapt within a changing environment may contribute to the extinction of that species.
Where to Check It Out Unit 5, Lesson 1

Sample Question Circle the correct answer.

4 Which of these conditions is **least likely** to cause a species to become extinct due to environmental changes?

A. less genetic variation

B. more genetic variation

C. specific food preferences

D. more competition for food

Big Idea 16 Heredity and Reproduction

What It Means to You

You are a storehouse of information. In each of your cells is a blueprint with the instructions that made you. These instructions are encoded in a substance called DNA. All living things have DNA. Each parent passes half of their DNA to their children, and this is why children and their parents share certain traits. Life on our planet depends on living things reproducing and passing their DNA to succeeding generations. Scientists even have succeeded in manipulating the DNA of some plants, such as corn, to yield varieties with more calories and better resistance to disease.

Cornstalks

Benchmarks

SC.7.L.16.1 Understand and explain that every organism requires a set of instructions that specifies its traits, that this hereditary information (DNA) contains genes located in the chromosomes of each cell, and that heredity is the passage of these instructions from one generation to another.
Where to Check It Out Unit 6, Lesson 4

SC.7.L.16.2 Determine the probabilities for genotype and phenotype combinations using Punnett Squares and pedigrees.
Where to Check It Out Unit 6, Lesson 5

SC.7.L.16.3 Compare and contrast the general processes of sexual reproduction requiring meiosis and asexual reproduction requiring mitosis.
Where to Check It Out Unit 6, Lessons 1, 2, & 3

SC.7.L.16.4 Recognize and explore the impact of biotechnology (cloning, genetic engineering, artificial selection) on the individual, society and the environment.
Where to Check It Out Unit 7, Lesson 2

Sample Question Circle the correct answer.

5 Delia is teaching her sister about important molecules in the body. She tells her sister that one type of molecule carries a set of instructions that determines traits, such as eye color or hair color. Which molecule is Delia describing?

A. DNA

B. glucose

C. cellulose

D. cholesterol

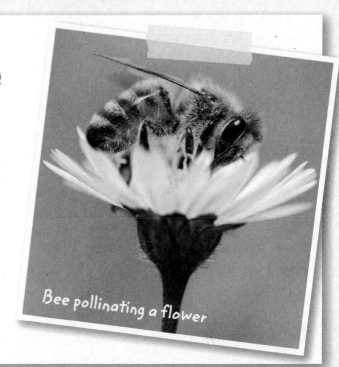

Bee pollinating a flower

Life Science

Big Idea 17 Interdependence

What It Means to You

You can't make it on your own. Every organism depends on others and the resources in its environment to survive. All organisms must share space, food, water, and other resources with the other organisms around them. Some organisms compete violently for these resources. Sometimes, they find it's better to work together to get them. Regardless of who is stronger or how well some may work together, there is only so much of any particular resource to go around. Resources can become even more limited through natural events, such as drought, and human activities that alter the environment.

Benchmarks

SC.7.L.17.1 Explain and illustrate the roles of and relationships among producers, consumers, and decomposers in the process of energy transfer in a food web.
Where to Check It Out Unit 8, Lesson 2

SC.7.L.17.2 Compare and contrast the relationships among organisms such as mutualism, predation, parasitism, competition, and commensalism.
Where to Check It Out Unit 8, Lesson 3

SC.7.L.17.3 Describe and investigate various limiting factors in the local ecosystem and their impact on native populations, including food, shelter, water, space, disease, parasitism, predation, and nesting sites.
Where to Check It Out Unit 8, Lesson 4

Sample Question Circle the correct answer.

6 Ecosystems have producers, decomposers, and consumers. Carnivores and scavengers are both types of consumers in an ecosystem. Which of the following is a characteristic of scavengers that makes them different from carnivores?

A. Scavengers eat only plant materials.

B. Scavengers eat only living organisms.

C. Scavengers eat only dead organisms.

D. Scavengers produce their own food.

Big Idea 18 Matter and Energy Transformations

What It Means to You

Ecosystems never sleep. Matter and energy are constantly moving through them. The light energy that plants get from the sun gets changed into chemical energy, which passes to animals when they eat the plants. When plants and animals die, their remains can provide energy and nutrients for other organisms.

Benchmarks

SC.8.L.18.1 Describe and investigate the process of photosynthesis, such as the roles of light, carbon dioxide, water and chlorophyll; production of food; release of oxygen.
Where to Check It Out Unit 9, Lesson 1

SC.8.L.18.2 Describe and investigate how cellular respiration breaks down food to provide energy and releases carbon dioxide.
Where to Check It Out Unit 9, Lesson 1

SC.8.L.18.3 Construct a scientific model of the carbon cycle to show how matter and energy are continuously transferred within and between organisms and their physical environment.
Where to Check It Out Unit 9, Lesson 2

SC.8.L.18.4 Cite evidence that living systems follow the Laws of Conservation of Mass and Energy.
Where to Check It Out Unit 9, Lesson 2

Sample Question Circle the correct answer.

7 Jamal is running a race this afternoon. He eats a big breakfast to make sure that he can reach the finish line because food provides the energy his cells need to complete any activity. What kind of energy is stored in food?

A. chemical energy

B. kinetic energy

C. light energy

D. mechanical energy

Additional Standards

The following standards from math, language arts, and health are part of this year's science curriculum. You will find them throughout the book, in the lessons where they best align.

Benchmarks

MA.6.S.6.2 Select and analyze the measures of central tendency or variability to represent, describe, analyze, and/or summarize a data set for the purposes of answering questions appropriately.

MA.6.A.3.6 Construct and analyze tables, graphs, and equations to describe linear functions and other simple relations using both common language and algebraic notation.

LA.6.2.2.3 The student will organize information to show understanding (e.g., representing main ideas within text through charting, mapping, paraphrasing, summarizing, or comparing/contrasting).

LA.6.4.2.2 The student will record information (e.g., observations, notes, lists, charts, legends) related to a topic, including visual aids to organize and record information and include a list of sources used.

HE.6.C.1.4 Recognize how heredity can affect personal health.

HE.6.C.1.8 Explain how body systems are impacted by hereditary factors and infectious agents.

UNIT 1
Nature of Science

Big Idea 1
The Practice of Science

Big Idea 2
The Characteristics of Scientific Knowledge

Big Idea 3
The Role of Theories, Laws, Hypotheses, and Models

Big Idea 4
Science and Society

Skier testing aerodynamic properties in a wind tunnel

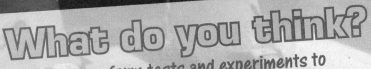
What do you think?

Scientists perform tests and experiments to answer questions, increase our knowledge, and improve the products we use. How can you apply scientific thought in your everyday activities?

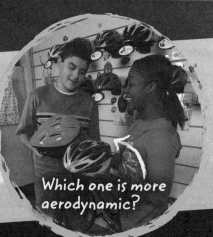
Which one is more aerodynamic?

Weather Myths

People have passed down many stories about predicting weather. Groundhog Day is a holiday based on a myth about predicting the end of winter. The story says that if a groundhog leaves its hole and does not see its shadow, winter will end in six weeks. This traditional method for predicting weather has no basis in science. Are any weather myths supported by science?

1 Think About It

Many people believe that the number of times a cricket chirps in a given time period is a way to determine the temperature. Why is it possible that this myth could be scientifically supported?

_____

_____

_____

✔ Count the number of chirps in 14 seconds, then add 40 to get the temperature in degrees Fahrenheit.

© Houghton Mifflin Harcourt Publishing Company • Image Credits: ©Nature Pics/Alamy Images

② Ask A Question

How can people test whether or not this is accurate?

As a class, design a plan for testing whether or not cricket chirps can accurately determine the temperature. Remember that crickets do not chirp all day long.

Things to Consider

✔ ☐ Is the temperature the same where your thermometer and cricket are located?

✔ ☐ Have you collected enough data and performed enough trials?

③ Apply Your Knowledge

A Determine what materials you will need to carry out your class plan.

_____
_____
_____

B Describe the procedure you will use to run your experiment. What will you specifically do to ensure your data lead to reliable results?

_____
_____
_____
_____
_____
_____
_____
_____

C Carry out your plan to test the cricket chirp theory. Record your data and results in a notebook. Analyze your results and write your conclusion below.

_____
_____
_____
_____
_____
_____
_____

Take It Home

Research other weather myths, especially any that are unique to your area. Do they have any basis in science? Share your findings with your class.

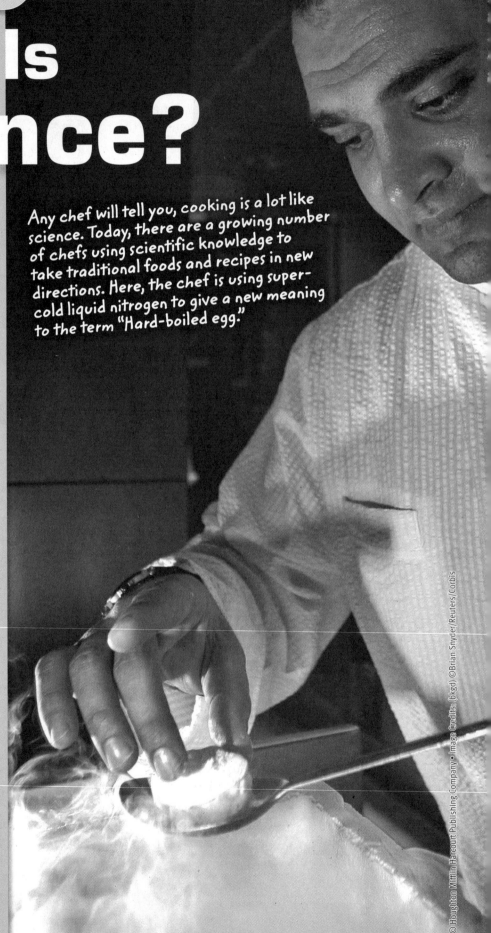

What Is Science?

ESSENTIAL QUESTION

What are the characteristics of science?

By the end of this lesson, you should be able to distinguish what characterizes science and scientific explanations, and differentiate between science and pseudoscience.

🔍 Sunshine State Standards

SC.6.N.1.5 Recognize that science involves creativity, not just in designing experiments, but also in creating explanations that fit evidence.

SC.6.N.2.1 Distinguish science from other activities involving thought.

SC.7.N.1.6 Explain that empirical evidence is the cumulative body of observations of a natural phenomenon on which scientific explanations are based

SC.8.N.1.6 Understand that scientific investigations involve the collection of relevant empirical evidence, the use of logical reasoning, and the application of imagination in devising hypotheses, predictions, explanations and models to make sense of the collected evidence.

SC.8.N.2.1 Distinguish between scientific and pseudoscientific ideas.

SC.8.N.2.2 Discuss what characterizes science and its methods.

LA.6.4.2.2 The student will record information (e.g., observations, notes, lists, charts, legends) related to a topic, including visual aids to organize and record information and include a list of sources used.

Any chef will tell you, cooking is a lot like science. Today, there are a growing number of chefs using scientific knowledge to take traditional foods and recipes in new directions. Here, the chef is using super-cold liquid nitrogen to give a new meaning to the term "Hard-boiled egg."

Engage Your Brain

1 Predict Check T or F to show whether you think each statement is true or false.

T F

☐ ☐ Science is the study of the natural world.

☐ ☐ Scientific explanations should be logical and testable.

☐ ☐ The methods of science can be used in other fields.

☐ ☐ Scientific explanations do not change.

☐ ☐ Creativity does not play a role in science.

2 Compose In this lamp, heating of the liquid at the bottom causes the wax globs in it to rise and fall in interesting patterns. What is a scientific question you could ask about this lamp? What is a non-scientific question you could ask about this lamp?

_____

_____

_____

_____

_____

Active Reading

3 Synthesize You can often define an unknown word if you know the meaning of its word parts. Use the word parts and sentence below to make an educated guess about the meaning of the word *pseudoscience*.

Word part	Meaning
pseudo-	false; pretending to be
science	the systematic study of the natural world

Example Sentence
Their belief that space aliens visited the Earth in ancient times is based on <u>pseudoscience</u> and faulty logic.

pseudoscience:

_____

_____

_____

Vocabulary Terms

• science
• empirical evidence
• pseudoscience

4 Apply As you learn the definition of each vocabulary term in this lesson, create your own definition or sketch to help you remember the meaning of the term.

Character Witness

What characterizes science?

Many people think of science as simply a collection of facts. **Science** is the systematic study of natural events and conditions. Scientific subjects can be anything in the living or nonliving world. In general, all scientific subjects can be broken down into three areas—life science, Earth science, and physical science.

Life science, or biology, is the study of living things. Life scientists may study anything from how plants produce food to how animals interact in the wild. Earth science, or geology, is the study of the surface and interior of Earth. An Earth scientist may study how rocks form or what past events produced the volcano you see in the photo. Physical science includes the subjects of physics and chemistry. Physicists and chemists study nonliving matter and energy. They may study the forces that hold matter together or the ways electromagnetic waves travel through space.

Of course, the three areas contain much more than this. Indeed, the subjects of science can seem practically limitless. As you will see, however, they all share some common characteristics and methods.

Community Consensus

One aspect that really sets the study of science apart from other pursuits is its need for openness and review. Whatever information one scientist collects, others must be able to see and comment upon.

The need for openness is important, because scientific ideas must be testable and reproducible. This means that if one scientist arrives at an explanation based on something he or she observed, that scientist must make the data available to other scientists. This allows others the chance to comment upon the results. For example, a scientist may claim that her evidence shows the volcano will erupt in five days. If the scientist declines to describe what that evidence is or how she collected it, why should anyone else think the claim is accurate?

5 Identify As you read, underline three areas of science.

Visualize It!

6 Predict What kinds of evidence might the scientists in the photo be collecting about the volcano?

_____

_____

7 Explain How might the study of volcanoes affect the people who live near them?

_____

_____

_____

Use of Empirical Evidence

If scientific evidence must be open to all, it needs to be the kind of evidence all can observe. It must be something measurable and not just one person's opinion or guess. Evidence in science must be evidence that can be gained by the senses or empirical evidence. **Empirical evidence** includes observations and measurements. It includes all the data that people gather and test to support and evaluate scientific explanations.

For example, a scientist studying a volcano would visit the volcano to get empirical evidence. The scientist might use specialized tools to make observations and take measurements. Many tools help scientists collect more accurate evidence. Tools often make collecting data safer. For example, few scientists would want to go to the top of the volcano and look down into it. Mounting a thermal camera on an airplane allows scientists to get an aerial shot of the volcano's mouth. Not only does the shot show the detail they want, but also it's a lot safer.

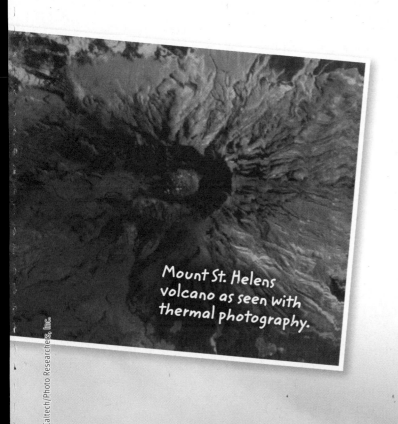

Mount St. Helens volcano as seen with thermal photography.

Scientists use special thermal cameras to take photographs that show the temperature regions of volcanoes.

"Give me an explanation..."

What is a scientific explanation?

Empirical evidence is the basis for scientific explanations. A scientific explanation provides a description of how a process in nature occurs. Scientific explanations are based on observations and data. Beliefs or opinions that are not based on explanations that can be tested are not scientific.

Scientists may begin developing an explanation by gathering all the empirical evidence they have. This could be the observations and measurements they have made or those from other scientists. Then they think logically about how all of this evidence fits together. The explanation they propose must fit all the available evidence.

Often, other scientists will then further evaluate the explanation by testing it for themselves. The additional observations and tests may provide data that further support the explanation. If the results do not support the explanation, the explanation is rejected or modified and retested.

Consider a scientific explanation for how metal rusts. Rust is a compound of oxygen and a metal, usually iron. Oxygen makes up one-fifth of the air we breathe. Therefore, rust may form when oxygen in the air combines with metal. We observe that most rusted metals have also been exposed to large amounts of water. We also observe that the rate of rusting increases if the water contains salt, as it does near oceans. A scientist would propose that water causes metal to rust and that salt increases the rate of rusting. How might you test this statement?

Active Reading

8 Apply As you read, underline the characteristics of a scientific explanation.

How is a scientific explanation evaluated?

So, how would you evaluate the explanation of why some metals rust? Look at the explanation below and start to consider what you know.

First, look at your empirical evidence. Think of all the evidence you could gather to support the statement. A few examples are there for you. Think carefully about what you notice when you look at rusty metal.

Second, consider if the explanation is logical. Does it contradict anything you know or other evidence you have seen?

Third, think of other tests you could do to support your ideas. Could you think of a test that might contradict the explanation?

Last, evaluate the explanation. Do you think it has stood up to the tests? Do you think the tests have addressed what they were supposed to?

> **The Scientific Explanation:**
> Many metals that rust contain iron that reacts with water and oxygen.

The Evidence

9 Identify What evidence do you have about when some metal objects rust?

- I've seen bridges, cars, and many metal objects exposed to the outdoors rust
- I left several garden tools outside that rusted

The Logic

Second, consider if the explanation is consistent with other evidence you have seen. Think about if all metals rust in the same way.

10 Infer Describe how well your explanation fits all of the evidence you have, with all that you know.

- Some metals, like aluminum, don't rust
- Older metals rust more than newer ones

The Tests

Next, think of other tests you could do that would support the explanation.

11 Predict How might you test the conditions under which different metals rust?

- Expose different metals to the same conditions and see if they rust
- Could put metals in regular water and saltwater and note the rate of rusting

The Conclusion

Only after gathering evidence, thinking logically, and doing additional testing do you evaluate the scientific explanation.

12 Evaluate Does this empirical evidence support your explanation? Explain your answer.

Common Habits

What is involved in scientific work?

Even though science and the people who study it are very diverse, scientists have several characteristics in common. Scientists are curious, creative, and careful observers. They are also logical, skeptical, and objective.

You do not have to be a scientist to have these characteristics. When you use these habits of mind, you are thinking like a scientist!

Active Reading

13 Apply Which of the characteristics above do you use most often?

_____

_____

_____

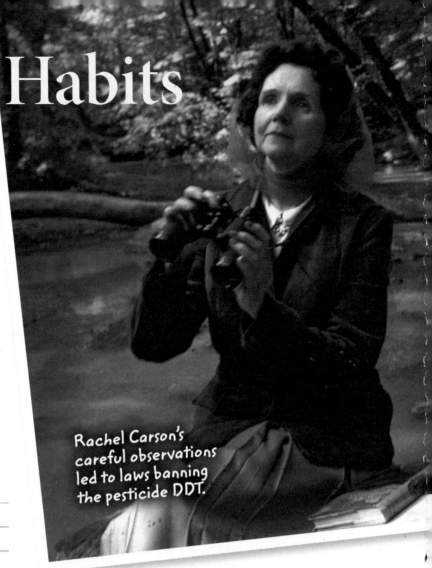

Rachel Carson's careful observations led to laws banning the pesticide DDT.

Careful Observation

Scientists observe with their senses as well as with scientific tools. All observations contribute to the understanding of a subject.

For example, ecologist Rachel Carson spent her entire life observing the natural world around her. She studied the oceans and wrote books and articles about them. She spent years researching and documenting the effects of pesticides, like DDT, on the environment. Her book, *Silent Spring,* drew the world's attention to the problem.

Curiosity

Scientists are curious about the world around them and about the things they observe. Most scientific discoveries are the result of someone asking why or how something happens.

For example, Rachel Carson was curious about all of nature. This curiosity drove her to identify the connections in it. It allowed her to understand how one part affects another.

14 List Name two things you are curious about.

_____

_____

Creativity

Being creative means to be original. Creative people think for themselves and always try to see other ways things might be.

In science, creativity is used when scientists design experiments and other investigations to test their hypotheses. Scientists must also use creative thinking to develop new explanations based on their data and other available evidence.

15 Identify Name an activity you do in which you are creative.

_____

_____

19 Apply Research shows that interaction with animals can benefit humans. In the discussion of dolphin therapy to the right, fill in the blanks with the appropriate characteristics scientists are showing.

Scientists saw how well people responded to animals and imagined _____ that these interactions might be helpful in some types of therapy.

Scientists were _____ about whether dolphins could be used as therapy animals.

Early studies showed that dolphin therapy has helped to improve certain conditions in humans. But scientists must be _____. They must not draw conclusions too quickly.

They need to conduct more tests and make _____ to determine the effects of dolphin therapy.

When they have more data, they will assess it _____ before drawing a conclusion.

They will consider all the evidence _____ before making decisions about the advantages and disadvantages of dolphin therapy.

Logic

Thinking logically involves reasoning through information and making conclusions supported by the evidence. Logical thinking is an important tool for the scientist.

For example, toothpaste helps to prevent tooth decay. Some mouthwash also helps to prevent tooth decay. It is logical to think that if the two products are used together they might work even better. This logical conclusion should then be tested.

16 Infer What is another career that relies on logic?

_____

_____

Skepticism

Being skeptical means that you don't accept everything you hear or read immediately. You ask questions before deciding whether you will accept information as factual. Scientists are skeptical of drawing conclusions too quickly. Instead, they repeat observations and experiments, and they review and try to replicate the work of others.

17 Conclude Why should you be skeptical of some advertisements?

_____

_____

_____

Objectivity

Being objective requires that you set aside your personal feelings, moods, and beliefs while you evaluate something. Science requires unbiased observations, experiments, and evaluations. Scientists want their tests to support their ideas. Scientists must be careful not to let this hope influence what they see.

18 Explain Describe a time when it was difficult to be objective.

_____

_____

_____

"Space Aliens built the Pyramids"

How is pseudoscience similar to and different from science?

People have marveled at the pyramids for thousands of years. Even today, scientists still question how ancient people could have built such awesome structures. Some have given a possible explanation for this—the pyramids were built by an advanced race of beings from outer space. Because it is unclear how ancient people could have built the pyramids, supporters of this idea think it provides one possible answer.

Some people will claim to have scientific evidence to support an explanation when in fact they do not. **Pseudoscience** is a belief or practice that is based on incorrectly applied scientific methods. Pseudoscience can seem like real science, but pseudoscientific ideas are based on faulty logic and are supported by claims that can't be tested.

Similarities

Pseudoscience is like science in that it often involves topics related to the natural world. People who believe in pseudoscience have explanations that can sound logical. Like science, pseudoscience uses technical language or scientific-sounding terms. Both science and pseudoscience claim to be based on empirical evidence.

Differences

The biggest difference between science and pseudoscience is that pseudoscience does not use accepted scientific methods. The evidence that supports pseudoscience may be very vague or lack any measurements. Some pseudoscientific claims lack the ability to be tested at all. Other pseudoscientific beliefs are supported only by personal experiences. Unlike scientists, pseudoscientists might claim that results not proven false must be true. This is faulty logic. Scientists must offer evidence for their conclusions. Pseudoscience asks skeptics to prove it false. In the case of the pyramids, pseudoscientists claim the pyramids' complexity is proof of their alien origin. To disprove the claim, you must prove aliens did not visit Earth 5,000 years ago. This is almost impossible to do.

Active Reading **20 Identify** Name two traits of pseudoscience.

Evidence is vauge & can't be tested.

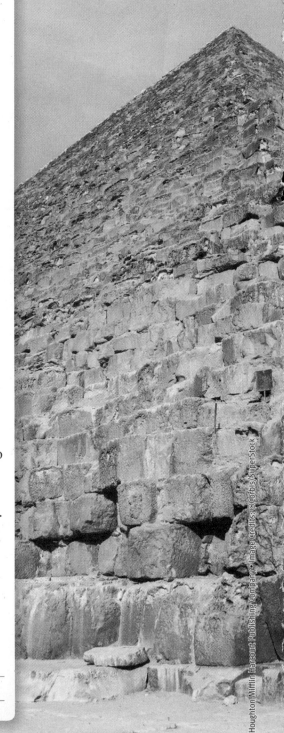

Science vs. Pseudoscience

Science	Pseudoscience
Based on logic	Not based on logic or logic is exaggerated
Has testable explanations	Explanations generally not testable
Relies on empirical evidence	Empirical evidence is not available; personal opinions often are used as empirical evidence
Results can be reproduced by others	Results cannot be reproduced by others
Explanations that are not proven false continue to be tested	Explanations that are not proven false are assumed to be true
Explanations are modified by new evidence	Explanations do not change with new evidence

21 Explain Would it be possible for something to initially be regarded as pseudoscience and then later be supported by science? Explain your answer.

No, because "Pseudo science can seem like real sciences but Pseudo seience ideas are based on faultly logic & supported by claims that can't be tested.

22 Analyze Someone tells you they've heard of a powder that, if worn in a pouch around the neck, will cure a cold. This person claims that the powder has cured everyone with a cold who has worn it. How do you explain to this person that, despite the positive results, this is a pseudoscientific claim?

Explain it by saying, It has no logical science to back it up, despite the good reviews. So, it's a pseudoscientific claim.

Even today, researchers don't know how ancient people hauled the large stones needed to build the pyramids. Does this prove that aliens did it?

No, because THEU don't know that aliens did it also

Think Outside the Book

23 Evaluate A popular hoax on the Internet warned of the dangers of the chemical dihydrogen monoxide. The supposed opponents claimed the chemical could cause death if inhaled and severe burns if touched. Do some research to find out what this chemical is. How are the claims made about it like the claims made by pseudoscientists?

Visual Summary

To complete this summary, fill in the blanks with the correct word or phrase. Then use the key below to check your answers. You can use this page to review the main concepts of the lesson.

What Is Science?

Science is the systematic study of natural events and conditions.

24 Explanations in science must be testable and have_____ of other scientists.

25 The _____ collected in scientific investigations is often in the form of measurements.

Scientists may study very different things, but they share many common traits.

26 Scientists use empirical evidence, logical thinking, and tests to_____ a scientific explanation.

27 Scientists are _____ about the subjects they study.

Science and pseudoscience both deal with the natural world, but pseudoscience only deceptively appears to be science.

28 Many claims of pseudoscience are not refutable because they can't be _____

Answers: 24 consensus; 25 empirical evidence; 26 evaluate; 27 curious; 28 tested

29 **Hypothesize** How might the characteristics of a scientist be displayed in a person of your age?

Lesson Review

Vocabulary

Fill in the blank with the term that best completes the following sentences.

1 _____ is the systematic study of the natural world.

2 _____ is often mistakenly regarded as being based on science.

3 _____ _____ is the name for the observations and data on which a scientific explanation can be based.

Key Concepts

4 **Describe** What are two things that characterize the practice of science?

_____

_____

_____

5 **Sequence** What are the three steps scientists take to evaluate a scientific explanation?

_____

_____

_____

_____

6 **Describe** What are six traits of a good scientific observer?

_____

_____

_____

_____

_____

7 **Justify** Why is it good for scientists to be skeptical?

_____

_____

_____

Critical Thinking

Use the table below to answer the following questions.

Characteristic	Science	Pseudoscience
Concerns the natural world		
Explanations can sound logical		
Results can always be tested by others		
Explanations can be proven false		
Allows personal opinions to be used as evidence		

8 **Assess** Place an "x" in the appropriate box if the characteristic could describe science, pseudoscience, or both. What might this tell you about the relationship between science and pseudoscience?

_____

_____

_____

_____

_____

9 **Judge** Good scientists use their imagination. What do you think is the difference between being imaginative in doing science and doing pseudoscience?

_____

_____

_____

_____

_____

Scientific Knowledge

ESSENTIAL QUESTION

How do scientists develop explanations?

By the end of this lesson, you should be able to analyze how scientists chose their methods, develop explanations, and identify support for a theory.

Sunshine State Standards

SC.6.N.2.2 Explain that scientific knowledge is durable because it is open to change as new evidence or interpretations are encountered.

SC.6.N.3.1 Recognize and explain that a scientific theory is a well-supported and widely accepted explanation of nature and is not simply a claim posed by an individual. Thus, the use of the term theory in science is very different than how it is used in everyday life.

SC.7.N.1.7 Explain that scientific knowledge is the result of a great deal of debate and confirmation within the science community.

SC.7.N.2.1 Identify an instance from the history of science in which scientific knowledge has changed when new evidence or new interpretations are encountered.

SC.7.N.3.1 Recognize and explain the difference between theories and laws and give several examples of scientific theories and the evidence that supports them.

SC.8.N.1.3 Use phrases such as "results support" or "fail to support" in science, understanding that science does not offer conclusive 'proof' of a knowledge claim.

SC.8.N.1.5 Analyze the methods used to develop a scientific explanation as seen in different fields of science.

SC.8.N.3.2 Explain why theories may be modified but are rarely discarded.

LA.6.4.2.2 The student will record information (e.g., observations, notes, lists, charts, legends) related to a topic, including visual aids to organize and record information and include a list of sources used.

Tiny radio transmitters allow scientists to track animals such as this tortoise in the wild. The information about the animal's behavior helps scientists better understand and possibly even protect it.

© Houghton Mifflin Harcourt Publishing Company • Image Credits: (bkgd) ©Olivier Grunewald/Photolibrary/Getty Images

Engage Your Brain

1 Describe Fill in the blank with the word or phrase that you think correctly completes the following sentences.

Scientists can study in the field or in the _____.

A good scientific theory is often_____ when new evidence is found but is rarely completely rejected.

The results of a scientific investigation either support or do not support a claim; they do not offer conclusive _____

2 Hypothesize Describe how you might study the butterfly coming out of the cocoon. What actions would you take? What tools would you use? What might you want to avoid doing?

_____
_____
_____
_____
_____
_____

 Active Reading

3 Apply Many scientific words such as *method* have everyday meanings. Use context clues to write your own definition for the meaning of the word *method*.

Example Sentence
Gloria felt there was only one <u>method</u> for cooking spaghetti.

_____

_____

Vocabulary

4 Identify As you read, place a question mark next to any words that you don't understand. When you finish reading the lesson, go back and review the words that you marked. If the information is still confusing, consult a classmate or a teacher.

Method Acting

How do scientists choose their methods?

Scientists plan investigations to address a specific problem or question. The goal is to come up with a scientific explanation. Each problem or question is unique and so requires a unique method and the proper tools.

You wouldn't lock yourself in a closet to study the birds in your neighborhood. You wouldn't use a microscope to measure the force propelling a model rocket. Science also has methods and tools to study different kinds of problems. Learning to be a scientist is learning how to use these methods and tools properly.

Visualize It!

6 Infer Scientists have all kinds of tools available to them. They select them based on what they study. Can you tell where or how scientist might use the tools in each of the two photos?

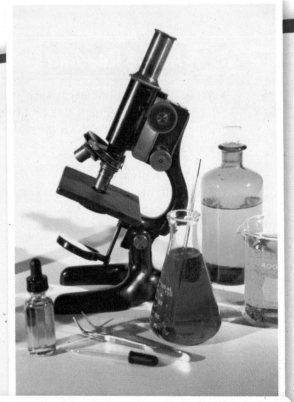

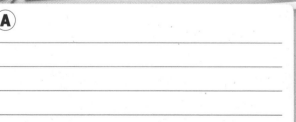

Ⓐ
_____
_____
_____
_____

Ⓑ
_____
_____
_____
_____

By the Tools Available

Scientists did not know about cells before there was a microscope. No one had seen the moons of the planet Jupiter before there was the telescope. Severe weather tracking and prediction reached a new level of sophistication with the invention of doppler radar. Scientists need their tools.

Scientists, however, know that they can't always have the tools they may need. Some might be too expensive. Others simply may not exist. So, scientists also need to be creative in the ways they use their tools. For example, astronomers study the light from a star to get an idea of its chemical makeup. Similarly, geologists study what Earth's interior is like by looking at seismograph readings during an earthquake. Tools are only useful if the scientist using them can interpret the data they provide. This skill is a large part of the education of a scientist.

By the Subject Under Study

Generally, scientific investigations fall into two types: experiments and fieldwork. Experiments involve scientists controlling different variables during an investigation. Experiments usually are done under very precise and controlled conditions in a laboratory. Physicists and chemists generally do a lot of experiments.

In contrast, scientists doing fieldwork make observations of what is around them. They watch and observe and try to make sense of what they see. Instead of controlling variables, they try to determine what variables are at work and how they relate to each other. A large part of doing fieldwork is often coming to understand the variables that exist. Biologists and geologists generally do a lot of fieldwork. Sometimes, a scientist will do fieldwork and then take a specimen back to a laboratory to do more testing.

Visualize It!

7 Identify For each photo, identify some tools a scientist might use to study the subject of the photo. Use examples from the photos on the other page for suggestions.

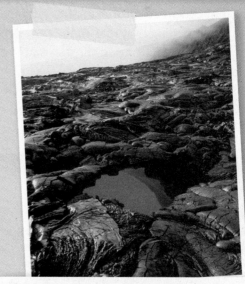

(A)
_____
_____
_____
_____

(B)
_____
_____
_____
_____

Well, Prove It!

How do scientific theories become accepted?

Active Reading **8 Identify** As you read, underline an example of new evidence supporting a theory.

In science, a theory is not the same as an educated guess. A theory is not an explanation for a single fact. A scientific *theory* is a system of ideas that explains many related observations and is supported by a large body of evidence acquired through scientific investigation. Scientific theories may be modified but are rarely rejected.

Being Supported by Evidence

About 65 million years ago, dinosaurs and many other organisms suddenly became extinct. Scientists have offered many explanations for why this happened, from widespread disease to sudden climate change.

In the 1970s, Walter and Luis Alvarez found a thin layer of iridium-rich clay at various places on Earth. These layers dated to 65 million years ago, the same time as the mass extinction. Iridium is a rare element on Earth but is found in large amounts in meteorites. The Alvarezes proposed that perhaps Earth had been struck by a large meteorite at that time. They proposed that this massive impact was what caused the dinosaurs' extinction.

In the 1990s, evidence of a crater of the right size, type, and age was found near the city of Chicxulub (CHIK-shuh-loob) in Mexico. With this evidence, most scientists agreed that a meteorite impact did play a role in the extinction of the dinosaurs.

This rock specimen was collected from the Chicxulub crater. Scientists used samples like this to determine when the meteorite struck Earth. The map shows the location of the crater.

Incorporating New Evidence

Many scientists were skeptical that a single meteorite impact could result in a mass extinction. Further research was needed.

Evidence was found of major volcanic eruptions in India occurring at the end of the dinosaur age. Volcanic ash in the atmosphere can block sunlight and contribute to global cooling. Thus, many scientists thought that volcanoes were the main cause of the mass extinction, and a volcanic-eruption explanation was put forth. But further research showed that these volcanoes had been erupting for about 500,000 years before the Chicxulub impact without having a massive effect on the global environment.

For years scientists studied the evidence using tools and technology from many different fields. Recently, scientists around the world have come to agree that the Chicxulub impact was most likely the trigger that caused tidal waves, earthquakes, landslides, and blasts of dust that, together with the volcanic ash that was already present, darkened the skies. This led to global cooling and reduced plant life, which killed the dinosaurs. With the evidence unified into a well-supported explanation, the meteorite impact explanation for dinosaur extinction could now be called a theory.

Think Outside the Book Inquiry

9 Infer The mass extinction of 65 million years ago is one of the most significant events in Earth's history. Write an essay about why this event was so significant.

The Chicxulub meteorite was about 6 mi (10 km) in diameter. It formed a crater about 3300 ft (1000 m) deep and 110 mi (180 km) wide. The meteorite's impact triggered waves thousands of feet high and darkened the skies with dust.

The modern site for the Chicxulub crater is found buried under limestone in the Yucatan peninsula of Mexico. Finding the crater was evidence in support of the meteorite impact theory.

Chicxulub Crater

Visualize It!

10 Infer Why would the Chicxulub crater be covered up now?

_____

_____

How can you know who's right?

The most reliable scientific information is found in professional science journals. These contain articles written and reviewed by other scientists. The reason the information is reliable is simple. It has been checked and rechecked by experts in the same area of science as the journal articles. The downside to reading scientific journals is that they are not easy to understand. They contain many words that nonscientists may not recognize.

You should be very cautious of accepting scientific explanations from advertisers or anyone trying to sell you something. They can be more concerned with getting you to buy their products than with teaching you science.

When you read anything, or assess any scientific claim, you need to ask yourself if it makes sense logically. You should always think critically. When presented with a claim, ask yourself whether the results support it. Do the results agree with what you know about the world? Remember, scientists do not claim to prove anything. Scientists attempt to provide an explanation that agrees with the results of observation and testing.

Active Reading

11 **Identify** As you read, underline an example of what you need to be aware of when reading a scientific explanation.

12 **Appraise** Conduct library or Internet research to investigate the scientific claims below. Check the appropriate box according to whether you find the theory is supported or not supported by scientific evidence.

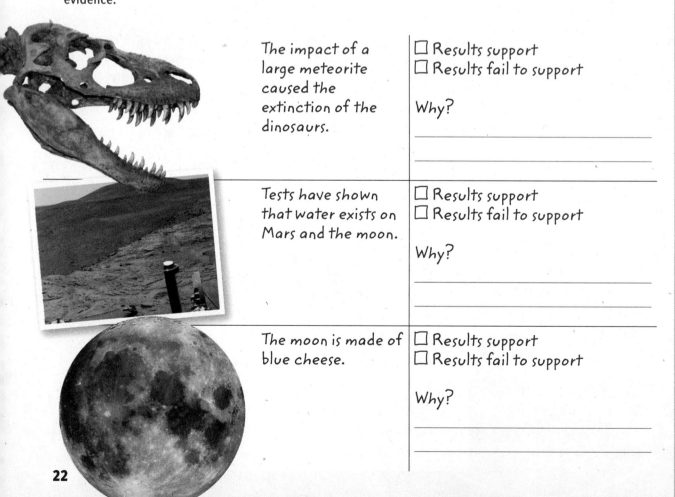

The impact of a large meteorite caused the extinction of the dinosaurs.

☐ Results support
☐ Results fail to support

Why?
_____
_____

Tests have shown that water exists on Mars and the moon.

☐ Results support
☐ Results fail to support

Why?
_____
_____

The moon is made of blue cheese.

☐ Results support
☐ Results fail to support

Why?
_____
_____

A Theory for the Birds

Dinosaurs Take Flight

The fossil *archaeopteryx*, shown to the right, gave the first solid evidence linking dinosaurs to modern birds. Although it had wings and feathers and may even have been able to fly, it seems to be more dinosaur than bird. It had jaws with teeth, three-fingered claws, and a tail.

Gone But Not Forgotten

Not all dinosaurs of the past were large, like the ones we see reconstructed in museums. Some were small. *Archaeopteryx* was about as big as a medium-sized dog.

Family Resemblance?

Pigeons are thought to be one modern bird that closely resembles its ancient counterpart. Few scientists today debate the dinosaur origins of birds. They do, however, debate how it may have occurred.

Extend

Inquiry

13 Determine Do the fossil remains appear to support or fail to support the idea that today's birds are the descendants of dinosaurs?

14 Relate How might the theory of dinosaurs' relation to birds be modified?

15 Infer Recent DNA evidence shows that dinosaurs and birds are genetically closer than either are to alligators. What does this say about the strength of the theory that birds and dinosaurs are related?

Visual Summary

To complete this summary, fill in the blanks with the correct word or phrase. Then use the key below to check your answers. You can use this page to review the main concepts of the lesson.

Scientific Knowledge

Scientists in different fields use different methods to develop scientific explanations.

16 What might a scientist be doing with the tools shown below?

_____

Good scientific theories are supported by a lot of evidence.

17 A good scientific theory is often _____ with new evidence but is rarely discarded.

18 Scientists don't claim to _____ the theory. They just claim that the results _____it.

Answers: 16 lab work/experimenting; 17 modified; 18 prove; support

19 **Integrate** Why do you think scientists claim to offer only supporting evidence for a theory and not proof?

Lesson Review

Vocabulary

Fill in the blank with the term that best completes the following sentence.

1 An explantion in science that has a lot of evidence to back it up is a scientific

_____

2 Scientists never say a theory is proven or not. They only say if the evidence

_____ or _____ it.

Key Concepts

3 List What are two types of scientific investigations?

_____

_____

4 Infer You've been assigned to observe the habits of the birds living in your neighborhood. What tools might you take along?

_____

_____

_____

5 Describe What kinds of tools might you use in a laboratory?

_____

_____

6 Judge Any time a scientific theory is challenged, it means it's not a good theory. Do you agree with this statement? Explain.

_____

_____

_____

7 Discriminate Why would you be cautious of scientific information you hear from advertisers?

_____

_____

Critical Thinking

Use the photo below to answer the following questions.

8 Relate What type of investigation would a scientist studying this sinkhole use? What tools might be used to study it?

_____

_____

9 Apply What are some questions a scientist might want to find out about this sinkhole?

_____

_____

_____

10 Assess Do you think it's wise for scientists not to accept a theory immediately, even if the theory has a lot of evidence to support it?

_____

_____

_____

Scientific Investigations

ESSENTIAL QUESTION

How do scientists discover things?

By the end of this lesson, you should be able to summarize the processes and characteristics of different kinds of scientific investigations.

Sunshine State Standards

SC.6.N.1.2 Explain why scientific investigations should be replicable.

SC.7.N.1.2 Differentiate replication (by others) from repetition (multiple trials).

SC.8.N.1.1 Define a problem from the eighth grade curriculum using appropriate reference materials to support scientific understanding, plan and carry out scientific investigations of various types, such as systematic observations or experiments, identify variables, collect and organize data, interpret data in charts, tables, and graphics, analyze information, make predictions, and defend conclusions.

SC.8.N.1.2 Design and conduct a study using repeated trials and replication.

SC.8.N.1.4 Explain how hypotheses are valuable if they lead to further investigations, even if they turn out not to be supported by the data.

SC.8.N.1.5 Analyze the methods used to develop a scientific explanation as seen in different fields of science.

SC.8.N.1.6 Understand that scientific investigations involve the collection of relevant empirical evidence, the use of logical reasoning, and the application of imagination in devising hypotheses, predictions, explanations and models to make sense of the collected evidence.

LA.6.4.2.2 The student will record information (e.g., observations, notes, lists, charts, legends) related to a topic, including visual aids to organize and record information and include a list of sources used.

This scientist is studying DNA, the molecule of life!

Engage Your Brain

1 Discriminate Circle the word or phrase that best completes the following sentences.

A *hypothesis / dependent variable* is a possible explanation of a scientific problem.

Scientists conduct controlled experiments because this method enables them to test the effects of a single *variable / theory*.

Graphing of results is most often done as part of *writing hypotheses / analyzing data*.

Making observations *in the field / in laboratories* allows a scientist to collect data about wildlife in their natural environments.

2 Explain Draw a picture of what you think a scientific investigation might look like. Write a caption to go with your picture.

Active Reading

3 Synthesize Many English words have their roots in other languages. Use the Latin words below to make an educated guess about the meaning of the words *experiment* and *observation*.

Latin word	Meaning
experiri	to try
observare	to watch

Example sentence:
Shaun's favorite <u>experiment</u> involved pouring vinegar onto baking soda.

Experiment:

_____

_____

Example sentence:
Telescopes are used to make <u>observations</u>.

Observation:

_____

_____

Vocabulary Terms

- experiment
- observation
- hypothesis
- independent variable
- dependent variable
- data

4 Apply As you learn the definition of each vocabulary term in this lesson, write a sentence that includes the term to help you remember it.

Testing, Testing, 1, 2, 3

What are some parts that make up scientific investigations?

An **experiment** is an organized procedure to study something under controlled conditions. Scientists often investigate the natural world through experiments. But scientists must learn about many things through observation. **Observation** is the process of obtaining information by using the senses. The term can also refer to the information obtained by using the senses. Scientific investigations may also involve the use of models, which are representations of an object or system.

Elements of Investigations

Hypothesis

A **hypothesis** (hy•PAHTH•eh•sys) is a testable idea or explanation that leads to scientific investigation. A scientist may think of a hypothesis after making observations or after reading findings from other scientists' investigations.

Hypotheses must be carefully constructed so they can be tested in a practical and meaningful way. For example, suppose you find a bone fossil, and you form the hypothesis that it came from a dinosaur that lived 200 million years ago. You might test your hypothesis by comparing the fossil to other fossils that have been found and by analyzing the fossil to determine its age.

If an investigation does not support a hypothesis, it is still useful. The information from the investigation can help scientists form a better hypothesis. Scientists may go through many cycles of testing and analysis before they arrive at a hypothesis that is supported.

Active Reading 5 **Explain** Why should hypotheses be testable?

_____

_____

_____

This young plant is growing in a hostile environment.

Visualize It!

6 **Infer** Write a hypothesis offering a possible explanation of what will happen to the plant above.

_____

_____

_____

Independent and Dependent Variables

A variable is any factor that can change in a scientific investigation. An **independent variable** is the factor that is deliberately manipulated. A **dependent variable** changes as a result of manipulation of one or more independent variables.

Imagine that you want to test the hypothesis that increasing the heat under a pot of water will cause the water to boil faster. You fill three pots with the same amount of water, then heat them until the water boils. The independent variable is the amount of heat. The dependent variable is the time it takes for the water to boil. You measure this variable for all three pots to determine whether your hypothesis is supported.

If possible, a controlled experiment should have just one independent variable. Scientists try to keep other variables constant, or unchanged, so they do not affect the results. For example, in the experiment described above, both pots should be made of the same material because some materials change temperature more easily than others.

Observations and Data

Data are information gathered by observation or experimentation that can be used in calculating or reasoning. This information may be anything that a scientist perceives through the senses or detects through instruments.

In an investigation, everything a scientist observes must be recorded. The setup and procedures need to be recorded. By carefully recording this information, scientists make sure they will not forget anything.

Scientists analyze data to determine the relationship between the independent and dependent variables in an investigation. Then they draw conclusions about whether the data support the investigation's hypothesis.

7 Apply Suppose you want to test the hypothesis that plants grow taller when they receive more sunlight. Identify an independent variable and a dependent variable for this investigation.

_____

_____

_____

_____

_____

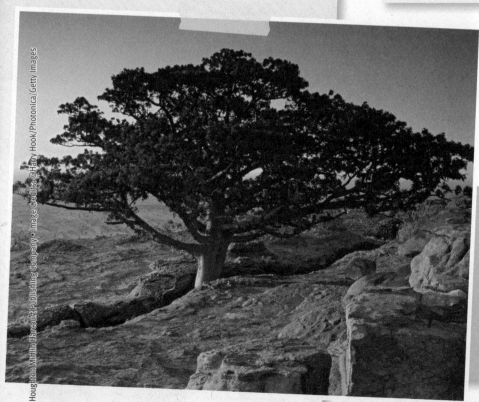

You may have thought that the plant at the left will die. But as this photograph shows, plants can get enough nutrients to thrive under similar conditions.

© Houghton Mifflin Harcourt Publishing Company • Image Credits: © Harry Hook/Photonica/Getty Images

Many Methods

What are some scientific methods?

Conducting experiments and other scientific investigations is not like following a cookbook recipe. Scientists do not always use the same steps in every investigation or use steps in the same order. They may even repeat some of the steps. The following graphic shows one path that a scientist might follow while conducting an experiment.

Visualize It!

8 Diagram Using a highlighter, trace the path a scientist might follow if the data from an experiment did not support the hypothesis.

Defining a Problem

After making observations or reading scientific reports, a scientist might be curious about some unexplained aspect of a topic. A scientific problem is a specific question that a scientist wants to answer. The problem must be well-defined, or precisely stated, so that it can be investigated.

Planning an Investigation

A scientific investigation must be carefully planned so that it tests a hypothesis in a meaningful way. Scientists need to decide whether an investigation should be done in the field or in a laboratory. They must also determine what equipment and technology are required and how materials for the investigation will be obtained.

Forming a Hypothesis and Making Predictions

When scientists form a hypothesis, they are making an educated guess about a problem. A hypothesis must be tested to see if it is true. Before testing a hypothesis, scientists usually make predictions about what will happen in an investigation.

Identifying Variables

The independent variable of an experiment is identified in the hypothesis. But scientists need to decide how the independent variable will change. They also must identify other variables that will be controlled. In addition, scientists must determine how they will measure the results of the experiment. The dependent variable often can be measured in more than one way. For example, if the dependent variable is fish health, scientists could measure size, weight, or number of offspring.

Collecting and Organizing Data

The data collected in an investigation must be recorded and properly organized so that they can be analyzed. Data such as measurements and numbers are often organized into tables, spreadsheets, or graphs.

Interpreting Data and Analyzing Information

After they finish collecting data, scientists must analyze this information. Their analysis will help them draw conclusions about the results. Scientists may have different interpretations of the same data because they analyze it using different methods.

Drawing and Defending Conclusions

Scientists conclude whether the results of their investigation support the hypothesis. If the hypothesis is not supported, scientists may think about the problem some more and try to come up with a new hypothesis to test. Or they may repeat an experiment to see if any mistakes were made. When they publish the results of their investigation, scientists must be prepared to defend their conclusions if they are challenged by other scientists.

Life Lessons

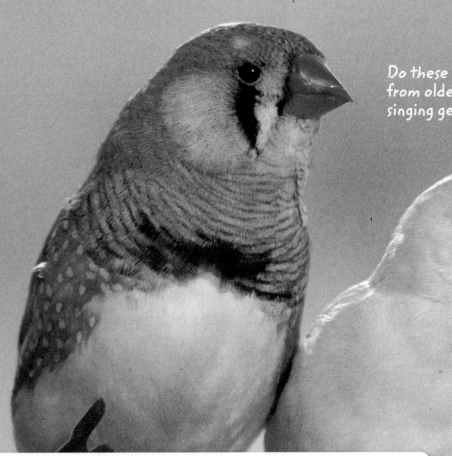

Do these birds learn their songs from older birds? Or is their singing genetic?

How are scientific methods used?

Scientific methods are used in physical, life, and earth sciences. Which methods are used depends on the type of investigation that is to be conducted.

Different Situations Require Different Methods

Scientists choose the setting for an investigation very carefully. Some problems are suited for field investigations. For example, many life scientists work in the field in order to study living things in their natural habitat. Many geologists begin in the field, collecting rocks and samples. But, those same geologists might then study their samples in a laboratory, where conditions can be controlled.

Sometimes scientists study things that are very large, very small, or that occur over a very long period of time. In these cases, scientists can use models in their investigations. A scientific model is a representation of an object or a process that allows scientists to study something in detail. Scientists can conduct experiments and make observations using models.

Think Outside the Book Inquiry

9 **Describe** Do research to learn about a new hypothesis that has replaced an older explanation of something in the natural world. Describe the process that led to this change in thinking.

When finches were first isolated, they didn't sing like wild finches. But later generations of isolated finches sang just like wild birds.

Active Reading

10 Identify As you read, underline the scientific methods used in the study.

Scientific Methods Are Used in Life Science

Life scientists use scientific methods to study how traits are passed from parents to offspring.

One team of scientists recently studied birds called zebra finches. Zebra finches learn songs by imitating the singing of older relatives. But the scientists thought that genes might play a role in how the birds learn their songs.

To test this hypothesis, they isolated a group of young zebra finches from older birds. When these young birds grew up, they sang differently than wild finches did. Then, the scientists placed another group of young males in with the isolated finches. The younger finches imitated the songs of the older ones, but the songs were slightly different. As the scientists continued to add new groups of young finches in with the isolated ones, each new group started to sing more like wild finches. The scientists concluded that genes influence the way zebra finches learn how to sing.

High Quality

What are some characteristics of good scientific investigations?

Scientists may use different ways to test the same hypothesis. But good scientific investigations share some important characteristics. Scientific observations should be well-documented and have supporting evidence. In an experiment, the variables should be controlled as much as possible.

Experiments should be repeated multiple times by the original investigator. Scientific investigations should also be able to be replicated by scientists not involved with the original work. If the investigation is valid, the same results will be found.

Before publishing a study, scientific journals ask other scientists to review an article. This is called peer review. Scientists must provide answers to the questions raised by their peers.

Visualize It!

11 Infer When scientists replicate experiments, they will often do so under different conditions than the original investigations. Why might this be helpful? Why do you think the astronaut replicated Galileo's investigation on the moon?

_____

_____

_____

_____

_____

_____

According to legend, Galileo dropped two balls from the Leaning Tower of Pisa to demonstrate that objects of different masses fall at the same rate.

Over 300 years later, scientists were still replicating Galileo's investigation. In 1971, astronaut David Scott traveled to the moon, which has no air. When he dropped a hammer and a feather, they hit the ground at the same time.

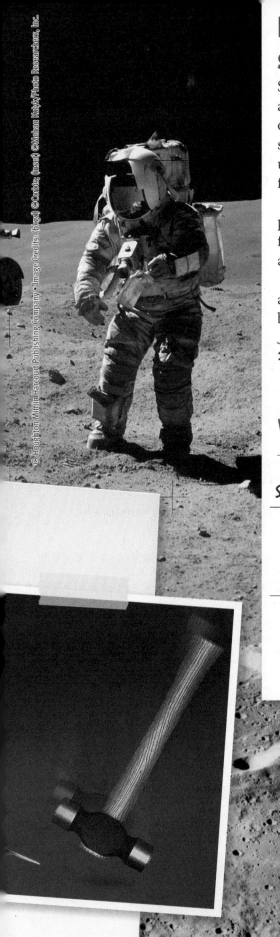

How can you evaluate the quality of scientific information?

Scientific information is available on the Internet, on television, and in magazines. Some sources are more trustworthy than others. The most reliable scientific information is published in scientific journals. However, these articles are often difficult to understand. Sometimes, summaries of these articles are published for the public.

Many scientists write books for the general public. These publications are trustworthy if the scientist is writing about his field of study. Reliable books may also be written by people who aren't scientists but who are knowledgeable about a particular field.

Usually, the most reliable Internet sources are government or academic webpages. Commercial webpages are often unreliable because they are trying to sell something.

---

12 Apply Find two sources of information about the same scientific investigation. Then, fill out the chart below to explain why you think each source is trustworthy or untrustworthy.

What is this investigation about? _____

_____

Source	Trustworthy? Why or why not?

Think Outside the Book

13 Design Suppose that you are conducting a field experiment with plants. You are testing the hypothesis that plants grow faster when mulch covers the soil. Plan how you would conduct the experiment. Then plan how you would repeat it.

Visual Summary

To complete this summary, fill in the blanks with the correct word or phrase. Then, use the key below to check your answers. You can use this page to review the main concepts of the lesson.

Scientific Investigations

Scientific investigations include experiments, fieldwork, surveys, and models.

14 A type of investigation that allows scientists to control variables is a(n)
_____

15 Scientific experiments test relationships between _____ and _____ variables.

16 A scientific hypothesis must be
_____

There is no single correct way to conduct a scientific investigation.
Some methods include making and testing hypotheses, collecting data, analyzing data, and drawing conclusions.

17 A(n) _____ is either supported or unsupported by the results of an investigation.

18 The results of an investigation are the
_____

Reliable scientific information comes from investigations with reproducible results.
Sources of reliable scientific information include scientific journals and government web sites.

19 An investigation that has been done by more than one scientist with similar findings has been _____

20 The most reliable scientific information is published in _____
_____

Answers: 14 experiment; 15 independent, dependent; 16 testable 17 hypothesis; 18 data; 19 replicated; 20 scientific journals

21 Apply Choose an organism that you can observe in its environment. Write a hypothesis that you could test about this organism.

Answers: 14 experiment; 15 independent, dependent; 16 testable 17 hypothesis; 18 data; 19 replicated; 20 scientific journals

21 Apply Choose an organism that you can observe in its environment. Write a hypothesis that you could test about this organism.

36 Unit 1 Nature of Science

© Houghton Mifflin Harcourt Publishing Company • Image Credits: (tl) ©Wayne Lawler/Photo Researchers, Inc.; (tr) ©Hill Street Studios/Blend Images/Corbis; (bc) ©Corbis

Lesson Review

Vocabulary

Fill in the blank with the term that best completes the following sentences.

1 A scientific _Investigation_ is a proposed explanation that can be tested.

2 A(n) _Independant factor_ is the factor that is deliberately changed in an experiment.

3 The information gathered in an investigation is called _Variables_

4 A(n) _Scientific Investigation_ should have only one independent variable.

5 _____ can be made in the field or in the laboratory.

Key Concepts

6 Infer What kinds of scientific investigations involve making observations?

_____

_____

7 Apply In an experiment, which variable changes in response to the manipulation of another variable?

_____

8 Explain When might a scientist use a model?

_____

_____

_____

9 Compare How are repetition and replication alike and different?

_____

_____

_____

_____

_____

Critical Thinking

Use the table below to answer the following questions.

Plant	Amount of Water Given	Amount of Fertilizer Given	Height
1	10 mL	none	6 cm
2	20 mL	5 g	8 cm
3	30 mL	10 g	7 cm
4	40 mL	15 g	12 cm

10 Evaluate The table above shows the data collected during an experiment about plant height. Based on the data collected, is this a controlled experiment? Why or why not?

_____

_____

_____

_____

_____

11 Describe How would you experiment to find out how much water this plant type needs for optimal growth?

_____

_____

_____

_____

12 Recommend Write a checklist with at least three entries for how you can evaluate whether scientific information is reliable.

_____

_____

_____

_____

Supporting Hypotheses

Scientists repeat investigations whenever possible to test the validity of hypotheses. A hypothesis is more strongly supported when more than one investigation gives similar results. But sometimes investigations with similar hypotheses give different results. When this happens, it is important that scientists ask questions to help them judge whether the differences in the results are insignificant or meaningful.

Sunshine State Standards

SC.6.N.1.4 Discuss, compare, and negotiate methods used, results obtained, and explanations among groups of students conducting the same investigation.

SC.8.N.1.4 Explain how hypotheses are valuable if they lead to further investigations, even if they turn out not to be supported by the data.

MA.6.A.3.6 Construct and analyze tables, graphs, and equations to describe linear functions and other simple relations using both common language and algebraic notation.

Tutorial

Two groups of students worked together to test a hypothesis. Each group collected four samples of seawater and four samples of drinking water to test. Their hypothesis and the measurements that the students made are shown below. The two groups shared their data and asked the following questions as they evaluated their results.

Conductivity Report

Background: Seawater contains dissolved salts in the form of positive and negative ions. These ions may allow seawater to conduct electric current. Conductivity is a measure of how well a material conducts an electric current.

Hypothesis: The conductivity of seawater is higher than the conductivity of drinking water.

Average Conductivity in Siemens per Meter

	Group 1 Values (S/m)	Group 2 Values (S/m)
Seawater	3.97	4.82
Drinking water	0.005	0.0045

Are the results of the two investigations similar or different? The average conductivity of seawater measured by each group was different.

Do the different results still support the original hypothesis? Even though the groups had different results for seawater conductivity, both groups' results supported the hypothesis that the conductivity of seawater is higher than that of drinking water.

What additional investigations would help to explain the groups' results? The students designed a second investigation in which they would bring all of their samples to the same temperature and then repeat their measurements.

What could account for differences in the results? Students examined the following factors:
- type of equipment
- procedure
- conditions
- materials used

One student did more research and learned that temperature affects conductivity. The students realized that the two groups had made conductivity measurements of seawater samples at different temperatures.

You Try It!

A class was divided into two groups and instructed to investigate the conductivity of rock salt (NaCl) and of quartz (SiO_2). The hypothesis and supporting data collected by the groups are shown below.

Hypothesis: The conductivity of a solid substance increases when the substance is placed in water.

Results of Conductivity Tests

	Group A			Group B		
	NaCl	SiO_2	H_2O	NaCl	SiO_2	H_2O
Conductivity (solid)	No	No	—	No	No	—
Conductivity (in water)	Yes	Yes	No	Yes	No	No

1 Evaluating Data Compare the results of the two groups.

_____
_____
_____
_____
_____
_____
_____

2 Judging Results Based on the results, what would each group conclude about whether their original hypothesis is supported? Explain your reasoning.

_____
_____
_____
_____
_____
_____

3 Evaluating Methods When the students examined their procedures, they found that Group A used a single beaker for both solids, and Group B used a different beaker of water for each solid and for the H_2O. How might this difference in methods explain the difference in their results?

_____
_____
_____
_____
_____
_____
_____
_____
_____
_____

Take It Home

With an adult, find a book or article about experiments in cold fusion. Were the results reproduced? Did they support the original hypothesis? Write a paragraph about your findings.

Lesson **4**

Representing Data

This clay tablet, which dates back to 2400 BCE, displays accounting records written in cuneiform script. Cuneiform is a picture-writing system that uses symbols. Today the tablet is located in the Louvre, in Paris, France.

ESSENTIAL QUESTION

How do scientists show the results of investigations?

By the end of this lesson, you should be able to use tables, graphs, and models to display and analyze scientific data.

🌞 Sunshine State Standards

SC.6.N.3.4 Identify the role of models in the context of the sixth grade science benchmarks.

SC.7.N.3.2 Identify the benefits and limitations of the use of scientific models.

SC.8.N.1.5 Analyze the methods used to develop a scientific explanation as seen in different fields of science such as biology, geology, and physics.

SC.8.N.1.6 Understand that scientific investigations involve the collection of relevant empirical evidence, the use of logical reasoning, and the application of imagination in devising hypotheses, predictions, explanations and models to make sense of the collected evidence.

SC.8.N.3.1 Select models useful in relating the results of their own investigations.

MA.6.A.3.6 Construct and analyze tables, graphs, and equations to describe linear functions and other simple relations using both common language and algebraic notation.

LA.6.4.2.2 The student will record information (e.g., observations, notes, lists, charts, legends) related to a topic, including visual aids to organize and record information and include a list of sources used.

40 Unit 1 Nature of Science

Engage Your Brain

1 Evaluate Check T or F to show whether you think each statement is true or false.

T   F

☐   ☐   A graph should always have a title describing what the graph is about.

☐   ☐   The factor that is manipulated in an experiment is usually plotted on the vertical axis of a graph.

☐   ☐   A model can be used to represent something that is too small to see with the naked eye.

2 Assemble Write a word or phrase beginning with each letter of the word MODEL that is an example or use of a model. Think of a model as anything that represents something else.

M _____

O _____

D _____

E _____

L _____

Active Reading

3 Apply Use context clues to write your own definition for the words *independent* and *dependent*.

Example sentence
After <u>independent</u> studies, the two scientists reached very different conclusions.

independent:

_____

_____

Example sentence
The cost of the service is <u>dependent</u> on its availability.

dependent:

_____

_____

Vocabulary Terms

- independent variable
- dependent variable
- model

4 Apply As you learn the definition of each vocabulary term in this lesson, create your own definition or sketch to help you remember the meaning of the term.

Modeling Data with Graphs

How do scientists make sense of data?

There are many different kinds of scientific investigations conducted in science, all of which involve the collection of data. *Data* are the facts, figures, and other evidence scientists gather when they conduct an investigation.

Scientists Organize the Data

Scientists use data tables to organize and record the data that they collect. By creating a data table, they can record their observations and measurements in an orderly way.

Data tables often have two columns. One column lists the **independent variable**. This is the variable that is deliberately manipulated in an investigation. The other column lists the **dependent variable**. This is the variable that changes as a result of the manipulation of the independent variable. When creating a data table, any units of measurement, such as seconds or degrees, should be included in the table's column headings and not in the individual cells.

The data table below shows the high temperatures for certain days and the number of cold drinks sold at a concession stand on those days.

Drink Sales

High temperature (°F)	Number of cold drinks sold
25	43
40	55
58	60
70	72
81	70

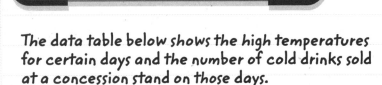

Visualize It!

5 Apply Name the independent variable and the dependent variable in the data table. Explain your answer.

_____

_____

_____

_____

© Houghton Mifflin Harcourt Publishing Company • Image Credits: (bkgd) ©David Madison/Photographer's Choice/Getty Images; ©Burazin/Photographer's Choice/Getty Images

Scientists Graph and Analyze the Data

Scientists often analyze data for patterns or trends by constructing graphs of the data. The type of graph they construct depends upon the data they collected and what they want to show.

A *scatter plot* is a graph with points plotted to show a possible relationship between two sets of data. A scatter plot has a horizontal *x*-axis and a vertical *y*-axis. The *x*-axis usually represents the independent variable in the data table. The *y*-axis usually represents the dependent variable.

To show the general relationship between the two variables in the graph, a "line of best fit" is often used. A line of best fit is a line that is drawn to "fit," or come close to, most of the data points.

The graphs below show steps used to construct a scatter plot of the drink sales data at the left.

Active Reading

6 Identify Which axis of a graph usually represents the independent variable?

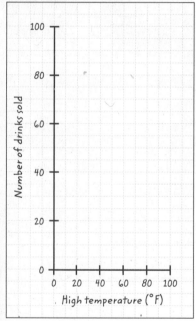 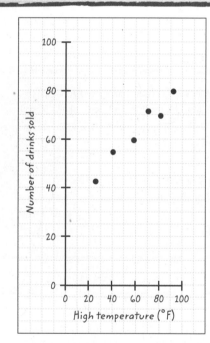 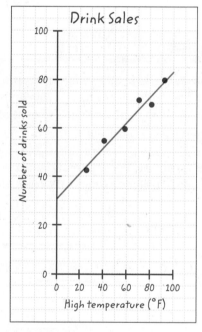

Step 1 Label the Axes Label each axis on a graph with the name of the variable that is represented. Each axis can have its own range and scale so that the data can be seen easily. The range is the difference between the greatest value and the least value of a variable. The scale is the size that is used for each box or grid mark on the graph.

Step 2 Plot the Data Points Plot the data from the table as data points on the graph.

7 Analyze Do you see a trend in these data? Explain.

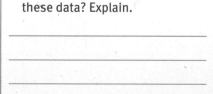

Step 3 Draw a Line of Best Fit Draw a line that comes close to most of the data points. The line shows the pattern described by the data. It also shows how the data differ from the pattern.

More Graphing!

What do graphs show?

Different types of graphs are used to show different types of information about data. On the previous pages, you read about scatter plots. Other graphs include bar graphs and circle graphs. A *bar graph* is used to display and compare data in a number of separate, or distinct, categories. Data about the number of inches it rained each month can be displayed in a bar graph. A *circle graph* is used when you are showing how each group of data relates to all of the data. Data about the number of boys and girls in your class can be displayed in a circle graph.

Active Reading **8 List** Name three different types of graphs.

_____

_____

_____

Visualize It!

Dwayne has been training for several weeks for cross-country tryouts. To make the team, he must be able to run 1 mile in less than 8 minutes. The data at the right shows the amount of time in minutes that it took Dwayne to run a mile each week.

Week 1	11.95 min
Week 2	11.25 min
Week 3	11.40 min
Week 4	10.10 min
Week 5	9.25 min
Week 6	8.60 min

9 Complete Use the empty table below to organize Dwayne's running data. Include a title for the table, the column heads, and all of the data.

Title

Headings

Data

© Houghton Mifflin Harcourt Publishing Company • Image Credits: ©Daniel Schoenen/age fotostock

Use the steps below to construct a graph of Dwayne's running data. The horizontal and vertical axes have been drawn for you.

Step 1
Label each axis with the name of the variable that is represented.

Step 2
Find the range for each axis. For the running data, the range of the independent variable is 6 weeks. Thus, the *x*-axis must cover at least 6 weeks.

Step 3
Decide the scale for each axis. For the running data, use a scale of 1 week for each grid mark on the *x*-axis.

Step 4
Graph the points by putting a dot on the graph for each pair of data in the data table.

Step 5
Title the graph. A good title tells a reader what the graph is all about.

10 Graph Use the steps at the left to construct a scatter plot of the running data given.

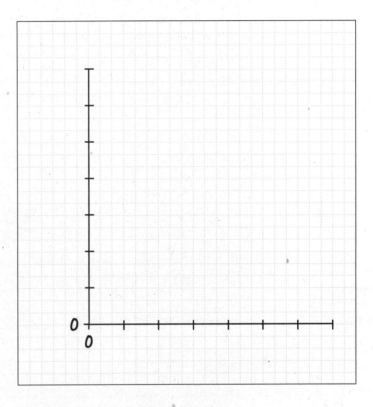

11 Assess Explain how you could use the graph to predict whether Dwayne will run 1 mile in less than 8 minutes.

_____
_____
_____
_____
_____
_____
_____
_____
_____
_____
_____
_____

Throw Me a Curve!

What kinds of patterns can be shown using graphs?

When you graph data, you can identify what the pattern, or *trend*, of the data is. A trend shows the relationship between the two variables studied in the experiment. Graphs make it easy to tell if something is increasing, decreasing, or staying the same.

Linear Relationships

A line can sometimes be used to show the trend of data on a graph. A graph in which the relationship between the independent variable and dependent variable can be shown with a straight line is called a *linear graph*. A straight line shows that the rate of change of the dependent variable with respect to the independent variable is constant. In other words, *y* always increases or decreases by the same value in relation to *x*.

◉ Visualize It!

12 Interpret Use the graph to determine the mass of 7 cm³ of water.

_____

_____

_____

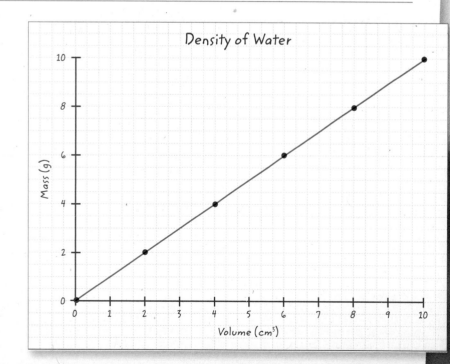

The density of water is an example of a linear relationship.

Nonlinear Relationships

Sometimes, the graph of the relationship between the independent variable and dependent variable studied is not a straight line but a smooth curve. Any graph in which the relationship between the variables cannot be shown with a straight line is called a *nonlinear graph*.

Graphs allow scientists to determine the relationship between variables. In a direct relationship, the value of one variable increases as the value of the other variable increases. In contrast, an inverse relationship is one in which the value of one variable decreases as the other increases. The graph of a direct relationship is an upward sloping line. The graph of an inverse relationship is a downward sloping line.

Active Reading **13 Apply** Describe the difference between linear and nonlinear relationships on a graph.

_____

_____

_____

_____

_____

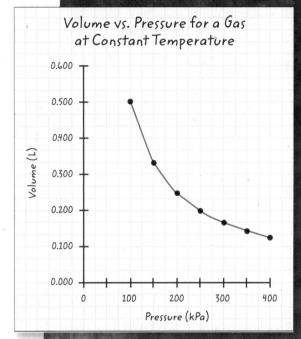

Both of these graphs show nonlinear relationships.

Visualize It!

14 Infer Describe the relationship shown in the graph of Suzi's Surf Shop Sales. Then use the graph to find the approximate sales of the surf shop in 2007.

_____

_____

_____

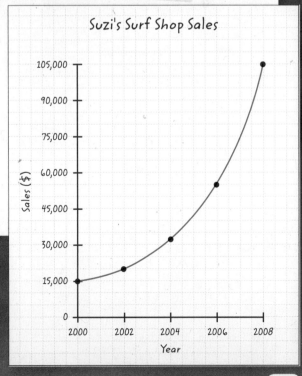

The Perfect Model

How do scientists select a model?

A **model** is a representation of an object or a process that allows scientists to study something in greater detail. The best models are those that most closely resemble the system, process, or object they represent.

By the Kind of Information It Shows

Scientists use many different kinds of physical and mathematical models. A physical model is something that is drawn or built. Maps and globes are some of the oldest types of physical models. These are two-dimensional models. Two-dimensional models have length and width but not height. A three-dimensional model has length, width, and height. A diorama of a classroom is a three-dimensional model. Scientists also use mathematical models to represent how the natural world functions. With mathematical models, you can predict the results of changes in a system. A computer simulation is one type of mathematical model.

Active Reading

15 Apply As you read, underline some examples of models.

Visualize It!

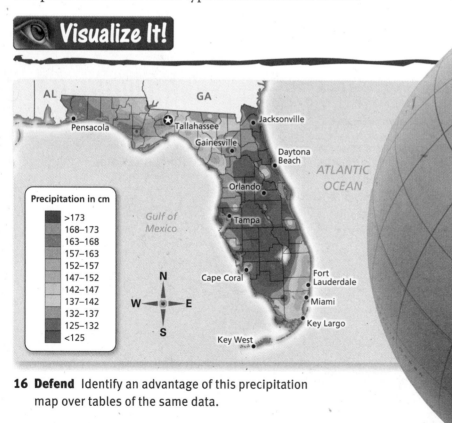

Precipitation in cm

	>173
	168–173
	163–168
	157–163
	152–157
	147–152
	142–147
	137–142
	132–137
	125–132
	<125

16 Defend Identify an advantage of this precipitation map over tables of the same data.

_____

_____

_____

By How It Can Be Used

A two-dimensional floor plan of a building would give you a good idea of the building's layout. You could add furniture to the floor plan to see how you would use the space, but you would not be able to determine anything about the height of the furniture in the room. A three-dimensional model would allow you to see the walls and windows, and get a better feeling for how objects fit in the room. A computerized simulation of the building could enable you to see what it would be like to move through the building.

Similar models could be made of a molecule such as DNA. A two-dimensional drawing of the molecule would show the atoms that make up the molecule and how those atoms are arranged. A three-dimensional model would enable you to study the molecule from different angles. A simulation would enable you to see how the molecule functions. Today, many processes in science can be modeled in great detail. The information needed from the model determines the type of model that is used.

Think Outside the Book Inquiry

19 Criticize Many advertisements feature models. Find an example of a nonhuman model in a magazine. Write a critique of the model. Consider the following questions: "How useful is the model? What has been left out or exaggerated? How could the model be improved?"

18 Predict Scale is the relationship between the dimensions of a model and the dimensions of the real object. How could the scale on this map be helpful when taking a trip?

_____

_____

_____

_____

_____

Inquiry

17 Infer What are two advantages of the globe over the precipitation map of Florida for understanding characteristics of Florida? What are two advantages of the map over the globe?

_____

_____

_____

© Houghton Mifflin Harcourt Publishing Company • Image Credits: ©Cartesia/PhotoDisc/Getty Images

Visual Summary

To complete this summary, circle the correct word. Then use the key below to check your answers. You can use this page to review the main concepts of the lesson.

A graph in which the relationship between the independent and dependent variable can be shown with a straight line is a linear graph.

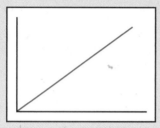

20 The dependent / independent variable is usually found on the x-axis of a graph.

A graph in which the relationship between the variables cannot be shown with a straight line is called a nonlinear graph.

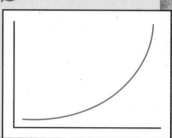

21 If the rate of change of the dependent variable with respect to the independent variable is not constant, then the relationship between the variables is linear / nonlinear.

Representing Data

A scientific model is a representation of an object or system.

22 A globe is an example of a mathematical / physical model.

23 An equation is an example of a mathematical / physical model.

Scientists select models based on their advantages and limitations.

24 A road map is a two-dimensional / three-dimensional model.

25 Conclude You and a friend each decide to build the same model airplane. After the airplanes are built, you decide to conduct an investigation to determine which airplane can glide through the air the longest. Outline a plan to conduct your investigation.

Lesson Review

Vocabulary

Fill in the blank with the term that best completes the following sentences.

1 The _____ variable in an investigation is the variable that is deliberately manipulated.

2 The _____ variable in an investigation is the variable that changes in response to changes in the investigation.

3 A(n) _____ can be a physical or mathematical representation of an object or a process.

Key Concepts

4 Identify Alfonso is conducting an experiment to determine whether temperature affects how fast earthworms move. What are the independent and dependent variables in his experiment?

_____
_____
_____
_____

5 Apply When creating a graph, why is an appropriate title for a graph important?

_____
_____
_____

6 Provide Give an example of a model used in science that is larger than the real object and an example of a model that is smaller than the real object.

_____
_____
_____
_____

Critical Thinking

Use this graph to answer the following questions.

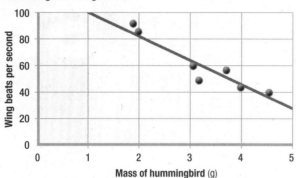

Hummingbird Wing Beats

7 Interpret In this graph, what are the independent and dependent variables?

_____
_____
_____
_____

8 Describe Explain a trend or pattern you observe in the graph.

_____
_____
_____
_____
_____
_____

9 Analyze Both a globe and a flat world map can model features of Earth. Give an example of when you would use each of these models.

_____
_____
_____
_____
_____

Science and Society

ESSENTIAL QUESTION

How do science and society work together?

By the end of this lesson, you should be able to describe the impact that science has had on society and society has had on science, especially in regard to political, social, and economic concerns and decisions.

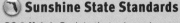

Sunshine State Standards

SC.8.N.4.1 Explain that science is one of the processes that can be used to inform decision making at the community, state, national, and international levels.

SC.8.N.4.2 Explain how political, social, and economic concerns can affect science, and vice versa.

LA.6.4.2.2 The student will record information (e.g., observations, notes, lists, charts, legends) related to a topic, including visual aids to organize and record information and include a list of sources used.

Science and society work hand in hand. For example, when society requires high-security measures, science answers with iris scanners, such as this one. An iris scanner uses unique patterns in a person's eye to identify the person.

Engage Your Brain

1 Discriminate Circle the word that best completes the following sentences.

Few / Most parts of our lives today have been influenced by science.

Political, economic, and social decision-making is *often / never* based on scientific information.

All / Many important scientific discoveries have been made within the past 100 years.

2 Relate You may have seen the icon above on recycling containers. Write your impression of how the recycling icon might symbolize the effects of science on society.

_____

_____

_____

_____

_____

_____

 ## Active Reading

3 Synthesize Many English words have their roots in other languages. The word science comes from the Latin word *scientia*, which means *knowledge*. Use the word *scientist* or *scientific* in a sentence.

_____

_____

_____

_____

Vocabulary

4 Apply In this lesson, you'll learn about *society*, *economics*, and *politics* in relation to science. As you learn about each term in this lesson, create your own explanation or sketch to remind you what each term refers to.

In what areas does science help us make decisions?

Science has led to lifesaving discoveries and has taught us to protect our resources, too. Science also helps people make decisions that affect us all. For example, scientists can gather data about the health of our environment. Then, decision-makers use this data to make rules and laws.

Water-quality rules and laws depend on science. Over 150 years ago, doctor John Snow found that bacteria in polluted water could make people sick with cholera, a deadly disease. The polluted water was not safe to drink! Now, decision-makers use science to decide how much bacteria and other substances can be found in water before it is unsafe to drink.

 Active Reading

5 Diagram As you read, complete the graphic organizer below about science and decisions.

Science affects decisions made

In Communities

Community governments make decisions about a local area. For example, they make sure the water in their area follows water-quality rules and laws. Water supplies are tested often. If levels of bacteria are too high, your community leaders may decide to warn you to boil water before drinking it.

In States

State governments make decisions that affect the whole state or many parts of the state. For example, state agencies test water used by more than one community. They may decide to close a beach if they find levels of bacteria that scientists say are harmful. They also may make rules against fishing if fish show high levels of dangerous substances.

WARNING
RUNOFF/STORM DRAIN WATER MAY CAUSE ILLNESS
AVOID CONTACT WITH PONDED OR FLOWING RUNOFF AND THE AREA WHERE RUNOFF ENTERS THE OCEAN

AVISO
CORRIENTE DE AGUA/AGUA DEL DRENAJE DE TORMENTA PUEDE CAUSAR ENFERMEDADES
EVITE CONTACTO CON AGUA DE DESAGÜE QUE ESTE ESTANCADA O CORRIENDO Y EL AREA DONDE DESEMBOCA AL OCEANO
ORANGE COUNTY ENVIRONMENTAL HEALTH DIVISION
FOR FURTHER INFORMATION, CALL (714) 667-3752

everywhere!

Throughout the Nation

Some decisions affect the whole country. The United States government created the Environmental Protection Agency (EPA) in 1970. The EPA sets rules and laws for water quality for the entire country. These laws are often based on science. The EPA may make rules about how industries can use our country's water. For example, there are rules about whether waste materials can be dumped into lakes and rivers. The rules help us keep our water safe.

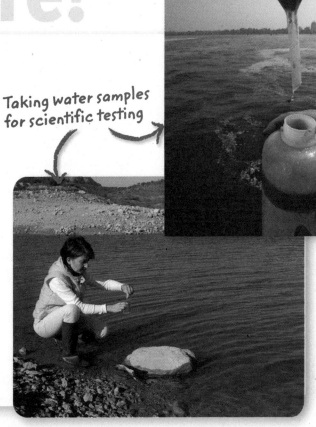

Taking water samples for scientific testing

6 Explain How does science help us protect our nation's resources?

_____

_____

_____

At the International Level

Some decisions affect more than one country. Oceans, rivers, and other bodies of water often affect more than one country. For example, the Great Lakes touch both the United States and Canada. Any action taken by one country could affect the other in matters of health and environmental policy. So, nations also need to adhere to agreed-upon rules for the proper use of shared water resources. Science gives a country's representatives the data they need to talk about and make decisions about important matters like these.

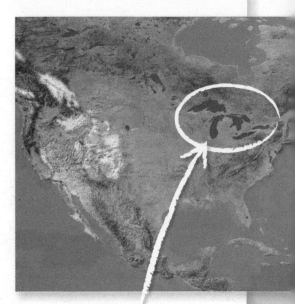

The Great Lakes are bordered by Canada to the north and the United States to the south.

7 Describe How might a nation be affected if another nation did not follow agreed-upon water rules?

_____

_____

_____

_____

High Goals

How can science and politics affect each other?

Scientific investigations have led to new technologies that have improved human lives. How do scientists decide what to investigate? The direction of science is influenced by many things, such as political, societal, and economic concerns. Science, in turn, affects politics, society, and the economy.

The Space Race is an example of how science and politics affect each other. In 1957, the former Soviet Union sent the first satellite into orbit. American leaders wanted to show that we could excel in space exploration, too.

Government Sets a Goal

The Space Race was not only a scientific rivalry. It was part of a bigger political contest between nations. Politics and government leaders sometimes set a direction or goal for science. In 1961, U.S. president John F. Kennedy announced the goal that the United States would put an American on the moon within the decade. Kennedy made it clear the country would give all the resources it could to this task. Without such political drive, scientists would not have had the funding and other resources to take on space exploration.

Active Reading

8 Apply As you read, underline events that influenced the path of science.

The Space Race: A Decade of Science

Americans responded to the Space Race with supreme scientific effort and enormous funding.

9 Predict How do you think you would have reacted to President Kennedy's call to Americans to support the Space Race?

_____

_____

_____

_____

In 1961, President Kennedy announced the goal of putting a person safely on the moon. Scientists got to work on the goal!

Science Meets the Goal

Researchers from all fields of science worked on the challenges of space flight. Many scientists worked on how to support human life in space. For example, they dehydrated food to ensure an adequate supply for astronauts. They also learned how to communicate from thousands of miles away. When *Apollo 11* landed on the moon in 1969, it was a win for both the nation and science. The work of the scientists and engineers had put two Americans on the moon.

The United States landed on the moon because government and politics made the work of scientists possible. But was the Space Race worth our effort and money? Some people say we should have focused on problems here on Earth. Other people say the Space Race led to other discoveries that improved the lives of everyone. For example, the Space Race taught us ways to preserve food. As a result, we can get more nourishment to people all over the world.

10 List Use the table below to list some pros and cons of using resources for the Space Race.

Pros	Cons

11 Devise If you were an astronaut in space, what would you want to explore to help society?

_____

_____

_____

_____

1969: An American on the moon!

Where do we go from here?

Big Help!

How do science, society, and economics interact?

Politics are not the only drivers of science. Societal needs and economics influence science, too. If society sees no value in certain research, scientists may not get funding for the research. Also, people may not buy or use new technologies when they are made.

Society Has a Need

One example of societal needs driving science happens when there are outbreaks of diseases, such as polio, AIDS, or the H1N1 influenza. Polio, AIDS, and H1N1 are diseases caused by viruses. These diseases can cause suffering and even death. Society needs solutions when diseases threaten the health of the nation and world. So, society turns to science.

Active Reading

12 Identify What is an example of a societal need that science can address? _____

13 Apply Influenza, also called the flu, is a viral infection. In addition to getting vaccinated, what are some ways that you can avoid influenza?

_____
_____
_____
_____
_____
_____

One way to stop the spread of disease is to limit exposure of sick people to healthy people. This airport scanner allows airport employees to see if passengers have fevers, a sign of illness.

Science Addresses the Need

Scientists find many ways to meet the needs of society. Societal needs may lead some scientists to prioritize research such as vaccine development. Vaccines prevent people from getting viral diseases. After an outbreak of polio in the early 1950s, Jonas Salk pioneered the first successful polio vaccine. This vaccine was given as a shot. Later, Albert Sabin developed another polio vaccine that was taken by mouth. Scientists continue to explore and learn new things. Sometimes, new scientific knowledge improves upon or challenges existing knowledge.

Science and Economics Affect Each Other

Preventing disease is just one example of how science benefits society. But science can be expensive. Priorities for how to spend money on science must be set. Science, in turn, affects the economy. Lifesaving improvements allow people to live longer, which changes how much money we make over our lifetimes. Making more money allows us to spend more. And spending more puts money back into the economy.

Think Outside the Book *Inquiry*

14 Investigate In 1900, the three leading causes of death in the United States were all infectious diseases. In 2000, none of the three leading causes were infectious diseases. Do research to find out the current leading causes of death. Then, make a poster describing prevention methods that you and your family can use.

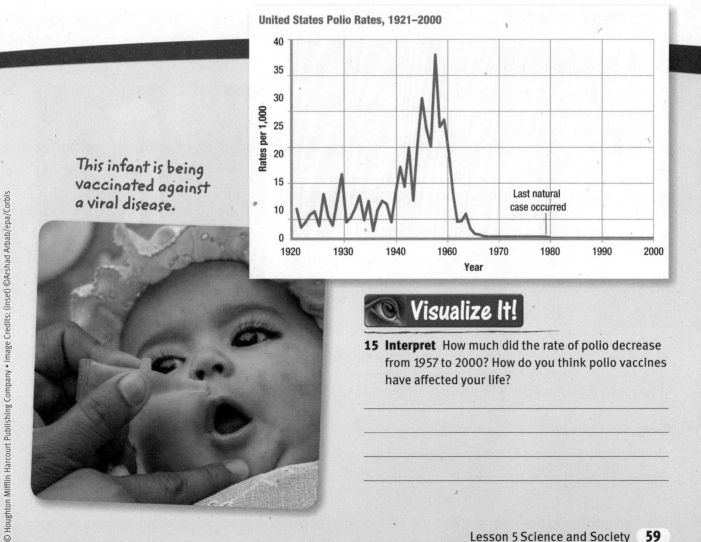

This infant is being vaccinated against a viral disease.

United States Polio Rates, 1921–2000

Last natural case occurred

Visualize It!

15 Interpret How much did the rate of polio decrease from 1957 to 2000? How do you think polio vaccines have affected your life?

_____

_____

_____

_____

Visual Summary

To complete this summary, check the box that indicates true or false. Then, use the key below to check your answers. You can use this page to review the main concepts of the lesson.

Science and Society

Science helps society.

Scientific advancements improve our quality of life.

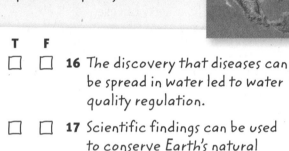

T	F	
☐	☐	**16** The discovery that diseases can be spread in water led to water quality regulation.
☐	☐	**17** Scientific findings can be used to conserve Earth's natural resources.

Society promotes science.

Societal needs are some of the issues addressed by science.

T	F	
☐	☐	**18** Science sets its own goals without influence from society.
☐	☐	**19** Society, economics, and politics drive the direction of science.

Science is affected by politics, economics, and culture.

Priorities for science are often based on political, economic, cultural, and other nonscientific considerations.

T	F	
☐	☐	**20** Political considerations played a great role in the decision for the United States to enter the Space Race.
☐	☐	**21** The Space Race provided no direct technological or other benefits to society.

Answers: 16 T; 17 T; 18 F; 19 T; 20 T; 21 F

22 Debate Some scientific discoveries have no obvious practical application. Are you in favor of funding scientific endeavors that don't seem to have an obvious application in the near future?

Lesson Review

Vocabulary

Draw a line to connect the following terms to how they affect science.

1 economics

2 politics

3 society

A leaders may promote certain scientific research

B events, such as disease outbreak, prioritize scientific research

C funding is not available for all potential research

Key Concepts

4 Discriminate What was Jonas Salk's scientific contribution to society?

A He developed a cure for polio.

B He convinced Americans to support the Space Race.

C He developed a vaccine to prevent polio.

D He demonstrated that a disease could be spread in water.

5 List Science helps policy-makers decide which laws and rules to make. At what levels does science affect policies?

_____

_____

_____

_____

6 Determine Give an example of how politics can affect science.

_____

_____

_____

_____

_____

_____

Critical Thinking

The table below shows the sources of power for the people in the city of Riverview. Use this table to answer the following questions.

Power Sources for City of Riverview		
Source	**Percent from Source**	**Type**
Coal burning	20%	Nonrenewable resource
Hydroelectric power	70%	Renewable resource
Wind power	10%	Renewable resource

7 Apply What is the main source of power in Riverview?

_____

_____

8 Conclude Ten years ago, the only power source in Riverview came from coal burning. Why might the people of Riverview have wanted to change their power source?

_____

_____

_____

_____

_____

_____

9 Infer What role did science play in this change?

_____

_____

_____

_____

_____

My Notes

Unit 1 **Summary**

Representing Data —— is critical for ——> **Scientific Investigations**

What is Science?

Scientific Knowledge —— impacts the relationship between ——> **Science and Society**

1 Interpret Science is the systematic study of natural events and conditions. Explain how the Graphic Organizer above illustrates this definition.

_____
_____
_____
_____

2 Relate How can scientific knowledge impact a decision about treating a disease outbreak?

_____
_____
_____
_____

3 Explain Why is empirical evidence used to support scientific explanations?

_____
_____
_____
_____

4 Apply Why is it important to organize scientific data?

_____
_____
_____
_____

© Houghton Mifflin Harcourt Publishing Company • Image Credits: (l) ©Vincent Realmuto, JPL-Caltech/Photo Researchers, Inc.; (r) ©Pierre Vauthey/Corbis Sygma

Multiple Choice
Identify the choice that best completes the statement or answers the question.

1 Astrologers relate the location of stars and planets to events in human lives. Many years ago, people classified astrology as a science. Why do modern scientists consider astrology to be a pseudoscience?

   A. Astrology does not involve the use of telescopes.

   B. Astrology does not offer conclusive proof of its claims.

   C. Astrology is based on observations of extremely distant objects.

   D. Astrology is not supported by empirical evidence.

2 A physician performed an experiment to investigate the effects of exercise on students. He examined 25 volunteers and found them to be in good health. He then had the students perform exercises such as jogging and bicycling. The doctor recorded the students' pulse rates before, during, and after each activity. Which was the dependent variable in this experiment?

   F. the students' health

   G. the exercise

   H. the number of volunteers

   I. the students' pulse rates

3 In 1897, Joseph Thomson discovered that atoms contained electrons. He proposed a change in the atomic theory of that time, and the theory was modified because of his discovery. Since Thomson's discovery, atomic theory has been further modified. What is the **best** explanation for why scientific theories are modified?

   A. Theories more than ten years old are usually out of date.

   B. Scientists want to prove that the work of other scientists is wrong.

   C. New evidence that supports a revision prompts scientists to modify earlier theories.

   D. So much information is available today that it is harder to focus research and disprove theories.

4 Ana did an experiment to find out whether spider plants grow faster under fluorescent lighting or incandescent lighting. Under fluorescent lighting, Ana's plants grew 1.5 cm taller in two months. She gave her notes to Al, who did the same experiment with similar results. Which term describes Al's experiment?

   F. plagiarism

   G. replication

   H. pseudoscience

   I. repetition

5   Scientific investigations involve many steps and processes. Which characteristics define a laboratory experiment?

　　A.   hypothesis, models, and calculations

　　B.   test variables, data, and uncontrolled conditions

　　C.   data, conclusions, and unregulated environment

　　D.   independent and dependent variables, data, and controlled conditions

6   Which of the following is an example of how economics can affect science?

　　F.   Limited funding may lead scientists to research one topic instead of another.

　　G.   Legislators may create new laws about the use of natural resources based on the recommendations of scientists.

　　H.   A health crisis may drive scientists to prioritize research on new medications or vaccines.

　　I.   Community leaders may use scientific data to support a recommendation for costly pollution clean-ups.

7   Imagine that the label on a sunscreen product reads, "Recommended by nine out of ten doctors." No other information regarding this claim is provided. Why would a scientist tell a consumer to be wary of this statistical claim?

　　A.   Sunscreen products are ineffective.

　　B.   The supporting scientific data are missing.

　　C.   The claim cannot be confirmed or refuted.

　　D.   The claim cannot be reevaluated when new information emerges.

8   Scientists think that about 65 million years ago, an asteroid struck Mexico and created a huge cloud of dust in the atmosphere. The dust contained iridium, an element found in asteroids. The dust cloud blocked the sun, killing most of the plants on Earth. Plant-eating dinosaurs starved. Without herbivores to eat, meat-eating dinosaurs died, too. Scientists studied rock layers from the time of the strike to confirm their theory. What evidence would support the theory that an asteroid impact could have contributed to the extinction of the dinosaurs?

　　F.   a rock layer containing no iridium

　　G.   a rock layer containing fossils of human beings

　　H.   a rock layer containing greater than usual amounts of iridium

　　I.   a rock layer containing fossils from 100 million years ago

9 A map is a type of model. The map below shows the migratory range of the Florida manatee.

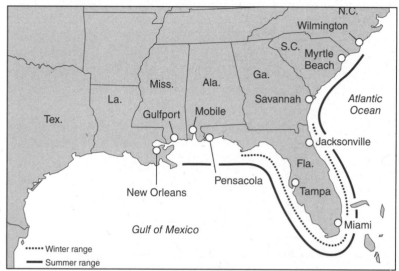

Which of the following statements is **not** supported by the map?

A. The summer migratory range of manatees includes Myrtle Beach, South Carolina.

B. The winter migratory range of manatees includes Pensacola, Florida.

C. Manatees have a greater migratory range in summer than in winter.

D. Manatees can be found near Tampa, Florida, throughout the year.

10 The graph below shows the number of people who visited doctors because of influenza-like illnesses over a two-year period.

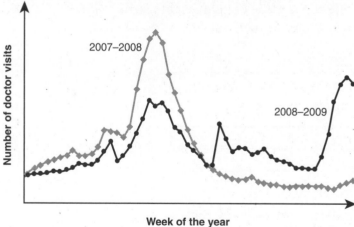

What can you conclude from this graph?

F. Influenza-like illnesses follow a steady pattern throughout the year.

G. Scientists can predict that the number of influenza-like illnesses will decrease for 2009–2010.

H. The severity of influenza-like symptoms decreased in 2008-2009.

I. The number of people who developed influenza-like illnesses did not peak at the same time in 2008–2009 as it did in 2007–2008.

11 Ms. Adam, a high school coach, counts the male and female athletes on her school's teams over the last four years. The bar graph below shows the number of male and female high school athletes over a four-year period of time.

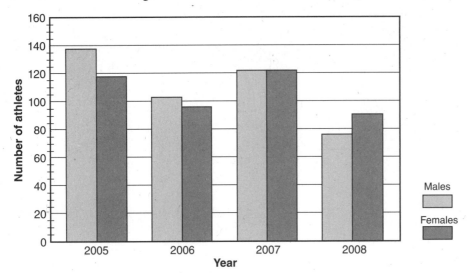

What was the **increase** in the number of female athletes from 2006 to 2007?

A. 22

B. 26

C. 31

D. 45

12 Clara tests a hypothesis that the heavier of two materials will insulate cold drinks better than the lighter-weight material. She adds equal volumes of the same cold beverage to two cups. One cup is made of lightweight plastic foam, and the other cup is made of a heavier, ceramic material. She records her results in a chart.

Material	Time for beverage to warm to room temperature (hours)
plastic foam	3.25
ceramic	2.50

How are these experimental results valuable to Clara?

F. The results explain why the materials perform differently.

G. Clara has to accept that her hypothesis was not supported.

H. Clara can use a different heavier material to see if she obtains different results.

I. The results can be communicated with others through newspapers, magazines, and the Internet to increase the validity of her results.

The Cell

Big Idea 14

Organization and Development of Living Organisms

Big Idea 15

Diversity and Evolution of Living Organisms

Colorized picture of the organelles of a cell through a modern microscope

What do you think?

As microscopes have become more powerful, our understanding of cells and their functions has also increased. What kinds of questions would you use a microscope to answer?

Cells seen through an early microscope

Unit 2
The Cell

CITIZEN SCIENCE
Seeing through Microscopes

Microscopes have come a long way. Today, we can see the details of the surface of metals at the atomic level. Microscopes have allowed us to study our world at some of the smallest levels.

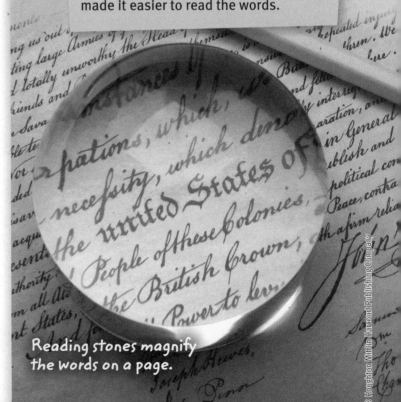

Circa 1000 CE
Although people may have used rock crystals to magnify things thousands of years ago, it wasn't until about 1000 CE that people were able to form and polish clear-glass partial spheres. Placing these reading stones on top of a page made it easier to read the words.

Reading stones magnify the words on a page.

© Houghton Mifflin Harcourt Publishing Company

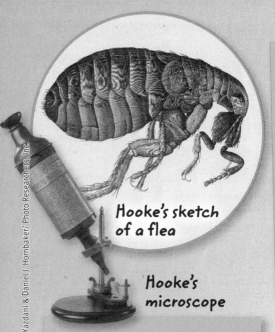

Hooke's sketch of a flea

Hooke's microscope

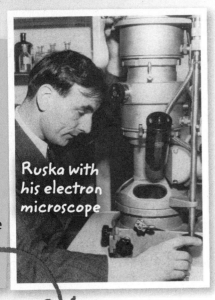

Ruska with his electron microscope

1931

Ernst Ruska developed the electron microscope, which shows much greater detail than light microscopes do. The electron microscope uses an electron beam instead of light to show things as small as the structure of viruses. Ruska received the Nobel Prize in Physics in 1986 for his breakthrough.

1665

Robert Hooke was interested in many areas of science. In 1665, Hooke invented a light microscope to look at small creatures like fleas. Hooke's microscope was similar to a telescope, but it also had a way to shine light on the object.

Atoms at platinum's surface

1981

The scanning tunneling microscope changed the way scientists look at things again. Using this microscope, we can look at images of surfaces at the atomic level. The microscope uses a beam of electrons to map a surface. This information is collected and processed so that it can be viewed on a computer screen.

What's in a Microscope?

① Think About It

A What characteristics do different microscopes have?

_____

_____

_____

_____

B Why are they used?

_____

_____

_____

_____

_____

② Conduct Research

Choose a specific kind of microscope and research how it is used, whether it is used to view live or dead samples, and its range of magnification.

_____

_____

_____

_____

_____

_____

Take It Home

With an adult, prepare an oral presentation for your class on the microscope that you have researched.

© Houghton Mifflin Harcourt Publishing Company • Image Credits: (tl) ©Photo by SSPL/Getty Images; (microscope) ©Dave King/Dorling Kindersley/Getty Images; (tr) AP Photo/HO; (c) ©Drs. Ali Yazdani & Daniel J. Hornbaker/Photo Researchers, Inc.

The Characteristics of Cells

ESSENTIAL QUESTION

What are living things made of?

By the end of this lesson, you should be able to explain the components of the scientific theory of cells.

Sunshine State Standards

SC.6.N.2.2 Explain that scientific knowledge is durable because it is open to change as new evidence or interpretations are encountered.

SC.6.L.14.2 Investigate and explain the components of the scientific theory of cells (cell theory): all organisms are composed of cells (single-celled or multi-cellular), all cells come from pre-existing cells, and cells are the basic unit of life.

LA.6.4.2.2 The student will record information (e.g., observations, notes, lists, charts, legends) related to a topic, including visual aids to organize and record information and include a list of sources used.

MA.6.A.3.6 Construct and analyze tables, graphs, and equations to describe linear functions and other simple relations using both common language and algebraic notation.

People communicate to others through talking, signing, body language, and other methods. Inside your body, cells communicate too. Brain cells, like the ones shown here, control balance, posture, and muscle coordination.

Engage Your Brain

1 Predict Check T or F to show whether you think each statement is true or false.

T	F	
☐	☐	All living things are made up of one or more cells.
☐	☐	Rocks are made up of cells.
☐	☐	All cells are the same size.
☐	☐	Cells perform life functions for living things.

2 Describe Sketch your idea of what a cell looks like. Label any parts you include in your sketch.

Active Reading

3 Synthesize Many English words have their roots in other languages. Use the Greek words below to make an educated guess about the meanings of the words *prokaryote* and *eukaryote*. Here *kernel* refers to the nucleus where genetic material is contained in some cells.

Word part	Meaning
pro-	before
eu-	true
karyon	kernel

Vocabulary Terms

- cell
- organism
- cell membrane
- cytoplasm
- organelle
- nucleus
- prokaryote
- eukaryote

4 Apply As you learn the definition of each vocabulary term in this lesson, create your own sketches of a prokaryotic cell and a eukaryotic cell and label the parts in each cell.

prokaryote:

_____

_____

eukaryote:

_____

_____

Cell-ebrate!

What is a cell?

Like all living things, you are made up of cells. A **cell** is the smallest functional and structural unit of all living organisms. An **organism** is any living thing. All organisms are made up of cells. Some organisms are just one cell. Others, like humans, contain trillions of cells. An organism carries out all of its own life processes.

Robert Hooke was the first person to describe cells. In 1665, he built a microscope to look at tiny objects. One day, he looked at a thin slice of cork from the bark of a cork tree. The cork looked as if it was made of little boxes. Hooke named these boxes *cells*, which means "little rooms" in Latin.

Visualize It!

6 Compare Looking at the photos of the three different cells, what do the cells have in common?

_____

_____

_____

_____

Active Reading

5 Identify As you read, underline the reasons why cells are important.

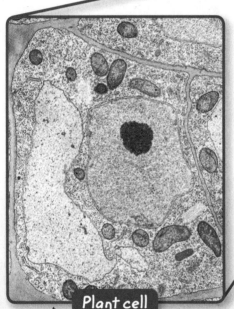

Plant cell

Plant cells range in size from 10 μm to 100 μm. They can be much larger than animal cells.

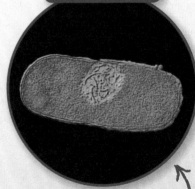

Bacterial cell

Bacterial cells are up to 1000 times smaller than human cells.

The average size of a human cell is 10 μm. It would take about 50 average human cells to cover the dot on this letter i.

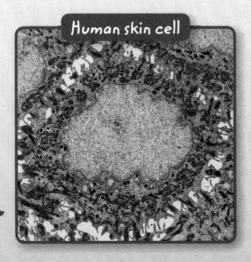

Human skin cell

Why are most cells small?

Most cells are too small to be seen without a microscope. Cells are small because their size is limited by their outer surface area. Cells take in food and get rid of wastes through their outer surface. As a cell grows, it needs more food and produces more waste. Therefore, more materials pass through its outer surface. However, as a cell grows, the cell's volume increases faster than the surface area. If a cell gets too large, the cell's surface area will not be large enough to take in enough nutrients or pump out enough wastes. The ratio of the cell's outer surface area to the cell's volume is called the *surface area-to-volume ratio*. Smaller cells have a greater surface area-to-volume ratio than larger cells.

Do the Math

Here's an example of how to calculate the surface area-to-volume ratio of the cube shown at the right.

Sample Problem

A Calculate the surface area.

surface area of cube =

number of faces × area of one face

surface area of cube = $6(2 \text{ cm} \times 2 \text{ cm})$

surface area of cube = 24 cm^2

B Calculate the volume.

volume of cube = side × side × side

volume of cube = $2 \text{ cm} \times 2 \text{ cm} \times 2 \text{ cm}$

volume of cube = 8 cm^3

C Calculate the surface area-to-volume ratio. A ratio is a comparison between numbers. It can be written by placing a colon between the numbers being compared.

surface area : volume = $24 \text{ cm}^2 : 8 \text{ cm}^3$

surface area : volume = $3 \text{ cm}^2 : 1 \text{ cm}^3$

You Try It

7 Calculate What is the surface area-to-volume ratio of a cube whose sides are 3 cm long?

A Calculate the surface area.

B Calculate the volume.

C Calculate the surface area-to-volume ratio.

Cell *Hall of Fame*

What is the cell theory?

Scientific knowledge often results from combining the work of several scientists. For example, the discoveries of Matthias Schleiden (muh•THY•uhs SHLY•duhn), Theodor Schwann (THEE•oh•dohr SHVAHN), and Rudolf Virchow (ROO•dawlf VIR•koh) led to one very important theory called the *cell theory*. The cell theory lists three basic characteristics of all cells and organisms:

- All organisms are made up of one or more cells.
- The cell is the basic unit of all organisms.
- All cells come from existing cells.

The cell theory is fundamental to the study of organisms, medicine, heredity, evolution, and all other aspects of life science.

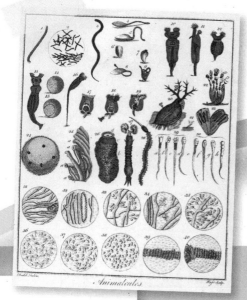

Animalcules.

Visualize It!

8 Provide As you read, fill in the missing events on the timeline.

Model of Hooke's microscope

1673
Anton van Leeuwenhoek made careful drawings of the organisms he observed.

1665
Robert Hooke sees tiny, box-like spaces when using a microscope like this to observe thin slices of cork. He calls these spaces cells.

1858
Rudolf Virchow proposed that cells could form only from the division of other cells.

9 Explain How can microscopes help you see cells? First, think of a good place to collect a sample of cells. Then, in a paragraph, describe how to prepare a microscope slide to observe those cells.

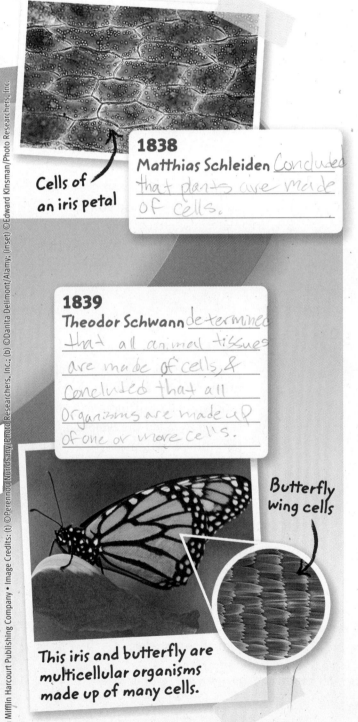

Cells of an iris petal

1838
Matthias Schleiden _Concluded that plants are made of cells._

1839
Theodor Schwann _determined that all animal tissues are made of cells, & concluded that all organisms are made up of one or more cells._

Butterfly wing cells

This iris and butterfly are multicellular organisms made up of many cells.

All Organisms Are Made Up of One or More Cells

Anton van Leeuwenhoek (AN•tahn VAN LAY•vuhn•huk) was the first person to describe actual living cells when he looked at a drop of pond water under a microscope. These studies made other scientists wonder if all living things were made up of cells. In 1838, Matthias Schleiden concluded that plants are made of cells. Then in 1839, Theodor Schwann determined that all animal tissues are made of cells. He concluded that all organisms are made up of one or more cells.

Organisms that are made up of just one cell are called _unicellular organisms_. The single cell of a unicellular organism must carry out all of the functions for life. Organisms that are made up of more than one cell are called _multicellular organisms_. The cells of multicellular organism often have specialized functions.

The Cell Is the Basic Unit of All Organisms

Based on his observations about the cellular make up of organisms, Schwann made another conclusion. He determined that the cell is the basic unit of all living things. Thus, Schwann wrote the first two parts of the cell theory.

All Cells Come from Existing Cells

In 1858, Rudolf Virchow, a doctor, proposed that cells could form only from the division of other cells. Virchow then added the third part of the cell theory that all cells come from existing cells.

Active Reading

10 Summarize What is the cell theory?

_____

_____

_____

_____

_____

On the Cellular

What parts do all cells have in common?

Different cells vary in size and shape. However, all cells have some parts in common, including cell membranes, cytoplasm, organelles, and DNA. These different parts help the cell to carry out all the tasks needed for life.

Active Reading

11 Identify As you read, underline the function of cell membranes, organelles, and DNA.

Cell Membrane

A **cell membrane** is a protective layer that covers a cell's surface and acts as a barrier between the inside of a cell and the cell's environment. It also controls materials, such as water and oxygen, that move into and out of a cell.

Cytoplasm

The region enclosed by the cell membrane that includes the fluid and all of the *organelles* of the cell is called the **cytoplasm** (SY•tuh•plaz•uhm).

Organelles

An **organelle** is a small body in a cell's cytoplasm that is specialized to perform a specific function. Cells can have one or more types of organelles. Most, but not all, organelles have a membrane.

DNA

Deoxyribonucleic acid, or DNA, is genetic material that provides instructions for all cell processes. Organisms inherit DNA from their parent or parents. In some cells, the DNA is contained in a membrane-bound organelle called the **nucleus**. In other types of cells, the DNA is not contained in a nucleus.

What are the two types of cells?

Although cells have some basic parts in common, there are some important differences. The way that cells store their DNA is the main difference between the two cell types.

 **Active Reading**

12 Define As you read, underline the differences between prokaryotes and eukaryotes.

Prokaryotic

A **prokaryote** (proh•KAIR•ee•oht) is a single-celled organism that does not have a nucleus or membrane-bound organelles. Its DNA is located in the cytoplasm. Prokaryotic cells contain organelles called *ribosomes* that do not have a membrane. Some prokaryotic cells have hairlike structures called *flagella* that help them move. Prokaryotes, which include all bacteria and archaea, are smaller than eukaryotes.

Eukaryotic

A **eukaryote** (yoo•KAIR•ee•oht) is an organism made up of cells that contain their DNA in a nucleus. Eukaryotic cells contain membrane-bound organelles, as well as ribosomes. Not all eukaryotic cells are the same. Animals, plants, protists, and fungi are eukaryotes. All multicellular organisms are eukaryotes. Most eukaryotes are multicellular. Some eukaryotes, such as amoebas and yeasts, are unicellular.

Visualize It!

13 Identify Use the list of terms below to fill in the blanks with the matching cell parts in each cell. Some terms are used twice.

DNA in cytoplasm
DNA in nucleus
Cytoplasm
Cell membrane
Organelles

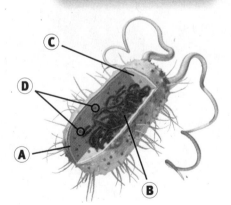

Prokaryotic

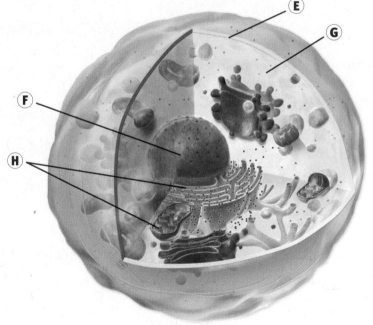

Eukaryotic

A _____

B _____

C _____

D _____

E _____

F _DNA in nucleus_

G _____

H _____

Visual Summary

To complete this summary, fill in the blanks with the correct word or phrase. Then use the key below to check your answers. You can use this page to review the main concepts of the lesson.

Cells and Cell Theory

A cell is the smallest unit that can perform all the processes necessary for life.

14 The cell of a _____ organism must carry out all of its life functions; an organism made up of more than one cell is called a _____ organism.

The cell theory lists three basic principles of all cells and organisms.

15 All cells come from existing _____

All cells have a cell membrane, cytoplasm, organelles, and DNA.

16 The organelle that contains DNA in eukaryotic cells is called a _____

Eukaryotic

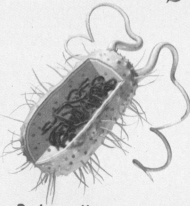

Prokaryotic

Answers: 14 unicellular, multicellular; 15 cells; 16 nucleus

17 Relate Choose an organism that you are familiar with, and explain how the three parts of the cell theory relate to that organism.

Lesson Review

Vocabulary

Fill in the blank with the term that best completes the following sentences.

1 The _____ is the smallest functional and structural unit of all living things.

2 All cells are surrounded by a(n) _____

3 A living thing is called a(n) _____

Key Concepts

4 Describe Discuss two ways that all cells are alike.

_____
_____
_____
_____

5 List What are the main ideas of the cell theory?

_____
_____
_____
_____
_____

6 Compare How do prokaryotes differ from eukaryotes? How are they similar?

_____
_____
_____
_____
_____
_____

Critical Thinking

Use this figure to answer the following questions.

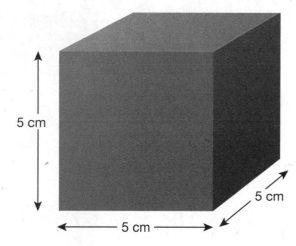

7 Apply What is the surface area-to-volume ratio of this cube?

_____
_____
_____

8 Apply Cells are not as large as this cube. Explain why in terms of a cell's surface area-to-volume ratio.

_____
_____
_____
_____

9 Compare How is the structure of a unicellular organism different than the structure of a multicellular organism? How does this affect function?

_____
_____
_____
_____
_____

Chemistry of Life

ESSENTIAL QUESTION

What are the building blocks of organisms?

By the end of this lesson, you should be able to discuss the chemical makeup of living things.

Sunshine State Standards

SC.6.N.1.1 Define a problem from the sixth grade curriculum, use appropriate reference materials to support scientific understanding, plan and carry out scientific investigation of various types, such as systematic observations or experiments, identify variables, collect and organize data, interpret data in charts, tables, and graphics, analyze information, make predictions, and defend conclusions.

SC.6.L.14.1 Describe and identify patterns in the hierarchical organization of organisms from atoms to molecules and cells to tissues to organs to organ systems to organisms.

LA.6.4.2.2 The student will record information (e.g., observations, notes, lists, charts, legends) related to a topic, including visual aids to organize and record information and include a list of sources used.

These fungi are bioluminescent, which means they produce light from chemical reactions in their bodies. The light attracts insects that disperse the fungi's spores.

Engage Your Brain

1 Describe Fill in the blank with the word or phrase that you think correctly completes the following sentences.

The chemical formula for _____

is H_2O. The *H* stands for hydrogen and the

_____ stands for oxygen.

If you don't get enough water, you might

_____

_____

2 Relate What do you think you are made of?

_____

_____

_____

_____

_____

 ## Active Reading

3 Synthesize You can often define an unknown word if you know the meaning of its word parts. Use the word parts and sentence below to make an educated guess about the meaning of the word *atom*.

Word part	Meaning
a–	not
tom	to cut

Example sentence
Air is mostly made up of oxygen and nitrogen <u>atoms</u>.

atom: _____

_____

_____

Vocabulary Terms

- atom
- molecule
- lipid
- protein
- carbohydrate
- nucleic acid
- phospholipid

4 Identify This list contains the key terms you'll learn in this lesson. As you read, circle the definition of each term.

It's Elementary

What are atoms and molecules?

Think about where you live. The streets are lined with many types of buildings. But these buildings are made from a lot of the same materials, such as bricks, glass, wood, and steel. Similarly, all cells are made from the same materials. The materials in cells are made up of atoms that can join together to form molecules.

Atoms Are the Building Blocks of Matter

The matter that you encounter every day, both living and nonliving, is made up of basic particles called **atoms.** Not all atoms are the same. There are nearly one hundred types of atoms that occur naturally on Earth. These different types of atoms are known as *elements.* Each element has unique properties. For example, oxygen is a colorless gas made up of oxygen atoms. The element gold is a shiny metal made up of gold atoms. Just six elements make up most of the human body. These and other elements are important for cell processes in all living things.

Active Reading

5 Relate How do atoms relate to cells?

Both atoms & Cells are made up of atoms.

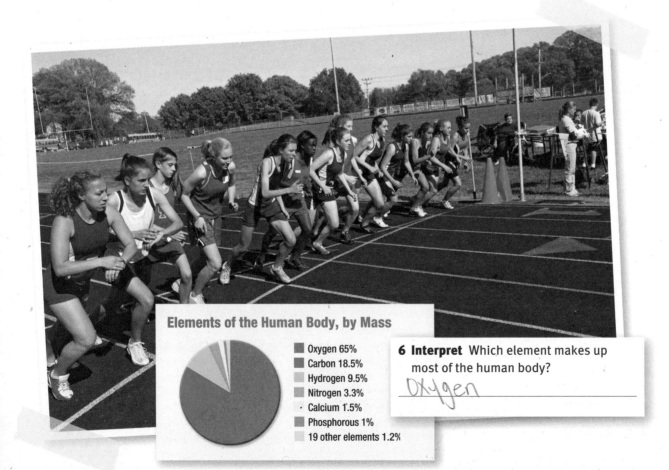

Elements of the Human Body, by Mass

- Oxygen 65%
- Carbon 18.5%
- Hydrogen 9.5%
- Nitrogen 3.3%
- Calcium 1.5%
- Phosphorous 1%
- 19 other elements 1.2%

6 Interpret Which element makes up most of the human body?

Oxygen

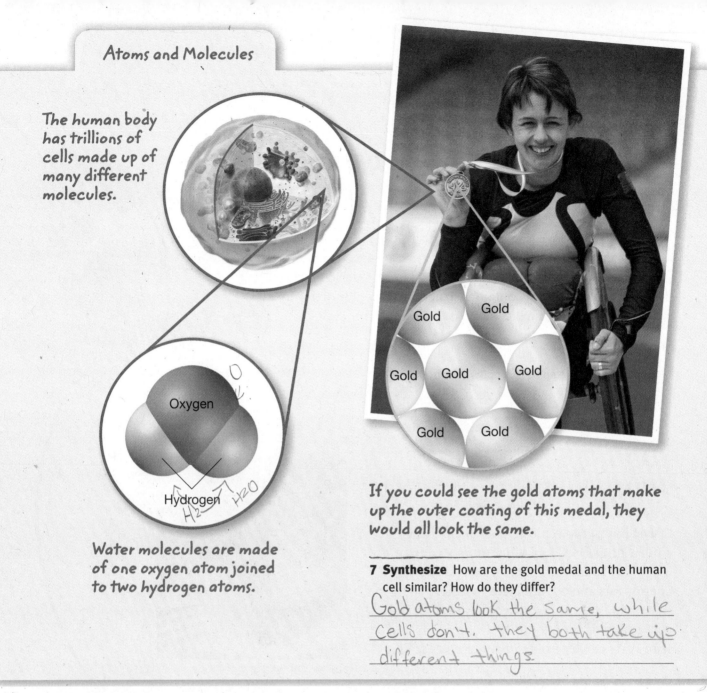

Atoms and Molecules

The human body has trillions of cells made up of many different molecules.

Oxygen

Hydrogen

Water molecules are made of one oxygen atom joined to two hydrogen atoms.

If you could see the gold atoms that make up the outer coating of this medal, they would all look the same.

7 Synthesize How are the gold medal and the human cell similar? How do they differ?

Gold atoms look the same, while cells don't. they both take up different things.

Molecules Are Made of Two or More Atoms

A **molecule** is a group of atoms that are held together by chemical bonds. For example, the molecule of water shown above is made of one oxygen atom bonded to two hydrogen atoms. If you separated the oxygen and hydrogen atoms, then you would no longer have a water molecule.

Some molecules are made up of only one type of atom. For example, a molecule of oxygen gas is made of two oxygen atoms. Other molecules contain different types of atoms. A substance made up of atoms of two or more elements joined by chemical bonds is called a *compound*. Most of the molecules found in cells are also compounds.

Cell Fuel

What are some important types of molecules in cells?

Organisms need certain types of molecules for growth, repair, and other life processes. For example, organisms use nutrients such as lipids, proteins, and carbohydrates for energy and as building materials. You get these nutrients from the food you eat. Nucleic acids are molecules that contain instructions for cell functions. Each of these types of molecules has a role in cell processes.

 **Active Reading**

8 Identify What are some examples of nutrients?

_____

_____

_____

Lipids

A **lipid** is a fat molecule or a molecule that has similar properties. Lipids do not mix with water. They have many jobs in cells, such as storing energy. Fats and oils are lipids that store energy that organisms can use when they need it. Your cells get lipids from foods such as olive oil and fish. Waxes and steroids are other types of lipids.

Proteins

A **protein** is a molecule made up of smaller molecules called *amino acids*. When you eat foods high in proteins, such as peanut butter and meat, the proteins are broken down into amino acids. Amino acids are used to make new proteins. Proteins are used to build and repair body structures and to regulate body processes. Proteins called *enzymes* (EHN•zymz) help chemical processes happen in cells.

9 Describe What are the building blocks of proteins?

_____

© Houghton Mifflin Harcourt Publishing Company • Image Credits: (c) ©Purestock/Alamy; (b) © MBI/Alamy

Carbohydrates

Molecules that include sugars, starches, and fiber are called **carbohydrates**. Cells use carbohydrates as a source of energy and for energy storage. Cells break down carbohydrates to release the energy stored in them. Carbohydrates contain carbon, hydrogen, and oxygen atoms. Simple carbohydrates, such as table sugar, are made up of one sugar molecule or a few sugar molecules linked together. Complex carbohydrates, such as starch, are made of many sugar molecules linked together. Pasta, made from grains, is a good source of complex carbohydrates.

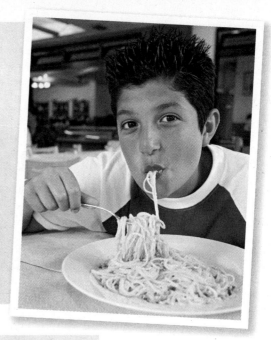

Nucleic Acids

A **nucleic acid** is a molecule that carries information in cells. Nucleic acids are made up of smaller molecules called *nucleotides* (NOO•klee•oh•TYDZ). Deoxyribonucleic acid, or DNA, is one type of nucleic acid that is found in all cells. DNA contains the information that cells need to make molecules, such as proteins. The order of nucleotides in DNA reads like a recipe. Each nucleotide tells the cell the order of amino acids needed to build a certain protein.

DNA

10 Summarize Fill in the table with a function of each nutrient in the cell.

Nutrient	Function in the cell
Lipids	
Proteins	
Carbohydrates	
Nucleic acids	

© Houghton Mifflin Harcourt Publishing Company • Image Credits: (t) ©Xenia Demetriou - xeniaphotos.com/Alamy

Waterworks

What are phospholipids?

All cells are surrounded by a cell membrane. The cell membrane helps protect the cell and keep the internal conditions of the cell stable. A lipid that contains phosphorus is called a **phospholipid** (FOSS•foh•LIH•pyd). Phospholipids form much of the cell membrane. The head of a phospholipid molecule is attracted to water. The tail repels water, or pushes it away. Because there is water inside and outside the cell, the phospholipids form a double layer. One layer lines up so that the heads face the outside of the cell. A second layer of phospholipids line up so the heads face the inside of the cell. The tails from both layers face each other, forming the middle of the cell membrane. Molecules, such as water, are regulated into and out of a cell through the cell membrane.

Active Reading **11 Explain** Describe how phospholipids form a barrier between water inside the cell and water outside the cell.

_____

_____

_____

_____

Visualize It!

12 Identify Write *attracts* next to the end of the phospholipid that attracts water. Write *repels* next to the end that repels water.

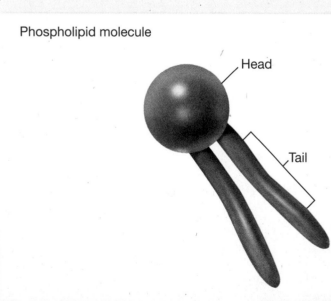

Phospholipid molecule

Head

Tail

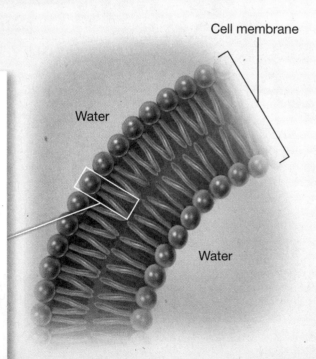

Cell membrane

Water

Water

Why is water important?

Many cell processes require water, which makes up nearly two-thirds of the mass of the cell. Thus, water is an important nutrient for life. Water moves through the cell membrane by a process called *osmosis*. Osmosis depends on the concentration of the water inside and outside of the cell. Pure water has the highest concentration of water molecules. If the water concentration inside the cell is lower than the water concentration outside the cell, then water will move into the cell. If the environment outside a cell has a low concentration of water, such as in a salty solution, water will move out of the cell.

Think Outside the Book Inquiry

14 **Associate** Think of an object that could be an analogy to the cell membrane. Draw a picture of the object and explain how it is similar to and different from a cell membrane.

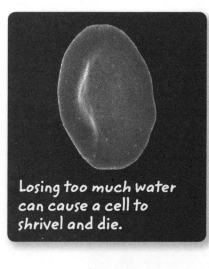

Losing too much water can cause a cell to shrivel and die.

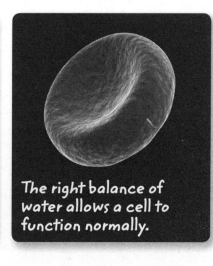

The right balance of water allows a cell to function normally.

If too much water enters a cell, it may swell up and burst.

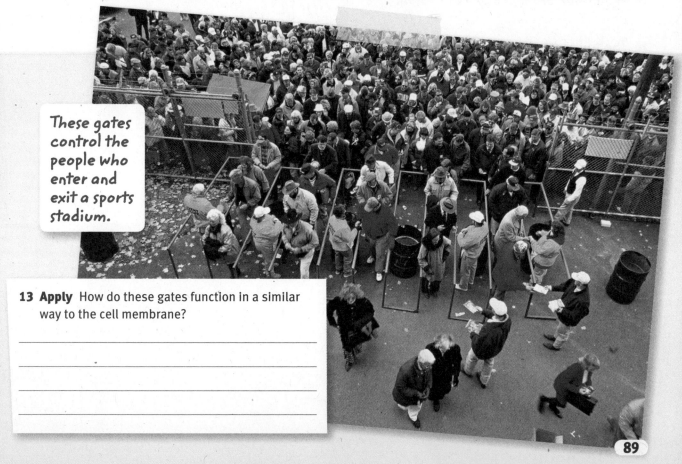

These gates control the people who enter and exit a sports stadium.

13 **Apply** How do these gates function in a similar way to the cell membrane?

_____

_____

_____

_____

Visual Summary

To complete this summary, circle the correct word and fill in the blanks with the correct word or phrase. Then, use the key below to check your answers. You can use this page to review the main concepts of the lesson.

Cell Chemistry

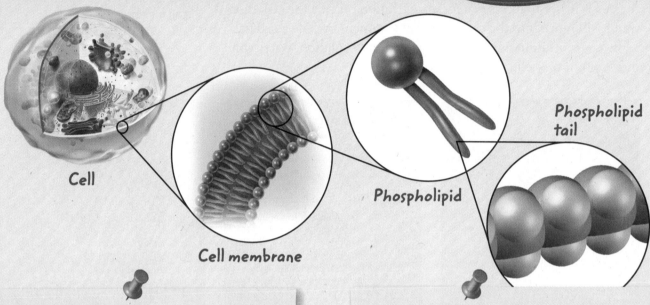

Cell

Cell membrane

Phospholipid

Phospholipid tail

Cells are made up of atoms and molecules.

15 A cell membrane is made of phospholipid atoms / molecules.

16 The tail of the phospholipid is made up of carbon and hydrogen atoms / molecules.

Cells use different molecules for life processes.

17 List four types of molecules important for cell processes.

_____

_____

_____

_____

18 Water moves into and out of a cell through the

_____

Answers: 15 molecules, 16 atoms; 17 lipids, carbohydrates, proteins, nucleic acids; 18 cell membrane

19 Relate Explain how atoms and molecules are important to cell processes.

90 Unit 2 The Cell

Lesson Review

Vocabulary

Fill in the blank with the term that best completes the following sentences.

1 The smallest unit of an element is a(n)

_____

2 A(n) _____ is a group of atoms joined by chemical bonds.

Key Concepts

3 Contrast What is the difference between atoms and molecules?

_____

_____

_____

_____

4 Identify What are the functions of proteins in organisms?

_____

_____

_____

_____

5 List Name four important types of molecules found in cells.

_____

_____

_____

_____

6 Describe How does the structure of the cell membrane help the cell regulate water?

_____

_____

_____

_____

_____

_____

_____

Critical Thinking

Use this diagram to answer the following questions.

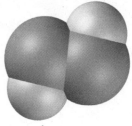

7 Identify Is this an atom or a molecule? Explain.

_____

_____

_____

_____

_____

8 Recognize The red spheres represent oxygen atoms, and the blue spheres represent hydrogen atoms. Is this substance a compound? Explain.

_____

_____

_____

_____

_____

_____

_____

9 Summarize Why is water important in cells?

_____

_____

_____

_____

_____

_____

_____

_____

Cell Structure and Function

ESSENTIAL QUESTION

What are the different parts that make up a cell?

By the end of this lesson, you should be able to compare the structure and function of cell parts in plant and animal cells.

Sunshine State Standards

SC.6.L.14.4 Compare and contrast the structure and function of major organelles of plant and animal cells, including cell wall, cell membrane, nucleus, cytoplasm, chloroplasts, mitochondria, and vacuoles.

LA.6.2.2.3 The student will organize information to show understanding (e.g., representing main ideas within text through charting, mapping, paraphrasing, summarizing, or comparing/contrasting).

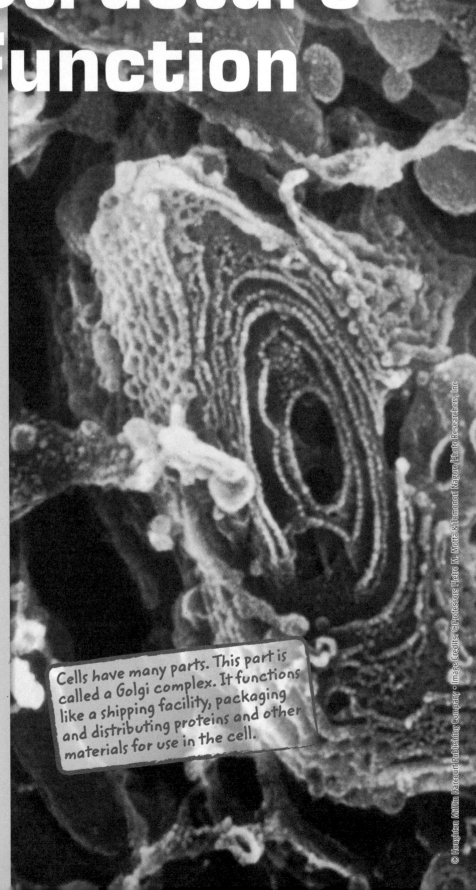

Cells have many parts. This part is called a Golgi complex. It functions like a shipping facility, packaging and distributing proteins and other materials for use in the cell.

Engage Your Brain

1 Predict Check T or F to show whether you think each statement is true or false.

T	F	
☐	☐	All cells have the same structure and function.
☐	☐	Prokaryotes do not have a nucleus.
☐	☐	Plant cells are the same as animal cells.
☐	☐	All organisms are multicellular.

2 Relate How does the structure of this umbrella relate to its function?

_____

_____

_____

_____

_____

Active Reading

3 Synthesis You can often define an unknown word if you know the meaning of its word parts. Use the word parts and sentence below to make an educated guess about the meaning of the word *chloroplast*.

Word part	Meaning
chloro-	green
plast	structure

Example sentence
Plant cells have <u>chloroplasts</u>, which contain a green pigment used for making their own food.

chloroplast:

_____

_____

Vocabulary Terms

- cytoskeleton
- mitochondrion
- ribosome
- endoplasmic reticulum
- Golgi complex
- cell wall
- vacuole
- chloroplast
- lysosome

4 Apply As you learn the definition of each vocabulary term in this lesson, create your own definition or sketch to help you remember the meaning of the term.

Being Eu-nique

What are the characteristics of eukaryotic cells?

Visualize It!

6 Apply A euglena is a unicellular organism. Why is it a eukaryote like the plant and animal cells shown here?

Can differ from each other depending on their structure and function.

All organisms are made up of one or more cells, but what kinds of cells? There are two types of organisms: prokaryotes and eukaryotes. Prokaryotes are made up of a single prokaryotic cell. Eukaryotes are made up of one or more eukaryotic cells. Prokaryotic cells do not have a nucleus or membrane-bound organelles. Eukaryotic cells have membrane-bound organelles, including a nucleus.

Eukaryotic cells can differ from each other depending on their *structure* and *function*. A cell's structure is the arrangement of its parts. A cell's function is the activity the parts carry out. For example, plant cells and animal cells have different parts that have different functions for the organism. This is what make plants and animals so different from each other. Even cells within the same organism can differ from each other depending on their function. Most of the cells in multicellular organisms are specialized to perform a specific function. However, all eukaryotic cells share some characteristics. They all have a nucleus, membrane-bound organelles, and parts that protect and support the cell.

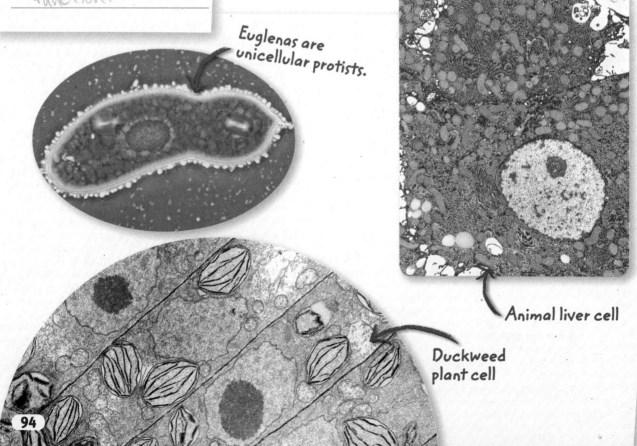

Euglenas are unicellular protists.

Animal liver cell

Duckweed plant cell

Parts that Protect and Support the Cell

Every cell is surrounded by a cell membrane. The cell membrane acts as a barrier between the inside of a cell and the cell's environment. The cell membrane protects the cell and regulates what enters and leaves the cell.

The cytoplasm is the region between the cell membrane and the nucleus that includes fluid and all of the organelles. Throughout the cytoplasm of eukaryotic cells is a **cytoskeleton**. The cytoskeleton is a network of protein filaments that gives shape and support to cells. The cytoskeleton is also involved in cell division and in movement. It may help parts within the cell to move. Or it may form structures that help the whole organism to move.

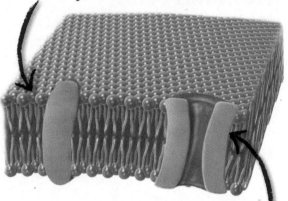

The cell membrane is a double layer of phospholipids. Water molecules and some gas molecules can pass through the cell membrane.

Other larger materials must pass through protein channels in the membrane.

Genetic Material in the Nucleus

The nucleus is an organelle in eukaryotic cells that contains the cell's genetic material. Deoxyribonucleic acid, or DNA, is stored in the nucleus. DNA is genetic material that contains information needed for cell processes, such as making proteins. Proteins perform most actions of a cell. Although DNA is found in the nucleus, proteins are not made there. Instead, instructions for how to make proteins are stored in DNA. These instructions are sent out of the nucleus through pores in the nuclear membrane. The nuclear membrane is a double layer. Each layer is similar in structure to the cell membrane.

7 Describe What are two functions of the cell membrane?

protects the cell &
regulates what enters
& leaves the cell.

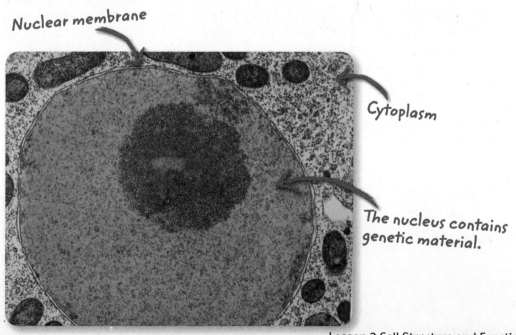

Nuclear membrane

Cytoplasm

The nucleus contains genetic material.

© Houghton Mifflin Harcourt Publishing Company • Image Credits: (b) ©Biophoto Associates/Photo Researchers, Inc.

Part-iculars

What organelles are found in plant and animal cells?

Even though plant and animal cells are microscopic, they are very complex. They have many parts that function to keep the cell alive. Many of these parts are membrane-bound organelles that perform a specific function.

Mitochondria

Organisms need energy for life processes. Cells carry out such processes for growth and repair, movement of materials into and out of the cell, and chemical processes. Cells get energy by breaking down food using a process called *cellular respiration*. Cellular respiration occurs in an organelle called the **mitochondrion** (my•TOH•kahn•dree•ahn). In cellular respiration, cells use oxygen to release energy stored in food. For example, cells break down the sugar glucose to release the energy stored in the sugar. The mitochondria then transfer the energy released from the sugar to a molecule called adenosine triphosphate, or ATP. Cells use ATP to carry out cell processes.

Mitochondria have their own DNA and they have two membranes. The outer membrane is smooth. The inner membrane has many folds. Folds increase the surface area inside the mitochondria where cellular respiration occurs.

8 Explain Why are mitochondria called the powerhouses of cells?

Moitochondria transfers energy from broken down sugar or food

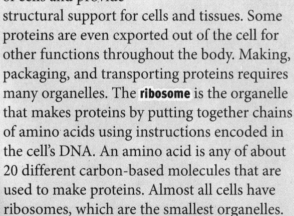

Ribosomes

Ribosomes

Proteins control most chemical reactions of cells and provide structural support for cells and tissues. Some proteins are even exported out of the cell for other functions throughout the body. Making, packaging, and transporting proteins requires many organelles. The **ribosome** is the organelle that makes proteins by putting together chains of amino acids using instructions encoded in the cell's DNA. An amino acid is any of about 20 different carbon-based molecules that are used to make proteins. Almost all cells have ribosomes, which are the smallest organelles.

Ribosomes are not enclosed in a membrane. In prokaryotes, the ribosomes are suspended freely in the cytoplasm. In eukaryotes, some ribosomes are free, and others are attached to another organelle called the *endoplasmic reticulum*.

9 Describe How do ribosomes make proteins?

Puts together chains of amino acids using instructions encoded in the cell's DNA

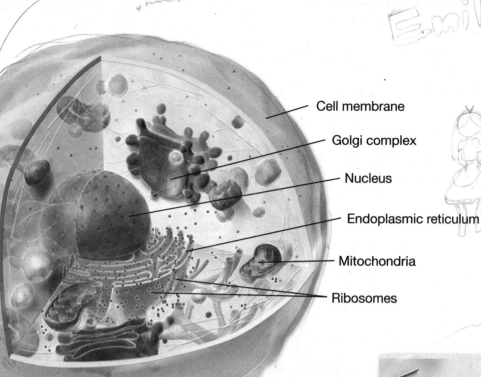

Cell membrane

Golgi complex

Nucleus

Endoplasmic reticulum

Mitochondria

Ribosomes

Emily

Golgi complex

Golgi Complex

The membrane-bound organelle that packages and distributes materials, such as proteins, is called the **Golgi complex** (GOHL•ghee COHM•plehkz). It is named after Camillo Golgi, the Italian scientist who first identified the organelle.

The Golgi complex is a system of flattened membrane sacs. Lipids and proteins from the ER are delivered to the Golgi complex where they may be modified to do different jobs. The final products are enclosed in a piece of the Golgi complex's membrane. This membrane pinches off to form a small bubble, or vesicle. The vesicle transports its contents to other parts of the cell or out of the cell.

11 Describe What is the function of the Golgi complex?

Golgi modifies membrane sacs

Endoplasmic Reticulum

In the cytoplasm is a system of membranes near the nucleus called the **endoplasmic reticulum** (ehn•doh•PLAHZ•mick rhett•ICK•yoo•luhm), or ER. The ER assists in the production, processing, and transport of proteins and in the production of lipids. The ER is either smooth or rough. Rough ER has ribosomes attached to its membrane, while smooth ER does not. Ribosomes on the rough ER make many of the cell's proteins. Some of these proteins move through the ER to different places in the cell. The smooth ER makes lipids and breaks down toxic materials that could damage the cell.

10 Compare How does rough ER differ from smooth ER in structure and function?

Rough ER has ribosomes attached to it's membrane, Smooth ER doesn't

Now Showing: The Plant Cell

What additional parts are found in plant cells?

Think about some ways that plants are different from animals. Plants don't move around, and some have flowers. Plant cells do have a cell membrane, cytoskeleton, nucleus, mitochondria, ribosomes, ER, and a Golgi complex just like animal cells do. In addition, plant cells have a cell wall, large central vacuole, and chloroplasts.

Cell Wall

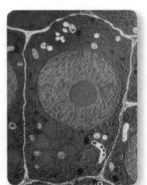

In addition to the cell membrane, plant cells have a **cell wall**. The cell wall is a rigid structure that surrounds the cell membrane, identified by the yellow line around the plant cell in this photo. Cell walls provide support and protection to the cell. Plants don't have a skeleton like many animals do, so they get their shape from the cell wall. The cells of fungi, archaea, bacteria, and some protists also have cell walls.

Large Central Vacuole

A **vacuole** (VAK•yoo•ohl) is a fluid-filled vesicle found in the cells of most animals, plants, and fungi. A vacuole may contain enzymes, nutrients, water, or wastes. Plant cells also have a large central vacuole that stores water. Central vacuoles full of water help support the cell. Plants may wilt when the central vacuole loses water.

13 Compare How do large central vacuoles differ from vacuoles?

large central vacuoles store water

Emily

Visualize It!

14 Identify Label these cell parts on the plant cell shown here:
- Mitochondrion
- Golgi complex
- Nucleus
- Endoplasmic reticulum
- Ribosomes
- Cell wall
- Cell membrane
- Cytoskeleton

Large central vacuole

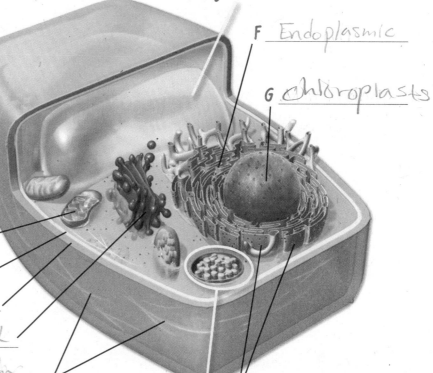

F _Endoplasmic_

G _Chloroplasts_

A _Mitochondria_

B _Cell membrane_

C _Cell wall_

D _Golgi complex_

E _Cyto skeleton_

H _Ribosomes_

Chloroplasts

Animals must eat food to provide their cells with energy. However, plants, and some protists, can make their own food using photosynthesis. These organisms have **chloroplasts** (KLOHR•oh•plahstz), organelles where photosynthesis occurs. Photosynthesis is the process by which cells use sunlight, carbon dioxide, and water to make sugar and oxygen. Chloroplasts are green because they contain a green pigment called *chlorophyll* (KLOHR•oh•fill). Chlorophyll absorbs the energy in sunlight. This energy is used to make sugar, which is then used by mitochondria to make ATP. Chloroplasts have two outer membranes.

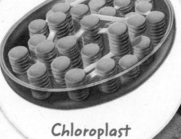

Chloroplast

15 Describe What is the role of chlorophyll inside chloroplasts?

Absorbs the energy in sunlight

Think Outside the Book Inquiry

16 Describe Cyanobacteria and green algae are similar to plants. Choose one of these organisms and explain why they are similar to plants but are not classified as plants.

Introducing: The Animal Cell

What additional part is found in animal cells?

Animal cells are eukaryotic cells that contain a nucleus and are surrounded by a cell membrane. They contain many of the same organelles as most plant cells, including mitochondria, ribosomes, ER, and a Golgi complex. Most animal cells also contain a membrane-bound organelle called a *lysosome*.

Active Reading 17 **Recognize** As you read, underline the function of lysosomes.

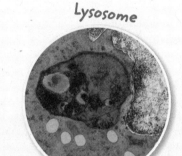

Lysosome

Lysosomes

Organelles called **lysosomes** (LY•soh•zohmz) contain digestive enzymes, which break down worn-out or damaged organelles, waste materials, and foreign invaders in the cell. Some of these materials are collected in vacuoles. A lysosome attaches to the vacuole and releases the digestive enzymes inside. Some of these materials are recycled and reused in the cell. For example, a human liver cell recycles half of its materials each week.

18 **Compare** How are lysosomes similar to vacuoles?

Breaks down things that are sometimes stored in vacuoles.

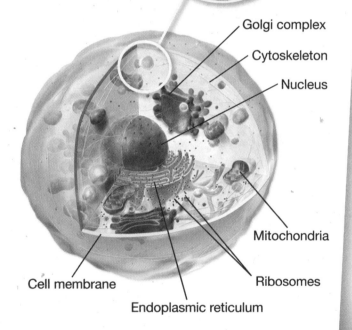

Golgi complex
Cytoskeleton
Nucleus
Mitochondria
Ribosomes
Endoplasmic reticulum
Cell membrane

19 Compare Draw a sketch for each organelle identified in the *Structure* column. Put check marks in the last two columns to identify whether the cell structure can usually be found in plant cells, animal cells, or both.

Structure	Function	In plant cell?	In animal cell?
Nucleus	Contains the genetic material		✓
Endoplasmic reticulum	Processes and transports proteins and makes lipids	✓	✓
Golgi complex	Packages and distributes materials within or out of the cell	✓	
Ribosome	Makes proteins		
Chloroplast	Uses sunlight, carbon dioxide, and water to make food by photosynthesis		
Mitochondrion	Breaks down food molecules to release energy by cellular respiration		
Large central vacuole	Stores water and helps give shape to the cell		
Lysosome	Produces enzymes that digest wastes, cell parts, and foreign invaders		

Visual Summary

To complete this summary, fill in the blanks to identify the organelles in each cell. Then, use the key below to check your answers. You can use this page to review the main concepts of the lesson.

Compare
Plant Cells and Animal Cells

Structures in plant cells

20 _____

21 _____

Structures in animal cells

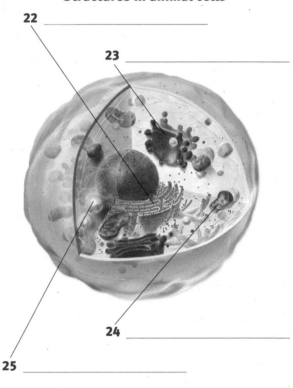

22 _____

23 _____

24 _____

25 _____

Plants and animals are eukaryotes. The structures inside a eukaryotic cell work together to keep the cell and the entire organism alive.

Answers: 20 large central vacuole; 21 cell wall; 22 endoplasmic reticulum; 23 Golgi complex; 24 mitochondrion; 25 lysosome

26 **Summarize** How do eukaryotic cells differ from each other?

Lesson Review

Vocabulary

Circle the term that best completes the following sentences.

1 A *Golgi complex / ribosome* makes proteins that are transported through the endoplasmic reticulum.

2 The *nucleus / large central vacuole* contains genetic material of a eukaryotic cell.

3 The *cell membrane / cytoplasm* acts as a barrier between the inside of a cell and the cell's environment.

4 The organelle in which photosynthesis takes place is the *cell wall / chloroplast*.

Key Concepts

5 Recognize What do all eukaryotic cells have in common?

_____

_____

_____

_____

6 Compare How are the functions of the cytoskeleton and the cell wall similar?

_____

_____

_____

_____

7 Contrast What structures are found in plant cells that are not found in animal cells?

_____

_____

_____

_____

Critical Thinking

Use this diagram to answer the following questions.

8 Identify What is this organelle?

_____

9 Explain How does its structure affect its function?

_____

_____

_____

_____

_____

10 Compare Which cells contain this organelle: plant cells, animal cells, or both?

11 Apply Explain the function of ribosomes and why cells need them.

_____

_____

_____

_____

_____

_____

Levels of **Cellular Organization**

ESSENTIAL QUESTION

How are living things organized?

By the end of this lesson, you should be able to describe the different levels of organization in living things.

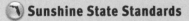 **Sunshine State Standards**

SC.6.L.14.1 Describe and identify patterns in the hierarchical organization of organisms from atoms to molecules and cells to tissues to organs to organ systems to organisms.

LA.6.4.2.2 The student will record information (e.g., observations, notes, lists, charts, legends) related to a topic, including visual aids to organize and record information and include a list of sources used.

Eyes may seem like small and simple body parts, but they are organs made up of millions of cells and many layers of tissues.

Engage Your Brain

1 Describe Fill in the blank with the word or phrase that you think correctly completes the following sentences.

Your body has many organs, such as a

heart and _____

Plant organs include stems and

_____

Animal and plant organs are organized into organ systems, much like you organize your

homework in _____

2 Explain How is the structure of a hammer related to its function?

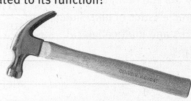

_____

_____

_____

_____

_____

_____

Active Reading

3 Relate Many scientific words, such as *organ* and *tissue*, also have everyday meanings. Use context clues to write your own definition for each underlined word.

It is helpful to use a <u>tissue</u> when sneezing to prevent the spread of droplets carrying bacteria.

tissue:

_____

_____

_____

An <u>organ</u> can be very difficult to play.

organ:

_____

_____

_____

Vocabulary Terms

- organism
- tissue
- organ
- organ system
- structure
- function

4 Apply As you learn the definition of each vocabulary term in this lesson, create your own definition or sketch to help you remember the meaning of the term.

Body Building

How are living things organized?

An **organism** is a living thing that can carry out life processes by itself. *Unicellular organisms* are made up of just one cell that performs all of the functions necessary for life. Unicellular organisms do not have levels of organization. Having only one cell has advantages and disadvantages. For example, unicellular organisms need fewer resources and can live in harsh conditions, such as hot springs and very salty water. However, unicellular organisms are very small, which means they may be eaten by larger organisms. Another disadvantage of being unicellular is that the entire organism dies if the single cell dies.

Active Reading

5 Identify As you read, underline the characteristics of unicellular organisms and multicellular organisms.

Cells

Multicellular organisms are made up of more than one cell. These cells are grouped into different levels of organization, including tissues, organs, and organ systems. The cells that make up a multicellular organism, such as humans and plants, may be specialized to perform specific functions. Different cells have different functions in the body. This specialization makes the multicellular organism more efficient. Other benefits of being multicellular are larger size and longer life span.

There are disadvantages to being multicellular, too. Multicellular organisms need more resources than unicellular organisms do. Also, the cells of multicellular organisms are specialized for certain jobs, which means that cells must depend on each other to perform all of the functions that an organism needs.

Humpback whales are multicellular organisms.

Diatoms are unicellular organisms that live in water.

© Houghton Mifflin Harcourt Publishing Company • Image Credits: (bkgd) ©Kim Westerskov/Getty Images; (inset) ©Eye of Science/Photo Researchers, Inc.

Tissues

A **tissue** is a group of similar cells that perform a common function. Humans and many other animals are made up of four basic types of tissue: nervous, epithelial, connective, and muscle. Nervous tissue functions as a messaging system within the body. Epithelial tissue is protective and forms boundaries, such as skin. Connective tissue, including bones and blood, holds parts of the body together and provides support and nourishment to organs. Muscle tissue helps produce movement.

Plants have three types of tissues: transport, protective, and ground. Transport tissues move water and nutrients throughout the plant. Protective tissues protect the outside of the plant. Ground tissues provide support and storage. They absorb light energy to make food in photosynthesis (foh•toh•SYN•thuh•sys).

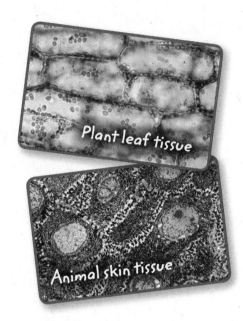

Plant leaf tissue

Animal skin tissue

6 Explain Fill in the Venn diagram to compare the functions of animal tissues and plant tissues. What functions do they share?

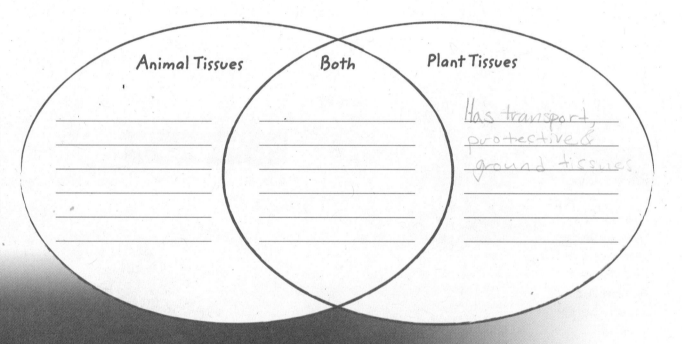

Animal Tissues

Both

Plant Tissues

Has transport, protective & ground tissues.

Visualize It!

7 Compare In which organism shown on the opposite page are cells organized into tissues? Explain your answer.

_____

_____

_____

_____

_____

Organs

A structure made up of a collection of tissues that carries out a specialized function is called an **organ**. The stomach is an organ that breaks down food for digestion. Different types of tissues work together to accomplish this function. For example, nervous tissue sends messages to muscle tissue to tell the muscle tissue to contract. When the muscle tissue contracts, food and stomach acids are mixed and the food breaks down.

Plants also have organs that are made up of different tissues working together. For example, a leaf is an organ that contains protective tissue to reduce water loss, ground tissue for photosynthesis, and transport tissue to distribute nutrients from leaves to stems. Stems and roots are organs that function to transport and store water and nutrients in the plant. The trunk of most trees is a stem. Roots are usually below ground.

 **Active Reading**

8 Apply How do organs relate to cells and tissues?

_____

_____

_____

Plants have two organ systems: the shoot system that includes stems and leaves, and the root system that is usually below ground.

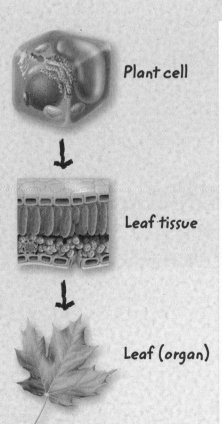

Plant cell

Leaf tissue

Leaf (organ)

 **Visualize It!**

9 Identify Label the different organ systems on the tree shown here.

A tree has organ systems.

The digestive system is an organ system in many animals, including humans.

Stomach
muscle cell

Stomach
muscle tissue

Stomach (organ)

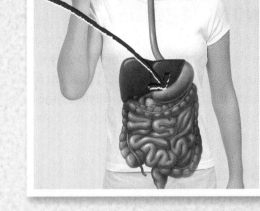

Digestive system in humans

10 Infer The cells that make up the stomach lining are tightly packed together to form a boundary of the stomach. Explain which basic type of tissue makes up this boundary of the stomach.

_____

_____

_____

Organ Systems

An **organ system** is a group of organs that work together to perform body functions. Each organ system has a specific job to do for the organism. For example, the stomach works with other organs of the digestive system to digest and absorb nutrients from food. Other organs included in the digestive system are the esophagus and the small and large intestines.

Humans are made up of many organ systems. All of the systems have specific functions to keep the body alive.

Think Outside the Book Inquiry

11 Illustrate Research an organ system of the human body other than the digestive system and draw a sketch of the organs included in that organ system.

What's Your Function?

How do the levels of organization work together?

Cells, tissues, organs, and organ systems make up the structure of multicellular organism. **Structure** is the arrangement of parts in an organism or an object. The structure of a cell, tissue, or organ then determines their **function**, or the activity of each part in an organism. In fact, the structure of any object can determine its function.

Active Reading

12 Recognize As you read, underline examples of cellular structures.

Structure

A sports car differs from a dump truck even though they are both vehicles. The structure of the parts in a sports car allow it to go fast. A dump truck is large and sturdy, which allows it to haul things. Cells, tissues, and organs also vary in structure. For example, bone cells look different than plant leaf cells. A lung differs from a stomach because they have different functions.

Function

The structure of each vehicle determines what function the vehicle performs. The relationship of structure and function is true for cells, too. Cells, tissues, and organs are specialized to perform specific functions. Those that have similar structures likely have similar functions. For example, a lung is an organ made up of cells and tissues that work together to help you breathe. The lungs are made up of millions of tiny air sacs called *alveoli* (ahl•VEE•oh•lye). The large number of alveoli increases the surface area of the lungs to allow enough oxygen and carbon dioxide to move between the lungs and the blood.

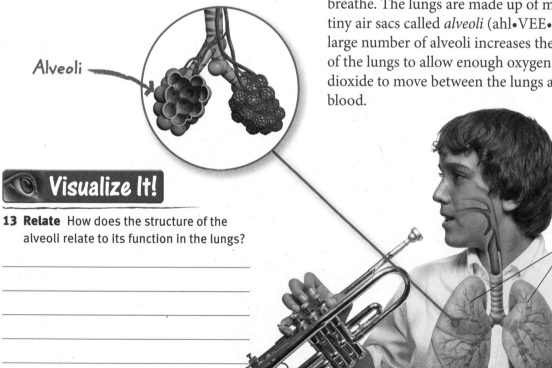

Alveoli

Visualize It!

13 Relate How does the structure of the alveoli relate to its function in the lungs?

_____

_____

_____

_____

_____

_____

lungs

Odd Bodies

With the millions of different organisms that exist on Earth, it's no wonder there are so many different body structures. Some organisms have special structures that can help them eat or not be eaten!

Can't Touch This!
Named for its prickly body, the spiny katydid doesn't make much of a meal for its predator. Male katydids sing loudly at night to attract female katydids. The singing can also attract predators, such as bats, who hunt for food at night. Its spines provide the katydid with some protection from being eaten.

Blow on Your Food
The longhorn cowfish is a marine organism that lives on the sandy bottom at up to 50 m deep. Its permanently puckered mouth helps the cowfish find food. The cowfish blows jets of water into the sand to find and feed on tiny organisms.

Night Vision
The tarsier's huge eyes provide excellent vision for hunting insects at night. Its eyes average 16 mm in diameter, while the tarsier's overall body size ranges from 85 mm to 165 mm. If a tarsier were your height, its eyes would be about the size of apples! When the tarsier spots its prey, it leaps through the air to pounce on it. The tarsier's long fingers help it grasp branches when it's on the move.

Extend

Inquiry

14 Relate How does the body structure of each of these organisms contribute to a particular function?

15 Contrast How do structures in organisms compare with structures of nonliving things such as construction cranes, buildings, ships, airplanes, or bridges?

16 Imagine Describe an organism that might live in an extreme environment like inside a volcano, deep in the ocean, or in an icy cave. Is it a plant or an animal? What special structures would it have in order to survive in that environment?

Visual Summary

To complete this summary, check the box that indicates true or false. Then, use the key below to check your answers. You can use this page to review the main concepts of the lesson.

Cellular Organization

All organisms are made up of one or more cells.

T F
17 ☐ ☐ A plant is a unicellular organism.

The structures of cells, tissues, and organs determine their functions.

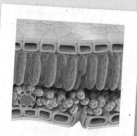

T F
18 ☐ ☐ The protective tissue on a leaf has a structure that keeps the plant from drying out.

Multicellular organisms are organized into tissues, organs, and organ systems.

T F
19 ☐ ☐ This leaf is an example of a plant organ.

T F
20 ☐ ☐ Organs form organ systems.

Answers: 17 F; 18 T; 19 T; 20 T

21 **Synthesize** How do cells, tissues, organs, and organ systems work together in a multicellular organism?

Lesson Review

Vocabulary

Fill in the blank with the term that best completes the following sentences.

1 Animals have four basic types of
_____: nervous, epithelial, muscle, and connective.

2 Together, the esophagus, stomach, and intestines are part of a(n) _____.

Key Concepts

3 Describe What are the levels of organization in multicellular organisms?

_____

_____

_____

_____

_____

4 Analyze Discuss two benefits of multicellular organisms having some specialized cells rather than all the cells being the same.

_____

_____

_____

_____

_____

_____

_____

5 Relate How do the structures in an organism relate to its function?

_____

_____

_____

_____

_____

Critical Thinking

Use the figure to answer the next two questions.

Human heart

6 Apply What level of organization is shown here?

_____

7 Relate How does this level of organization relate to cells? To organ systems?

_____

_____

_____

_____

_____

_____

_____

8 Hypothesize Birds that fly have lightweight bones, some of which are hollow. How might this unique body structure benefit the bird?

_____

_____

_____

_____

_____

_____

_____

_____

Think Science

Making Predictions

Sunshine State Standards

MA.6.A.3.6 Construct and analyze tables, graphs, and equations to describe linear functions and other simple relations using both common language and algebraic notation.

Scientists try to answer questions about the world by developing hypotheses, making predictions, and conducting experiments to test those predictions. To make a prediction, a scientist will analyze a general idea and then predict specific results. Predictions often take the form of "if–then" statements. For example, "If living organisms are made of small units called cells, then we predict that we will see cells if we look at organisms up close under a microscope."

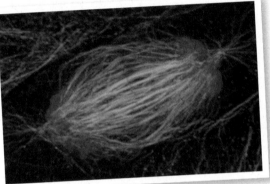

A dividing frog cell showing microtubules (green) and DNA (blue)

Tutorial

For an organism to grow and reproduce, chromosomes must replicate and cells must divide. The following steps will teach you how to make predictions from hypotheses about the role of protein fibers, called microtubules, in cell division.

Question: How do chromosomes move and separate during cell division?

Hypothesis: Microtubules play an important role in the movement of the chromosomes during cell division.

Prediction: If microtubules were inhibited during cell division, then chromosomes would not be able to move and separate from each other during cell division.

Observations: When microtubules are exposed to a drug that blocks microtubule formation, movement of chromosomes is inhibited and cell division stops.

What is the hypothesis? A hypothesis is a plausible answer to a scientific question. Form a hypothesis based on prior experience, background knowledge, or your own observations.

What would we expect or predict to see if the hypothesis were true? When scientists summarize their data, they look for observations and measurements that will support their hypothesis.

Does the prediction match the observations? If the data matches the predictions generated by the hypothesis, then the hypothesis is supported. Sometimes errors occur during the scientific investigation, which can lead to incorrect results. There is also the possibility that correct data will not match the hypothesis. When this happens, generate a new hypothesis.

You Try It!

Scientists often propose hypotheses about the causes of events they observe. Read the following scenario, and answer the questions that follow.

Scenario: A cell biologist has three cell cultures of human skin cells. The cells in each culture are taken from the same cell line. Each cell culture is placed in a solution for observation. The cells in culture A are growing faster than the cells in cultures B and C.

Question: Why are the cells in culture A growing at a faster rate than the cells in cultures B and C?

Hypothesis 1: The waste level is higher in cultures B and C than in culture A.

Hypothesis 2: The nutrient levels are higher in culture A than in cultures B and C.

1 Making Predictions Read each of the hypotheses above and then make a prediction for each about what might be observed.

Hypothesis 1:

_____
_____
_____

Hypothesis 2:

_____
_____
_____

2 Testing a Hypothesis Identify a possible experiment for each hypothesis that you can perform or observations that you can make to find out whether the hypothesis is supported.

Hypothesis 1:

_____
_____
_____

Hypothesis 2:

_____
_____
_____

3 Predicting Outcomes Fill in the two tables below with plausible data that supports each hypothesis.

Culture	Waste level	Rate of growth (cells/hour)
A		
B		
C		

Culture	Nutrient level	Rate of growth (cells/hour)
A		
B		
C		

Take It Home

Find a recent newspaper or magazine article that makes a conclusion based on a scientific study. Carefully evaluate the study and identify the predictions that were tested in the study. Bring the article to class and be prepared to discuss your analysis of the article.

Homeostasis and Cell Processes

ESSENTIAL QUESTION

How do organisms maintain homeostasis?

By the end of this lesson, you should be able to explain the important processes that organisms undergo to maintain stable internal conditions.

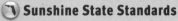

Sunshine State Standards

SC.6.L.14.3 Recognize and explore how cells of all organisms undergo similar processes to maintain homeostasis, including extracting energy from food, getting rid of waste, and reproducing.

LA.6.4.2.2 The student will record information (e.g., observations, notes, lists, charts, legends) related to a topic, including visual aids to organize and record information and include a list of sources used.

These American alligators are warming themselves in the sun. Temperature is one factor that an organism can control to maintain stable internal conditions.

Engage Your Brain

1 Explain How is this person able to stay on the skateboard?

_____

_____

2 Describe Fill in the blanks with the word or phrase that you think correctly completes the following sentences.

Eating _____ provides your body with nutrients it needs for energy.

Cells can _____ to make more cells.

Trucks, airplanes, and trains are used to _____ people and supplies from one place to another.

Active Reading

3 Synthesis You can often define an unknown word if you know the meaning of its word parts. Use the word parts and sentence below to make an educated guess about the meaning of the word *photosynthesis*.

Word part	Meaning
photo-	light
synthesis	to make

Example sentence
Plants use a process called <u>photosynthesis</u> to make their own food.

Vocabulary Terms
- homeostasis
- photosynthesis
- cellular respiration
- mitosis
- passive transport
- diffusion
- osmosis
- active transport
- endocytosis
- exocytosis

4 Identify As you read, place a question mark next to any words that you don't understand. When you finish reading the lesson, go back and review the text that you marked. If the information is still confusing, consult a classmate or a teacher.

photosynthesis:

_____

_____

Stayin' Alive

What is homeostasis?

We all feel more comfortable when our surroundings are ideal—not too hot, not too cold, not too wet, and not too dry. Cells are the same way. However, a cell's environment is constantly changing. **Homeostasis** (hoh•mee•oh•STAY•sis) is the maintenance of a constant internal state in a changing environment. In order to survive, your cells need to be able to obtain and use energy, make new cells, exchange materials, and eliminate wastes. Homeostasis ensures that cells can carry out these tasks in a changing environment.

Active Reading 6 **Summarize** What are four things that cells can do to maintain homeostasis?

_____

_____

_____

Visualize It!

7 **Apply** Think about how this girl is feeling after she exercises. What things can you see that are helping to keep her body temperature stable?

_____

_____

_____

© Houghton Mifflin Harcourt Publishing Company • Image Credits: ©Dave & Les Jacobs/Blend Images/Corbis

Balance in Organisms

All cells need energy and materials in order to carry out life processes. A unicellular organism exchanges materials directly with its environment. The cell membrane and other parts of the cell regulate what materials get into and out of the cell. This is one way that unicellular organisms maintain homeostasis.

Cells in multicellular organisms must work together to maintain homeostasis for the entire organism. For example, multicellular organisms have systems that transport materials to cells from other places in the organism. The main transport system in your body is your cardiovascular system. The cardiovascular system includes the heart, blood vessels, and blood. The heart pumps blood through branched blood vessels that come close to every cell in the body. Blood carries materials to the cells and carries wastes away from the cells. Other multicellular organisms have transport systems, too. For example, many plants have two types of vascular tissues that work together as a transport system. *Xylem* is the tissue that transports water and minerals from the roots to the rest of the plant. Another tissue called *phloem* transports food made within plant cells.

© Houghton Mifflin Harcourt Publishing Company • Image Credits: (t) ©Biophoto Associates/Photo Researchers, Inc.; (b) ©Steve Gschmeissner/Photo Researchers, Inc.

Active Reading

8 Compare As you read, underline how unicellular organisms and multicellular organisms exchange materials.

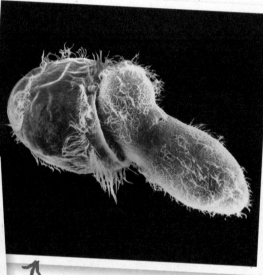

A unicellular organism, **Didinium**, is eating another unicellular organism, called a **Paramecium**.

Xylem transports water and minerals.

Phloem transports food to different parts of the plant.

Plants have two types of vascular tissue that they use to transport materials.

Get Growing!

How do cells get energy?

Cells need energy to perform cell functions. Cells get energy by breaking down materials, such as food, in which energy is stored. Breaking down food also provides raw materials the cell needs to make other materials for cell processes.

Photosynthesis

The sun provides the energy for plants to grow and make food. Plants use sunlight to change carbon dioxide and water into sugar and oxygen. This process by which plants, algae, and some bacteria make their own food is called **photosynthesis**. Inside plant and algal cells are special organelles, called chloroplasts, where photosynthesis takes place.

Cellular Respiration

All living things need food to produce energy for cell processes. The process by which cells use oxygen to produce energy from food is called **cellular respiration**. Plants, animals, and most other organisms use cellular respiration to get energy from food.

Nearly all the oxygen around us is made by photosynthesis. Animals and plants use oxygen during cellular respiration to break down food. Cellular respiration also produces carbon dioxide. Plants need carbon dioxide to make sugars. So, photosynthesis and respiration are linked, each one depending on the products of the other.

Plants provide the food for nearly all living thing on land. Some organisms eat plants for food. Other organisms eat animals that eat plants.

---

9 Synthesize Fill in the blanks with the materials that are involved in photosynthesis and cellular respiration.

Photosynthesis	_____ + carbon dioxide $\xrightarrow{\text{sunlight}}$ _____ + oxygen
Cellular respiration	sugar + _____ $\longrightarrow$ water + _____ + energy

How do cells divide?

Cells grow, divide, and die. Some cells divide more often than others. For example, cells in the skin are constantly dividing to replace those that have died or are damaged. Some cells, such as nerve cells, cannot divide to produce new cells once they are fully formed. Multicellular organisms grow by adding more cells. These new cells are made when existing cells divide.

The Cell Cycle

Cell division in eukaryotes is a complex process. Before a cell can divide, its DNA is copied. Then, the DNA copies are sorted into what will become two new cells. In order to divide up the DNA evenly between the new cells, the DNA needs to be packaged. The packages are called *chromosomes* (croh•moh•SOHMS). Equal numbers of chromosomes are separated, and the nucleus splits to form two identical nuclei. This process is called **mitosis**. Then, the rest of the cell divides, resulting in two identical cells. Because the two new cells have DNA identical to that found in the original cell, all the cells in an organism have the same genetic material.

Active Reading

10 Explain Why is it important for DNA to be copied before cell division?

_____

_____

_____

_____

11 Compare How do new cells form in plants and animal?

_____

_____

_____

_____

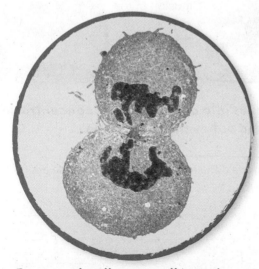

In animal cells, the cell membrane pinches inward through the cell to form two new cells.

When a plant cell divides, a cell plate forms and the cell splits into two cells.

Move It!

How do cells exchange materials?

What would happen to a factory if its supply of raw materials never arrived or it couldn't get rid of its garbage? Like a factory, an organism must be able to obtain materials for energy, make new materials, and get rid of wastes. The exchange of materials between a cell and its environment takes place at the cell's membrane. Cell membranes are *semi-permeable* because they allow only certain particles to cross into or out of the cell.

Passive Transport

Active Reading

12 Relate As you read, underline the similarity between diffusion and osmosis.

The movement of particles across a cell membrane without the use of energy by the cell is called **passive transport**. For example, when a tea bag is added to a cup of water, the molecules in the tea will eventually spread throughout the water. **Diffusion** is the movement of molecules from high concentrations to low concentrations. Some nutrients move into a cell by diffusion. Some waste products move out of the cell by diffusion. **Osmosis** is the diffusion of water through a semi-permeable membrane. Many molecules are too large to diffuse through the cell membrane. Some of these molecules enter and exit cells through protein channels embedded in the cell membrane. When molecules move through these protein channels from areas of higher concentration to areas of lower concentration, the process usually requires no energy.

The tea has a higher concentration of molecules in the tea bag than in the rest of the mug.

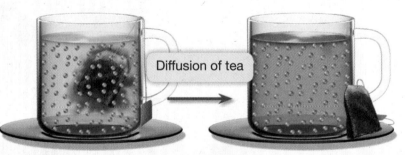

Diffusion of tea

Tea moves into areas of lower concentration, spreading out evenly in the mug.

13 Apply How is diffusion related to smelling the odor of a skunk that is far away?

_____

_____

_____

_____

Active Transport

Cells often need to move materials across the cell membrane from areas of low concentration into areas of higher concentration. This is the opposite direction of passive transport. **Active transport** is the movement of particles against a concentration gradient and requires the cell to use energy. Some large particles that do not fit through the protein channels may require active transport across the cell membrane by processes called *endocytosis* and *exocytosis*.

Visualize It!

14 Identify Place a check mark next to the box that describes diffusion. Explain your answer.

_____

_____

_____

_____

Chemical energy

Passive transport moves materials into and out of a cell to areas of lower concentration. ☐

Active transport uses energy to move materials into and out of a cell to areas of higher concentration. ☐

© Houghton Mifflin Harcourt Publishing Company

Endocytosis

The process by which a cell uses energy to surround a particle and enclose the particle in a vesicle to bring the particle into the cell is called **endocytosis** (en•doh•sye•TOH•sis). Vesicles are sacs formed from pieces of the cell membrane. Unicellular organisms, such as amoebas, use endocytosis to capture smaller organisms for food.

The cell comes into contact with a particle.

The cell membrane begins to wrap around the particle.

15 Describe What is happening in this step?

_____

_____

_____

_____

Exocytosis

When particles are enclosed in a vesicle and released from a cell, the process is called **exocytosis** (ek•soh•sye•TOH•sis). Exocytosis is the reverse process of endocytosis. Exocytosis begins when a vesicle forms around particles within the cell. The vesicle fuses to the cell membrane and the particles are released outside of the cell. Exocytosis is an important process in multicellular organisms.

Large particles that must leave the cell are packaged in vesicles.

16 Describe What is happening in this step?

_____

_____

_____

_____

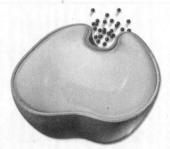

The cell releases the particles to the outside of the cell.

How do organisms maintain homeostasis?

As you have read, cells can obtain energy, divide, and transport materials to maintain stable internal conditions. In multicellular organisms, the cells must work together to maintain homeostasis for the entire organism. For example, when some organisms become cold, the cells respond in order to maintain a normal internal temperature. Muscle cells will contract to generate heat, a process known as shivering.

Some animals adapt their behavior to control body temperature. For example, many reptiles bask in the sun or seek shade to regulate their internal temperatures. When temperatures become extremely cold, some animals hibernate. Animals such as ground squirrels are able to conserve their energy during the winter when food is scarce.

Some trees lose all their leaves around the same time each year. This is a seasonal response. Having bare branches during the winter reduces the amount of water loss. Leaves may also change color before they fall. As autumn approaches, chlorophyll, the green pigment used for photosynthesis, breaks down. As chlorophyll is lost, other yellow and orange pigments can be seen.

© Houghton Mifflin Harcourt Publishing Company • Image Credits: (bkgd) ©Ben Muir/Corbis; (inset) ©Digital Vision

The leaves of some trees change colors when the season changes.

Active Reading

17 Identify As you read, underline the different ways that organisms can respond to changes in the environment.

Visualize It!

18 Describe How is this boy's body responding to the cold weather?

_____

_____

_____

Visual Summary

To complete this summary, fill in the blanks with the correct word or phrase. Then use the key below to check your answers. You can use this page to review the main concepts of the lesson.

Cells need energy to perform cell functions.

19 Food is made during _____ Energy is produced from food during

_____

Cell division allows organisms to grow and repair damaged parts.

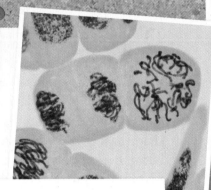

20 _____ occurs when cells divide to form two new nuclei that are identical to each other.

Maintaining Homeostasis: Balance In Organisms

Materials move into and out of cells through the cell membrane.

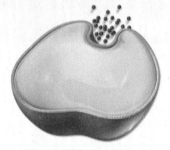

21 _____ uses energy to release particles from a cell.

Organisms respond to changes in the environment.

22 The change in leaf color on these trees is one way the trees maintain _____

Answers: 19 photosynthesis; cellular respiration; 20 Mitosis; 21 Active transport; 22 homeostasis

23 **Summarize** Explain why organisms need to maintain homeostasis.

Lesson Review

Vocabulary

In your own words, define the following terms.

1 homeostasis

_____

_____

2 endocytosis

_____

_____

Key Concepts

3 Compare What is the difference between passive and active transport?

_____

_____

_____

4 List List four things that cells do to maintain homeostasis.

_____

_____

_____

5 Describe What happens during mitosis?

_____

_____

_____

6 Apply How do the cells in your body get energy?

_____

_____

_____

_____

_____

Critical Thinking

Use the graphs to answer the next two questions.

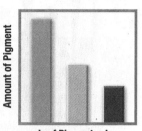
Summer

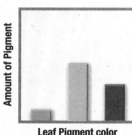
Fall

7 Compare How do the amounts of green pigment, chlorophyll, differ from summer to fall?

_____

_____

_____

8 Infer How do you think the change in chlorophyll levels is a response to changes in the length of day from summer to fall?

_____

_____

_____

_____

_____

_____

_____

_____

9 Explain Why is homeostasis important for cells as well as for an entire organism?

_____

_____

_____

_____

_____

Classification of Living Things

ESSENTIAL QUESTION

How are organisms classified?

By the end of this lesson, you should be able to describe how people sort living things into groups based on shared characteristics.

Scientists use physical and chemical characteristics to classify organisms. Is that an ant? Look again. It's an ant-mimicking jumping spider!

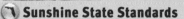

Sunshine State Standards

SC.6.N.2.2 Explain that scientific knowledge is durable because it is open to change as new evidence or interpretations are encountered.

SC.6.N.3.4 Identify the role of models in the context of the sixth grade science benchmarks.

SC.6.L.15.1 Analyze and describe how and why organisms are classified according to shared characteristics with emphasis on the Linnaean system combined with the concept of Domains.

LA.6.2.2.3 The student will organize information to show understanding (e.g., representing main ideas within text through charting, mapping, paraphrasing, summarizing, or comparing/contrasting).

Engage Your Brain

1 Predict Check T or F to show whether you think each statement is true or false.

T	F	
☐	☐	The classification system used today has changed very little since it was introduced.
☐	☐	To be classified as an animal, organisms must have a backbone.
☐	☐	Organisms can be classified by whether they have nuclei in their cells.
☐	☐	Scientists can study genetic material to classify organisms.
☐	☐	Organisms that have many physical similarities may be related.

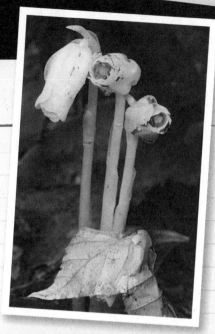

2 Analyze The flowering plant shown above is called an Indian pipe. It could be mistaken for a fungus. Write down how the plant is similar to and different from other plants you know.

_____

_____

_____

_____

Active Reading

3 Synthesize Often, you can define an unknown word if you know the meaning of its word parts. Use the word parts and sentence below to make an educated guess about the meaning of the term *dichotomous key*.

Word part	Meaning
dich-	in two
-tomous	to cut

Example sentence
Sophie used the paired statements in a <u>dichotomous key</u> to identify the animal she found during the field trip.

dichotomous key:

_____

_____

_____

Vocabulary Terms

- species
- genus
- domain
- Bacteria
- Archaea
- Eukarya
- Animalia
- Plantae
- Protista
- Fungi
- dichotomous key

4 Apply As you learn the definition of each vocabulary term in this lesson, write your own definition or make a sketch to help you remember the meaning of each term.

Sorting Things Out!

Why do we classify living things?

There are millions of living things on Earth. How do scientists keep all of these living things organized? Scientists *classify* living things based on characteristics that living things share. Classification helps scientists answer questions such as:

- How many kinds of living things are there?
- What characteristics define each kind of living thing?
- What are the relationships among living things?

Sharks have fins and gills.

Dolphins also have fins, but not gills.

Visualize It!

5 Analyze The photos below show two organisms. In the table, place a check mark in the box for each characteristic that the organisms have.

Miami blue butterfly

Scrub jay

	Wings	Antennae	Beak	Feathers
Miami blue butterfly				
Scrub jay				

6 Summarize What characteristics do Miami blue butterflies have in common with scrub jays? How do they differ?

_____

_____

_____

How do scientists know living things are related?

If two organisms look similar, are they related? To classify organisms, scientists compare physical characteristics. For example, they may look at size or bone structure. Scientists also compare the chemical characteristics of living things.

 **Active Reading**

7 Identify As you read this page, underline the characteristics used to classify living things.

Physical Characteristics

How are chickens similar to dinosaurs? If you compare dinosaur fossils and chicken skeletons, you'll see that chickens and dinosaurs share many physical characteristics. Scientists look at physical characteristics, such as skeletal structure. They also study how organisms develop from an egg to an adult. Organisms that have similar skeletons and development may be related.

Chemical Characteristics

Scientists can identify the relationships among organisms by studying genetic material such as DNA and RNA. They use mutations and genetic similarities to find relationships among organisms. Organisms that have very similar gene sequences or have the same mutations are likely related. Other chemicals, such as proteins and hormones, can also be studied to learn how organisms are related.

Kaibab squirrels live on the North Rim of the Grand Canyon.

Abert's squirrels live on the South Rim of the Grand Canyon.

Kaibab squirrels and Abert's squirrels look different, and they are separated by the Grand Canyon. However, DNA testing showed that these squirrels are very closely related.

8 Synthesize In addition to canyons, what other kinds of geologic formations might separate similar organisms?

_____

_____

_____

What's in a Name?

How are living things named?

Early scientists used names as long as 12 words to identify living things, and they also used common names. So, classification was confusing. In the 1700s, a scientist named Carolus Linnaeus (KAR•uh•luhs lih•NEE•uhs) simplified the naming of living things. He gave each kind of living thing a two-part *scientific name*.

Scientific Names

Each species has its own scientific name. A **species** (SPEE•sheez) is a group of organisms that are very closely related. They can mate and produce fertile offspring. Consider the scientific name for a mountain lion: *Puma concolor*. The first part, *Puma,* is the genus name. A **genus** (JEE•nuhs; plural, *genera*) includes similar species. The second part, *concolor,* is the specific, or species, name. No other species is named *Puma concolor*.

A scientific name always includes the genus name followed by the specific name. The first letter of the genus name is capitalized, and the first letter of the specific name is lowercase. The entire scientific name is written either in italics or underlined.

HELLO
my name is
Carolus Linnaeus

The A.K.A. Files

Some living things have many common names. Scientific names prevent confusion when people discuss organisms.

Scientific name:
Puma concolor

Common names:
Mountain lion
Puma
Cougar
Panther

Scientific name:
Acer rubrum

Common names:
Red maple
Swamp maple
Soft maple

9 Apply In the scientific names above, circle the genus name and underline the specific name.

What are the levels of classification?

Linnaeus's ideas became the basis for modern taxonomy (tak•SAHN•uh•mee). *Taxonomy* is the science of describing, classifying, and naming living things. At first, many scientists sorted organisms into two groups: plants and animals. But many organisms did not fit into either group.

Today, scientists use an eight-level system to classify living things. Each level gets more definite. Therefore, it contains fewer kinds of living things than the level before it. Living things in the lower levels are more closely related to each other than they are to organisms in the higher levels. From most general to most definite, the levels of classification are domain, kingdom, phylum (plural, *phyla*), class, order, family, genus, and species.

Think Outside the Book Inquiry

10 **Analyze** With a partner, investigate how Linnaeus's development of scientific names affected taxonomy. Make an informative brochure that describes your findings.

Classifying Organisms

Domain | **Domain Eukarya** includes all protists, fungi, plants, and animals.

Kingdom | **Kingdom Animalia** includes all animals.

Phylum | Animals in **Phylum Chordata** have a hollow nerve cord in their backs. Some have a backbone.

Class | Animals in **Class Mammalia**, or mammals, have a backbone and nurse their young.

Order | Animals in **Order Carnivora** are mammals that have special teeth for tearing meat.

Family | Animals in **Family Felidae** are cats. They are carnivores that have retractable claws.

Genus | Animals in **Genus *Felis*** are cats that cannot roar. They can only purr.

Species | The **species *Felis domesticus***, or the house cat, has unique traits that other members of genus *Felis* do not have.

From domain to species, each level of classification contains a smaller group of organisms.

Visualize It!

11 **Apply** How does the shape of a pyramid relate to the number of organisms in each level of the classification system?

Triple Play

What are the three domains?

Once, kingdoms were the highest level of classification. Scientists used a six-kingdom system. But scientists noticed that organisms in two of the kingdoms differed greatly from organisms in the other four kingdoms. So, scientists added a new classification level: domains. A **domain** represents the largest differences among organisms. The three domains are Bacteria (bak•TIR•ee•uh), Archaea (ar•KEE•uh), and Eukarya (yoo•KEHR•ee•uh).

Active Reading

12 Identify As you read, underline the three domains of life.

Bacteria

All bacteria belong to domain Bacteria. Domain **Bacteria** is made up of prokaryotes that usually have a cell wall and reproduce by cell division. *Prokaryotes* are single-celled organisms that lack a nucleus in their cells. Bacteria live in almost any environment—soil, water, and even inside the human body!

Archaea

Domain **Archaea** is also made up of prokaryotes. They differ from bacteria in their genetics and in the makeup of their cell walls. Archaea were discovered living in harsh environments, such as hot springs and thermal vents, where other organisms could not survive. Some archaea are found in the open ocean and soil.

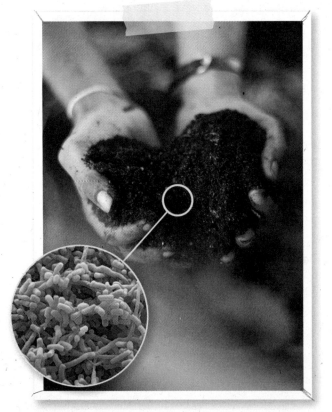

Bacteria from the genus *Streptomyces* are commonly found in soil.

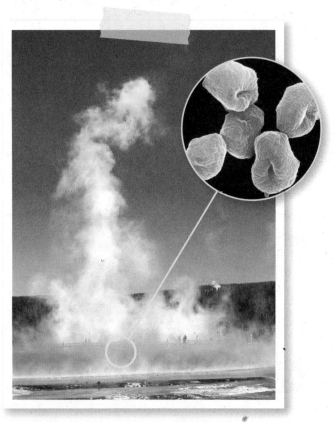

Archaea from genus *Sulfolobus* are found in hot springs.

Eukarya

What do algae, mushrooms, trees, and humans have in common? All of these organisms are *eukaryotes*. Eukaryotes are made up of cells that have a nucleus and membrane-bound organelles. The cells of eukaryotes are more complex than the cells of prokaryotes. For this reason, the cells of eukaryotes are usually larger than the cells of prokaryotes. Some eukaryotes, such as many protists and some fungi, are single-celled. Many eukaryotes are multicellular organisms. Some protists and many fungi, plants, and animals are multicellular eukaryotes. Domain **Eukarya** is made up of all eukaryotes.

It may look like a pinecone, but the pangolin is actually an animal from Africa. It is in domain Eukarya.

13 Analyze To demonstrate your understanding of domains, fill in the concept map below.

The Three Domains

include

A Bacteria

Archaea

B Eukarya

which are

which includes

protists

C Made up of prokaryotes

D fungi

E plants

F animals

My Kingdom for a Eukaryote!

What kingdoms are in Eukarya?

Eukaryotes are found throughout the world. They vary in size from single-celled organisms, such as plankton, to multicellular organisms, such as blue whales. Currently, four kingdoms make up the domain Eukarya: Protista, Fungi, Plantae, and Animalia.

Kingdom Animalia

Kingdom **Animalia** contains multicellular organisms that lack cell walls, are usually able to move around, and have specialized sense organs. They eat other organisms for food. Birds, fish, reptiles, insects, and mammals are just a few examples of animals.

Kingdom Protista

Members of the kingdom **Protista**, called *protists*, are single-celled or simple multicellular organisms such as algae, protozoans, and slime molds. Protists are a very diverse group of organisms, with plantlike, animal-like, or funguslike characteristics.

Kingdom Plantae

Kingdom **Plantae** consists of multicellular organisms that have cell walls, cannot move around, and make their own food. Plants are found on land and in water that light can pass through.

Kingdom Fungi

The members of kingdom **Fungi** get energy by absorbing materials and have cells with cell walls but no chloroplasts. Fungi are single-celled or multicellular. Yeasts, molds, and mushrooms are fungi. Fungi use digestive juices to break down materials around them for food.

Visualize It!

14 Synthesize For which kingdom would you most likely need a magnifying lens or microscope to study the organisms?

_____

How do classification systems change?

Thousands of organisms have been identified, but millions remain to be named. Many new organisms fit into the existing system. However, scientists often find organisms that don't fit. Not only do scientists identify new species, but they find new genera and even phyla. In fact, many scientists argue that protists are so different from each other that they should be classified into several kingdoms instead of one. Classification continues to change as scientists learn more about living things.

15 Predict How might the classification of protists change in the future?

_____

_____

_____

_____

How are classification relationships illustrated?

How do you organize your closet? What about your books? People organize things in many different ways. Scientists use different tools to organize information about classification. Among those tools are *branching diagrams*.

Branching Diagrams

Scientists often use a type of branching diagram called a *cladogram* (KLAD•uh•gram). A cladogram shows relationships among species. Organisms are grouped based on common characteristics. Usually, these characteristics are listed along a line that points to the right. Branches extend from this line. Organisms on branches to the right of each characteristic have the characteristic. Organisms on branches to the left lack the characteristic.

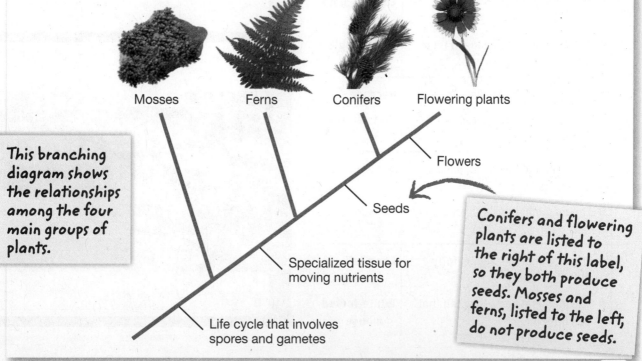

Mosses   Ferns   Conifers   Flowering plants

This branching diagram shows the relationships among the four main groups of plants.

Flowers

Seeds

Specialized tissue for moving nutrients

Life cycle that involves spores and gametes

Conifers and flowering plants are listed to the right of this label, so they both produce seeds. Mosses and ferns, listed to the left, do not produce seeds.

Keys to Success

How can organisms be identified?

Imagine walking through the woods. You see an animal sitting on a rock. It has fur, whiskers, and a large, flat tail. How can you find out what kind of animal it is? You can use a dichotomous key.

Dichotomous Keys

A **dichotomous key** (di•KOT•uh•muhs KEE) uses a series of paired statements to identify organisms. Each pair of statements is numbered. When identifying an organism, read each pair of statements. Then choose the statement that best describes the organism. Either the chosen statement identifies the organism or you will be directed to another pair of statements. By working through the key, you can eventually identify the organism.

---

16 Apply Use the dichotomous key below to identify the animals shown in the photographs.

Dichotomous Key to Six Mammals in the Eastern United States

1	**A** The mammal has no hair on its tail.	**Go to step 2**
	B The mammal has hair on its tail.	**Go to step 3**
2	**A** The mammal has a very short, naked tail.	**Eastern mole**
	B The mammal has a long, naked tail.	**Go to step 4**
3	**A** The mammal has a black mask.	**Raccoon**
	B The mammal does not have a black mask.	**Go to step 5**
4	**A** The mammal has a flat, paddle-shaped tail.	**Beaver**
	B The mammal has a round, skinny tail.	**Possum**
5	**A** The mammal has a long, furry tail that is black on the tip.	**Long-tail weasel**
	B The mammal has a long tail that has little fur.	**White-footed mouse**

A _Beaver_

B _Long-tail weasel_

17 Apply Some dichotomous keys are set up as diagrams instead of tables. Work through the key below to identify the unknown plant.

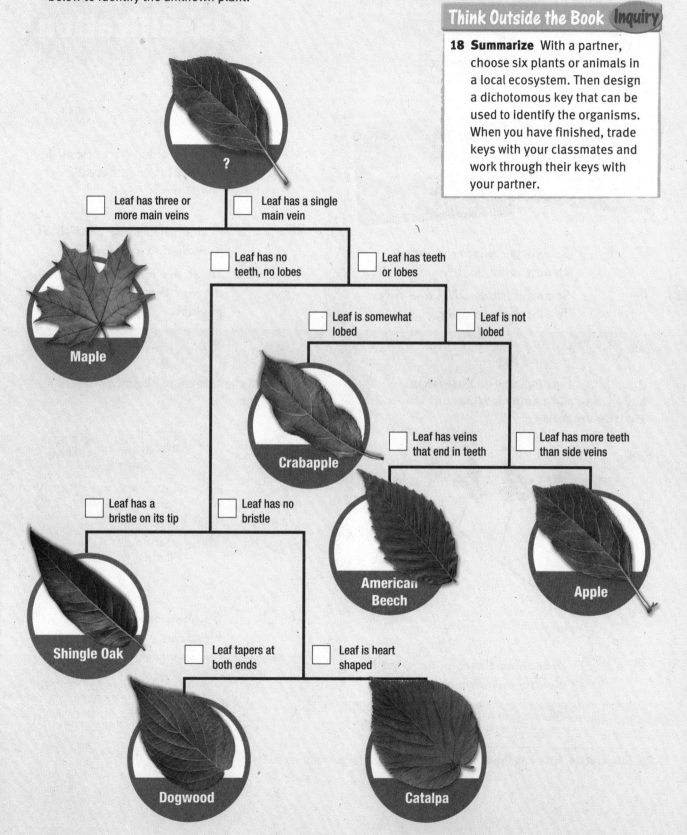

Leaf has three or more main veins

Leaf has a single main vein

Maple

Leaf has no teeth, no lobes

Leaf has teeth or lobes

Leaf is somewhat lobed

Leaf is not lobed

Crabapple

Leaf has veins that end in teeth

Leaf has more teeth than side veins

Leaf has a bristle on its tip

Leaf has no bristle

American Beech

Apple

Shingle Oak

Leaf tapers at both ends

Leaf is heart shaped

Dogwood

Catalpa

Think Outside the Book Inquiry

18 Summarize With a partner, choose six plants or animals in a local ecosystem. Then design a dichotomous key that can be used to identify the organisms. When you have finished, trade keys with your classmates and work through their keys with your partner.

Visual Summary

To complete this summary, check the box that indicates true or false. Then use the key below to check your answers. You can use this page to review the main concepts of the lesson.

Classification

Scientists use physical and chemical characteristics to classify organisms.

    T F

19 ☐ ☐ Scientists compare skeletal structure to classify organisms.

20 ☐ ☐ Scientists study DNA and RNA to classify organisms.

All species are given a two-part scientific name and classified into eight levels.

    T F

21 ☐ ☐ A scientific name consists of domain and kingdom.

22 ☐ ☐ There are more organisms in a genus than there are in a phylum.

Branching diagrams and dichotomous keys are used to help classify and identify organisms.

    T F

23 ☐ ☐ Branching diagrams are used to identify unknown organisms.

The highest level of classification is the domain.

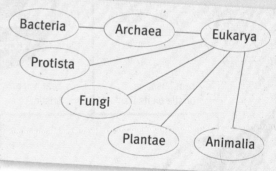

    T F

24 ☐ ☐ Domains are divided into kingdoms.

Answers: 19 T; 20 T; 21 F; 22 F; 23 F; 24 T

25 Summarize How has the classification of living things changed over time?

Lesson Review

Vocabulary

Fill in the blanks with the term that best completes the following sentences.

1 A _____ contains paired statements that can be used to identify organisms.

2 The kingdoms of eukaryotes are _____, Fungi, Plantae, and Animalia.

3 Domains _____ and _____ are made up of prokaryotes.

Key Concepts

4 List Name the eight levels of classification from most general to most definite.

_____

_____

_____

5 Explain How did scientific names impact classification?

_____

_____

_____

_____

6 Identify What two types of evidence are used to classify organisms?

_____

_____

7 Compare Dichotomous keys and branching diagrams organize different types of information about classification. How are these tools used differently?

_____

_____

_____

_____

_____

Critical Thinking

Use the figure to answer the following questions.

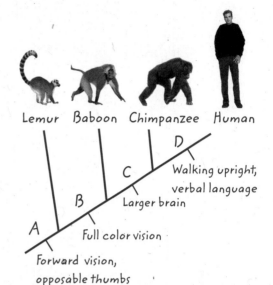

8 Identify Which traits do baboons have?

_____

_____

9 Analyze Which animal shares the most traits with humans?

_____

10 Synthesize Do both lemurs and humans have the trait listed at point D? Explain.

_____

_____

_____

_____

11 Classify A scientist finds an organism that cannot move. It has many cells, produces spores, and gets food from its environment. In which kingdom does it belong? Explain.

_____

_____

_____

_____

_____

My Notes

Unit 2 Summary

Chemistry of Life

is a component of the

Classification of Living Things

The Characteristics of Cells

Cell Structure and Function

Levels of Cellular Organization

Homeostasis and Cell Processes

---

1 Interpret The Graphic Organizer above shows that the characteristics of cells are related to cell structure and function. For example, all cells have a cell membrane. Explain the role of this characteristic in a cell's structure and function.

_____

_____

_____

2 Distinguish Describe the difference between the four levels of cellular organization.

_____

_____

_____

_____

3 Infer Why is waste removal a necessary cellular process for a cell to maintain homeostasis?

_____

_____

_____

_____

4 Apply If two animals have almost identical physical characteristics, can you assume that they are related species? Why or why not?

_____

_____

_____

_____

Benchmark Review

Name _____

Multiple Choice

Identify the choice that best completes the statement or answers the question.

1 Serena knows that scientists use physical characteristics to classify organisms. She studies the figures of four different organisms.

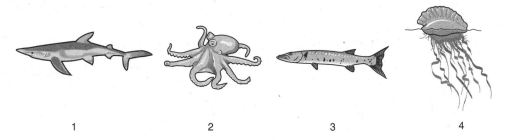

1   2   3   4

Which two organisms should Serena conclude are **most** closely related?

A. 1 and 2

B. 1 and 3

C. 2 and 3

D. 2 and 4

2 Eukaryotic cells and prokaryotic cells have some parts in common. Which of the following pairs of parts would you find in **both** types of cells?

F. cytoplasm and nucleus

G. cell membrane and cytoplasm

H. DNA and membrane-bound organelles

I. cell membrane and membrane-bound organelles

3 Robert Hooke was the first person to describe cells. Which of the following instruments did he use to make his observations?

A.   C.

B.   D.

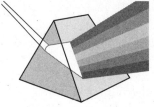

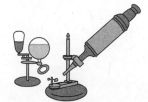

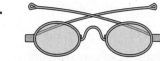

4 Cells use energy to carry out various cell processes. Which of the following molecules stores energy for the cell to use?

F. ATP

G. DNA

H. water

I. chloroplast

5 In biology class, Zach observes cells. Each cell has a structure that separates the inside of the cell from the environment. Which structure is Zach observing?

A. nucleus

B. cytoskeleton

C. cell membrane

D. genetic material

6 Imagine a cell that has the shape of a cube with sides that are 3 cm long. What is the surface area-to-volume ratio of this cell?

F. 27 cm³

G. 54 cm²

H. 27 cm³ : 54 cm²

I. 54 cm² : 27 cm³

7 Jemin made a poster to compare unicellular organisms with multicellular organisms. Which of the following statements that she included is **not** true?

A. Unicellular organisms live longer.

B. Multicellular organisms are larger.

C. Unicellular organisms are made of just one cell.

D. Multicellular organisms can have groups of cells that work together.

8 Gerard listed four levels of structural organization within multicellular organisms. He listed them in order from the smallest structure to the largest structure. Which of the following lists is correct?

F. cells, tissues, organ systems, organs

G. cells, tissues, organs, organ systems

H. tissues, cells, organ systems, organs

I. tissues, cells, organs, organ systems

9 The following picture shows a single cell.

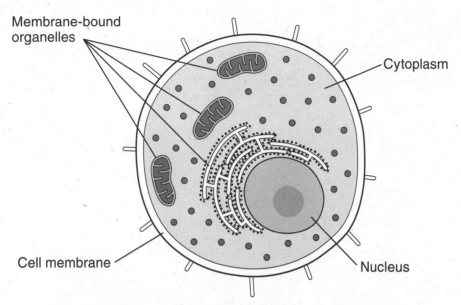

Membrane-bound organelles

Cytoplasm

Cell membrane

Nucleus

What is the function of the structure labeled *Nucleus*?

A. to hold the cell's DNA

B. to hold the cell's organelles

C. to hold the cell's cytoplasm

D. to hold the cell's cell membrane

10 Kayla summarizes the cell theory to her class. She states that all organisms are made up of one or more cells. Which pair of statements correctly completes her summary?

F. All cells come from existing cells, and all cells have the same parts.

G. All cells are the same size, and the cell is the basic unit of all organisms.

H. The cell is the basic unit of all organisms, and all cells have the same parts.

I. The cell is the basic unit of all organisms, and all cells come from existing cells.

Benchmark Review

11 The following diagram shows the basic steps of photosynthesis.

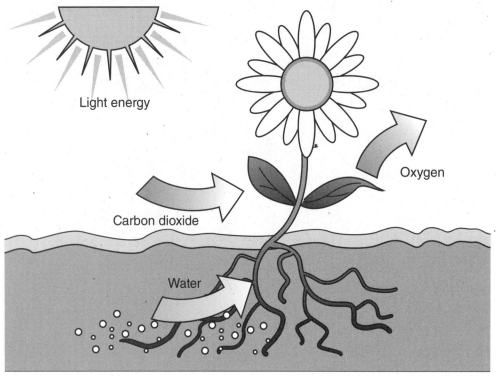

What label would you add to complete this illustration so that it shows the products of photosynthesis?

A. ATP

B. Fat

C. Protein

D. Sugar

12 Mariella is observing the cells of an organism that has ribosomes, mitochondria, and lysosomes. She notes that the cells do not have a cell wall. What type of organism is Mariella **most likely** observing?

F. a plant

G. a fungus

H. an animal

I. a prokaryote

13 Lilly is writing a report about nutrients. Which of the following is a **true** statement about nutrients that she could include in her report?

  A. Some organisms do not need nutrients.

  B. Lipids and carbohydrates are two types of nutrients.

  C. Nutrients are cells in the bodies of animals but not plants.

  D. Nutrients are chemical compounds that have no function in animals.

14 Tina looks in her science book at a diagram of a cellular organelle. The diagram is shown below.

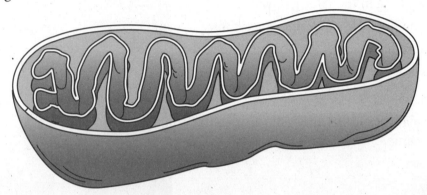

Which organelle is Tina observing?

  F. cytoskeleton

  G. large central vacuole

  H. mitochondrion

  I. ribosome

15 Plant cells use photosynthesis to make food. Plant cells also use cellular respiration to get energy from the food they make. How is cellular respiration **different** from photosynthesis?

  A. Photosynthesis produces ATP, and cellular respiration produces sugars.

  B. Photosynthesis requires oxygen, and cellular respiration requires carbon dioxide.

  C. Photosynthesis produces oxygen, and cellular respiration produces carbon dioxide.

  D. Photosynthesis requires energy from food, and cellular respiration requires energy from the sun.

16 Jelal subscribes to a nature magazine. An article about the classification of mammals included the following table.

	Mammal 1	Mammal 2	Mammal 3
Height at shoulder	42 cm	62 cm	77 cm
Length without tail	68 cm	81 cm	110 cm
Weight	22 lb	30 lb	80 lb
Scientific name	*Canis mesomelas*	*Canis latrans*	*Canis lupus*

Which of the following is a statement that Jelal might read in the article?

F. The organisms belong in the same genus.

G. The organisms do not have a common ancestor.

H. The organisms are members of the domain Archaea.

I. The organisms lack common chemical characteristics.

17 Mike is trying to explain scientific names to a classmate. What are the two parts of a scientific name?

A. genus and species

B. phylum and class

C. domain and genus

D. domain and kingdom

18 Roger explains to his sister the importance of water in cell processes. He describes the chemical structure of water to her. Which of the following is a **true** statement about water?

F. Water is an element.

G. Water is a molecule because it contains carbon.

H. Water is a molecule because it has two different elements.

I. Water is a molecule because it is made up of two or more atoms.

Human Body Systems

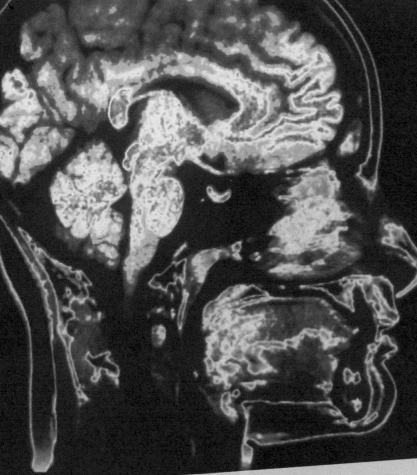

Big Idea 14

Organization and Development of Living Organisms

A brain scan can show whether the brain is functioning normally.

What do you think?

In the Middle Ages, people dug up the dead and operated on them to learn about the body. Today, technology like the MRI scanner allows us to study the living body. How does the living body work?

A patient must stay still to get an accurate MRI scan.

CITIZEN SCIENCE
Muscles at Work

Design a test for muscle endurance or strength.

① Define the Problem

Unlike many things that wear out with use, our muscles actually get stronger the more often they are used. Doing different kinds of exercises helps different groups of muscles. But how can you tell if you are improving? How can you tell how strong a group of muscles are?

Muscles become larger as they become stronger.

Strength moves like this hold take practice and training.

② Think About It

Design a test for a group of muscles.

Choose a group of muscles that you would like to work with. Then, come up with one or two simple exercises that can be done to show either how strong the muscles are or how well they are able to work continuously. Place a time limit on your tests so that the tests don't take too long.

Check off the points below as you use them to design your test.

☐ The kind of action the muscles can do.

☐ To do the test safely, remember to isolate the group of muscles. (Research how to do an exercise safely.)

☐ The equipment you will need for the test.

③ Plan and Test Your Design

A Write out how you will conduct your test in the space below. Check your plan with your teacher before proceeding.

_____

_____

_____

_____

_____

_____

B Conduct the test on yourself. Have a classmate time you, help you count, or make any other measurements that you might need help with. Briefly state your findings.

_____

_____

_____

_____

_____

Take It Home

Do the same exercises at home throughout the week. Then conduct your test again. See if there is any improvement. Report your findings to the class.

Introduction to Body Systems

ESSENTIAL QUESTION

How do the body systems work together to maintain homeostasis?

By the end of this lesson, you should be able to describe the functions of the human body systems, including how they work together to maintain homeostasis.

🌴 Sunshine State Standards

SC.6.L.14.5 Identify and investigate the general functions of the major systems of the human body (digestive, respiratory, circulatory, reproductive, excretory, immune, nervous, and musculoskeletal) and describe ways these systems interact with each other to maintain homeostasis.

HE.6.C.1.4 Recognize how heredity can affect personal health.

HE.6.C.1.8 Explain how body systems are impacted by hereditary factors and infectious agents.

LA.6.4.2.2 The student will record information (e.g., observations, notes, lists, charts, legends) related to a topic, including visual aids to organize and record information and include a list of sources used.

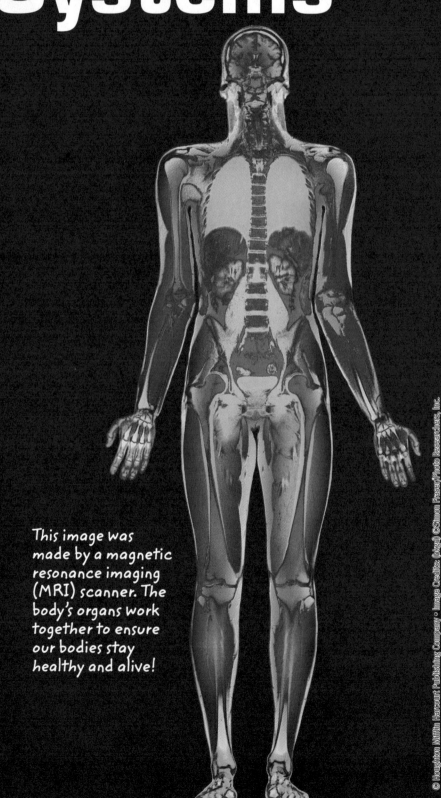

This image was made by a magnetic resonance imaging (MRI) scanner. The body's organs work together to ensure our bodies stay healthy and alive!

Engage Your Brain

1 Predict Check T or F to show whether you think each statement is true or false.

T   F

☐   ☐   Your muscles provide a framework that supports and protects your body.

☐   ☐   When you breathe in and out, you're using your lungs.

☐   ☐   Your nervous system gets rid of wastes from your body.

☐   ☐   When you eat food, it enters your digestive system.

2 Identify Draw a diagram of your body showing at least four organs. As you read the lesson, write down the organ system that each organ is a part of.

Active Reading

3 Synthesize You can often define an unknown word if you know the meaning of its word parts. Use the word parts and sentence below to make an educated guess about the meaning of the word *homeostasis*.

Greek word	Meaning
homoios	same
stasis	standing

Example Sentence
In order to maintain <u>homeostasis</u>, the cardiovascular system and the respiratory system work together to move oxygen-carrying blood around the body.

homeostasis:

_____

_____

_____

_____

Vocabulary Terms

- **homeostasis**

4 Apply As you learn the definition of the vocabulary term in this lesson, make a sketch that shows the meaning of the term or an example of that term. Next to your drawing, write your own definition of the term.

What do the body systems do?

Humans and other organisms need to get energy. They need to use energy to run their bodies and move. They need to reproduce. They need to get rid of waste and protect their bodies. Body systems, also called *organ systems*, help organisms to do all of these things. They also coordinate all the functions of a body.

Groups of organs that work together form body systems. Nerves detect a stimulus in the environment and send a signal through the spinal cord to the brain. The brain sends a signal to respond. Without all the parts, the system would not work. Some organs work in more than one organ system.

Active Reading **5 Identify** As you read about body systems on these pages, underline the main function of each body system.

The respiratory system gathers oxygen from the environment and gets rid of carbon dioxide from the body. The exchange occurs in the lungs.

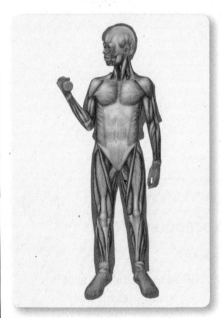

The muscular system allows movement of body parts. It works with the skeletal system to help you move.

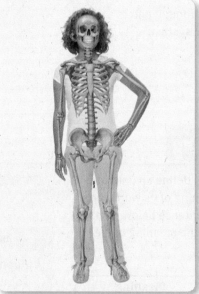

The skeletal system is made up of bones, ligaments, and cartilage. It supports the body and protects important organs. It also makes blood cells.

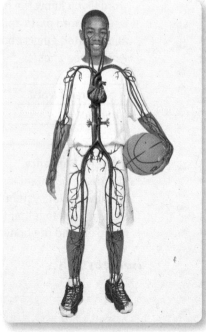

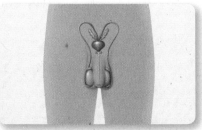

The male reproductive system produces sperm and delivers it to the female reproductive system.

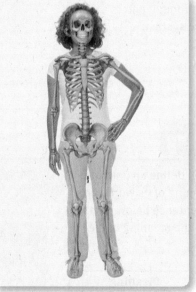

The female reproductive system produces eggs and nourishes a developing fetus.

The cardiovascular system moves blood through the body. The heart is the pump for this system. Blood flows through blood vessels.

6 Analyze Look closely at the body systems shown on these pages. Then circle the two systems that send messages around the body.

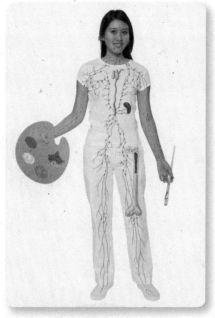

The lymphatic system returns leaked fluid back to the blood. As a major part of the immune system, it has cells that help get rid of invading bacteria and viruses.

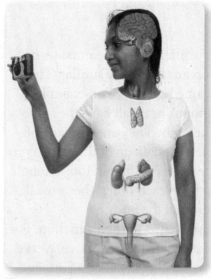

The endocrine system makes chemical messages. These messages help to regulate conditions inside the body. They also influence growth and development.

The integumentary system is the protective covering of the body. It includes the skin, hair, and nails. As part of the immune system, the skin acts as a barrier that protects the body from infection.

The excretory system gets rid of the body's wastes. The urinary system, shown here, removes wastes from blood. The skin, lungs, and digestive system also remove wastes from the body.

The digestive system breaks down food into nutrients that can be used by the body. The stomach breaks down food into tiny pieces. Nutrients are absorbed in the small intestine.

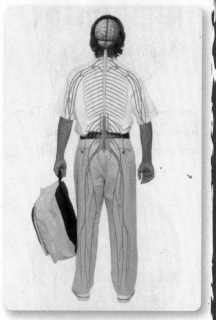

The nervous system collects information and responds to it by sending electrical messages. This information may come from outside or inside the body. The brain is the center of the nervous system.

A Closer Look

How are structure and function linked?

Even though animals may look very different on the outside, on the inside, their cells, tissues, and organs look very similar. This is because these structures do the same basic job. For example, a frog's heart, a bird's heart, and a human's heart all have the same function, to pump blood around the body. They are all made of the same type of muscle tissue, which is made up of the same type of muscle cells. The structure of the hearts is similar, too. Though their shape may be a little different from each other, they are all muscular pumps that push blood around the body.

The shapes and sizes of cells are related to their function. For example, sperm cells have long tails that are used to move. Nerve cells are long and thin to send messages long distances. Surface skin cells are broad and flat. The diagram below shows how skin cells form the skin, which covers and protects the body.

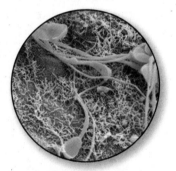

Sperm cells can "swim." They have long tails that whip around to move the cells.

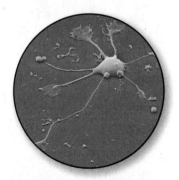

Nerve cells have long, thin branches to send electrical messages between the brain and far-away body parts.

Skin is made up of different cells in many layers. The epidermis is the outer layer of skin. The dermis is the second layer of skin and contains glands, hair follicles, and blood vessels.

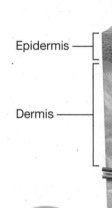

Epidermis

Dermis

7 Infer Muscle cells can get longer and shorter. How does this ability fit in with their job in the body?

_____

_____

_____

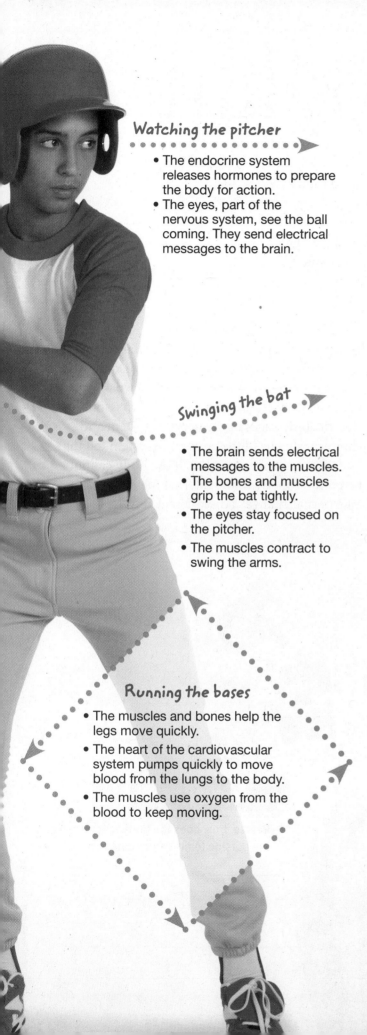

Watching the pitcher
- The endocrine system releases hormones to prepare the body for action.
- The eyes, part of the nervous system, see the ball coming. They send electrical messages to the brain.

Swinging the bat
- The brain sends electrical messages to the muscles.
- The bones and muscles grip the bat tightly.
- The eyes stay focused on the pitcher.
- The muscles contract to swing the arms.

Running the bases
- The muscles and bones help the legs move quickly.
- The heart of the cardiovascular system pumps quickly to move blood from the lungs to the body.
- The muscles use oxygen from the blood to keep moving.

How do body systems work together?

Our body systems can do a lot, but they can't work alone! Almost everything we need for our bodies to work properly requires many body systems to work together. For example, the nervous system may sense danger. The endocrine system releases hormones that cause the heart to beat faster to deliver more oxygen through the circulatory system to muscles. The muscular system and skeletal system work together to run away from danger.

Active Reading **8 Identify** As you read the captions on the left, underline examples of body systems working together.

Body Systems Share Organs

Many organs are part of several body systems. Reproductive organs are part of the reproductive system and part of the endocrine system. The liver works in the digestive system but also is part of the excretory system. The heart is part of the muscular system and the cardiovascular system. Blood vessels too are shared. For example, blood vessels transport chemical messages from the endocrine system and cells from the lymphatic and cardiovascular systems.

Body Systems Communicate

There are two basic ways cells communicate: by electrical messages and by chemical messages. Nerve cells transfer information between the body and the spinal cord and brain. Nerves pass electrical messages from one cell to the next along the line. The endocrine system sends chemical messages through the bloodstream to certain cells.

9 Apply When you are finished running the bases, you are sweating and you feel thirsty. What body systems are interacting in this case?

_____
_____
_____
_____

Keeping the Balance

What is homeostasis?

Cells need certain conditions to work properly. They need food and oxygen and to have their wastes taken away. If body conditions were to change too much, cells would not be able to do their jobs. **Homeostasis** (hoh•mee•oh•STAY•sis) is the maintenance of a constant internal environment when outside conditions change. Responding to change allows all systems to work properly.

Responding to Change

If the external environment changes, body systems work together to keep conditions stable within the body. For example, if body cells were to get too cold, they would not work properly and they could die. So, if the brain senses the body temperature is getting too low, it tells the muscles to shiver. Shivering muscles release energy as heat which warms the body. Your brain will also tell you to put on a sweater!

Maintaining a Balance

To maintain homeostasis, the body has to recognize that conditions are changing and then respond in the right way. In order to work, organ systems need to communicate properly. The electrical messages of the nervous system and chemical signals of the endocrine system tell the body what changes to make. If the body cannot respond properly to the internal messages or to an external change, a disease may develop.

Too cold

Just right

Too hot

A thermostat keeps an even temperature in a room by turning the heater off when it gets too warm, and on when it gets too cold. Your body does the same thing but in a different way.

Visualize It!

10 Relate How does the body react when the outside temperature gets too hot?

_____

_____

_____

_____

What can go wrong with homeostasis?

If one body system does not work properly, other body systems can be affected. For example, body cells that do not get enough energy or nutrients cannot work properly. A lack of food harms many systems and may cause disease or even death. The presence of toxins or pathogens also can disrupt homeostasis. Toxins can prevent cells from carrying out life processes and pathogens can break down cells. Problems also occur if the body's messages do not work, or they are not sent when or where they are needed. Many diseases which affect homeostasis are hereditary.

Active Reading

11 Identify As you read this page, underline what can happen if homeostasis is disrupted.

Structure or Function Diseases

Problems with the structure or function of cells, tissues, or organs can affect the body. For example, diabetes is a disease that affects cell function. Certain changes in body cells stop them from taking glucose in from the blood as they normally do. If cells cannot get energy in the form of glucose, they cannot work properly.

Pathogens and Disease

When the body cannot maintain homeostasis, it is easier for pathogens to invade the body. Pathogens can also cause a disruption in homeostasis. For example, tuberculosis is a lung disease caused by bacteria. It weakens the lungs and body. Weakened lungs cannot take in oxygen well. Low oxygen levels affect the whole body.

12 Apply Alcoholism is a disease that disrupts homeostasis. Below are three body systems that are affected by alcohol. The effects on the nervous system are filled in. In the space provided, predict what might happen when the function of the two remaining systems is affected.

Body systems affected	What are the effects?
Nervous system	Disrupts proper functioning of the brain. The brain cannot respond properly to internal or external messages.
Digestive system	
Reproductive system	

Alcoholism can damage the structure and function of the liver and reduce its ability to remove toxins from the blood.

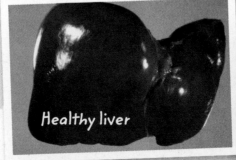
Healthy liver

Unhealthy liver

Visual Summary

To complete this summary, fill in the blanks with the correct word or phrase. Then use the key below to check your answers. You can use this page to review the main concepts of the lesson.

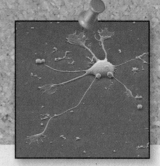

Body systems each have specific jobs.

13 The _____ system brings oxygen into the blood and releases carbon dioxide from the body.

The structure of cells, tissues, and organs are linked to their functions.

14 The long, thin cells of the

_____ system help transmit messages around the body. The muscular heart pushes

_____ around the body.

Body Systems and Homeostasis

Body systems work together, which allows the body to work properly.

15 The _____

and _____ systems work together to allow the player to swing the bat.

The body maintains homeostasis by adjusting to change.

16 If body temperature goes up, the

_____ senses the change and will work to reduce the body temperature to normal.

Answers: 13 respiratory; 14 nervous; blood; 15 nervous; muscular (either order) 16 brain

17 **Explain** How might disruption of the respiratory system affect homeostasis of the body?

Lesson Review

Vocabulary

Use a term from the lesson to complete each sentence below.

1 _____ is maintaining stable conditions inside the body.

2 A group of organs that work together is called a(n) _____ .

Key Concepts

3 Compare How are the functions of the skeletal and muscular systems related?

_____

_____

_____

_____

4 Identify What body system receives information from inside and outside the body and responds to that information?

_____

_____

5 Explain How is skin part of the integumentary system and the excretory system?

_____

_____

_____

_____

_____

6 Describe What are the basic needs of all cells in the body?

_____

_____

_____

7 Relate Give an example of how a cell's structure relates to its function in the body.

_____

_____

_____

Critical Thinking

Use the graph to answer the following questions.

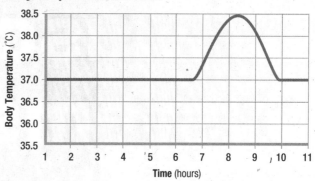

Body Temperature over Time

8 Analyze Is the body in homeostasis during the entire time shown in the graph? Explain your answer.

_____

_____

_____

_____

9 Predict What would happen to the body if the graph continued to decrease during the tenth hour instead of leveling off?

_____

_____

_____

10 Apply The body loses water and salts in sweat. Explain why drinking large volumes of plain water after exercising may affect the salt balance in the body.

_____

_____

_____

_____

_____

_____

The Skeletal and Muscular Systems

ESSENTIAL QUESTION

How do your skeletal and muscular systems work?

By the end of this lesson, you should be able to explain how the skeletal and muscular systems work together to allow movement of the body.

🌞 Sunshine State Standards

SC.6.L.14.5 Identify and investigate the general functions of the major systems of the human body (digestive, respiratory, circulatory, reproductive, excretory, immune, nervous, and musculoskeletal) and describe ways these systems interact with each other to maintain homeostasis.

HE.6.C.1.4 Recognize how heredity can affect personal health.

HE.6.C.1.8 Explain how body systems are impacted by hereditary factors and infectious agents.

LA.6.4.2.2 The student will record information (e.g., observations, notes, lists, charts, legends) related to a topic, including visual aids to organize and record information and include a list of sources used.

By working together, your muscular and skeletal systems allow you to do many things such as stand up, sit down, type a note, or run a race.

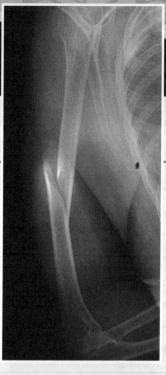

Engage Your Brain

1 Identify Circle the terms that best complete the following sentences.

The *skeletal / muscular* system is responsible for supporting the body.

Bones are part of your *skeletal / muscular* system.

Your heart is made up of *bone / muscle* tissue.

You can increase your flexibility by stretching your *bones / muscles*.

2 Infer This x-ray shows a broken arm. How might this injury affect your ability to move?

_____

_____

_____

_____

 ## Active Reading

3 Synthesize You can often identify functions of a body part if you know what its name means. Use the Latin words below and context clues to make an educated guess about a function of *ligaments* and *tendons*.

Latin word	Meaning
ligare	to tie
tendere	to stretch

Example Sentence
Ligaments are found at the ends of bones.

ligament:

_____

Example Sentence
Tendons connect muscles to bones.

tendon:

_____

Vocabulary Terms

- skeletal system
- ligament
- joint
- muscular system
- tendon

4 Apply As you learn the definition of each vocabulary term in this lesson, create your own definition or sketch it to help you remember the meaning of the term.

What's Inside?

What are the main functions of the skeletal system?

When you hear the word *skeleton*, you might think of the dry, white bones that you see in the models in your science class. You might think your bones are lifeless, but they are very much alive. The **skeletal system** is the organ system that supports and protects the body and allows it to move. Its other jobs include storing minerals and producing red blood cells. A human's skeleton is inside the body, so it is called an *endoskeleton*.

 **Active Reading**

5 Identify As you read, underline the main functions of the skeletal system.

Visualize It!

6 Relate How might a suit of armor be a good analogy for a function of the skeletal system?

_____

_____

_____

_____

Protection

Bones provide protection to organs. For example, your ribs protect your heart and lungs, your vertebrae protect your spinal cord, and your skull protects your brain.

Storage

The hard outer layer of bone, called *compact bone*, stores important minerals such as calcium. These minerals are necessary for nerves and muscles to work properly.

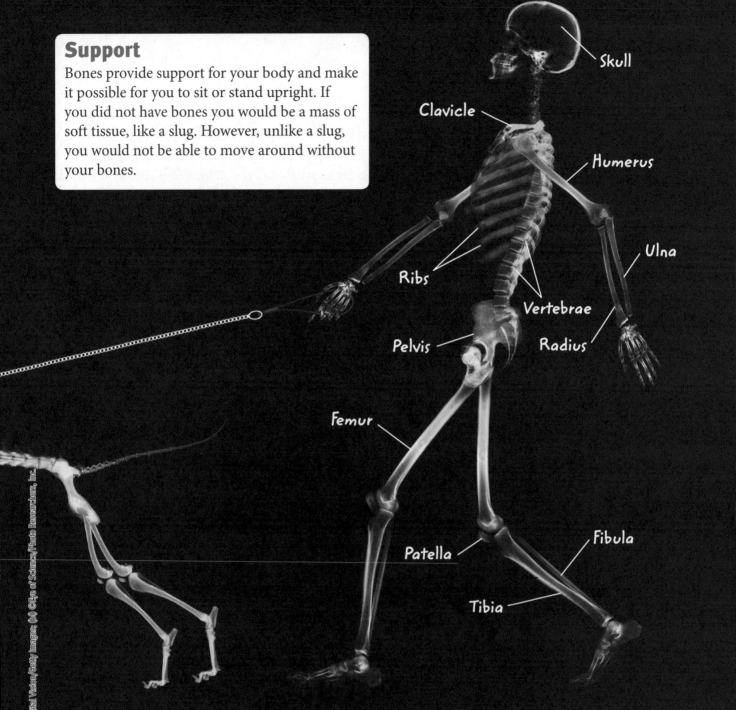

Support

Bones provide support for your body and make it possible for you to sit or stand upright. If you did not have bones you would be a mass of soft tissue, like a slug. However, unlike a slug, you would not be able to move around without your bones.

Skull

Clavicle

Humerus

Ulna

Ribs

Vertebrae

Radius

Pelvis

Femur

Fibula

Patella

Tibia

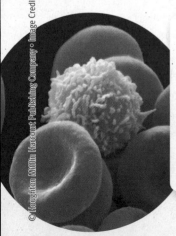

Blood Cell Production

At the center of bones, such as the long bones in the man's and dog's legs, is soft tissue called *marrow*. Red marrow, a type of marrow that makes blood cells, is found mostly in flat bones such as the ribs, pelvis and skull. The red and white blood cells shown here are made in the red bone marrow.

Movement

Bones play an important role in movement by providing a place for muscles to attach. Muscles pull on bones to move the body. Without bones, muscles could not do their job of moving the body.

No Bones About It!

What are the parts of the skeletal system?

Bones, ligaments, and cartilage make up your skeletal system. The skeletal system is divided into two parts. The skull, vertebrae, and ribs make up the *axial skeleton*, which supports the body's weight and protects internal organs. The arms, legs, shoulders, and pelvis make up the *appendicular skeleton*, which allows for most of the body's movement.

Bones

Bones are alive! They have blood vessels which supply nutrients and nerves which signal pain. The body of a newborn baby has about 300 bones, but the average adult has only 206 bones. As a child grows, some bones fuse together.

Ligaments

The tough, flexible strand of connective tissue that holds bones together is a **ligament**. Ligaments allow movement, and are found at the end of bones. Some ligaments, such as the ones on your vertebrae, prevent too much movement of bones.

7 Compare How does the axial skeleton differ from the appendicular skeleton?

_____

_____

_____

_____

Cartilage

Cartilage is a strong, flexible, and smooth connective tissue found at the end of bones. It allows bones to move smoothly across each other. The tip of your nose and your ears are soft and bendy because they contain only cartilage. Cartilage does not contain blood vessels.

What are bones made of?

Bones are hard organs made of minerals and connective tissue. If you looked inside a bone, you would notice two kinds of bone tissue. One kind, called *compact bone*, is dense and does not have any visible open spaces. Compact bone makes bones rigid and hard. Tiny canals within compact bone contain blood capillaries. The other kind of bone tissue, called *spongy bone*, has many open spaces. Spongy bone provides most of the strength and support for a bone. In long bones, such as those of the arm or the leg, an outer layer of compact bone surrounds spongy bone and another soft tissue called *marrow*.

Active Reading **8 Identify** As you read, underline the name of a protein found in bone.

Minerals

Calcium is the most plentiful mineral in bones. The minerals in bones are deposited by bone cells called *osteoblasts*. Minerals such as calcium make the bones strong and hard.

Connective Tissue

The connective tissue in bone is made mostly of a protein called *collagen*. Minerals make the bones strong and hard, but the collagen in bones allows them to be flexible enough to withstand knocks and bumps. Otherwise, each time you bumped a bone, it would crack like a china cup.

Marrow

Bones also contain a soft tissue called *marrow*. There are two types of marrow. Red marrow is the site of platelet and red and white blood cell production. Red marrow is in the center of flat bones such as the ribs. Yellow marrow, which is found in the center of long bones such as the femur, stores fat.

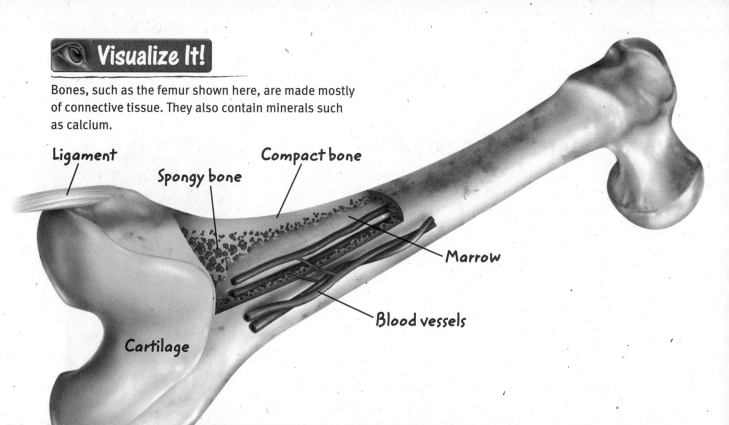

Visualize It!

Bones, such as the femur shown here, are made mostly of connective tissue. They also contain minerals such as calcium.

Ligament

Spongy bone

Compact bone

Marrow

Blood vessels

Cartilage

9 Summarize In the chart below, fill in the main functions of each part of the skeletal system.

Structure	Function
Spongy bone	
Compact bone	
Cartilage	
Ligaments	

How do bones grow?

The skeleton of a fetus growing inside its mother's body does not contain hard bones. Instead, most bones start out as flexible cartilage. When a baby is born, it still has a lot of cartilage. As the baby grows, most of the cartilage is replaced by bone.

The bones of a child continue to grow. The long bones lengthen at their ends, in areas called *growth plates*. Growth plates are areas of cartilage that continue to make new cells. Bone cells called *osteocytes* move into the cartilage, hardening it and changing it into bone. Growth continues into adolescence and sometimes even into early adulthood. Most bones harden completely after they stop growing. Even after bones have stopped growing, they can still repair themselves if they break.

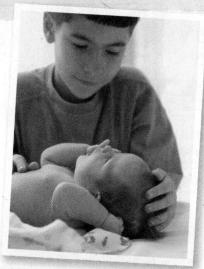

This baby's skeleton has more cartilage than his older brother's skeleton has.

Bone Connections

How are bones connected?

The place where two or more bones connect is called a **joint**. Some joints allow movement of body parts, others stop or limit movement. Just imagine how difficult it would be to do everyday things such as tying your shoelaces if you could not bend the joints in your arms, legs, neck, or fingers!

Joints

Bones are connected to each other at joints by strong, flexible ligaments. The ends of the bone are covered with cartilage. Cartilage is a smooth, flexible connective tissue that helps cushion the area in a joint where bones meet. Some joints allow little or no movement. These *fixed joints* can be found in the skull. Other joints, called *movable joints*, allow movement of the bones.

Your joints allow you to do everyday tasks easily.

Some Examples of Movable Joints

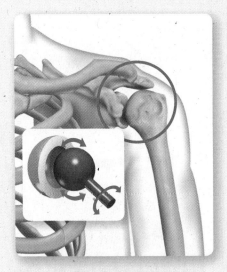

Ball and Socket joint
Shoulders and hips are ball-and-socket joints. Ball-and-socket joints allow one of the bones of the joint to rotate in a large circle.

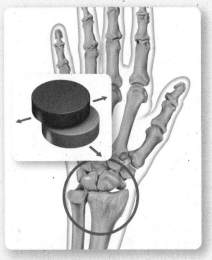

Gliding joint
Wrists and ankles are gliding joints. Gliding joints allow a great deal of flexibility in many directions.

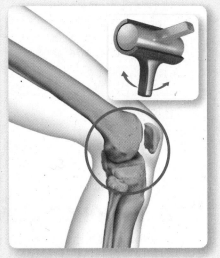

Hinge joint
Knees and elbows are hinge joints. Hinge joints work like door hinges, allowing bones to move back and forth.

10 **Apply** Some joints, such as the ones in your skull, do not move at all. Why do you think it is important that skull joints cannot move?

_____

_____

_____

_____

What are some injuries and disorders of the skeletal system?

Sometimes the skeletal system can become injured or diseased. Injuries and diseases of the skeletal system affect the body's support system and ability to move. Hereditary factors may play a role in the incidence of diseases such as osteoporosis and arthritis.

Active Reading

11 Identify As you read, underline the characteristics of each injury and disease.

Fractures

Bones may be fractured, or broken. Bones can be broken by a high-force impact such as a fall from a bike. A broken bone usually repairs itself in six to eight weeks.

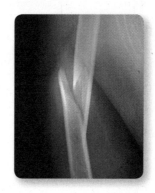

Sprains

A sprain is an injury to a ligament that is caused by stretching a joint too far. The tissues in the sprained ligament can tear and the joint becomes swollen and painful to move. Sprains are common sports injuries.

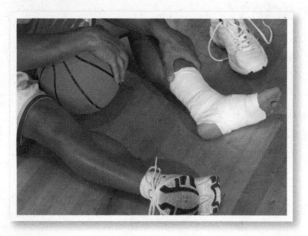

12 Apply How could someone sprain a ligament?

_____

_____

_____

_____

_____

Osteoporosis

Osteoporosis is a disease that causes bone tissue to become thin. The bones become weak and break more easily. It is most common among adults who do not get enough calcium in their diet. What you eat now can affect your risk of developing osteoporosis later in life.

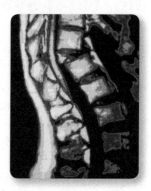

13 Infer Why is it important to get enough calcium in your diet?

_____

_____

_____

_____

Arthritis

Arthritis is a disease that causes joints to swell, stiffen, and become painful. It may also cause the joint to become misshapen, as shown in the photo. A person with arthritis finds it difficult to move the affected joint. Arthritis can be treated with drugs that reduce swelling.

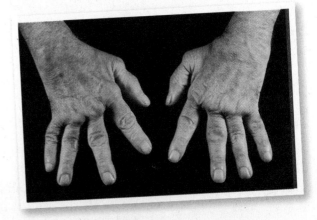

Keep Moving!

What are the main functions of the muscular system?

Muscles pump blood through your body, enable you to breathe, hold you upright, and allow you to move. All animals except the simplest invertebrates have muscles for movement. The **muscular system** is mostly made of the muscles that allow your body to move and be flexible. Other muscles move materials inside your body. *Muscle* is the tissue that contracts and relaxes, making movement possible. Muscle tissue is made up of muscle cells. Muscle cells contain special proteins that allow them to shorten and lengthen.

Active Reading **14 Identify** How do muscles make movement possible?

What are the three types of muscles?

Your body has three kinds of muscle tissue: *skeletal muscle, smooth muscle,* and *cardiac muscle.* Each muscle type has a specific function in your body.

You are able to control the movement of skeletal muscle, so it is called *voluntary muscle.* You are not able to control the movement of smooth muscle and cardiac muscles. Muscle action that is not under your control is *involuntary.* Smooth muscle and cardiac muscle are called *involuntary muscles.*

Smooth Muscle

Smooth muscle is found in internal organs and blood vessels. It helps move materials through the body. Arteries and veins contain a layer of smooth muscle that can contract and relax. This action controls blood flow through the blood vessel. Smooth muscle movement in your digestive system helps move food through your intestines. Smooth muscle is involuntary muscle.

Smooth muscle cells are spindle shaped. They are fat in the middle with thin ends.

Cardiac muscle cells are long, thin, and branched.

Cardiac Muscle

Cardiac muscle is the tissue that makes up the heart. Your heart never gets tired like your skeletal muscle can. This is because cardiac muscle cells are able to contract and relax without ever getting tired. In order to supply lots of energy to the cells, cardiac muscle cells contain many mitochondria. Your cardiac muscles do not stop moving your entire lifetime!

The contractions of cardiac muscle push blood out of the heart and pump it around the body. Cardiac muscle is involuntary; you cannot consciously stop your heart from pumping.

Skeletal muscle cells are long and thin with stripes, or striations.

Skeletal Muscle

Skeletal muscle is attached to your bones and allows you to move. You have control over your skeletal muscle. For example, you can bring your arm up to your mouth to take a bite from an apple. The tough strand of tissue that connects a muscle to a bone is called a **tendon**. When a muscle contracts, or shortens, the attached bones are pulled closer to each other. For example, when the bicep muscle shortens, the arm bends at the elbow.

Most skeletal muscles work in pairs around a joint, as shown below. One muscle in the pair, called a *flexor*, bends a joint. The other muscle, the *extensor*, straightens the joint. When one muscle of a pair contracts, the other muscle relaxes to allow movement of the body part. Muscle pairs are found all around the body.

15 Apply What would happen to the arm if the flexor was not able to contract?

_____

_____

_____

_____

_____

_____

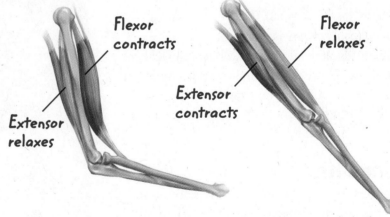

Flexor contracts

Extensor relaxes

Flexor relaxes

Extensor contracts

The biceps muscle is the flexor that contracts to bend the arm.

The triceps muscle is the extensor that contracts to straighten the arm.

16 Compare How do the three muscle tissue types look similar and different?

_____

_____

_____

_____

_____

_____

Move It or Lose It!

What are some injuries and disorders of the muscular system?

Like other systems, the muscular system can suffer injury or disease. As a result, muscles may lose normal function. Some muscle diseases are hereditary. Diseases that affect muscle function can also affect other body systems. For example, myocarditis is an inflammation of the heart muscle that can cause heart failure and harm the cardiovascular system.

Muscle Strain and Tears

A *strain* is a muscle injury in which a muscle is overstretched or torn. This can happen when muscles have not been stretched properly or when they are overworked. Strains cause the muscle tissue to swell and can be painful. Strains and tears need rest to heal.

Muscular Dystrophy

Muscular dystrophy is a hereditary disease that causes skeletal muscle to become weaker over time. It affects how muscle proteins form. A person with muscular dystrophy has poor balance and difficulty walking or doing other everyday activities.

Tendinitis

Tendons connect muscles to bones. Tendons can become inflamed or even torn when muscles are overused. This painful condition is called *tendinitis*. Tendinitis needs rest to heal. It may also be treated with medicines that reduce swelling.

17 Contrast What is the difference between a muscle strain and tendinitis?

_____

_____

_____

Physical therapy can help people gain full use of their muscles and joints after an injury.

Think Outside the Book

18 Plan With a classmate, research the recommendations for regular physical activity. Then design a poster to show how people can fit 30–60 minutes of physical activity into their daily lives.

What are some benefits of exercise?

Exercising is one of the best things you can do to keep your body healthy. *Exercise* is any activity that helps improve physical fitness and health. Exercise benefits the muscular system by increasing strength, endurance, and flexibility. Exercise helps other body systems, too. It helps keep your heart, blood vessels, lungs, and bones healthy. Exercise also reduces stress, helps you sleep well, and makes you feel good.

Exercises that raise your heart rate to a certain level for at least 60 minutes improve the fitness of the heart. A fit heart is a more efficient pump. It can pump more blood around the body with each beat. It is also less likely to develop heart disease. Good muscle strength and joint flexibility may help a person avoid injuries. Weight training helps bones stay dense and strong. Dense, strong bones are less likely to break. Thirty to sixty minutes of physical activity every day can help improve the health of people of all ages, from children to older adults.

Active Reading **19 Identify** As you read, underline the characteristics of anaerobic and aerobic exercise.

Muscle Strength

Resistance exercise helps improve muscle strength by building skeletal muscle and increasing muscle power. Resistance exercise involves short bursts of intense effort lasting no more than a few minutes. Resistance exercises are also called *anaerobic exercises* because the muscle cells contract without using oxygen. Lifting weights and doing pushups are examples of anaerobic exercises.

Muscle Endurance

Endurance exercises allow muscles to contract for a longer time without getting tired. Endurance exercises are also called *aerobic exercises* because the muscle cells use oxygen when contracting. Aerobic exercises involve moderately intense activity from about 30 to 60 minutes at a time. Some examples of aerobic exercises are walking, jogging, bicycling, skating, and swimming.

Flexibility

Can you reach down and touch your toes? If a joint can move through a wide range of motions, it has good flexibility. *Flexibility* refers to the full range of motion of a joint. Stretching exercises help improve flexibility of a joint. Having good flexibility can help prevent ligament, tendon, and muscle injuries. Stretching after aerobic or anaerobic exercises may also help prevent injuries.

Visual Summary

To complete this summary, fill in the blanks with the correct word or phrase. Then, use the key below to check your answers. You can use this page to review the main concepts of the lesson.

The Skeletal and Muscular Systems

The skeletal system supports and protects the body and allows for movement.

20 The three main parts of the skeletal system are bones, _____, and _____.

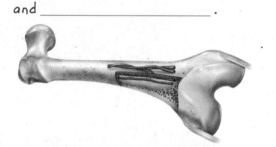

Joints connect two or more bones.

21 The shoulder is an example of a _____ joint.

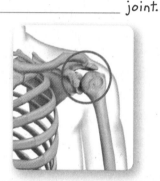

The muscular system allows for movement and flexibility.

22 Muscles work in _____ to move body parts.

Exercise benefits the body in many ways.

23 Aerobic exercises improve muscle _____.

Anaerobic exercises improve muscle _____.

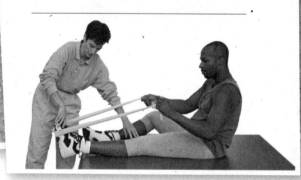

Answers: 20 cartilage; ligaments; 21 ball and socket; 22 pairs; 23 endurance; strength

24 **Synthesize** Explain why you need both muscles and bones to move your body.

Lesson Review

Vocabulary

Draw a line to connect the following terms to their definitions.

1 skeletal system

2 ligament

3 muscular system

4 joint

5 tendon

A groups of muscles that allow you to move and that move materials inside your body

B a place where two or more bones connect

C bones, cartilage, and the ligaments that hold bones together

D tough strands of tissue that connect muscles to bones

E a type of tough, flexible connective tissue that holds bones together

Key Concepts

6 List What are the functions of the skeletal system?

The skeletal system holds bones, cartilage, & ligaments together.

7 Analyze What are bones made of?

It's made of cartilage and joints to hold it in place.

8 Explain How do muscles work in pairs to move the body?

They're voluntary which means you have to control them on your own to make them work.

9 Identify What bone disease is caused by a lack of calcium in the diet?

Osoperosis

Critical Thinking

Use this graph to answer the following questions.

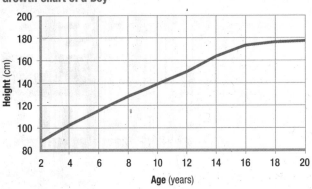

Growth Chart of a Boy

10 Analyze At which points in this graph is bone growing at the fastest rate?

_____

_____

_____

11 Infer At which times on this graph would you expect that the boy's growth plates have stopped creating new bone?

_____

_____

_____

12 Apply If aerobic exercise improves heart strength so that it pumps more blood with each beat, what likely happens to the heart rate as the cardiac muscle gets stronger? Explain your answer.

The heart rate would decrease because it becomes more efficient to beat less.

_____

_____

The Circulatory and Respiratory Systems

ESSENTIAL QUESTION

How do the circulatory and respiratory systems work?

By the end of this lesson, you should be able to relate the structures of the circulatory and respiratory systems to their functions in the human body.

🕐 Sunshine State Standards

SC.6.L.14.5 Identify and investigate the general functions of the major systems of the human body (digestive, respiratory, circulatory, reproductive, excretory, immune, nervous, and musculoskeletal) and describe ways these systems interact with each other to maintain homeostasis.

LA.6.4.2.2 The student will record information (e.g., observations, notes, lists, charts, legends) related to a topic, including visual aids to organize and record information and include a list of sources used.

HE.6.C.1.4 Recognize how heredity can affect personal health.

HE.6.C.1.8 Explain how body systems are impacted by hereditary factors and infectious agents.

This micrograph shows red blood cells inside a blood vessel in the lung. The blood cells are picking up oxygen to bring to the rest of the body.

Engage Your Brain

1 Identify Check T or F to show whether you think each statement is true or false.

T   F

☐   ☐   Air is carried through blood vessels.

☐   ☐   The cardiovascular system does not interact with any other body system.

☐   ☐   The respiratory system gets rid of carbon dioxide from the body.

☐   ☐   Smoking cigarettes can lead to lung disease.

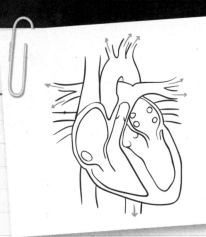

2 Identify What is the name of the organ, shown here, that makes the "lub-dub" sound in your chest?

_____

3 Infer What is the function of this organ?

_____

_____

_____

Active Reading

4 Synthesize You can sometimes tell a lot about the structure of an unknown object by understanding the meaning of its name. Use the meaning of the Latin word and the sentence below to write your own definition of *capillary*.

Latin word	Meaning
capillaris	thin and hairlike

Example Sentence
Oxygen that is carried by blood cells moves across the <u>capillary</u> wall and into body cells.

capillary:

_____

_____

_____

_____

Vocabulary Terms

- cardiovascular system
- blood
- lymphatic system
- lymph
- lymph node
- artery
- capillary
- vein
- respiratory system
- pharynx
- larynx
- trachea
- bronchi
- alveoli

5 Apply As you learn the definition of each vocabulary term in this lesson, create your own definition or sketch to help you remember the meaning of the term.

Go with the Flow!

What is the circulatory system?

![Active Reading icon] **Active Reading**

6 Identify As you read, underline the functions of the cardiovascular system and the lymphatic system.

When you hear the term *circulatory system,* what do you think of? If you said "heart, blood, and blood vessels," you are half right. The term circulatory system describes both the cardiovascular system and the lymphatic system. Both systems work closely together to move fluids around your body and protect it from disease. Your moving blood helps to keep all parts of your body warm. In these ways the two systems help maintain homeostasis.

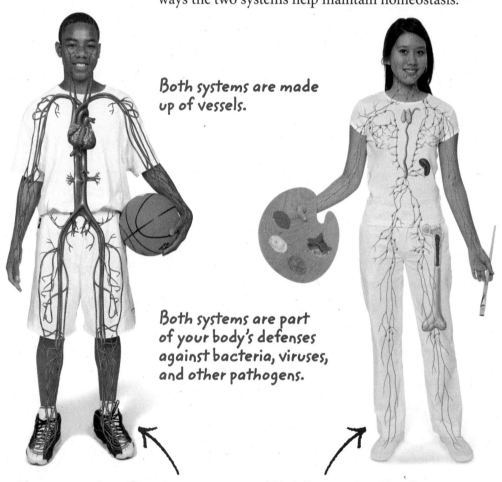

Both systems are made up of vessels.

Both systems are part of your body's defenses against bacteria, viruses, and other pathogens.

The Cardiovascular System

Your heart, blood, and blood vessels make up your **cardiovascular system**, which transports blood around your body. **Blood** is the fluid that carries gases, nutrients, and wastes through the body. The cardiovascular system is a closed circulatory system; the blood is carried in vessels that form a closed loop. The blood maintains homeostasis by transporting hormones, nutrients, and oxygen to cells and by carrying wastes away from cells.

The Lymphatic System

The **lymphatic system** is a group of organs and tissues that collect the fluid that leaks from blood and returns it to the blood. The leaked fluid is called **lymph**. The lymphatic system is an open circulatory system, and lymph can move in and out of the vessels. The lymphatic system is also part of the body's defenses against disease. Certain lymph vessels in the abdomen move fats from the intestine and into the blood.

7 Compare Fill in the Venn diagram to compare the structures and functions of both these systems. You can add more details as you read more about these systems in this lesson.

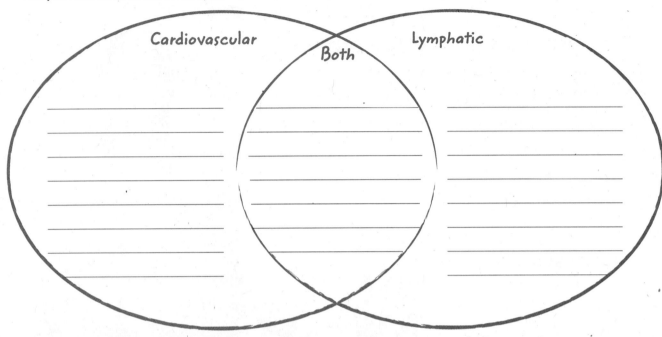

Cardiovascular

Both

Lymphatic

How do the systems work together?

Every time your heart pumps, a little fluid is forced out of the thin walls of the tiniest blood vessels, called *capillaries.* Most of this fluid is reabsorbed by the capillaries, and the remaining fluid is collected by lymph capillaries. *Lymph capillaries* absorb fluid, particles such as dead cells, and pathogens from around body cells. The lymph capillaries carry the fluid, now called *lymph,* to larger lymph vessels. Lymph is returned to the cardiovascular system when it drains into blood vessels at the base of the neck.

The lymphatic system is the place where certain blood cells, called *white blood cells,* mature. Some of these white blood cells stay in the lymphatic system where they attack invading pathogens.

 **Active Reading**

8 Synthesize How does returning leaked fluid from the blood help maintain homeostasis?

_____
_____
_____
_____
_____

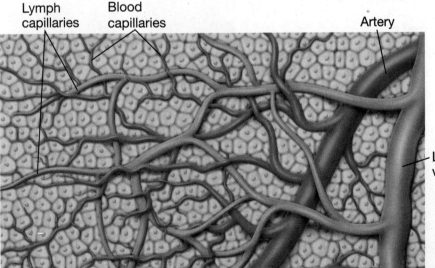

Lymph capillaries

Blood capillaries

Artery

Lymphatic vessel

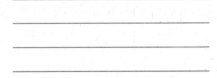 The fluid that leaks from blood capillaries moves into lymph capillaries and is eventually returned to the blood.

Node Doubt!

What are the parts of the lymphatic system?

As you have read, lymph vessels collect and return fluids that have leaked from the blood. In addition to these vessels, several organs and tissues are part of the lymphatic system.

9 Identify As you read these pages, underline the main function of each part of the lymphatic system.

Lymph Nodes

As lymph travels through lymph vessels, it passes through lymph nodes. **Lymph nodes** are small, bean-shaped organs that remove pathogens and dead cells from lymph. Lymph nodes are concentrated in the armpits, neck, and groin. Infection-fighting blood cells, called *white blood cells,* are found in lymph nodes. When bacteria or other pathogens cause an infection, the number of these blood cells may multiply greatly. The lymph nodes fill with white blood cells that are fighting the infection. As a result, some lymph nodes may become swollen and painful. Swollen lymph nodes might be an early clue of an infection.

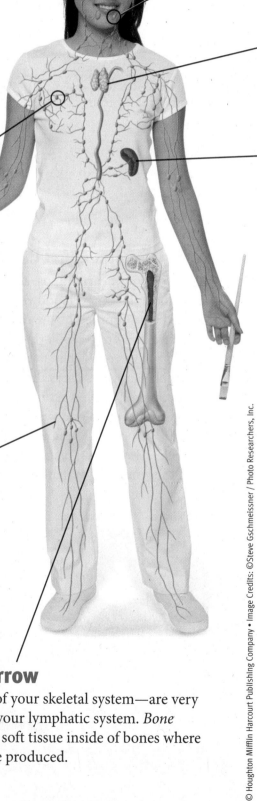

Lymph node

Lymph Vessels

Lymph vessels are the thin-walled vessels of the lymphatic system. They carry lymph back to lymph nodes. From the lymph nodes, the fluid is returned to the cardiovascular system through the lymph vessels. The vessels have valves inside them to stop lymph from flowing backward.

Bone Marrow

Bones—part of your skeletal system—are very important to your lymphatic system. *Bone marrow* is the soft tissue inside of bones where blood cells are produced.

© Houghton Mifflin Harcourt Publishing Company • Image Credits: ©Steve Gschmeissner / Photo Researchers, Inc.

Tonsils

Tonsils are small lymphatic organs at the back of the throat and tongue. The tonsils at the back of the throat are the most visible. Tonsils help defend the body against infection. White blood cells in the tonsil tissues trap pathogens. Tonsils in the throat sometimes get infected. An infection of the tonsils is called *tonsillitis*. When tonsils get infected, they may become swollen, as shown here.

Thymus

The *thymus* is an organ in the chest. Some white blood cells made in the bone marrow finish developing in the thymus. From the thymus, the white blood cells travel through the lymphatic system to other areas of the body. The thymus gets smaller as a person gets older. This organ is also a part of the endocrine system.

Spleen

The *spleen* is the largest lymphatic organ. It stores white blood cells and also allows them to mature. As blood flows through the spleen, white blood cells attack or mark pathogens in the blood. If pathogens cause an infection, the spleen may also release white blood cells into the bloodstream.

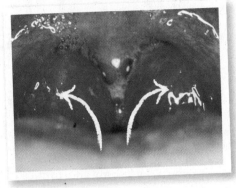

Swollen tonsils

Visualize It!

10 Predict A bad case of tonsillitis can sometimes affect a person's breathing. How is this possible?

_____

_____

_____

What are some disorders of the lymphatic system?

Lymphoma is a type of cancer that often begins in a lymph node. It can cause a swelling in the node called a *tumor*. There are many different types of lymphomas. Another disorder of the lymph system is lymphedema (lim•fih•DEE•muh). Lymphedema is a swelling of body tissues caused by a blockage or injury to lymph vessels. Lymph vessels are unable to drain lymph from a certain area, and that area becomes swollen. Filariasis is a disease caused by threadlike worms called *nematodes*. The nematodes may enter lymphatic vessels and block them, preventing lymph from moving around the body. Bubonic plague is a bacterial infection of the lymphatic system. The bacteria can enter the body through the bite of an infected flea. The bacteria grow inside lymph nodes, causing the nodes to swell.

Active Reading

11 Identify As you read, underline the names of the lymphatic system diseases discussed here.

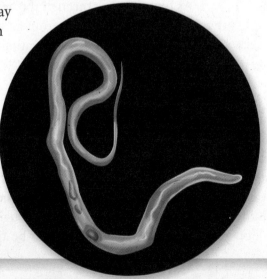

A person gets infected with filarial worms by being bitten by an infected fly. Filariasis is rare in the United States, but is common in developing countries.

The Heart of the Matter

What are the parts of the cardiovascular system?

Your cardiovascular system is the organ system that carries nutrients, gases, and hormones to body cells and waste products from body cells. It also helps keep the different parts of your body at an even temperature. Your cardiovascular system is made up of the heart, blood vessels, and blood.

Active Reading

12 Identify As you read this page, underline the parts of the heart that stop the blood from flowing backward.

Heart

The heart is the pump that sends blood around the body. Your heart is about the size of your fist and is almost in the center of your chest. When heart muscle contracts, it squeezes the blood inside the heart. This squeezing creates a pressure that pushes blood through the body.

Your heart has a left side and a right side. The two sides are separated by a thick wall. The right side of the heart pumps oxygen-poor blood to the lungs. The left side pumps oxygen-rich blood to the body. Each side has an upper chamber and a lower chamber. Each upper chamber is called an *atrium*. Each lower chamber is called a *ventricle*. Blood enters the atria and is pumped down to the ventricles. Flaplike structures called *valves* are located between the atria and the ventricles and in places where large vessels are attached to the heart. As blood moves through the heart, these valves close to prevent blood from going backward. The "lub-dub" sound of a beating heart is caused by the valves closing.

Left Atrium The left atrium receives oxygen-rich blood from the lungs.

Right Atrium The right atrium receives oxygen-poor blood from the body.

Right Ventricle The right ventricle pumps oxygen-poor blood to the lungs.

Left Ventricle The left ventricle pumps oxygen-rich blood to the body.

Blood

Blood is a type of connective tissue that is part of the cardiovascular system. It serves as a transport system, providing supplies for cells, carrying chemical messages, and removing wastes so cells can maintain homeostasis. Blood contains cells, fluid, and other substances. It travels through miles and miles of blood vessels to reach every cell in your body.

13 Infer Why is it important for your heart to keep oxygen-rich blood separate from oxygen-poor blood?

_____

_____

_____

_____

_____

Blood Vessels

Blood travels throughout your body in tubes called *blood vessels*. The three types of blood vessels are arteries, capillaries, and veins.

An **artery** is a blood vessel that carries blood away from the heart. Arteries have thick walls with a layer of smooth muscle. Each heartbeat pumps blood into your arteries at high pressure, which is your *blood pressure*. This pressure pushes blood through the arteries. Artery walls are strong and stretch to withstand the pressure. Nutrients, oxygen, and other substances must leave the blood to get to your body's cells. Carbon dioxide and other wastes leave body cells and are carried away by blood. A **capillary** is a tiny blood vessel that allows these exchanges between body cells and the blood. The gas exchange can take place because capillary walls are only one cell thick. Capillaries are so narrow that blood cells must pass through them in single file! No cell in the body is more than three or four cells away from a capillary.

Capillaries lead to veins. A **vein** is a blood vessel that carries blood back to the heart. Blood in veins is not under as much pressure as blood in arteries is. Valves in the veins keep the blood from flowing backward. The contraction of skeletal muscles around veins can help blood move in the veins.

Arteries carry oxygen-rich blood away from the heart.

Veins carry oxygen-poor blood back to the heart.

Capillaries deliver oxygen-rich blood to body cells and take oxygen-poor blood away from body cells.

14 Apply Complete the table below by naming the blood vessels and by sketching their function. Your sketch may be a symbol, as shown here.

Type of blood vessel		Vein
Sketch of function	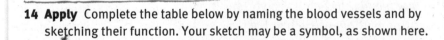	

It's in the Blood

What is blood made of?

An adult human body has about 5 liters of blood. Your body probably has a little less than that. Blood is made up of plasma, platelets, and red and white blood cells. Blood is a tissue because it is made of at least two different cell types. If you looked at blood under a microscope, you would see these differently shaped cells and platelets.

The Blood Files

Plasma

The fluid part of the blood is called *plasma*. Plasma is a mixture of water, minerals, nutrients, sugars, proteins, and other substances. This fluid also carries waste. Red blood cells, white blood cells, and platelets are found in plasma.

White blood cell

Red blood cell

Platelet

Platelets

Platelets are tiny pieces of larger cells found in bone marrow. Platelets last for only five to ten days, but they have an important role. When you cut or scrape your skin, you bleed because blood vessels have been cut open. As soon as bleeding starts, platelets begin to clump together in the cut area. They form a plug that helps reduce blood loss. Platelets also release chemicals that react with proteins in plasma. The reaction causes tiny fibers to form. The fibers help create a blood clot.

White Blood Cells

White blood cells help keep you healthy by fighting pathogens such as bacteria and viruses. Some white blood cells squeeze out of blood vessels to search for pathogens. When they find one they destroy it. Other white blood cells form antibodies. *Antibodies* are chemicals that identify pathogens. White blood cells also keep you healthy by destroying body cells that have died or been damaged.

Red Blood Cells

Most blood cells are red blood cells. *Red blood cells* are disk-shaped cells that do not have a nucleus. They bring oxygen to every cell in your body. Cells need oxygen to carry out life functions. Each red blood cell has hemoglobin. *Hemoglobin* is an oxygen-carrying protein; it clings to the oxygen molecules you inhale. Red blood cells can then transport oxygen to cells in every part of the body. The disk shape of red blood cells helps them squeeze into capillaries.

15 Predict How would the body be affected if red blood cells had low levels of hemoglobin?

_____

_____

_____

_____

_____

_____

How does blood move through the body?

Blood is pumped from the right side of the heart to the lungs. From the lungs it returns to the left side of the heart. The blood is then pumped from the left side of the heart to the body. It flows to the tiny capillaries around the body before returning to the right side of the heart. Blood in the arteries that come out of the heart is under great pressure because of the force from the pumping action of the heart. Blood in veins is under much less pressure than arterial blood because veins have larger internal diameters than arteries do. Veins carry larger volumes of blood more slowly.

Blood Moves in Circuits

Blood moves in two loops or circuits around the body. The beating heart moves blood to the lungs and also around the body. The flow of blood between the heart and the lungs is called the *pulmonary circulation*. As blood passes through the lungs, carbon dioxide leaves the blood and oxygen is picked up. The oxygen-rich blood then flows back to the heart, where it is pumped around the rest of the body. The circulation of blood between the heart and the rest of the body is called *systemic circulation*. Oxygen-poor blood returns to the heart from body cells in the systemic circulation.

Active Reading **16 Compare** What is the difference between the pulmonary and systemic circulations?

_____

_____

_____

How does circulation help maintain body temperature?

The circulation of blood also helps homeostasis. When the brain senses that body temperature is rising, it signals blood vessels in the skin to widen. As the vessels get wider, heat from the blood is transferred to the air around the skin. This transfer helps lower body temperature. When the brain senses that body temperature is normal, it signals the blood vessels to return to normal. When the brain senses the body temperature is getting too low, it signals the blood vessels near the skin to get narrower. This allows the blood to stay close to internal organs to keep them warm.

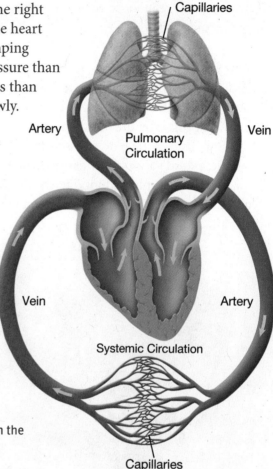

In pulmonary circulation, blood is pumped to the lungs where carbon dioxide leaves the blood and oxygen enters the blood.

Capillaries

Artery

Vein

Pulmonary Circulation

Vein

Artery

Systemic Circulation

Capillaries

In systemic circulation, blood moves around the body.

Visualize It!

17 Apply Put a box around the part of the diagram that shows the pulmonary circulation. Where in the diagram would you find oxygen-poor blood?

_____

_____

_____

_____

What are some problems that affect the cardiovascular system?

Cardiovascular disease is the leading cause of death in the United States. Cardiovascular disease can be caused by smoking, poor diet, stress, physical inactivity, or in some cases, heredity. Eating a healthy diet and regular exercise can reduce the risk of developing cardiovascular problems.

Atherosclerosis

A major cause of heart disease is a condition called *atherosclerosis* (ath•uh•roh•skluh•ROH•sis). Atherosclerosis is a hardening of artery walls caused by the build up of cholesterol and other lipids. The buildup causes the blood vessels to become narrower and less elastic. Blood cannot flow easily through a narrowed artery. When an artery supplying blood to the heart becomes blocked, oxygen cannot reach the heart muscle and the person may have a heart attack.

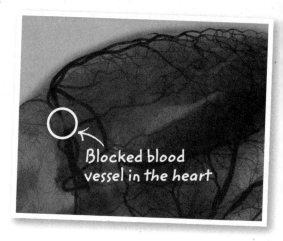

Blocked blood vessel in the heart

Blood pressure checks can help detect illness.

Hypertension

Hypertension is abnormally high blood pressure. Atherosclerosis may be caused in part by hypertension. The higher a person's blood pressure is, the greater their risk of developing cardiovascular problems such as heart attacks and strokes. Hypertension that is not treated can also cause kidney damage and shorten life expectancy. Regular check ups can help detect problems with blood pressure. Hypertension can be controlled with diet and sometimes with medication.

Heart Attacks and Strokes

A heart attack happens when an artery that supplies blood to the heart becomes blocked and the heart muscle tissue that depends on that blood supply does not get oxygen. Cells and tissues that do not get oxygen get damaged and can die. If enough heart muscle cells are damaged, the heart may stop beating.

A stroke can happen when a blood vessel in the brain becomes blocked or bursts. As a result, that part of the brain receives no oxygen. Without oxygen, brain cells die. Brain damage that occurs during a stroke can affect many parts of the body. People who have had a stroke may experience paralysis or difficulty in speaking.

Think Outside the Book (Inquiry)

18 **Research** Doctors often use an electrocardiogram (EKG) reading to see if there is something wrong with how a person's heart is beating. An EKG is a type of graph that "draws" the pumping activity of the heart. How might graphing the heartbeat help a doctor tell if there is a problem?

© Houghton Mifflin Harcourt Publishing Company • Image Credits: (t) ©SPL/Photo Researchers, Inc.; (c) ©MBI/Alamy

Take a Deep Breath

What are the functions of the respiratory system?

Your cells need a constant supply of oxygen to stay alive. Your cells must also be able to get rid of the waste product carbon dioxide, which is toxic to them. Breathing takes care of both of these needs. The **respiratory system** is the group of organs that takes in oxygen and gets rid of carbon dioxide. *Respiration,* or breathing, is the transport of oxygen from outside the body to cells and tissues, and the transport of carbon dioxide and wastes away from cells and to the environment.

 **Active Reading**

19 Identify As you read this page, underline the gas that is needed by your body for cellular respiration.

Takes in Oxygen

When a person inhales, air is drawn into the lungs. Oxygen in the air moves into the blood from the lungs. The oxygen-rich blood flowing away from the lungs is carried to all the cells in the body. Oxygen leaves the capillaries and enters the body cells. Inside each cell, oxygen is used for cellular respiration. During cellular respiration, the energy that is stored in food molecules is released. Without oxygen, body cells would not be able to survive.

Releases Carbon Dioxide

When a person exhales, carbon dioxide is released from the body. Carbon dioxide is a waste product of cellular respiration, and the body needs to get rid of it. Carbon dioxide moves from body cells and into capillaries where it is carried in the blood all the way to the lungs. Blood that flows to the lungs contains more carbon dioxide than oxygen. The carbon dioxide moves out of the lung capillaries and into the lungs where it is exhaled.

□ Oxygen
□ Carbon Dioxide

□ Oxygen
□ Carbon Dioxide

Visualize It!

20 Apply Scuba divers breathe air from the tanks strapped to their bodies. Check the box next to the gas you would expect to find in the greatest concentration in the air tank on the diver's back and in the air bubbles he is exhaling.

Breathe Easy

What are the parts of the respiratory system?

Breathing is made possible by your respiratory system. Air enters your respiratory system through your nose or mouth when you breathe in. From there, the air moves through a series of tubes to get to your lungs.

Nose, Pharynx, and Larynx

Air enters your respiratory system through your nose and your mouth. From the nose, air flows into the **pharynx** (FAIR•ingks), or throat. The pharynx branches into two tubes. One tube, the *esophagus*, leads to the stomach. The other tube, called the *larynx,* leads to the lungs. The **larynx** (LAIR•ingks) is the part of the throat that holds the vocal cords. When air passes across the vocal cords, they vibrate, making the voice.

Bronchioles and Alveoli

In the lungs, the bronchioles lead to tiny sacs called **alveoli** (singular, *alveolus*). Alveoli are surrounded by blood vessels. Gases in the air move across the thin walls of the alveoli and blood vessels. As you breathe, air is sucked into and forced out of alveoli. Breathing is carried out by the diaphragm and rib muscles. The *diaphragm* is a dome-shaped muscle below the lungs. As you inhale, the diaphragm contracts and moves down. The volume of the chest increases. As a result, a vacuum is created and air is sucked in. Exhaling reverses this process.

Trachea

The larynx is connected to a large tube called the **trachea** (TRAY•kee•uh), or windpipe. Air flows from the larynx through the trachea to the lungs. The trachea splits into two branches called **bronchi** (singular, *bronchus*). One bronchus connects to each lung. Each bronchus branches into smaller tubes called *bronchioles*.

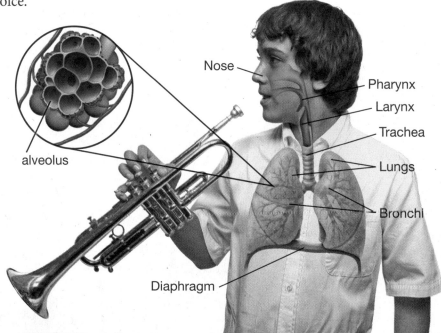

alveolus

Nose

Pharynx

Larynx

Trachea

Lungs

Bronchi

Diaphragm

👁 Visualize It!

21 Apply Draw arrows showing the direction of air flow into the lungs. How would an object blocking a bronchus affect this airflow?

_____

_____

What are some disorders of the respiratory system?

Millions of people suffer from respiratory disorders. These disorders include asthma, pneumonia, emphysema, and lung cancer. Some respiratory problems such as emphysema and lung cancer are strongly linked to cigarette smoke. Other respiratory disorders such as pneumonia are caused by pathogens, and some are genetic disorders. Depending on the cause, there are many different ways to treat respiratory diseases.

Asthma

Asthma is a condition in which the airways are narrowed due to inflammation of the bronchi. During an asthma attack, the muscles in the bronchi tighten and the airways become inflamed. This reduces the amount of air that can get into or out of the lungs. Asthma is treated with medicines that open the bronchioles.

Pneumonia

Pneumonia (noo•MOHN•yuh) is an inflammation of the lungs that is usually caused by bacteria or viruses. Inflamed alveoli may fill with fluid. If the alveoli are filled with too much fluid, the person cannot take in enough oxygen and he or she may suffocate. Pneumonia can be treated with medicines that kill the pathogens.

Emphysema

Emphysema (em•fuh•SEE•muh) occurs when the alveoli have been damaged. As a result, oxygen cannot pass across into the blood as well as it could in a normal alveolus. People who have emphysema have trouble getting the oxygen they need and removing carbon dioxide from the lungs. This condition is often linked to long-term use of tobacco.

Visualize It!

23 Compare How are these two lungs different? How can you tell the diseased lung from the healthy lung?

_____

_____

_____

_____

Emphysema lung

Healthy lung

Visual Summary

To complete this summary, fill in the blanks with the correct word or phrase. Then use the key below to check your answers. You can use this page to review the main concepts of the lesson.

The lymphatic system returns fluid to the blood.

25 The lymph organs found in your throat are called

_____.

Circulatory and Respiratory Systems

The cardiovascular system moves blood throughout the body and carries nutrients and oxygen to body cells.

26 The two gases that the blood carries around the body are

_____ and

_____.

The respiratory system takes oxygen into the body and releases carbon dioxide.

27 Oxygen enters the blood and carbon dioxide leaves the blood in the

_____ of the lungs.

Answers: 25 tonsils; 26 oxygen, carbon dioxide; 27 alveoli

28 **Relate** Describe how a problem with the respiratory system could directly affect the cardiovascular system.

Lesson Review

Vocabulary

In your own words, define the following terms.

1 Blood

_____

_____

2 Lymph

_____

_____

3 Alveoli

_____

_____

Key Concepts

Fill in the table below.

System	Structures
4 Identify What are the main structures of the lymphatic system?	
5 Identify What are the main structures of the cardiovascular system?	
6 Identify What are the main structures of the respiratory system?	

7 Explain How does blood help maintain homeostasis in the body?

_____

_____

_____

8 Contrast How are arteries and veins different?

_____

_____

_____

9 Relate How might a blockage of the lymph vessels affect the function of the cardiovascular system?

_____

_____

_____

Critical Thinking

Use this image to answer the following questions.

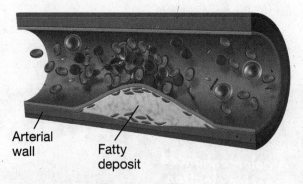

Arterial wall

Fatty deposit

10 Relate To what body system does this structure belong?

_____

11 Predict How might what is happening in this image affect the nervous system?

_____

_____

_____

_____

12 Infer Why is it important that lymph vessels are spread throughout the body?

_____

_____

_____

Olufunmilayo Falusi Olopade

MEDICAL DOCTOR

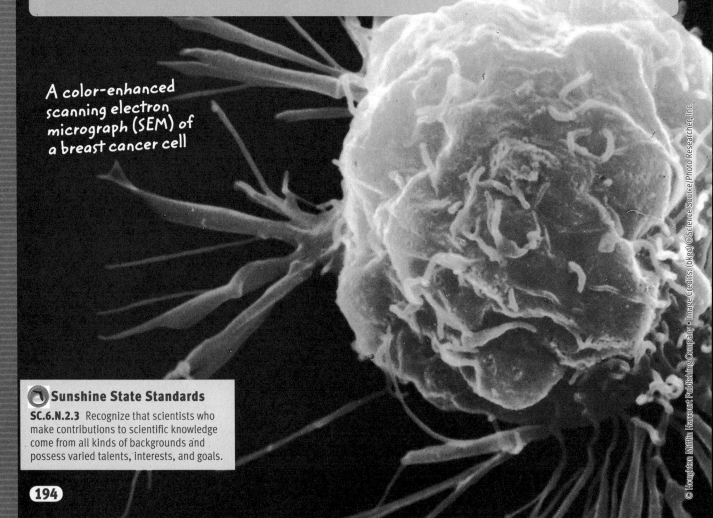

Dr. Olufunmilayo Olapade is the head of the University of Chicago's Cancer Risk Clinic. The MacArthur Foundation awarded her $500,000 for her creative work in breast cancer research.

Born in Nigeria, Dr. Olopade began her career as a medical officer at the Nigerian Navy Hospital in Lagos. She later came to Chicago to do cancer research. She became a professor at the University of Chicago in 1991. She founded the Cancer Risk Clinic shortly after this.

Dr. Olopade has found that tumors in African-American women often come from a different group of cells than they do in Caucasian women.

These tumors, therefore, need different treatment. Dr. Olopade designs treatments that address the source of the tumor. More importantly, her treatments try to address the particular risk factors of each patient. These can include diet, heredity, age, and activity. The MacArthur Foundation recognized Dr. Olopade for designing such new and practical treatment plans for patients. Studying cells has provided Dr. Olopade with clues on how to improve the lives of millions of African-American women.

A color-enhanced scanning electron micrograph (SEM) of a breast cancer cell

Sunshine State Standards

SC.6.N.2.3 Recognize that scientists who make contributions to scientific knowledge come from all kinds of backgrounds and possess varied talents, interests, and goals.

JOB BOARD

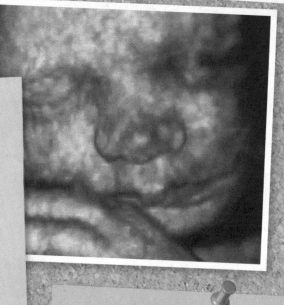

Diagnostic Medical Sonographer

What You'll Do: Operate and take care of the sonogram equipment that uses sound waves to create pictures of inside human bodies that a doctor can interpret.

Where You Might Work: Hospitals, clinics, and private offices that have sonogram equipment.

Education: A two- or four-year undergraduate degree or a special certification program is necessary.

Prosthetics Technician

What You'll Do: Create, test, fit, maintain, and repair artificial limbs and other prosthetic devices for people who need them.

Where You Might Work: Hospitals with prosthetic divisions and private companies.

Education: Technicians must have an associate, bachelor's, or post-graduate degree in orthotics and prosthetics. Some companies may require additional certification.

Physical Therapist

What You'll Do: Use exercise, ultrasound, heat, and other treatments when working with patients to help them improve their muscular strength, endurance, and flexibility.

Where You Might Work: Hospitals, clinics, and private physiotherapy offices, as well as some gyms and yoga studios.

Education: A master's degree from an accredited physical therapy program is required.

Language Arts Connection

Find one report of a new discovery in cancer prevention. Summarize the key points of the discovery in a paragraph. Be sure to include information about what the discovery is, who made it, how the discovery was made, and how it changes what we know about cancer.

The Digestive and Excretory Systems

ESSENTIAL QUESTION

How do your body's digestive and excretory systems work?

By the end of this lesson, you should be able to relate the parts of the digestive and excretory systems to their roles in the human body.

Sunshine State Standards

SC.6.L.14.5 Identify and investigate the general functions of the major systems of the human body (digestive, respiratory, circulatory, reproductive, excretory, immune, nervous, and musculoskeletal) and describe ways these systems interact with each other to maintain homeostasis.

HE.6.C.1.8 Explain how body systems are impacted by hereditary factors and infectious agents.

LA.6.4.2.2 The student will record information (e.g., observations, notes, lists, charts, legends) related to a topic, including visual aids to organize and record information and include a list of sources used.

Your digestive system works to get all of the nutrients out of the food you eat.

Engage Your Brain

1 Fill in the blanks with the words that you think best complete the following sentences.

Inside your ___mouth___, food is chewed and broken down by teeth and saliva.

The ___jaw___ is a muscle inside your mouth that helps you to swallow food and liquids.

If you eat too much food too quickly, you may get a ___stomach___ ache.

2 Imagine How is a blender like your stomach?

It churns and grinds up food to turn into a liquid.

Active Reading

3 Synthesize You can often define an unknown word if you see it used in a sentence. Use the sentence below to make an educated guess about the meaning of the word *enzyme*.

Example sentence
<u>Enzymes</u> in the mouth, stomach, and small intestine help in the chemical digestion of food.

enzyme:

___
___
___
___
___

Vocabulary Terms

- digestive system
- enzyme
- esophagus
- stomach
- small intestine
- large intestine
- pancreas
- liver
- excretory system
- kidney
- nephron
- urine

4 Apply As you learn the meaning of each vocabulary term in this lesson, create your own definition or sketch to help you remember the meaning of the term.

You are what you eat!

What is the digestive system?

Your cells need a lot of energy for their daily activities. Cells use nutrients, which are substances in food, for energy, growth, maintenance, and repair. The **digestive system** breaks down the food you eat into nutrients that can be used as building materials and that can provide energy for cells.

The digestive system interacts with other body systems to obtain and use energy from food. Blood, part of the circulatory system, transports nutrients to other tissues. In order to extract energy from nutrients, cells need oxygen. The respiratory system is responsible for obtaining this oxygen from the environment. The nervous system controls and regulates the functioning of the digestive system.

What are the two types of digestion?

Digestion is the process of breaking down food into a form that can pass from the digestive system into the bloodstream. There are two types of digestion: mechanical and chemical.

The Stomach

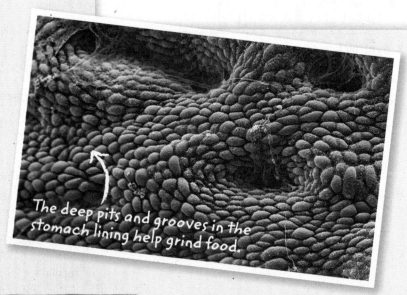

The deep pits and grooves in the stomach lining help grind food.

Inquiry

6 Infer The stomach lining is made up of deep muscular grooves. How do you think these structures help the stomach to break down food?

_____

_____

_____

_____

Mechanical Digestion

Mechanical digestion is the breaking, crushing, and mashing of food. Chewing is a type of mechanical digestion. Chewing creates small pieces of food that are easier to swallow and digest than large pieces are. Mechanical digestion increases the surface area of food for the action of chemical digestion.

Chemical Digestion

Chemical digestion is the process in which large molecules of food are broken down into smaller molecules so that they can pass into the bloodstream. An **enzyme** (EN•zym) is a chemical that the body uses to break down large molecules into smaller molecules. Enzymes act like chemical scissors. They "cut up" large molecules into smaller pieces. Mechanical digestion breaks up food and increases surface area so that enzymes can break nutrients into smaller molecules. Without mechanical digestion, chemical digestion would take days instead of hours!

 **Visualize It!**

7 Categorize Decide whether each of these steps in digestion is an example of mechanical digestion or chemical digestion. Then put a check in the correct box.

In your mouth, teeth grind food.

☐ mechanical

☐ chemical

Salivary glands release a liquid called saliva, which helps to break food down.

☐ mechanical

☐ chemical

In the stomach, muscles contract to grind food into a pulpy mixture.

☐ mechanical

☐ chemical

In the small intestine, most nutrients are broken down by enzymes.

☐ mechanical

☐ chemical

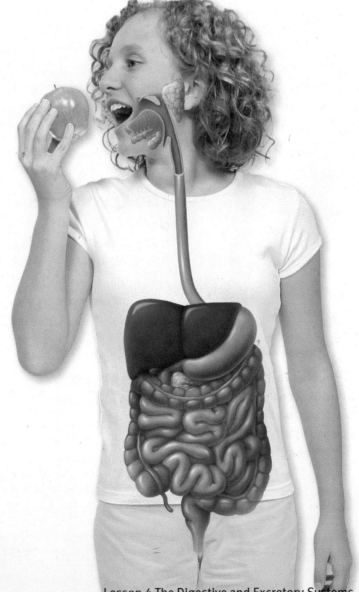

Chew on this

What are the parts of the digestive system?

Has anyone ever reminded you to chew your food? Chewing food is the first part of digestion. After food is chewed and swallowed, pieces of that food move through other organs in the digestive system, where the food is broken down even more.

8 As you read, underline the function of each organ of the digestive system.

The Mouth

Digestion begins in the mouth with both mechanical and chemical digestion. Teeth, with the help of strong jaw muscles, break and crush food.

As you chew, food is moistened by a liquid called *saliva*. Glands in your mouth make saliva. Saliva contains many substances, including an enzyme that begins the chemical digestion of starches in food.

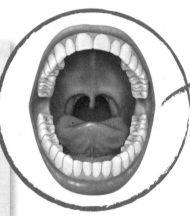

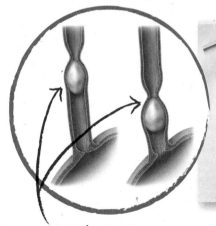

Muscles in the esophagus move this clump of food from your mouth to your stomach.

The Esophagus

Once food has been chewed, it is swallowed. The food moves through the throat and into a long tube called the **esophagus** (ih•SAWF•uh•gus). Waves of muscle contractions called *peristalsis* (per•ih•STAWL•sis) move the food into the stomach. The muscles move food along in much the same way as you move toothpaste from the bottom of the tube with your thumbs.

Visualize It!

9 Infer Consider the order of organs in the digestive system and their positions in the body. Why do you think digestion is more efficient if you are sitting up, rather than slumped over or lying down?

_____

_____

_____

_____

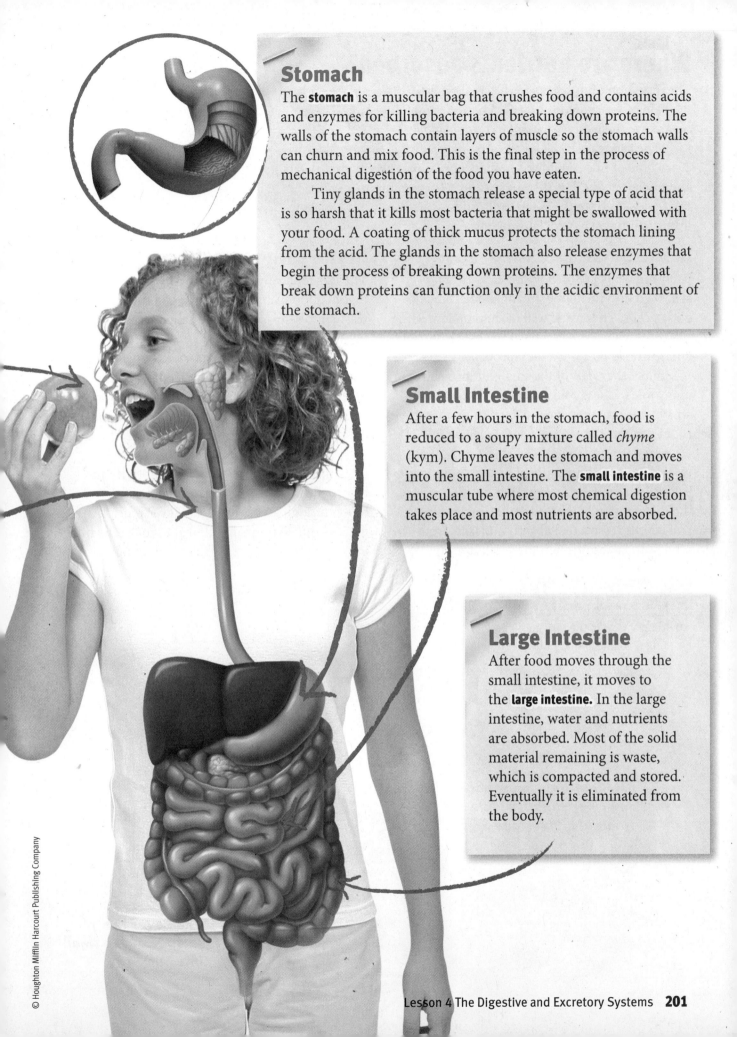

Stomach

The **stomach** is a muscular bag that crushes food and contains acids and enzymes for killing bacteria and breaking down proteins. The walls of the stomach contain layers of muscle so the stomach walls can churn and mix food. This is the final step in the process of mechanical digestión of the food you have eaten.

Tiny glands in the stomach release a special type of acid that is so harsh that it kills most bacteria that might be swallowed with your food. A coating of thick mucus protects the stomach lining from the acid. The glands in the stomach also release enzymes that begin the process of breaking down proteins. The enzymes that break down proteins can function only in the acidic environment of the stomach.

Small Intestine

After a few hours in the stomach, food is reduced to a soupy mixture called *chyme* (kym). Chyme leaves the stomach and moves into the small intestine. The **small intestine** is a muscular tube where most chemical digestion takes place and most nutrients are absorbed.

Large Intestine

After food moves through the small intestine, it moves to the **large intestine.** In the large intestine, water and nutrients are absorbed. Most of the solid material remaining is waste, which is compacted and stored. Eventually it is eliminated from the body.

Where are nutrients absorbed?

The digestion of nutrients in the small intestine takes place with the help of three organs that attach to the small intestine. These organs are the *pancreas*, *liver*, and *gall bladder*.

The **pancreas** (PANG•kree•uhz) makes fluids that break down every type of material found in foods: proteins, carbohydrates, fats, and nucleic acids. The **liver** makes and releases a mixture called *bile* that is then stored in the gall bladder. Bile breaks up large fat droplets into very small fat droplets.

In the Small Intestine

After nutrients are broken down, they are absorbed into the bloodstream and used by the body's cells. The inside wall of the small intestine has three features that allow it to absorb nutrients efficiently: folds, villi, and microvilli.

First, the walls of the small intestine have many folds. These folds increase the surface area inside the intestine wall, creating more room for nutrients to be absorbed. Each fold is covered with tiny fingerlike projections called *villi* (VIL•eye). In turn, the villi are covered with projections called microvilli. Microvilli increase the surface area of the villi. Villi contain blood and lymph vessels that absorb nutrients from food as it passes through the small intestine.

In the Large Intestine

The large intestine removes water from mostly-digested food, absorbs vitamins, and turns food waste into semi-solid waste called feces.

Some parts of food, such as the cell walls of plants, cannot be absorbed by the body. Bacteria live in the large intestine that feed off of this undigested food. The bacteria produce vitamins that are absorbed by the large intestine along with most of the water in the undigested food.

The *rectum* is the last part of the large intestine. The rectum stores feces until it can be expelled. Feces pass to the outside of the body through an opening called the *anus*. It takes about 24 hours for a meal to make the full journey through a person's digestive system.

Visualize It!

10 Relate How is the structure and function of this sponge similar to that of the small intestine?

_____

_____

_____

_____

This natural sponge has many crevasses, which increase its surface area.

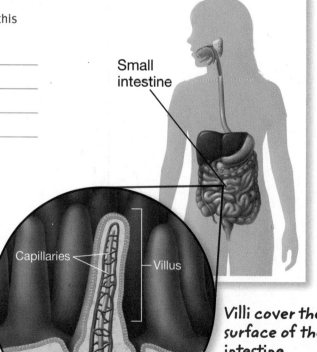

Small intestine

Capillaries

Villus

Villi cover the surface of the small intestine.

© Houghton Mifflin Harcourt Publishing Company • Image Credits: (bl) ©PhotoDisc/Getty Images

Toxic Waste!

What are the functions of the excretory system?

You have toxic waste in your body! As your cells perform the chemical activities that keep you alive, waste products, such as carbon dioxide and ammonia, are made. These waste products are toxic to cells. If waste builds up in a cell, homeostasis will be disrupted and the cell may die. The **excretory system** eliminates cellular wastes from the body through the lungs, skin, kidneys, and digestive system.

Waste Removal

To Sweat

Your skin is part of the excretory and the integumentary systems. Waste products such as excess salts are released through your skin when you sweat.

After you read the text, answer the associated questions below.

_____

11 Identify Sweat releases wastes through your _____

To Exhale

Your lungs are part of the excretory and respiratory systems. Lungs release water and toxic carbon dioxide when you exhale.

12 List Two waste products that are released when you exhale are _____ and _____

RESTROOM

To Produce Urine and Feces

Kidneys, part of the urinary system, remove all types of cellular waste products from your blood. Your digestive system eliminates feces from your body.

13 Identify The urinary system filters waste out of your

_____

Cleanup crew

What organs are in the urinary system?

The urinary system collects cellular waste and eliminates it from the body in the form of liquid waste. Waste products enter the urinary system through the kidneys.

14 Identify As you read, underline the functions of the organs in the urinary system.

Kidneys

The **kidney** is one of a pair of organs that remove waste from the blood. Inside each kidney are more than 1 million microscopic structures called **nephrons** (NEF•rahnz). Fluid is filtered from the blood into the nephron through a structure called the glomerulus (gloh•MEHR•yuh•luhs). Filtered blood leaves the glomerulus and circulates around the tubes that make up the nephron. These structures return valuable salts and ions to the blood. Tubes in the kidneys collect the wastes from the nephrons. Water and the wastes filtered out of the blood form a liquid known as **urine.**

Ureters

Urine forms in the kidneys. From the kidneys, urine travels through the *ureters*. The ureters are tubes that connect the kidneys to the bladder.

Bladder

The urine is transported from the kidneys to the bladder. The bladder is a saclike organ that stores urine. Voluntary muscles hold the urine until it is ready to be released. At that time, the muscles contract and squeeze urine out of the bladder.

Urethra

Urine exits the bladder through a tube called the urethra.

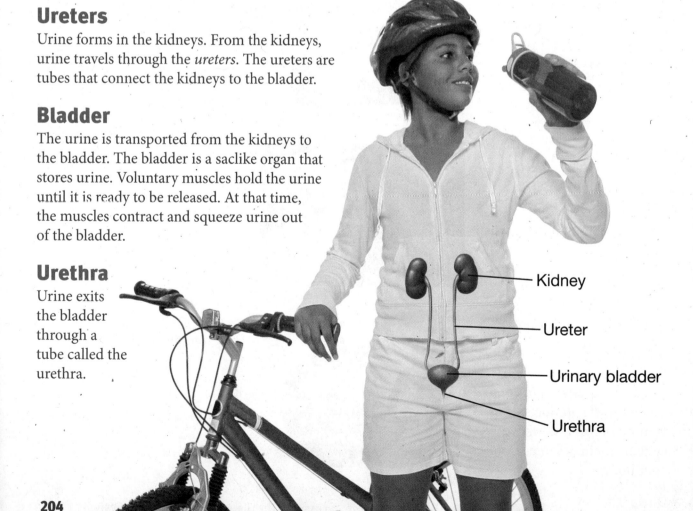

Kidney

Ureter

Urinary bladder

Urethra

Filtering Blood

Nephron

Unfiltered blood enters the kidney and flows into millions of tiny capillaries attached to the nephrons.

Artery

Unfiltered blood

Filtered blood

As blood flows through the capillaries, wastes are drawn out of the blood and into the nephron.

Vein

Ureter

Once the blood has been filtered, it flows back out of the kidney.

Urine

Urine is collected from all of the nephrons and then flows out of the kidney through the ureter.

Visualize It!

15 Identify After blood enters the kidneys, name the two paths the fluid takes.

_____
_____
_____
_____
_____
_____
_____
_____

How does the urinary system maintain homeostasis?

Your cells have to maintain a certain level of water and salt in order to function properly. The excretory system works with the endocrine system to help maintain homeostasis. Chemical messengers called *hormones* signal the kidneys to filter more or less water or salt, depending on the levels of water and salt in the body. For example, when you sweat a lot the water content of your blood can drop. When this happens, a hormone is released that signals the kidneys to conserve more water and make less urine. When your blood has too much water, less of the hormone is released. As a result, the nephrons conserve less water, and more urine is produced by the kidneys.

Household or environmental toxins that enter the body through the skin, lungs, or mouth eventually end up in the bloodstream. When the kidneys are damaged, many toxins can accumulate in the blood. Infections can also affect the kidneys. Bacterial infections can occur when bacteria around the opening of the urethra travels up to the bladder and possibly the kidneys.

Active Reading

16 Explain How does exercise affect the balance of salt and water in your body?

_____
_____
_____
_____
_____
_____
_____
_____

Visual Summary

To complete this summary, fill in the blanks with the correct word or phrase. Then, use the answer key to check your answers. You can use this page to review the main concepts of the lesson.

The digestive system breaks down the food you eat into nutrients that provide energy and building materials for cells.

17 The two types of digestion that take place in the mouth are _____ and _____

Digestion and Excretion

The excretory system removes waste from the body.

18 The _____ remove waste from the blood.

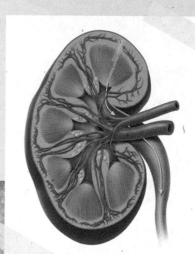

The digestive and excretory sytems work together to process the food that you eat.

19 To process this salad, food is broken down by the _____ _____ and wastes are removed by the _____

Answers: 17 mechanical, chemical; 18 kidneys; 19 digestive system, excretory system

20 **Summarize** What types of wastes does the excretory system remove?

Lesson Review

Vocabulary

Fill in the blank with the term that best completes the following sentences.

1 The _____ system helps the body maintain homeostasis by giving it the nutrients it needs to perform different functions.

2 The _____ system eliminates cellular waste through the lungs, skin, and kidneys.

3 The _____ is the name for the hollow muscular organ that stores urine.

Key Concepts

4 Compare What is the difference between mechanical digestion and chemical digestion in the mouth?

_____

_____

_____

_____

5 Describe Starting with the mouth, describe the pathway that food takes through the digestive system.

_____

_____

_____

_____

6 Explain How does the circulatory system interact with the digestive system?

_____

_____

_____

_____

7 Identify Where does urine go after it exits the kidneys?

_____

_____

_____

_____

8 Summarize How do kidneys work with other body systems to maintain homeostasis?

_____

_____

_____

_____

Use the diagram to answer the following question.

9 Apply Identify the organs numbered below.

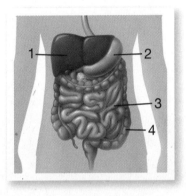

_____

_____

_____

Critical Thinking

10 Relate Why would damaged kidneys affect your health?

_____

_____

_____

11 Infer Suppose a person has a small intestine that has fewer villi than normal. Would the person most likely be overweight or underweight? Explain.

_____

_____

_____

_____

The Nervous and Endocrine Systems

ESSENTIAL QUESTION

How do the nervous and endocrine systems work?

By the end of this lesson, you should be able to relate the structures of the nervous and endocrine systems to their functions in the human body.

Sunshine State Standards

SC.6.L.14.5 Identify and investigate the general functions of the major systems of the human body (digestive, respiratory, circulatory, reproductive, excretory, immune, nervous, and musculoskeletal) and describe ways these systems interact with each other to maintain homeostasis.

HE.6.C.1.4 Recognize how heredity can affect personal health.

HE.6.C.1.8 Explain how body systems are impacted by hereditary factors and infectious agents.

LA.6.4.2.2 The student will record information (e.g., observations, notes, lists, charts, legends) related to a topic, including visual aids to organize and record information and include a list of sources used.

This sky diver can sense his surroundings and feel the rush of excitement with the help of his nervous and endocrine systems.

Engage Your Brain

1 Predict Check T or F to show whether you think each statement is true or false.

T   F

☐   ☐   The central nervous system allows us to sense the environment.

☐   ☐   The endocrine system functions by sending chemical signals.

☐   ☐   The spinal cord is part of the peripheral nervous system.

☐   ☐   The endocrine system helps regulate our blood sugar after we eat a meal.

2 Describe Think about a situation that makes you feel very nervous or anxious. Describe how this makes you feel inside. What do you think is going on in your body?

_____

_____

_____

_____

_____

Active Reading

3 Apply You can often understand the meaning of a word if you use it in a sentence. Use the following definition to write your own sentence that has the word *gland*.

Definition
gland: a group of cells that make special chemicals for the body

gland:

_____

_____

_____

_____

_____

Vocabulary Terms

- nervous system
- brain
- spinal cord
- neuron
- axon
- dendrite
- endocrine system
- hormone
- gland

4 Apply As you learn the definition of each vocabulary term in this lesson, create your own definition or sketch to help you remember the meaning of the term.

Brainiac!

What is the function of the nervous system?

The **nervous system** is made of the structures that control the actions and reactions of the body in response to stimuli from the environment. Your nervous system has two parts: the central nervous system (CNS) and the peripheral (puh•RIFF•uh•rahl) nervous system (PNS).

The CNS Processes Information

The brain and the spinal cord make up the CNS. The **brain** is the body's central command organ. It constantly receives impulses from all over the body. Your **spinal cord** allows your brain to communicate with the rest of your body. Your nervous system is mostly made up of specialized cells that send and receive electrical signals.

The PNS Connects the CNS to Muscles and Organs

Your PNS connects your CNS to the rest of your body. The PNS has two main parts—the sensory part and the motor part. Many processes that the brain controls happen automatically—you have no control over them. These processes are called *involuntary*. For example, you could not stop your heart from beating even if you tried. However, some of the actions of your brain you can control—these are *voluntary*. Moving your arm is a voluntary action.

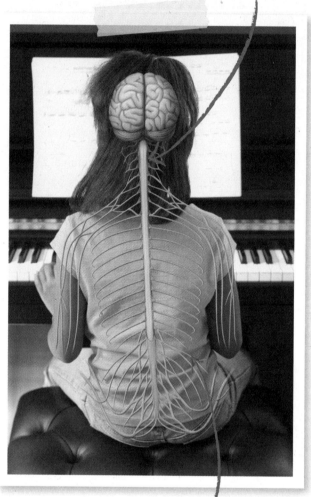

The CNS is shown in yellow.

The PNS is shown in green.

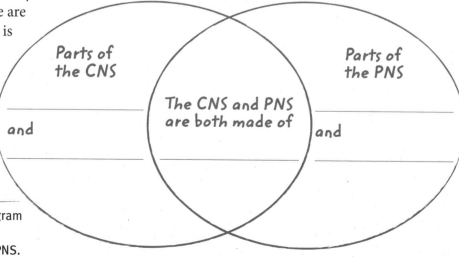

Parts of the CNS

_____
and
_____

The CNS and PNS are both made of
_____

Parts of the PNS

_____
and
_____

5 Compare Fill in the Venn diagram to compare and contrast the structure of the CNS and the PNS.

What are the parts of the CNS?

The CNS is made up of the brain and the spinal cord.

The Brain

The three main areas of the brain are the cerebrum, the cerebellum, and the brain stem. The largest part of the brain is the cerebrum. The cerebrum is where you think and problem-solve, and where most of your memories are stored. It controls voluntary movements and allows you to sense touch, light, sound, odors, taste, pain, heat, and cold. The second largest part of your brain is the cerebellum. It processes information from your body. This allows the brain to keep track of your body's position and coordinate movements. The brain stem connects your brain to your spinal cord. The medulla is part of the brain stem. It controls involuntary processes, such as blood pressure, body temperature, heart rate, and involuntary breathing.

6 Identify List a function of each part of the brain shown here.

Cerebrum

_____

_____

_____

Cerebellum

Brain stem

_____

_____

_____

The Spinal Cord

The spinal cord is made of bundles of nerves. A *nerve* is a collection of nerve cell extensions bundled together with blood vessels and connective tissue. Nerves are everywhere in your body. The spinal cord is surrounded by protective bones called *vertebrae*.

Special cells in your skin and muscles carry sensory information to the spinal cord. The spinal cord carries these impulses to the brain. The brain interprets these impulses as warmth, pain, or other sensations and sends information back to the spinal cord. Different cells in the spinal cord then send impulses to the rest of the body to create a response.

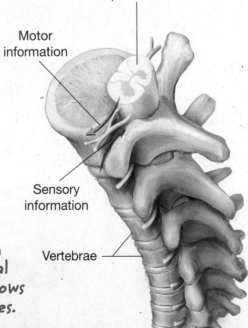

Spinal cord

Motor information

Sensory information

Vertebrae

Sensory information (red) flows in from the environment to the spinal cord. Motor information (blue) flows out from the spinal cord to muscles.

You've Got Nerves!

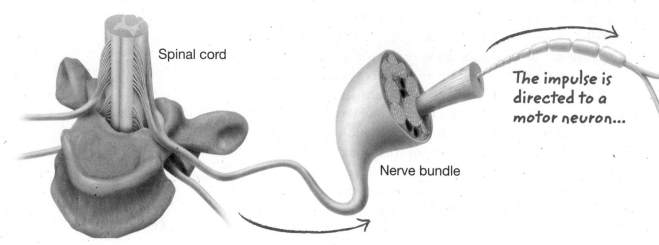

Spinal cord

Nerve bundle

The impulse is directed to a motor neuron...

If you notice that your shoe is untied, your brain interprets this information and sends an impulse down the spinal cord.

How do signals move through the nervous system?

Your nervous system works by receiving information from the environment and translating that information into electrical signals. Those electrical signals are sent from the brain to the rest of the body by special cells called *neurons*. A **neuron** is a cell that moves messages in the form of fast-moving electrical energy. These electrical messages are called *impulses*.

Signals move through the central and peripheral nervous systems with the help of glial (GLEE•uhl) cells. Glial cells do not transmit nerve impulses, but they protect and support neurons. Without glial cells, neurons would not work properly. Your brain has about 100 billion neurons, but there are about 10 to 50 times more glial cells in your brain.

Through Sensory and Motor Neurons

Neurons carry information from the body to the brain, and carry instructions from the brain back to the rest of the body. The two groups of neurons are sensory neurons and motor neurons.

Sensory neurons gather information from in and around your body. They then move this information to the brain. Motor neurons move impulses from the brain and spinal cord to other parts of the body. For example, when you are hot, motor neurons move messages from your brain to your sweat glands to tell the sweat glands to make sweat. Sweating cools your body.

Active Reading

7 Identify As you read, underline the special types of neurons that receive and send messages.

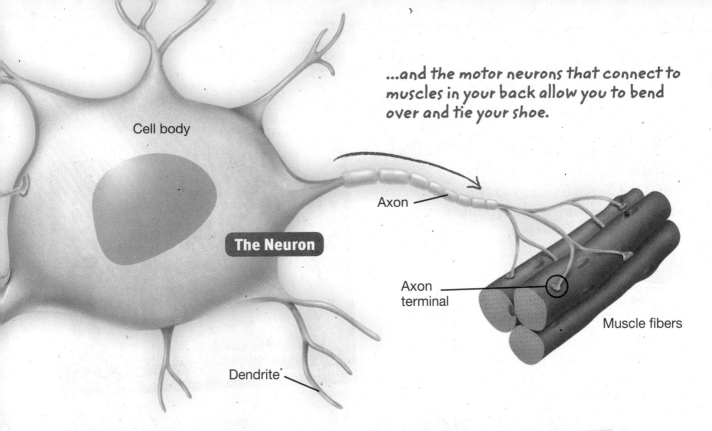

Cell body

...and the motor neurons that connect to muscles in your back allow you to bend over and tie your shoe.

Axon

The Neuron

Axon terminal

Muscle fibers

Dendrite

What are the parts of a neuron?

A neuron is made up of a large region called the *cell body*, a long extension called the *axon*, and short branches called *dendrites*. At the end of the axon is the *axon terminal*.

Like other cells, a neuron's cell body has a nucleus and organelles. But neurons have other structures that allow them to communicate with other cells. A **dendrite** (DEHN•dryt) is a usually short, branched extension of the cell body. A neuron may have one, two, or many dendrites. Neurons with many dendrites can receive impulses from thousands of cells at a time. The cell body gathers information from the dendrites and creates an impulse.

Impulses are carried away from the cell body by extensions of the neuron, called an **axon**. A neuron has only one axon, and they can be very short or quite long. Some long axons extend almost 1 m from your lower back to your toes! Impulses move in one direction along the axon.

At the end of an axon is the axon terminal, where a signal is changed from an electrical signal to a chemical signal. This chemical signal, called a *neurotransmitter*, is released into the gap between the neuron and other cells.

 **Visualize It!**

8 Apply In the boxes below, fill in the appropriate neuron parts, structures, or functions.

NEURON PART	STRUCTURE	FUNCTION
Cell body	region containing nucleus and organelles	
	branches of the cell body	gathers information from other cells
Axon		sends impulse away from cell body
	end of an axon	changes electrical signal to chemical signal

That Makes Sense!

What are the main senses?

The body senses the environment with specialized structures called *sensory organs*. These structures include the eyes, the skin, the ears, the mouth, and the nose.

9 Imagine If you were at this amusement park, what do you think you would see, hear, smell, taste, and feel?

_____

_____

An amusement park is full of sensory information! How do we sense it all?

Sight

Your eye allows you to see the size, shape, motion, and color of objects around you. The front of the eye is covered by a clear membrane called the *cornea*. Light from an object passes through an opening called the *pupil*. Light hits the eye's lens, an oval-shaped piece of clear, curved material. Eye muscles change the shape of the lens to focus light onto the retina. The *retina* (RET•nuh) is a layer of light-sensitive photoreceptor cells that change light into electrical impulses. These cells, called *rods* and *cones,* generate nerve impulses that are sent to the brain.

Rays form an upside-down image on the retina at the back of the eye. This image is translated by the brain.

Lens

Cornea

Retina

Pupil

Visualize It!

10 Identify What part of the eye focuses light on to the retina?

_____

_____

Light enters the eye through the lens. Light rays are bent by the cornea.

Touch

You feel a tap on your shoulder. The tap produces impulses in sensory receptors on your shoulder. These impulses travel to your brain. Once the impulses reach your brain, they create an awareness called a *sensation.* In this case, the sensation is that of your shoulder being touched. The skin has different kinds of receptors that detect pressure, temperature, pain, and vibration.

Hearing

Ears pick up sound wave vibrations. These sound waves push air particles, creating a wave of sound energy. The sensory cells of your ears turn sound waves into electrical impulses. These electrical impulses then travel to your brain. Each ear has an outer, a middle, and an inner portion. Sound waves reaching the outer ear are funneled toward the middle ear. There, the waves make the eardrum vibrate. The *eardrum* is a thin membrane separating the outer ear from the middle ear. The vibrating eardrum makes three tiny bones in the middle ear vibrate. The last of these bones vibrates against the *cochlea* (KOH•klee•uh), a fluid-filled organ of the inner ear. Inside the cochlea, the vibrations make waves in the fluid. Sensory receptors called *hair cells* move about in the fluid. Movement of the hair cells causes neurons in the cochlea to send electrical impulses. These impulses travel to the brain via the auditory nerve and are interpreted as sound.

The ears also help you maintain balance. Special fluid-filled canals in the inner ear are filled with hair cells that respond to changes in head orientation. These hair cells then send signals to the brain about the position of the head with respect to gravity.

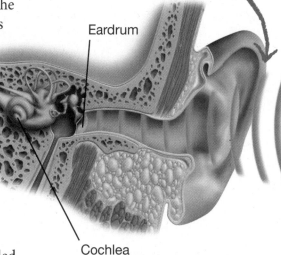

Sound waves enter the ear and cause the eardrum to vibrate. The vibrations are translated by receptors.

Eardrum

Cochlea

Taste

Your tongue is covered with taste buds. These taste buds contain clusters of *taste cells* that respond to signals in dissolved molecules in food. Taste cells react to five basic tastes: sweet, sour, salty, bitter, and savory. Your sense of taste can protect you from eating something that could be harmful.

Smell

The nose is your sense organ for smell. Receptors for smell are located in the upper part of your nasal cavity. Sensory receptors called *olfactory cells* react to chemicals in the air. These molecules dissolve in the moist lining of the nasal cavity and trigger an impulse in the receptors. The nerve impulses are sent to the brain, where they are interpreted as an odor. Your senses of taste and smell work together to allow you to taste a variety of food flavors. Both senses detect chemical cues in the environment.

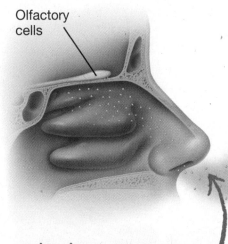

Olfactory cells

Molecules in the air enter your nose. There, they bind to receptors in the top of your nasal cavity.

11 Apply If you have a cold that causes congestion in your sinuses, how might that affect your sense of smell?

_____

_____

_____

_____

Keep Your Cool!

What is the function of the endocrine system?

Your **endocrine system** controls body functions and helps maintain homeostasis by using hormones. A **hormone** is a chemical messenger made in one cell or tissue that causes a change in another cell or tissue in a different part of the body. Hormones are produced by endocrine glands or tissues. A **gland** is a group of cells that make special chemicals for your body. Unlike direct signals of the nervous system, the signals sent by the endocrine system are indirect because they cycle through the whole body.

How do hormones work?

Hormones travel through the bloodstream. They travel from the endocrine gland where they are made and can reach every cell in the body. However, hormones affect only the cells that have specific *receptors*. Each hormone has its own receptor and affects only cells that have that receptor. These cells are called *target cells*. Many cells throughout the body have the same receptors, so hormones are able to perform many functions at the same time in different cells.

Active Reading

12 Identify As you read, underline the structure which allows hormones to affect only certain cells.

13 Apply Explain the difference between an endocrine cell and a target cell.

_____

_____

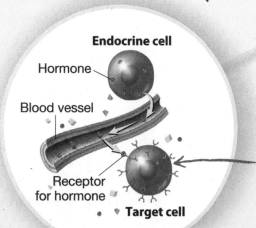

Endocrine cell

Hormone

Blood vessel

Receptor for hormone

Target cell

When you are surprised, a hormone called adrenaline makes you more alert.

Hormones are released from an endocrine cell and travel through the bloodstream to bind to a receptor on a target cell. Sometimes a target cell is very far away!

What glands make up the endocrine system?

Your body has several endocrine glands or tissues that make up the endocrine system.

- Your pituitary gland is very important because it secretes hormones that affect other glands. It also stimulates growth and sexual development.
- The hypothalamus is a gland in the brain that controls the release of hormones from the pituitary gland.
- The pineal gland, also in the brain, produces hormones essential in the control of sleep, aging, reproduction, and body temperature.
- Hormones from the thyroid control your metabolism.
- The parathyroid gland controls calcium levels in the blood.
- Hormones made in the reproductive organs (ovaries or testes) control reproduction.
- Other endocrine glands include the pancreas and adrenal glands. The pancreas regulates blood sugar levels and the adrenal glands control the body's fight or flight response in dangerous situations.

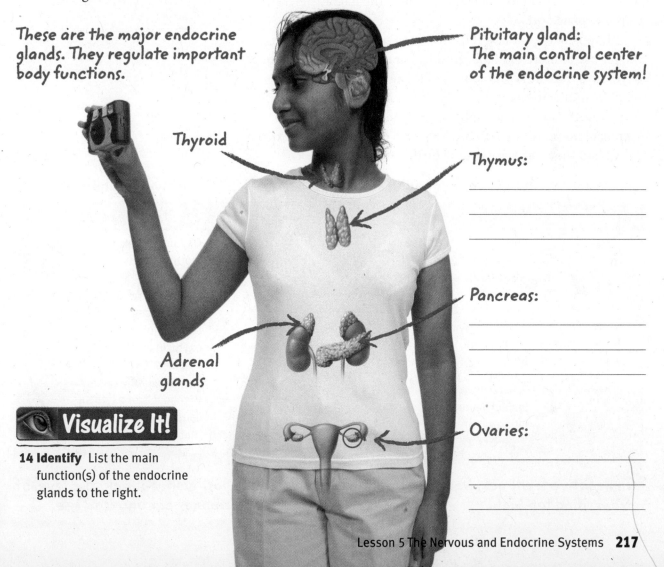

These are the major endocrine glands. They regulate important body functions.

Pituitary gland:
The main control center of the endocrine system!

Thyroid

Thymus:
_____
_____
_____

Pancreas:
_____
_____
_____

Adrenal glands

Ovaries:
_____
_____
_____

Visualize It!

14 Identify List the main function(s) of the endocrine glands to the right.

Feed◄─Back

How are hormone levels controlled?

The endocrine system keeps the body's internal environment in homeostasis. It does this by increasing or decreasing the amount of hormones in the bloodstream, some of which may have opposite effects on body cells. Such a process is called a feedback mechanism. A *feedback mechanism* is a cycle of events in which information from one step controls or affects a previous step.

By Feedback Mechanisms

There are two types of feedback, positive and negative. In negative feedback, the effects of a hormone in the body cause the release of that hormone to be turned down. For example, when you eat food, your blood sugar levels go up. Insulin is released and blood sugar levels are lowered. Once this happens, the lower blood sugar levels tell the pancreas to stop releasing insulin. In other words, when the proper level of blood sugar is reached, the insulin-releasing cells are turned off.

In positive feedback, the effects of a hormone stimulate the release of more of that hormone. For example, the hormone oxytocin stimulates contractions of the uterus. When a fetus matures in the uterus, both it and the mother produce oxytocin. The oxytocin stimulates contractions, and these contractions stimulate more oxytocin to be released. The contractions expel a baby from the mother's uterus at birth.

✏️ Active Reading

15 Compare Describe the difference between negative and positive feedback.

_____

_____

_____

_____

_____

Negative Feedback

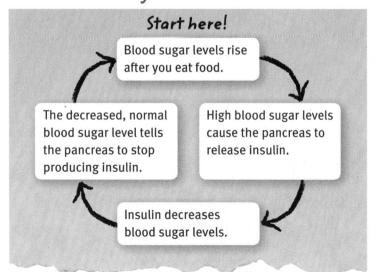

Start here!

Blood sugar levels rise after you eat food.

High blood sugar levels cause the pancreas to release insulin.

Insulin decreases blood sugar levels.

The decreased, normal blood sugar level tells the pancreas to stop producing insulin.

In negative feedback, hormone levels are kept from rising too high.

Positive Feedback

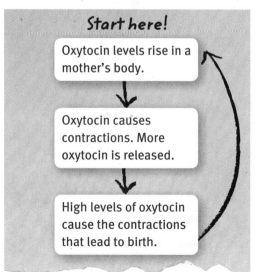

Start here!

Oxytocin levels rise in a mother's body.

Oxytocin causes contractions. More oxytocin is released.

High levels of oxytocin cause the contractions that lead to birth.

In positive feedback, the level of hormones continues to rise.

What are disorders of the endocrine and nervous systems?

The endocrine system and nervous system are both responsible for sending messages around our bodies. If a problem developed with one or more of these systems, other systems of the body would need to adjust to compensate for this loss.

Hormone Imbalances

Disorders of the endocrine system occur when an endocrine gland makes too much or not enough of a hormone. For example, a person whose pancreas does not make enough insulin has a condition called type 1 diabetes. This condition causes an imbalance of the blood sugar. A person who has diabetes may need daily injections of insulin to keep blood sugar levels within safe limits. Some patients receive their insulin automatically from a small pump worn next to the body. New technology allows people with type 1 diabetes to intake insulin using an inhaler.

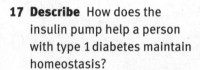

17 **Describe** How does the insulin pump help a person with type 1 diabetes maintain homeostasis?

_____

_____

_____

_____

_____

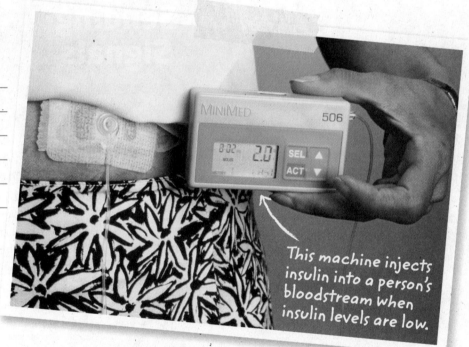

This machine injects insulin into a person's bloodstream when insulin levels are low.

Nerve Damage

Disorders of the nervous system include Parkinson's disease, multiple sclerosis, and spinal cord injury. In Parkinson's disease, the cells that control movement are damaged. Multiple sclerosis affects the brain's ability to send signals to the rest of the body.

A spinal cord injury may block information to and from the brain. For example, impulses coming from the feet and legs may be blocked. People with such an injury cannot sense pain in their legs. The person would also not be able to move his or her legs, because impulses from the brain could not get past the injury site.

Visual Summary

To complete this summary, fill in the blank to answer the question. Then, use the key below to check your answers. You can use this page to review the main concepts of the lesson.

The nervous system gathers information and responds by sending electrical signals.

18 Nerve cells called _____ carry electrical messages called _____

The endocrine system controls conditions in your body by sending chemical messages.

19 Hormones have specific actions by attaching to _____ on target cells.

Sending Signals

Hormones are controlled by feedback mechanisms.

20 _____ feedback is when higher levels of a hormone turn off the production of that hormone.

Negative Feedback
Start here!

Blood sugar levels rise after you eat food.

High blood sugar cause the pancreas to release insulin.

Insulin decreases blood sugar levels.

The decreased, normal blood sugar level tells the pancreas to stop producing insulin.

Answers: 18 neurons, impulses; 19 receptors; 20 Negative

21 **Apply** Describe how both your nervous and endocrine systems would be involved if you walked into a surprise party and were truly surprised.

Lesson Review

Vocabulary

Use a term from the section to complete each sentence below.

1 The _____ is made up of the brain and spinal cord.

2 Glands in the _____ send messages to target cells.

3 Use *gland* and *hormone* in the same sentence.

_____

_____

4 Use *hormone* and *feedback mechanism* in the same sentence.

_____

_____

Key Concepts

5 Identify Describe the function of the PNS and the CNS.

_____

_____

_____

6 Apply What are the parts of a neuron?

_____

_____

_____

7 Identify How are the messages of the endocrine system moved around the body?

_____

_____

_____

8 Identify What is the main sense organ for each of the five senses?

_____

_____

_____

Critical Thinking

The images below show how an eye responds to different light levels. Use the image to answer the following question.

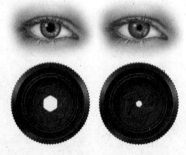

9 Interpret The pupil opens and closes automatically in response to light. What part of your nervous system controls this response?

_____

10 Infer Explain whether this is a voluntary or involuntary action.

_____

_____

_____

11 Predict How would your body be affected if your pituitary gland was not working properly?

_____

_____

_____

The Reproductive System

ESSENTIAL QUESTION

How does your reproductive system work?

By the end of this lesson, you should be able to relate the structure of the reproductive system to its function in the human body.

Sunshine State Standards

SC.6.N.3.4 Identify the role of models in the context of the sixth grade science benchmarks.

SC.6.L.14.5 Identify and investigate the general functions of the major systems of the human body (digestive, respiratory, circulatory, reproductive, excretory, immune, nervous, and musculoskeletal) and describe ways these systems interact with each other to maintain homeostasis.

MA.6.A.3.6 Construct and analyze tables, graphs, and equations to describe linear functions and other simple relations using both common language and algebraic notation.

HE.6.C.1.8 Explain how body systems are impacted by hereditary factors and infectious agents.

LA.6.4.2.2 The student will record information (e.g., observations, notes, lists, charts, legends) related to a topic, including visual aids to organize and record information and include a list of sources used.

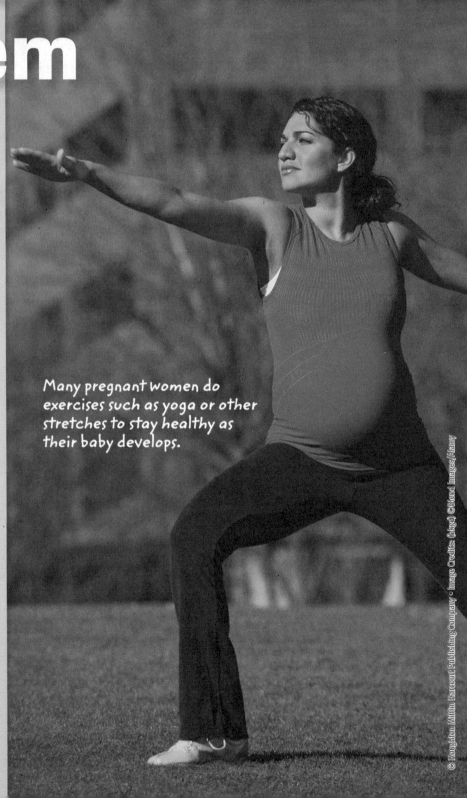

Many pregnant women do exercises such as yoga or other stretches to stay healthy as their baby develops.

Engage Your Brain

1 Predict Have you met a woman who was pregnant? Write a short answer describing what type of development you think is going on inside a pregnant woman.

The baby's cell grows from sperm/egg cell

2 Apply Name five things that have changed about you from your fifth to your tenth birthday.

- grew taller
- voice deeper

Active Reading

3 Explain You may be familiar with the eggs that farmers collect from chickens. Females of many species, including humans, produce eggs as part of the reproductive cycle. How do you think a human egg is similar to a chicken egg? How do you think they are different?

Vocabulary Terms

- sperm
- testes
- penis
- egg
- ovary
- uterus
- vagina
- embryo
- placenta
- umbilical cord
- fetus

4 Apply As you learn the definition of each vocabulary term in this lesson, create your own definition or sketch to help you remember the meaning of the term.

Reproduction

What are the main functions of the male reproductive system?

The male reproductive system functions to produce sperm and deliver sperm to the female reproductive system. **Sperm** are the male cells that are used for reproduction. Each sperm cell carries 23 chromosomes, half of the chromosomes of other body cells. The male reproductive system also produces hormones.

Hormones are chemical messengers that control many important body functions such as growth, development, and sex-cell production. The **testes** (singular, *testis*) are the main organs of the male reproductive system. These organs produce *testosterone*, the male sex hormone. Testosterone causes male characteristics to develop, such as facial hair and a deep voice.

The testes also make sperm. After sperm mature, they are stored in the *epididymis* (EH•puh•DIH•duh•miss). They leave the epididymis through a tube called the *vas deferens* and mix with fluids from several glands. This mixture of sperm and fluids is called *semen*. To leave the body, semen passes through the *urethra*, the tube that runs through the penis. The **penis** is the organ that delivers semen into the female reproductive system.

Male Reproductive System

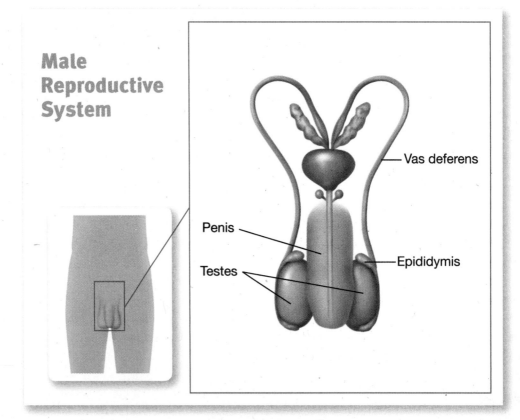

Vas deferens

Penis

Epididymis

Testes

What are the main functions of the female reproductive system?

The female reproductive system produces hormones and eggs, and provides a place to nourish a developing human. An **egg** is the female sex cell. Like sperm, egg cells have 23 chromosomes, only half the number of other body cells.

The female reproductive system produces the sex hormones *estrogen* and *progesterone*. These hormones control the development of female characteristics, such as breasts and wider hips. They also regulate the development and release of eggs, and they prepare the body for pregnancy.

An **ovary** is the reproductive organ that produces eggs. At sexual maturity, females have hundreds of thousands of immature eggs in their ovaries. Like sperm, eggs are produced through the process of meiosis. During a female's lifetime, usually about 400 of her eggs will mature and be released from the ovaries.

Female Reproductive System

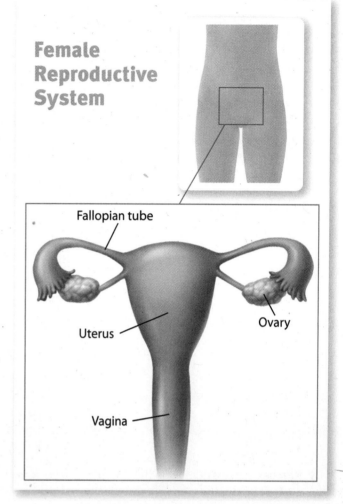

Fallopian tube

Uterus

Ovary

Vagina

6 Summarize Fill in the chart below to summarize the structures of the male and female reproductive systems.

Sex	Sex cell	Organ that produces sex cell	Other reproductive organs
Male			
Female			

7 Contrast What makes sperm cells and egg cells different from almost all other types of body cells?

_____

_____

_____

Fertile ground

How are eggs released?

A woman's reproductive system goes through changes that produce an egg, release the egg, and prepare the body for pregnancy. These changes are called the *menstrual cycle* and usually take about one month. About halfway through the cycle, an egg is released from the ovary. The egg travels through the *fallopian tube*, a pair of tubes that connect each ovary to the uterus. The **uterus** is the organ in which a fertilized egg develops into a baby. When a baby is born, it passes through the **vagina**, the canal between the uterus and the outside of the body.

If an egg is not fertilized, it is shed with the lining of the uterus. The monthly discharge of blood and tissue from the uterus is called *menstruation*. When menstruation ends, the lining of the uterus thickens and the cycle begins again.

Active Reading

8 Summarize As you read, underline the path an egg takes through the female reproductive system.

9 Number Place a number in the circles to order the steps of the menstrual cycle.

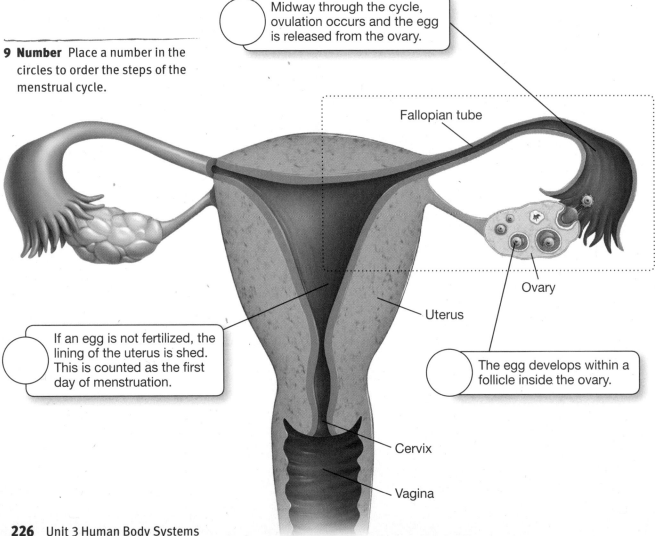

Midway through the cycle, ovulation occurs and the egg is released from the ovary.

If an egg is not fertilized, the lining of the uterus is shed. This is counted as the first day of menstruation.

The egg develops within a follicle inside the ovary.

Fallopian tube

Ovary

Uterus

Cervix

Vagina

How are eggs fertilized?

When sperm enter the female reproductive system, a few hundred make it through the uterus into a fallopian tube. There, the sperm release enzymes that help dissolve the egg's outer covering.

When a sperm enters an egg, the egg's membrane changes to stop other sperm from entering. During fertilization, the egg and sperm combine to form one cell. Once cell division occurs, the fertilized egg becomes an **embryo**. The genetic material from the father and the mother combine and a unique individual begins to develop. Usually, only one sperm gets through the outer covering of the egg. If more than one sperm enter the egg, multiple identical embryos can form. After fertilization, the embryo travels from the fallopian tube to the uterus over five to six days, and attaches to the thickened and nutrient-rich lining of the uterus.

Inquiry

10 Infer Sometimes more than one egg is released at a time. What do you think would happen if two eggs were released and both were fertilized? Explain your answer.

You get twins,

11 Summarize Determine what happens if an egg is fertilized and if it is not fertlized, and fill in both of the boxes below.

Was the egg fertilized?

yes → Goes to uterus, baby develops

no → flushed out through menstration

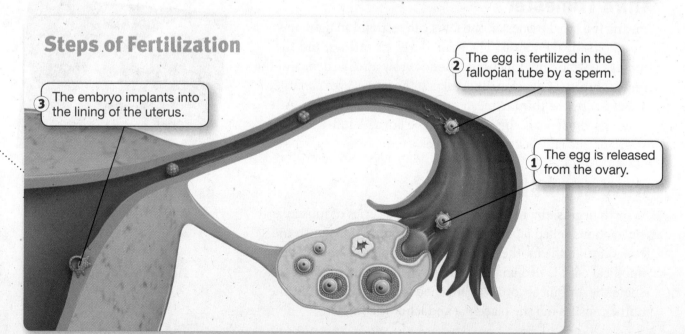

Steps of Fertilization

3 The embryo implants into the lining of the uterus.

2 The egg is fertilized in the fallopian tube by a sperm.

1 The egg is released from the ovary.

Happy Birthday!

What are the stages of pregnancy?

A normal pregnancy lasts about nine months. These nine months are broken down into three 3-month periods, called *trimesters*.

Active Reading **12 Identify** Underline three things that take place during each trimester.

First Trimester

Soon after implantation, the placenta begins to grow. The **placenta** is a network of blood vessels that provides the embryo with oxygen and nutrients from the mother's blood and carries away wastes. The embryo is surrounded by the *amnion,* a sac filled with fluid that protects the embryo. The embryo connects to the placenta by the **umbilical cord**. After week 10, the embryo is called a **fetus**. Many organs such as the heart, liver and brain form. Arms and legs as well as fingers and toes also form during this trimester.

Second Trimester

During the second trimester, joints and bones start to form. The fetus's muscles grow stronger. As a result, the fetus can make a fist and begins to move. The fetus triples its size within a month and its brain begins to grow rapidly. Eventually, the fetus can make faces. The fetus starts to make movements the mother can feel. Toward the end of the trimester, the fetus can breathe and swallow.

Third Trimester

During the third trimester, the fetus can respond to light and sound outside the uterus. The brain develops further, and the organs become fully functional. Bones grow and harden, and the lungs completely develop. By week 32, the fetus's eyes can open and close. By the third trimester the fetus can also dream. After 36 weeks, the fetus is almost ready to be born. A full-term pregnancy usually lasts about 40 weeks.

How are babies born?

As birth begins, the mother's uterus starts a series of muscular contractions called *labor*. Usually, these contractions push the fetus through the mother's vagina, and the baby is born. The umbilical cord is tied and cut. All that will remain of the place where the umbilical cord was attached is the navel. Finally, the mother pushes out the placenta, and labor is complete.

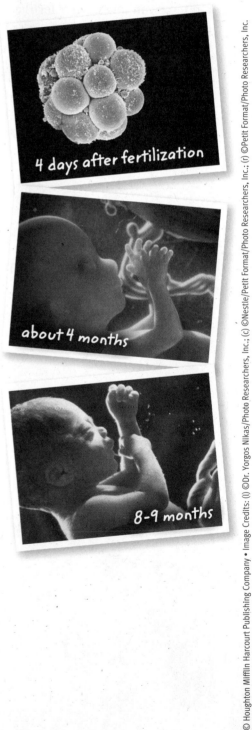

4 days after fertilization

about 4 months

8-9 months

What changes occur during infancy and childhood?

Development during infancy and childhood includes gaining control of skeletal muscles and learning to speak. Generally, infancy is the stage from birth to age 2. During infancy, babies grow quickly and baby teeth appear. The nervous system develops, and babies become more coordinated and start to walk. Many babies begin to say words by age 1. During this time, the body is growing rapidly. Childhood lasts from age 2 to puberty. Baby teeth are replaced by permanent teeth. Children learn to speak fluently and their muscles become more coordinated, allowing them to run, jump, and perform other activities.

What changes occur during adolescence and adulthood?

The stage from puberty to adulthood is *adolescence*. During adolescence, a person's reproductive system becomes mature. In most boys, puberty takes place between the ages of 9 and 16. During this time, the young male's body becomes more muscular, his voice becomes deeper, and body and facial hair appear. In most girls, puberty takes place between the ages of 9 and 15. During this time, the amount of fat in the hips and thighs increases, the breasts enlarge, body hair appears, and menstruation begins.

During adulthood, a person reaches physical and emotional maturity. A person is considered a young adult from about age 20 to age 40. Beginning around age 30, changes associated with aging begin. The aging process continues into middle age (between 40 and 65 years old). During this time, hair may turn gray, athletic abilities will decline, and skin may wrinkle. A person more than 65 years old is considered an older adult. Exercising and eating well-balanced diets help people stay healthy as they grow older.

Do the Math

Everyone grows as they age, but does the amount you grow change as you get older?

Sample Problem

To calculate growth rate, divide the difference in height by the difference in age. For example, the growth rate between the ages of one and five for the girl shown below is:

$(102 \text{ cm} - 71 \text{ cm}) \div (5 \text{ years} - 1 \text{ year}) = 8 \text{ cm/year}$

You Try It

13 Calculate Determine the growth rate for the girl between the ages of 14 and 19. Is the amount of growth greater between ages 1 and 5 or between ages 14 and 19?

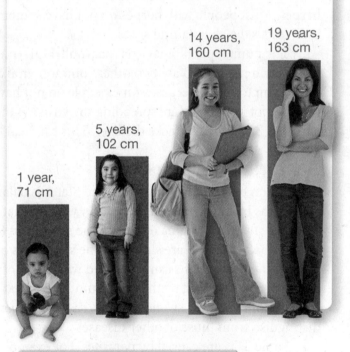

1 year, 71 cm

5 years, 102 cm

14 years, 160 cm

19 years, 163 cm

Think Outside the Book

14 Research Learning a new language can be easier for young children. This phenomenon is known as a "critical period." Research critical periods for language and write a short report describing what you learned.

Infections

What causes STIs?

Sexually transmitted infections (STIs) are infections that are passed from one person to another during sexual contact. STIs can be caused by viruses, bacteria, or parasites.

Active Reading **15 Identify** As you read, underline the symptoms of each STI listed below.

Viruses

Acquired immunodeficiency syndrome (AIDS) is caused by the human immunodeficiency virus (HIV). This virus infects and destroys immune system cells. As a result, people with AIDS usually show symptoms of many other illnesses that the immune system of a healthy person usually can fight. Most HIV infections are transmitted through sexual contact.

A much more common, but less deadly, viral STI is genital herpes. Most people with herpes do not have symptoms, but some individuals develop painful sores.

The human papillomavirus (paa•puh•LOH•muh•vy•russ) (HPV) and hepatitis B are two other common viral STIs that are often symptomless. Because some people do not have symptoms, they do not know they are spreading the virus. In the case of hepatitis B, the virus attacks the liver. This can lead to death.

Bacteria and Parasites

A common bacterial STI in the United States is chlamydia. Symptoms include a burning sensation when urinating or a discharge from the vagina or penis. The symptoms for gonorrhea, another bacterial STI, are similar to the symptoms of chlamydia. Both of these infections can be treated with antibiotics. Another STI, syphilis, is caused by the bacterium *Treponema pallidum*. Its symptoms, such as swollen glands, rash and fever, are hard to distinguish from those of other diseases.

Some STIs are caused by parasites. For example, the STI trichomoniasis is caused by the protozoan *Trichomonas vaginalis*. It is the most common curable STI for young women. Symptoms are more common in women and may include a genital discharge and pain during urination. Another parasitic STI is a pubic lice infestation. Pubic lice are tiny insects that feed on blood. The most common symptom of a pubic lice infection is genital itching.

16 Label For each photo below, label the type of infection as a virus, a bacterium, or a parasite.

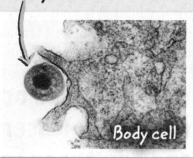

Chlamydia cell

Body cell

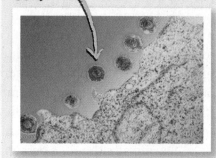

Herpes-infected immune cells

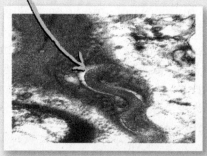

Syphilis cell

© Houghton Mifflin Harcourt Publishing Company • Image Credits: (t) ©David M. Phillips/Photo Researchers, Inc.; (c) ©Science Source/Photo Researchers, Inc.; (b) ©Biomedical Imaging Unit, Southampton General Hospital/Photo Researchers, Inc.

Seeing Double

HEALTH WATCH

Multiple births occur when two or more babies are carried during the same pregnancy. In humans, the most common type of multiple births occurs when the mother gives birth to two children, or twins. About 3% of all births in the United States result in twins.

Fraternal Siblings

Fraternal siblings form when two sperm fertilize two or more separate eggs. Fraternal siblings can be the same gender or different genders and are as different genetically as any ordinary siblings.

Identical Twins

Identical twins form when a single sperm fertilizes a single egg. The developing embryo then divides in two. Identical twins are always the same gender and are genetically identical.

Triplets

While twinning is the most common type of multiple birth, other multiples still occur. About 0.1% of all births are triplets.

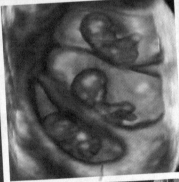

Extend

Inquiry

17 Infer Based on how identical twins form, infer how identical triplets could develop.

18 Research Describe some shared behavioral traits or language between twins and give an example.

19 Create Illustrate how fertilized eggs develop into fraternal triplets. You may choose to make a poster, make a model, or write a short story.

Visual Summary

To complete this summary, circle the correct word. Then, use the key below to check your answers. You can use this page to review the main concepts of the lesson.

The male reproductive system makes hormones and sperm cells.

20 Sperm are produced in the penis / testes.

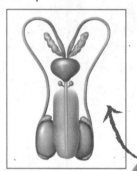

The female reproductive system makes hormones and egg cells, and protects a developing baby if fertilization occurs.

21 Eggs are produced in the ovary / vagina.

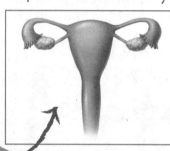

Reproduction and Development

A baby goes through many changes as it develops into an adult.

22 During pregnancy, a growing baby gets oxygen and nourishment from an organ called the embryo / placenta.

Sexually transmitted infections (STIs) are caused by viruses, bacteria, and parasites.

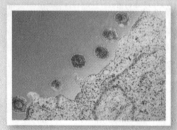

23 STIs are spread through the air / sexual contact.

Answers: 20 testes; 21 ovary; 22 placenta; 23 sexual contact

24 Applying Concepts Why does the egg's covering change after a sperm has entered the egg?

Lesson Review

Vocabulary

1 Use *uterus* and *vagina* in the same sentence.

_____

_____

_____

2 Use *sperm* and *egg* in the same sentence.

_____

_____

_____

Key Concepts

3 Compare Compare the functions of the male and female reproductive systems.

_____

_____

_____

_____

_____

4 Summarize Summarize the processes of fertilization and implantation.

_____

_____

_____

_____

5 Identify Explain what causes STIs and how they are transmitted.

_____

_____

_____

_____

6 Explain How does a fetus get nourishment up until the time it is born?

_____

_____

_____

Use the graph to answer the following question.

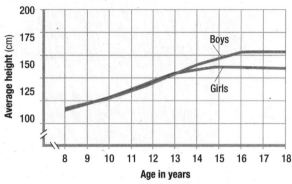

Growth Rates in Boys and Girls

Source: Centers for Disease Control and Prevention

7 Interpret At what age is the difference between the average height of boys and girls greatest? Estimate this difference to the nearest centimeter.

_____

_____

Critical Thinking

8 Predict How might cancer of the testes affect a man's ability to make sperm?

_____

_____

_____

_____

9 Apply Explain the difference beween identical twins and fraternal twins. Include in your answer how they form and their genetic makeup.

_____

_____

_____

_____

_____

_____

_____

My Notes

Unit 3 **Summary**

The Skeletal and Muscular Systems

The Circulatory and Respiratory Systems

Introduction to Body Systems

The Nervous and Endocrine Systems

The Reproductive System

The Digestive and Excretory Systems

---

1 Interpret The Graphic Organizer above shows the systems that must function well for a body to remain healthy. Describe what state the body is in when all of these systems are working well.

_____

_____

_____

2 Apply Provide an example for each system that describes how the nervous system and the endocrine system can affect other parts of the body.

_____

_____

_____

_____

3 Analyze Describe the two parts of the circulatory system, and explain how they work together.

_____

_____

_____

_____

4 Compare Name the two types of digestion, and describe how they are similar and different.

_____

_____

_____

_____

© Houghton Mifflin Harcourt Publishing Company • Image Credits: (tl) ©Stockbyte/Getty Images; (tr) ©Stem Jems/Photo Researchers, Inc.

Benchmark Review

Name _____

Multiple Choice

Identify the choice that best completes the statement or answers the question.

1 It is important for conditions inside the body to be stable as the external environment changes. The endocrine system helps the body do this through feedback mechanisms. Which of the following describes a feedback mechanism of the endocrine system?

A. an involuntary reaction that controls the way an organ works

B. a way to remove waste in response to more food being digested

C. a change in the amount of hormones that affect certain body cells

D. an increase in electrical signals from the nerves to the brain

2 Pierre is studying the organs in the human digestive system. He looks at a diagram of the intestines, similar to the one that follows.

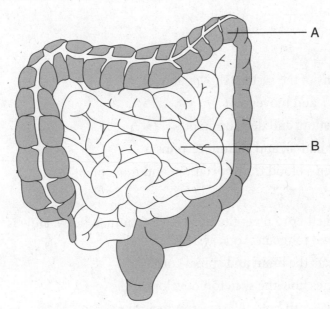

Which of the following **correctly** describes the diagram?

F. Structure A is the small intestine, and structure B connects the mouth to the stomach.

G. Structure A is the small intestine, and structure B absorbs water from digested material.

H. Structure A is the large intestine, and structure B absorbs nutrients from digested material.

I. Structure A is the large intestine, and structure B produces bile and stores it temporarily.

3 In science class, Rupert learns about the different systems of the human body.

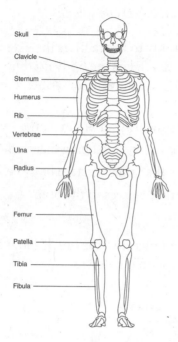

Skull
Clavicle
Sternum
Humerus
Rib
Vertebrae
Ulna
Radius
Femur
Patella
Tibia
Fibula

What are three functions of the system shown above?

A. support, protection, and movement

B. gas exchange, digestion, and development

C. waste removal, regulation, and stimuli response

D. removal of pathogens, blood transportation, and movement

4 Organ systems work together to meet the needs of the human body. How is the skeletal system related to the nervous system?

F. The skeleton protects the brain and spinal cord.

G. The brain determines how the skeleton develops.

H. The brain and spinal cord hold the skeleton together.

I. The skeletal system works as a part of the nervous system.

5 Groups of organs in the body work together as organ systems. Each organ system has a special role in the body. Organ systems include the nervous system, immune system, and endocrine system. What is the role of the endocrine system in the body?

A. It gets rid of wastes that the body produces.

B. It uses electrical signals to control body functions.

C. It uses chemical messages to control body functions.

D. It gets rid of pathogens that invade the body.

6 Kim is studying certain blood vessels in the body. Blood travels from the heart to the muscles in the upper arms. Which type of vessels is Kim studying?

F. veins

G. arteries

H. capillaries

I. lymph ducts

7 Muscles often work together to produce movement, as shown below.

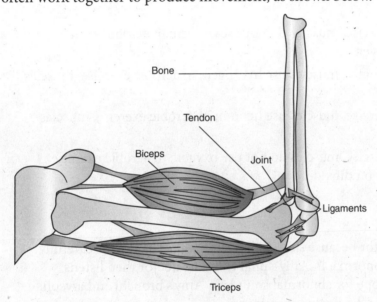

Bone

Tendon

Biceps

Joint

Ligaments

Triceps

When the bicep contracts and gets shorter, what does the tricep do?

A. It relaxes and gets longer.

B. It relaxes and gets shorter.

C. It contracts and gets longer.

D. It contracts and gets shorter.

8 The human muscular system can suffer injury or disease. Which of the following is an example of a genetic disease that affects the muscular system?

F. tendonitis

G. muscular dystrophy

H. a muscle strain

I. a muscle tear

Benchmark Review

9 The environment can affect a person's health. Which of the following diseases would be most adversely affected by cigarette smoke?

   A. emphysema and Parkinson's disease

   B. asthma and gonorrhea

   C. asthma and Parkinson's disease

   D. emphysema and asthma

10 Anaerobic exercise is an intense activity that lasts a short period of time. This kind of exercise increases muscle power. Aerobic exercise is a moderate activity that lasts a longer period of time. This kind of exercise strengthens the heart. Which of the following is another difference between anaerobic and aerobic exercise?

   F. In anaerobic exercise, muscles do not use oxygen; in aerobic exercise, muscles use oxygen.

   G. In anaerobic exercise, muscles use hydrogen; in aerobic exercise, muscles use nitrogen.

   H. In anaerobic exercise, muscles use helium; in aerobic exercise, muscles uses methane.

   I. In anaerobic exercise, muscles do not use oxygen; in aerobic exercise, muscles use carbon dioxide.

11 Amy goes to the doctor because she is not feeling well. The doctor carefully looks for anything abnormal in Amy's pharynx. The doctor then listens through his stethoscope for abnormal sounds in Amy's bronchi and alveoli. Which body system is the doctor examining?

   A. the lymphatic system

   B. the respiratory system

   C. the circulatory system

   D. the cardiovascular system

12 When he eats, Eli chews his food carefully. Which of these explains what Eli is doing as his teeth mash and crush the food into small pieces?

   F. He is performing peristalsis.

   G. He is chemically digesting his food.

   H. He is mechanically digesting his food.

   I. He is mixing his saliva with bile.

13 Sexually transmitted infections, called STIs, are illnesses that are transferred by sexual contact. STIs can be caused by viruses, bacteria, or parasites. Which of the following is an STI that is caused by a virus?

A. syphilis

B. pubic lice ✓

C. gonorrhea

D. genital herpes

14 Alice feels pain in her chest after she eats a big meal. Her doctor tells her that the pain is from stomach acid being pushed up into the tube that leads from her mouth to her stomach. To which structure is Alice's doctor referring?

F. liver

G. esophagus

H. large intestine

I. small intestine

15 Sergey runs a mile in gym class. After running, Sergey breathes heavily, pulling air into his lungs. Which statement **best** describes the path that the oxygen takes from his lungs to cells in his body?

A. Oxygen first enters his systemic circulation, then his heart, then his pulmonary circulation.

B. Oxygen first enters his pulmonary circulation, then his heart, then his systemic circulation.

C. Oxygen first enters his heart, then his systemic circulation, then his pulmonary circulation.

D. Oxygen first enters his heart, then his pulmonary circulation, then his systemic circulation.

16 Some diseases cause a person's kidneys to not function properly. A dialysis machine is a device that does the work of a person's kidneys. What does a dialysis machine do?

F. breaks down nutrients

G. filters waste from the blood

H. regulates the digestive system

I. delivers oxygen to the blood

17 At puberty, hormones trigger the development of sexual characteristics. Hormones also aid in reproduction. Which of the following are female sex hormones?

A. corpus and luteum

B. gonads and gametes

C. estrogen and progesterone

D. androgens and testosterone

18 The diagram shows the two main parts of the nervous system. The part labeled A processes and sends messages. The part labeled B transports the messages to and from the rest of the body.

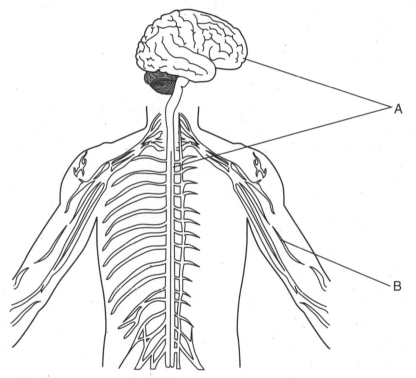

What structures make up the part of the nervous system labeled B?

F. the spinal cord only

G. the brain and spinal cord

H. blood vessels and muscle cells

I. motor nerves and sensory nerves

Immunity, Disease, and Disorders

© Houghton Mifflin Harcourt Publishing Company • Image Credits: (bkgd) ©Steve Gschmeissner/Photo Researchers, Inc.; (br) ©Myrleen Pearson/Alamy

Big Idea 14

Organization and Development of Living Organisms

Tapeworms attach themselves to the intestinal wall with these hooks.

What do you think?

Tapeworms can be passed between infected animals and people. Tapeworms make organisms sick by absorbing nutrients more quickly than their host can. How does your body respond to infectious disease?

Keeping your pets healthy can help keep you healthy.

Immunity, Disease, and Disorders

CITIZEN SCIENCE

Stop the Flu!

Many diseases spread through contact between infected people. Simple measures can help stop diseases from spreading.

① Think About It

A Take a quick survey of the students in your class to find out how many had the flu in the past year. Record your findings here.

_____

_____

_____

B Ask students who have had the flu to describe the symptoms they had. Record the symptoms below.

_____

_____

_____

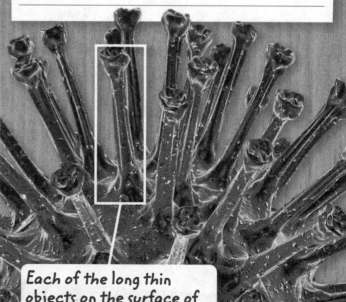

Each of the long thin objects on the surface of this cell is a single flu virus.

② Ask a Question

How do you fight a flu?

The flu is caused by a family of viruses. Viruses are tiny particles that attach to the surface of the cells in the body. But how do they get there? With your class, conduct research to answer the questions below:

A How is the flu spread?

_____

_____

B What are common ways to prevent the spread of the flu?

_____

_____

_____

Wash your hands.

Sneeze into your sleeve.

Use a tissue.

③ Make a Plan

A Choose one or two of the ways to fight the flu that you would like your whole school to do.

_____

_____

B In the space below, sketch out a design for a poster or pamphlet that would inform students of how they can avoid the flu.

C Once you have created your pamphlets or posters, write down how you plan to give out the pamphlets or where you would place the posters.

_____

_____

_____

_____

_____

_____

_____

_____

_____

Take It Home

Take your pamphlet or poster home. Use the pamphlet or poster to explain to everyone at home how they too can avoid the flu.

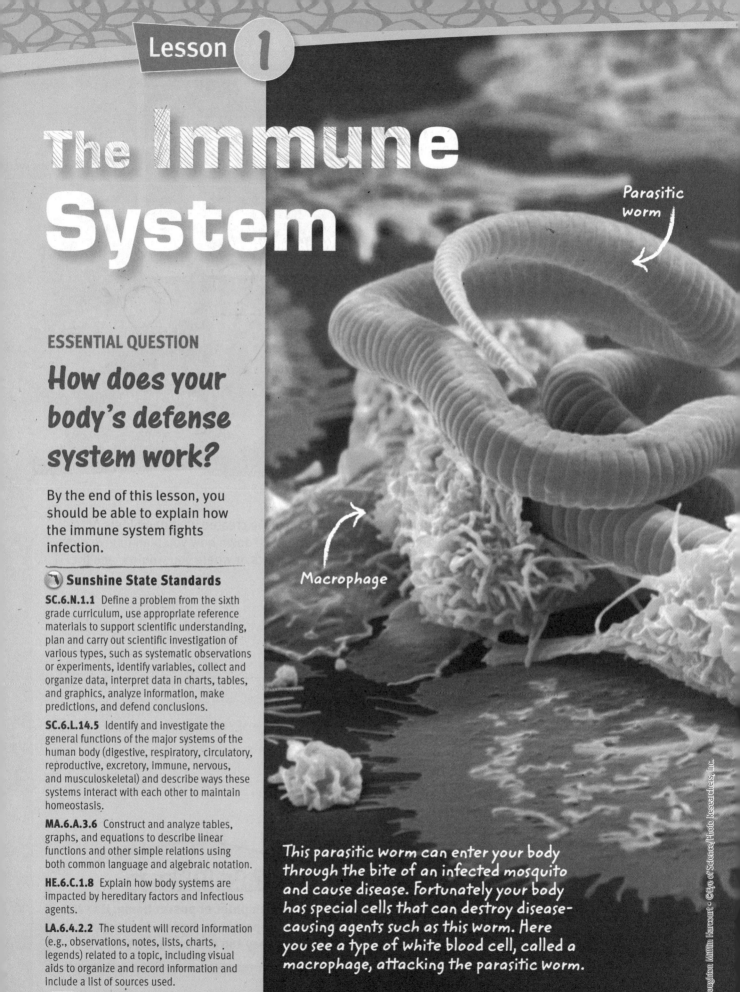

The Immune System

Parasitic worm

Macrophage

ESSENTIAL QUESTION

How does your body's defense system work?

By the end of this lesson, you should be able to explain how the immune system fights infection.

Sunshine State Standards

SC.6.N.1.1 Define a problem from the sixth grade curriculum, use appropriate reference materials to support scientific understanding, plan and carry out scientific investigation of various types, such as systematic observations or experiments, identify variables, collect and organize data, interpret data in charts, tables, and graphics, analyze information, make predictions, and defend conclusions.

SC.6.L.14.5 Identify and investigate the general functions of the major systems of the human body (digestive, respiratory, circulatory, reproductive, excretory, immune, nervous, and musculoskeletal) and describe ways these systems interact with each other to maintain homeostasis.

MA.6.A.3.6 Construct and analyze tables, graphs, and equations to describe linear functions and other simple relations using both common language and algebraic notation.

HE.6.C.1.8 Explain how body systems are impacted by hereditary factors and infectious agents.

LA.6.4.2.2 The student will record information (e.g., observations, notes, lists, charts, legends) related to a topic, including visual aids to organize and record information and include a list of sources used.

This parasitic worm can enter your body through the bite of an infected mosquito and cause disease. Fortunately your body has special cells that can destroy disease-causing agents such as this worm. Here you see a type of white blood cell, called a macrophage, attacking the parasitic worm.

1 Infer What happens when a computer gets a virus?

The computer is being hacked

2 Predict Check T or F to show whether you think each statement is true or false.

T	F	
☑	☐	Your body has cells that can help fight against disease.
☑	☐	Most microscopic organisms are harmless.
☑	☐	Skin can protect against infection.
☐	☑	Fever is always harmful to the body.

Active Reading

3 Synthesize You can often define an unknown word if you know the meaning of its word parts. Use the word parts and sentence below to make an educated guess about the meaning of the word *pathogen*.

Word part	Meaning
patho-	disease
-gen	to bring forth

Example sentence
Your body is constantly protecting itself against <u>pathogens</u>.

pathogen:

Vocabulary Terms

- pathogen
- immune system
- macrophage
- T cell
- B cell
- antibody
- immunity
- vaccine

4 Apply As you learn the definition of each vocabulary term in this lesson, create your own definition or sketch to help you remember the meaning of the term.

Playing DEFENSE

Inquiry

5 Describe How might watery eyes be a defensive response?

_____

_____

_____

What is your body's defense system?

Microscopic organisms and particles, such as bacteria and viruses, are all around you. Most are harmless, but some can make you sick. A **pathogen** is an organism, a virus, or a protein that causes disease. Fortunately, your body has many ways to protect you from pathogens.

External Defenses

Your skin provides external protection against pathogens that may enter the body. Skin also has structures, such as hair, nails, and sweat and oil glands, that help provide protection. For example, glands in your skin secrete oil that can kill pathogens. Mucous produced by mucous membranes in your nose and saliva in your mouth wash pathogens down into your stomach, where most are quickly digested. Hair, such as eyelashes and ear hairs, keep many particles in the air from entering the body. Nails protect your fingertips and toes. The skin and all of these structures make up the _integumentary system_.

External Defense Example

Your body loses and replaces approximately 1 million skin cells every 40 min. In the process, countless pathogens are removed.

6 Apply Why is it important to clean and care for cuts on your skin?

_____

_____

_____

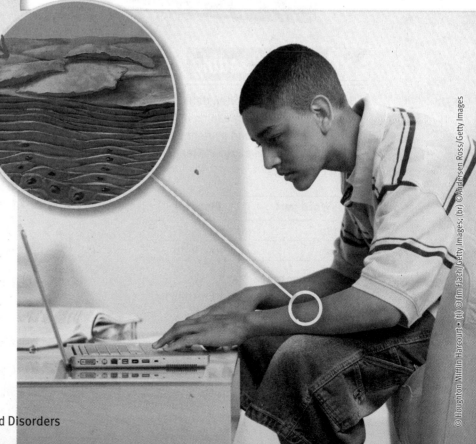

© Houghton Mifflin Harcourt • (t) ©Tim Flach/Getty Images; (br) ©Andersen Ross/Getty Images

Internal Defenses

Most of the time, pathogens cannot get past external defenses. Sometimes, skin is cut and pathogens can enter the body. The body responds quickly to keep out as many pathogens as possible. Blood flow increases to the injured area, causing it to swell and turn red. This swelling and redness is called *inflammation*. Cell pieces in the blood, called *platelets*, help seal the open wound so that no more pathogens can enter.

Your body may also respond by raising your body temperature. This response is called *fever*, which slows the growth of bacteria and some other pathogens. Both inflammation and fever are a part of the body's internal defenses. If a pathogen is not destroyed by inflammation or fever, then the immune system responds.

The **immune system** is made up of tissues and specialized white blood cells that recognize and attack foreign substances in the body. These white blood cells function in a coordinated way to identify and destroy pathogens.

7 Recognize List some of the body's external and internal defenses.

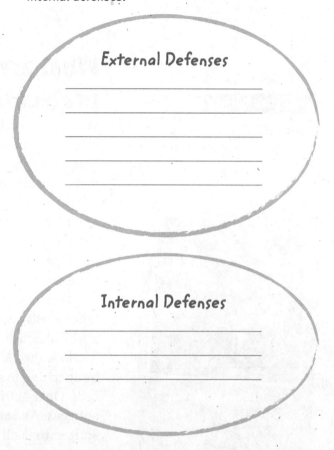

External Defenses

Internal Defenses

![Do the Math]

We usually measure temperature in degrees Fahrenheit (°F), but the standard scientific scale is in degrees Celsius (°C).

Sample Problems

To convert from °F to °C, first subtract 32 from the °F temperature, then multiply by 5, then divide by 9.

Normal body temperature is 98.6 °F. What is this temperature in °C?

$$(98.6\,°F - 32) \times 5 \div 9 = 37\,°C$$

To convert from °C to °F, first multiply the °C temperature by 9, then divide by 5, then add 32.

$$(37\,°C \times 9) \div 5 + 32 = 98.6\,°F$$

You Try It

8 Calculate If you have a fever, and your temperature is 39 °C, what is your temperature in °F?

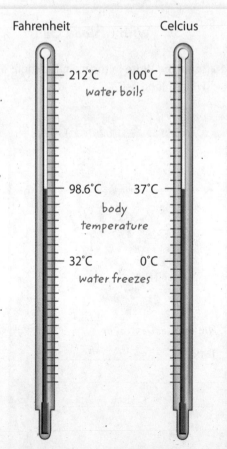

Fahrenheit   Celcius

212°C   100°C
water boils

98.6°C   37°C
body temperature

32°C   0°C
water freezes

Lesson 1 The Immune System **249**

© Houghton Mifflin Harcourt

Search and DESTROY

What are some white blood cells that protect the body?

9 Identify As you read, underline the characteristics of an antigen.

White blood cells destroy invading pathogens. Unlike red blood cells, white blood cells can move out of the blood vessels and "patrol" all the tissues of the body. Some of these cells attack pathogens directly. A **macrophage** (MAK•ruh•faj) is a white blood cell that destroys pathogens by engulfing and digesting them. Macrophages help start the body's immune response to *antigens*. An antigen is a substance that stimulates a response by the immune system. An antigen can be a pathogen or any foreign material in the body.

The immune system consists mainly of *T cells* and *B cells*. Some **T cells** coordinate the body's immune response, while others attack infected cells. T cells known as *helper T cells* activate other T cells, called *killer T cells*. Killer T cells attack infected body cells by attaching to specific antigens. Helper T cells also activate B cells. Once activated, **B cells** make antibodies that attach to specific antigens. An **antibody** is a specialized protein that binds to a specific antigen to tag it for destruction.

A macrophage is a white blood cell that attacks pathogens.

White Blood Cells

10 Identify Write in the main function, or task, of each white blood cell.

Macrophage	T cell	B cell
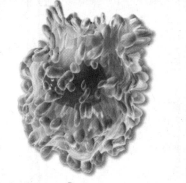	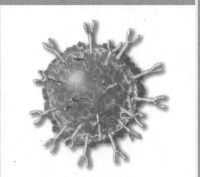	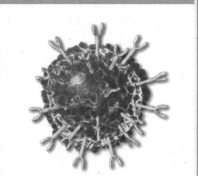
Nickname: Destroyer	Nickname: Activator/Attacker	Nickname: Responder
Task: _____ _____ _____ _____	Task: _____ _____ _____ _____	Task: _____ _____ _____ _____

Visualize It!

The Immune Response

11 Diagram Trace the path of the B cell response using a solid line. Trace the path of the T cell response using a dashed line.

Viral antigen

Virus

Virus

A virus that enters the body may be destroyed by macrophages, or the virus may get through to infect a body cell.

Macrophages engulf the virus particles and show the viral antigen. These macrophages activate helper T cells.

Macrophage

Receptor protein

Helper T cell

Helper T cells recognize the viral antigen on the macrophages. Helper T cells trigger two responses: the T cell response and the B cell response.

Helper T cell

B cell response

Helper T cells activate B cells to make and release antibodies that recognize the shape of the viral antigen.

T Cell Response

Helper T cells activate killer T cells.

B cell

Killer T cell

Activated B cell

Antibodies bind to the viral antigens forming clumps, and tag the virus for destruction. An antibody's shape is specialized to match an antigen like a key fits a lock.

Antibody

Viral antigen

Infected body cell

Killer T cells recognize the viral antigen on infected body cells. The killer T cells destroy the infected cells and cause the cells to release the virus particles.

Virus

12 Compare How do helper T cells differ from B cells?

_____

_____

_____

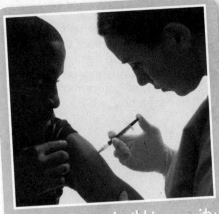

Vaccinations build immunity. This young person is receiving a vaccination shot.

Shields UP!

How does the body build immunity?

The body builds immunity against a disease when it is exposed to the pathogen that causes the disease. **Immunity** is the ability to resist or recover from an infectious disease. Immunity is passed from a mother to her fetus. Immunity can also results from the body being infected with the disease or from the body being vaccinated.

Producing Memory Cells

Your body produces billions of different kinds of T cells and B cells. However, it doesn't produce very many of each kind for specific pathogens. But, once your body has fought a pathogen, the body produces *memory cells*. Memory cells are T cells and B cells that "remember" a specific pathogen. Memory cells are not activated until the pathogen enters your body. Once the pathogen enters, your body immediately starts making large numbers of T cells and B cells that attack the pathogen. Your memory cells have made you immune to the pathogen.

Vaccination

A **vaccine** is a substance prepared from killed or weakened pathogens that is introduced into the body to produce immunity. The vaccine stimulates the body to make an immune response. B cells make antibodies to attack the specific pathogen being injected. Vaccination, or immunization, is a way to prevent illness from some diseases. Vaccines are used to trigger the body to make memory cells for a specific pathogen without causing illness.

How a Vaccine Works

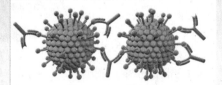

The vaccine is prepared from a killed or weakened pathogen and is introduced into the body.

The immune system responds, producing T cells and activated B cells. Memory cells are also produced.

If the pathogen infects the body, T cells and B cells begin a new immune response against the pathogen.

14 Synthesize How are vaccines related to memory cells?

_____

_____

What can challenge the immune system?

The immune system is a very effective body defense system. However, sometimes the immune system doesn't work properly and disease results. This can occur when a person inherits a gene that prevents the immune system from developing properly. It can also happen as a result of some kinds of infection.

Challenges to Immune System

Allergies	Sometimes, a person's immune system reacts to foreign antigens that are not dangerous to most people. An immune system reaction to a harmless or common substance is called an *allergy*. Allergies can be caused by certain foods such as peanuts, medicines such as penicillin, or certain types of pollen and molds.	**15 Relate** List different allergies that you or someone you know may have. peanut allergy, lactose (dairy)
Cancer	Healthy cells divide at a carefully controlled rate. Sometimes, cells don't respond to the body's controls. *Cancer* is a group of diseases in which cells divide at an uncontrolled rate. The immune system may not be able to stop the cancer cells from growing. Skin cancer is often caused by exposure to ultraviolet rays from sunlight, which can affect the cells that make pigment.	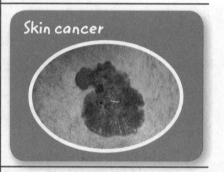 Skin cancer
Immune Deficiency	The immune system sometimes fails to develop properly or becomes weakened, resulting in an *immune deficiency disorder*. Acquired immune deficiency syndrome (AIDS) is caused by human immunodeficiency virus (HIV). This virus specifically infects the helper T cells. When the number of helper T cells becomes very low, neither T cell nor B cell immune responses can be activated. People who have AIDS can become very ill from pathogens that a healthy body can easily control.	**16 Relate** What is the relationship between HIV and AIDS?
Auto-immune Diseases	A disease in which the immune system attacks the body's own cells is called an *autoimmune disease*. In an autoimmune disease, immune system cells mistake body cells for foreign antigens. For example, rheumatoid arthritis (ROO•muh•toid ahr•THRY•tis) is a disease in which the immune system attacks the joints, most commonly the joints of the hands, as shown here.	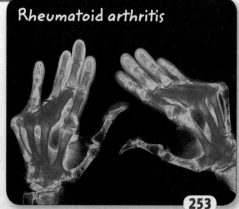 Rheumatoid arthritis

Visual Summary

To complete this summary, circle the correct word. Then use the key below to check your answers. You can use this page to review the main concepts of the lesson.

The **Immune** System

The human body has external and internal defenses.

17 This type of defense is external / internal.

39 °C

Celcius

18 This type of defense is external / internal.

The immune system has a specialized internal immune response when pathogens invade the body.

19 This is a macrophage/B cell engulfing a pathogen.

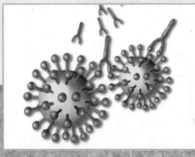

20 This is a(n) antibody /macrophage attaching to an antigen.

Answers: 17 external; 18 internal; 19 macrophage; 20 antibody

21 Summarize Explain three ways that your body can defend itself against pathogens.

Lesson Review

Vocabulary

In your own words, define the following terms.

1 pathogen

_____

_____

2 immune system

_____

_____

_____

Key Concepts

3 List What are some of your body's external defenses against pathogens?

_____

_____

_____

4 Summarize Explain how an immune response starts after a macrophage attacks a pathogen.

_____

_____

_____

_____

_____

_____

5 Compare How do T cells differ from B cells?

_____

_____

_____

_____

_____

Critical Thinking

Use the graph to answer the following question.

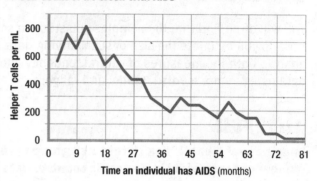

T Cell Count of a Person with AIDS

6 Interpret Over time, people with AIDS become very sick and are unable to fight off infection. Use the information in the graph to explain why this occurs.

_____

_____

_____

_____

_____

7 Explain How does your body respond differently the second time it is exposed to a pathogen than the first time it was exposed to the same pathogen?

_____

_____

_____

_____

_____

8 Infer Can your body make antibodies for pathogens that you have never been in contact with? Why or why not?

_____

_____

_____

_____

Mean, Median, Mode, and Range

Sunshine State Standards

MA.6.S.6.2 Select and analyze the measures of central tendency or variability to represent, describe, analyze, and/or summarize a data set for the purposes of answering questions appropriately.

You will often find that the samples you study in science vary in size. How do you estimate the size of such varying data sets? You can analyze both the measures of central tendency and the variability of data using mean, median, mode, and range.

Tutorial

Imagine that a public health research group is comparing the number of cases of flu in a specific country. Data has been collected for the last five years.

When working with numerical data, it is helpful to find a value that describes the data set. These representative values can describe a typical data value, or describe how spread out the data values are.

Number of Cases of Flu	
Year	**Number of Cases**
2004	800
2005	300
2006	150
2007	300
2008	200

Mean The mean is the sum of all of the values in a data set divided by the total number of values in the data set. The mean is also called the *average*.	$$\frac{800 + 300 + 150 + 300 + 200}{5}$$ **mean** = 350 cases/year
Median The median is the value of the middle item when data are arranged in numerical order. If there is an odd number of values, the median is the middle value. If there is an even number of values, the median is the mean of the two middle values.	If necessary, reorder the values from least to greatest: 150, 200, 300, 300, 800 → ← 300 is the middle value **median** = 300 cases/year
Mode The mode is the value or values that occur most frequently in a data set. If all values occur with the same frequency, the data set is said to have no mode. Values should be put in order to find the mode.	If necessary, reorder the values from least to greatest: 150, 200, 300, 300, 800 The value 300 occurs most frequently. **mode** = 300 cases/year
Range Range is another way to measure data. It measures how variable, or spread out, the data are. The range is the difference between the greatest value and the least value of a data set.	800 − 150 = 650 **range** = 650

You Try It!

The data table below shows the reported number of flu cases in four different countries.

Reported Number of Cases of Flu				
Year	Country 1	Country 2	Country 3	Country 4
2004	800	none	650	750
2005	300	350	450	450
2006	150	450	500	400
2007	300	200	550	350
2008	200	350	600	600

① **Using Formulas** Find the mean, median, and mode of the data for Country 2.

② **Using Formulas** Find the mean, median, and mode of the data for Country 3.

③ **Analyzing Data** Find the mean number of reported flu cases for only years in which cases were reported in Country 2. Compare this with the mean value for all years in Country 2. What conclusion can you draw about the effect of zeros on the mean of a data set?

Mean number of cases for years in which cases were reported: _____

Mean number of cases for all years: _____

Effect of zeros on the mean:

_____

_____

④ **Evaluating Data** Would the country with the greatest total number of flu cases from 2004 to 2008 have the greatest mean? Explain your reasoning.

_____

_____

_____

⑤ **Analyzing Methods** Calculate the range for Country 3.

When do you think you might need to use range instead of mean, median or mode?

_____

_____

_____

Infectious Disease

ESSENTIAL QUESTION

What causes disease?

By the end of this lesson, you should be able to compare types of infectious agents that may infect the human body.

Sunshine State Standards

SC.6.L.14.6 Compare and contrast types of infectious agents that may infect the human body, including viruses, bacteria, fungi, and parasites.

HE.6.C.1.3 Identify environmental factors that affect personal health.

HE.6.C.1.4 Recognize how heredity can affect personal health.

HE.6.C.1.8 Explain how body systems are impacted by hereditary factors and infectious agents.

LA.6.4.2.2 The student will record information (e.g., observations, notes, lists, charts, legends) related to a topic, including visual aids to organize and record information and include a list of sources used.

This may look like a spaceship landing and taking off of a planet. In fact, this is a virus injecting its DNA into a bacterial cell. The bacteria will copy the viral DNA, making more viruses.

258

Engage Your Brain

1 Predict Check T or F to show whether you think each statement is true or false.

T   F

☐   ☐   Diseases cannot be treated.

☐   ☐   Handwashing can help prevent the spread of disease.

☐   ☐   Only bacteria and viruses cause disease.

☐   ☐   All diseases can be spread from one person to another.

2 Explain Explain what you think the term *infection* means.

_____

_____

_____

_____

_____

_____

_____

_____

 Active Reading

3 Synthesize You can often define an unknown word if you know the meaning of its word parts. Use the word parts and sentence below to make an educated guess about the meaning of the word *antibiotic*.

Word part	Meaning
anti-	against
bio-	life

Example sentence

Antibiotics are used to treat bacterial illnesses such as strep throat.

Vocabulary Terms

- noninfectious disease
- infectious disease
- antibiotic
- antiviral drug

4 Identify This list contains the key terms you'll learn in this lesson. As you read, circle the definition of each term.

antibiotic:

_____

_____

_____

What is a noninfectious disease?

When you have a disease, your body does not function normally. You may feel tired, or have a sore throat, or have pain in your joints. Diseases have specific *symptoms,* or changes in how a person feels because of an illness. While there are many different kinds of diseases, all diseases can be categorized as either *noninfectious disease* or *infectious disease.*

Diseases that are caused by hereditary or environmental factors are called **noninfectious diseases**. For example, type I diabetes is caused by hereditary factors. Type 1 diabetes destroys cells that produce insulin. This makes it difficult for the body to use sugar for energy. Hemophilia is also caused by hereditary factors. The blood of people who have hemophilia does not clot properly when they get a cut. Some noninfectious diseases can be caused by environmental factors. *Mutagens* are environmental factors that cause mutations, or changes, in DNA. Sometimes, the changes cause a cell to reproduce uncontrollably. This results in a disease called *cancer.* X-rays, cigarette smoke, some air pollutants, and UV rays in sunlight can cause cancer. Cancer can have both hereditary and environmental causes.

Active Reading

5 List Name two types of factors that cause noninfectious disease.

_____

_____

_____

People who work around radiation, such as x-ray technicians, must protect themselves from overexposure.

X-RAYS CONTROLLED AREA

No unauthorised entry

Think Outside the Book Inquiry

6 Relate Think about a job that requires protection against some type of contamination. Then do the following:
- Explain why protection is necessary for that job.
- Draw the method of protection used for that job.

Air pollution can cause respiratory disease.

What is an infectious disease?

A disease that is caused by a *pathogen* is called an **infectious disease**. Pathogens include bacteria, fungi, and parasites, which are all alive. Pathogens also include viruses, which are noncellular particles that depend on living things to reproduce. Viruses cannot function on their own, so they are not considered to be alive.

Pathogens that cause disease can be picked up from the environment or passed from one living thing to another. Some pathogens travel through the air. Sneezing and coughing can release thousands of tiny droplets that may carry pathogens. If a person inhales these droplets, he or she may become infected. Some pathogens can be passed from nonliving things. A rusty nail can carry tetanus bacteria that may cause disease if a person is scratched by the nail. Pathogens can also be passed by other living things. Many diseases are carried by fleas, ticks, and mosquitoes.

A sneeze can force out thousands of droplets from your mouth and nose at speeds up to 160 km/h.

7 Apply What can you do to reduce the spread of droplets when you sneeze or cough?

_____

_____

_____

8 Categorize Determine whether each disease is infectious or noninfectious, and put a check mark in the correct box.

Example	Noninfectious Disease	Infectious Disease
Emphysema caused by cigarette smoke		
Strep throat that's been going around school		
Skin cancer caused by too much sun exposure		
The flu that you and your family members have		

That's Sick!

What can cause infectious disease?

Each type of pathogen causes a specific infectious disease. But diseases caused by similar types of pathogens share some common characteristics. Knowing what type of pathogen causes a disease helps doctors know how to treat the disease.

Viruses

Viruses are tiny particles that have their own genetic material but depend on living things to reproduce. Viruses insert their genetic material into a cell, and then the cell makes more viruses. Many viruses cause disease. Some, such as cold and flu viruses, are spread through the air or by contact. Others, such as the human immunodeficiency virus, or HIV, are spread through the transfer of body fluids. There are many types of cold and flu viruses, so preventing a cold or flu can be difficult.

👁 Visualize It!

9 Apply Once inside, what part of the cell do the viral particles go to? What do they do there?

_____

_____

_____

Bacteria

Most bacteria are beneficial to other living things. However, some bacteria cause disease. For example, the bacterium that causes tuberculosis infects about one-third of the world's population. It can infect a variety of organs, including the lungs, where it slowly destroys lung tissue. Strep throat, diarrheal illness, and some types of sinus infections are also caused by bacteria.

10 List Name some diseases caused by bacteria.

_____

_____

_____

_____

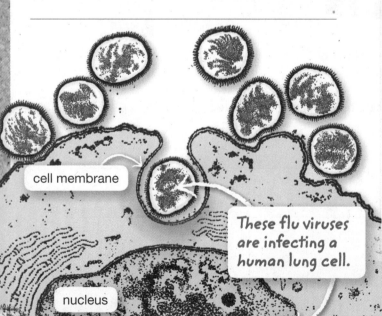

cell membrane

nucleus

These flu viruses are infecting a human lung cell.

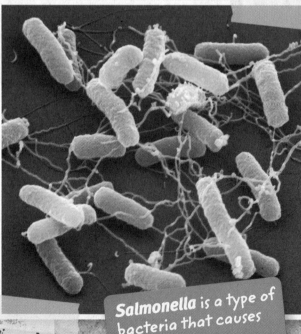

Salmonella is a type of bacteria that causes food poisoning.

Fungi

Most fungi are beneficial because they decompose, or break down, dead plants and animals into materials that other organisms use. However, some fungi are pathogens. The most common fungal diseases are skin infections. Two of the most common fungal skin infections are athlete's foot and ringworm of the body and scalp. These fungal skin infections can be passed on through contact with an infected person or contact with items such as socks, shoes, and shower surfaces where the fungus can grow.

11 Explain Why are most fungi beneficial?

_____

_____

_____

Parasites

A *parasite* is an organism that lives on and feeds on another organism, called a *host*. Parasites usually harm the host. Some of the most common parasites in humans are certain types of single-celled organisms called *protists*. For example, the protists that cause malaria infect as many as 500 million people each year. Another disease, called giardiasis, occurs when people consume water or food contaminated with the protist *Giardia lamblia*. Worms can also be parasites. The roundworm *Ascaris lumbricoides* is the most common cause of parasitic worm infections. It is spread in contaminated food, such as unwashed fruits and vegetables.

Active Reading **12 Define** What is a parasite?

_____

_____

_____

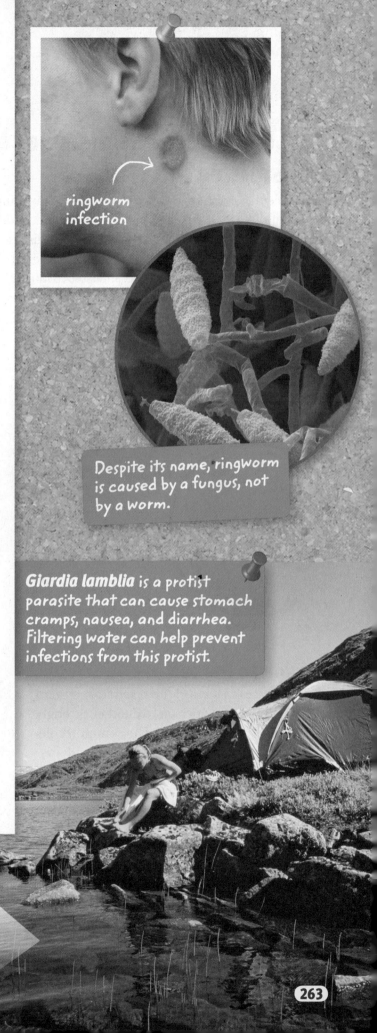

ringworm infection

Despite its name, ringworm is caused by a fungus, not by a worm.

Giardia lamblia is a protist parasite that can cause stomach cramps, nausea, and diarrhea. Filtering water can help prevent infections from this protist.

Giardia lamblia

Don't Pass It On

How can infectious diseases be transmitted?

Some scientists who investigate infectious diseases focus on the ways that diseases are passed on, or transmitted. A disease that spreads from person to person is a *contagious* disease. A person is also considered to be contagious if he or she has a disease that can spread to other people. Diseases can also be transmitted to people by other organisms and by contaminated food, water, or objects.

Water and Food

Drinking water in the United States is generally safe. But if a water treatment system fails, the water could become contaminated. Untreated water, such as rivers and streams, can also carry pathogens. Bacteria in foods can cause illness, too. For example, cattle and chickens often carry *Salmonella* bacteria. Raw beef, chicken, and eggs should be handled carefully during preparation to avoid contaminating food.

13 Infer Why should raw meats be kept separate from other foods?

_____

_____

Person to Person

Many diseases that affect the respiratory system are passed from one person to another through the air by a sneeze or cough. The common cold, the flu, and tuberculosis are usually spread this way. Pathogens can also be passed when an infected person touches another person. Other diseases, such as acquired immune deficiency syndrome, or AIDS, and hepatitis C can be passed during sexual contact.

14 Recognize List three ways that disease can be transmitted from one person to another.

_____

_____

_____

Deer tick that can transmit Rocky Mountain spotted fever

Animals to People

Quite a few human diseases are transmitted to humans by animals, especially insects and ticks. For example, humans can become infected with malaria when they are bitten by a mosquito infected with the malaria parasite. In a similar way, certain species of ticks can transmit diseases such as Rocky Mountain spotted fever and Lyme disease. Animals infected with the rabies virus can pass the disease on to other animals or people through a bite that cuts the skin.

Contaminated Objects

Objects that are handled by sick people or that come in contact with infected animals or contaminated food can pick up pathogens. Drinking glasses, utensils, doorknobs, towels, keyboards, and many other objects can transfer pathogens from one person to another. People who inject illegal drugs, such as heroin, can easily pick up pathogens from contaminated needles and related items. Traces of contaminated blood on a needle can infect a person who shares that needle.

15 Predict Read the scenario in the table below, and explain how disease could be transmitted to other people.

Scenario	How could disease be transmitted?
A person with a cold sneezes in a bus full of people.	
A person with a skin fungus shares a towel with another person.	

End Transmission

refrigeration

pasteurization

pickling

A variety of technologies used today allow some foods to be stored longer.

How can diseases be reduced?

Several important changes have helped decrease the occurrence of infectious disease. These changes include improved personal hygiene and improved technology used in medical procedures and food preservation.

Today, vaccines are used all over the world to prevent many serious diseases. Modern medical procedures using sterilized equipment, gloves, and masks help reduce contamination and improve patient recovery. Modern canning, freezing, dehydration, pickling, and refrigeration help prevent contamination of food. Pasteurization (pas•cher•ih•ZAY•shuhn) is the controlled heating of beverages or food, such as milk and cheese, to kill bacteria.

16 Apply Which methods of food preservation do you use at home?

_____
_____
_____

How can disease be treated?

Scientists are constantly discovering new ways to fight disease. *Antibiotics* have had a major impact on fighting some pathogens. An **antibiotic** is a medicine used to kill or slow the growth of bacteria and other microorganisms, such as fungi. Viruses, such as those that cause colds, are not affected by antibiotics. An antibiotic blocks cell processes. A virus relies on its host cell to survive, and does not have its own cell processes for the antibiotic to block. Today, *antiviral drugs* are being developed and used to treat viral infections. An **antiviral drug** is a drug that destroys viruses or prevents their replication.

📖 **Active Reading**

17 Identify As you read, underline the types of pathogens that are affected by antibiotics.

Resisting ARREST

A microscopic world of organisms exists all around us. Bacteria live in your mouth, on your skin, and on many objects that you touch every day. Most bacteria are harmless. However, some strains of bacteria that cause disease are no longer affected by antibiotics.

Tough guys
Some strains of *Staphylococcus aureus* bacteria have developed a resistance to antibiotics.

The Value of Money
Your money may carry more than just value. At least 93 different types of bacteria have been identified on dollar bills. Think of all the places each bill has traveled!

Soap It Up
Being in contact with different people and objects increases your exposure to a variety of microscopic organisms. Washing your hands throughout the day can help reduce your risk for some infections.

Extend

Inquiry

18 Identify What is the name and type of pathogen discussed in this article?

19 Research *Salmonella* is a pathogen that can be transmitted by contaminated food. Research and describe how *Salmonella* could be transmitted from a food processing factory to you.

20 Apply Find an object in your school that you and your classmates come in contact with nearly every day. How can you protect yourself and others from pathogens that may be on the object?

Visual Summary

To complete this summary, fill in the blanks with the correct word or phrase. Then, use the key below to check your answers. You can use this page to review the main concepts of the lesson.

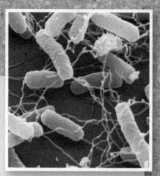

Diseases are categorized as noninfectious disease or infectious disease.

21 A disease that can be passed from one person to another is a(n)

_____

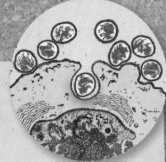

Infectious disease can be caused by different types of pathogens.

22 A type of pathogen that depends on living organisms to reproduce is a

_____

Infectious Disease

Infectious disease can be transmitted in many different ways.

23 List four ways an infectious disease can be transmitted.

_____

_____

_____

_____

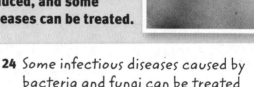

The spread of infectious diseases can be reduced, and some diseases can be treated.

24 Some infectious diseases caused by bacteria and fungi can be treated using

_____

Answers: 21 infectious disease; 22 virus; 23 another person, some animals, water and food, contaminated objects; 24 antibiotics

25 Synthesis Explain why antibiotics cannot be used to treat noninfectious disease.

_____

Lesson Review

Vocabulary

In your own words, define the following terms.

1 noninfectious disease

_____

_____

_____

2 infectious disease

_____

_____

_____

Key Concepts

3 Identify Name four types of pathogens that could cause infectious disease.

_____

_____

_____

4 Justify How has technology helped to reduce the spread of infectious disease?

_____

_____

_____

_____

_____

5 Compare How do viruses differ from bacteria, fungi, and parasites?

_____

_____

_____

_____

_____

_____

Critical Thinking

Use the graph to answer the following questions.

Reported Cases of Measles, United States, 1960–1996

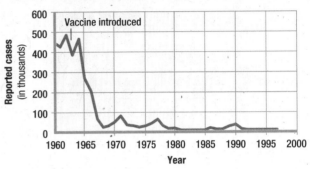

Source: U.S. Department of Health and Human Services

6 Compare How many cases of measles were reported in the United States in 1962, the year before the measles vaccine was licensed? How many cases were reported 5 years later?

_____

_____

7 Infer How many cases of measles would you predict were reported last year?

_____

_____

8 Hypothesize How can infectious and noninfectious diseases affect personal health?

_____

_____

_____

_____

_____

9 Apply Why might the risk of infectious disease be high in a community that has no water treatment facility?

_____

_____

_____

_____

My Notes

Unit 4 **Summary**

Immunity, Disease, and Disorders

involve

The Immune System

is part of the body's defense against

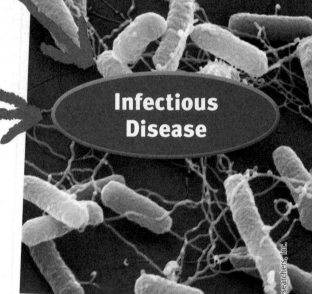

Infectious Disease

1 Interpret The Graphic Organizer above shows that the immune system defends against infectious disease. What other defenses, not shown on this organizer, protect your body against disease?

_____

_____

_____

2 Apply Name two differences between infectious disease and noninfectious disease.

_____

_____

_____

_____

3 Describe What are three ways that your body builds immunity?

_____

_____

_____

_____

4 Classify Name the category of pathogen that causes each of the following diseases: (1) athlete's foot, (2) influenza, (3) strep throat, and (4) malaria.

_____

_____

_____

Benchmark Review

Name _____

Multiple Choice
Identify the choice that best completes the statement or answers the question.

1 Sha-ree had been ill for 5 days. When her mother took her to the doctor, the doctor decided not to prescribe an antibiotic. He said Sha-ree had a virus. Why did the doctor **not** prescribe an antibiotic?

   A. Antibiotics target only white blood cells.

   B. Antibiotics are not used to fight any infections.

   C. Antibiotics cause fevers that make viruses stronger.

   D. Antibiotics kill some bacteria and fungi, not viruses.

2 Vaccinations can help build immunity. Vaccines stimulate the body to make an immune response. What is in a vaccine that causes the immune system to respond?

   F. antibiotic

   G. antiviral drug

   H. memory cells

   I. killed or weakened pathogen

3 The body's defense system uses cells that have different functions to fight against pathogens. Which of the cells pictured below engulfs pathogens and other foreign particles?

A.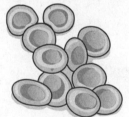
Red blood cells

C.
T cell

B.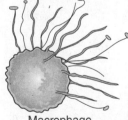
Macrophage

D.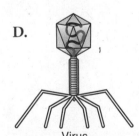
Virus

4   Mazie visited the school nurse because she felt ill. The nurse suggested that she might have a virus. Which of these words **best** describes a virus?

    F. antibody

    G. pathogen

    H. antibiotic

    I. macrophage

5   If a person eats food containing tapeworm eggs or larvae, the tapeworm can enter the intestines and grow there. The following picture shows a tapeworm.

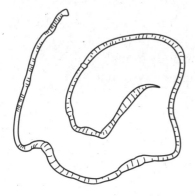

    Which type of organism is a tapeworm?

    A. bacterium

    B. fungus

    C. parasite

    D. virus

6   Jill is recovering from the flu. At lunchtime, she shares her water bottle with her friend Dara. The next day, Dara is sick. Which type of disease is the flu?

    F. autoimmune

    G. environmental

    H. infectious

    I. parasitic

x

z

w

v

u

s

r

q

p

o

n

m

l

k

j

i

h

g

f

e

d

c

b

a

!

@

$

%

^

&

(

)

-

=

+

/

?

.

,

;

:

1

2

3

4

5

6

7

8

9

0

A

B

C

D

E

Name _____

7 Insulin is a hormone that helps to control blood sugar levels in the body. Type 1 diabetes is a hereditary disease in which the body destroys the cells that produce insulin. What type of disease is type 1 diabetes?

A. infectious

B. autoimmune

C. allergy

D. virus

8 Jake has been sneezing a lot. Which defense is related to Jake's sneezing?

F. mucus

G. tears

H. skin

I. fever

9 Erik wants to avoid overexposure to mutagens as much as possible. Which strategy can **best** help him do this?

A. eat a balanced diet

B. exercise several days a week

C. wear sunscreen outdoors

D. wash his hands regularly

10 Jorge has a cold but feels well enough to study with his friends Lisa and Jin. Lisa and Jin become sick. Which term describes Jorge's condition when he was studying with his friends?

F. noninfectious

G. contagious

H. mutagen

I. pathogen

11 The human body has both internal and external defenses against disease. Which of these is an internal defense?

A. hair

B. tears

C. T cells

D. skin cells

F

G

H

I

J

12 The bacteria *Escherichia coli*, also called *E. coli*, are shown in the following picture.

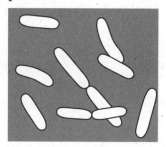

Some strains of these bacteria cause disease. Which term describes these organisms?

F.   genetic factors

G.   mutagens

H.   pathogens

I.   viruses

Life over Time

Big Idea 15

Diversity and Evolution of Living Organisms

Pitcher plants survive in environments that are often hostile to other varieties of plants.

This fly is about to become a meal!

What do you think?

Over time, different life forms change as the environment changes. This happened a number of times in Florida's prehistory. What kinds of organisms do you think lived in prehistoric Florida?

Prehistoric Florida

Fossils of land animals in Florida rocks and sediments date back to about 25 million years ago. The fossil record indicates that most of these land animals became extinct in Florida around 10,000 years ago. What do we know about fossils in Florida that are even older than these?

Age of the Dinosaurs, (245 million years ago to 65 million years ago)

The Florida peninsula was covered by ocean. Therefore, only marine fossils can be found in surface rocks of this age. No dinosaur fossils are known.

Beaked dolphin skeleton found in a Florida mine

In parts of Florida, the fossils of marine organisms and land animals are found in the same sediment. Why do you think that both types of fossils are found together?

_____

_____

_____

_____

_____

_____

_____

Fossil of a shark's jaw

Late Cenozoic Era (5 million years ago to Recent)

During the Ice Age, sea level rose and fell. Coral reefs formed in the warm waters off of the southeastern part of the peninsula. Fossils from this time include giant sloths, armadillos, bears, lions, sabertooth cats, and horses. Most of these animals became extinct around 10,000 years ago.

Middle Cenozoic Era (24.5 million years ago to 5 million years ago)

During this time, sea level generally dropped, and more of the Florida peninsula became exposed. Numerous mammals lived in forests and grassy plains. Fossils from this time include horses, rhinoceroses, bears, sabertooth cats, alligators, crocodiles, and birds.

Early Cenozoic Era (65 million years ago to 24.5 million years ago)

Most fossils from this time are marine organisms. These include fossils of shells, corals, sea urchins, sharks, sea turtles, and a very early whale.

Thousands of years ago, the Florida landscape looked like a cool, dry, and open savannah.

Take It Home | Your Neighborhood Through Time

Your neighborhood probably hasn't been around since the age of the dinosaurs but it has also changed over time. Do some research to find out when your town was founded. Create a timeline similar to the one above that shows the details of what changes your neighborhood and town might have experienced over time.

Theory of Evolution by Natural Selection

ESSENTIAL QUESTION

What is the theory of evolution by natural selection?

By the end of this lesson, you should be able to describe the role of genetic and environmental factors in the theory of evolution by natural selection.

Because this grass snake's skin color looks like the plant stalk, it is able to hide from predators! This form of camouflage is the result of natural selection.

🔍 Sunshine State Standards

SC.7.L.15.1 Recognize that fossil evidence is consistent with the scientific theory of evolution that living things evolved from earlier species.

SC.7.L.15.2 Explore the scientific theory of evolution by recognizing and explaining ways in which genetic variation and environmental factors contribute to evolution by natural selection and diversity of organisms.

SC.7.L.15.3 Explore the scientific theory of evolution by relating how the inability of a species to adapt within a changing environment may contribute to the extinction of that species.

LA.6.4.2.2 The student will record information (e.g., observations, notes, lists, charts, legends) related to a topic, including visual aids to organize and record information and include a list of sources used.

Engage Your Brain

1 Predict Check T or F to show whether you think each statement is true or false.

T   F

☑ ☐ Skin color can protect an animal from danger.

☑ ☐ The amount of available food can impact an organism's survival.

☐ ☑ Your parents' characteristics are not passed on to you.

☑ ☐ A species can go extinct if its habitat is destroyed.

2 Imagine How do you think phones have changed from the type in the photo below to what is used today?

Phones are mobile and they have touchscreens and you don't call an operator.

Active Reading

3 Synthesize You can often define an unknown word by clues provided in the sentence. Use the sentence below to make an educated guess about the meaning of the word *artificial*.

Example sentence
Many people prefer real sugar to artificial sweeteners made by humans.

artificial:

_____

_____

_____

Vocabulary Terms

- evolution
- artificial selection
- natural selection
- variation
- adaptation
- extinction

4 Apply As you learn the definition of each vocabulary term in this lesson, create your own definition or sketch to help you remember the meaning of the term.

Darwin's Voyage

What did Darwin observe?

You have already seen an example of how the telephone has changed over time. In biology, **evolution** refers to the process in which populations gradually change over time. A population is all the individuals of a species that live together in an area. A species is a group of closely-related organisms that can produce fertile offspring. A scientist named Charles Darwin developed a theory of how evolution takes place.

Charles Darwin was born in England in 1809. When he was 22 years old, Darwin graduated from college with a degree in theology. But he was most interested in plants and animals. So he signed on as the naturalist—a scientist who studies nature—on the British ship HMS *Beagle*. With the observations he made on this almost five-year journey, Darwin formed a theory about how biological evolution could happen.

Darwin kept a log during his voyage and this was published as *The Voyage of the Beagle*. Darwin observed and collected many living and fossil specimens. Darwin made his most influential observations on the Galápagos Islands of South America.

Darwin left England on December 27, 1831. He returned 5 years later.

ENGLAND

EUROPE

NORTH AMERICA

ATLANTIC OCEAN

AFRICA

The plants and animals on the Galápagos Islands differed from island to island. This is where Darwin studied birds called finches.

Galápagos Islands

Equator

SOUTH AMERICA

Cape of Good Hope

Think Outside the Book Inquiry

5 **Explore** Trace Darwin's route on the map, and choose one of the following stops on his journey: Galápagos Islands, Andes Mountains, Australia. Do some research to find out what plants and animals live there. Then write an entry in Darwin's log to describe what you saw.

Differences Among Species

Darwin collected birds from the Galápagos Islands and nearby islands. He observed that these birds differed slightly from those on the nearby mainland of South America. And the birds on each island were different from the birds on the other islands. After careful analysis back in England, he realized that they were all finches!

The most obvious difference between the finches was the shape of their beaks. Perhaps these differences related to the birds' diets. Birds with shorter, heavier beaks could eat harder foods than those that had skinnier, thinner beaks. Based on these observations, Darwin wondered if the birds had evolved from one species of finch.

This cactus finch has a narrow beak that it uses to cut into cactus and eat the tissue.

The vegetarian finch has a curved beak, ideal for taking large berries from a branch.

Visualize It!

6 Infer How do you think the pointed beak of this woodpecker finch helps it to get food?

_____

_____

_____

Woodpecker finch

ASIA

INDIAN OCEAN

Equator

AUSTRALIA

NEW ZEALAND

Darwin saw many plants and animals that were only found on certain continents, such as Australia.

km 0   1,000   2,000

mi 0   1,000   2,000

Darwin's Homework

What other ideas influenced Darwin?

The ideas of many scientists and observations of the natural world influenced Darwin's thinking. Darwin was influenced by ideas about how traits are passed on in selective breeding, Earth's history, and the growth of populations. All of these ideas helped him develop his theory of how populations could change over time.

Organisms Pass Traits On to Offspring

Farmers and breeders have been producing many kinds of domestic animals and plants for thousands of years. These plants and animals had traits that were desired by the farmers and breeders. A *trait* is a form of an inherited characteristic. For example, large tail feathers is a trait, and tail feather length is the corresponding characteristic. The practice by which humans select plants or animals for breeding based on desired traits is **artificial selection**. Artificial selection shows that traits can change and can spread through populations.

---

7 List Darwin studied artificial selection in the pigeons that he bred. List three other animals that have many different breeds.

_____

_____

_____

_____

_____

This chicken has been bred to have large tail feathers and a big red comb.

This chicken has been bred to have large head feathers.

This chicken has been bred to have feathers on its feet.

8 Identify As you read, underline the names of other important thinkers that influenced Darwin's theory.

Organisms Acquire Traits

Scientist Jean Baptiste Lamarck thought that organisms could bring about the changes they needed to survive in the environment. For example, a man could acquire stronger muscles over time. If the muscles were an advantage in the environment, he would pass these stronger muscles on to his offspring. We know now that acquired traits do not become part of an organism's DNA and can't be passed on to offspring. But the idea that an organism's traits help it survive influenced Darwin's theory.

9 Apply Is the size of your muscles acquired or part of your DNA? Explain.

_____

_____

_____

These rock layers formed over millions of years.

The Earth Changes Over Time

The presence of different rock layers, such as in the Grand Canyon to the left, show that Earth has changed over time. Geologist Charles Lyell theorized that small changes in rock have collected over hundreds of millions of years. Darwin reasoned that if Earth were very old, then there would be enough time for very small changes in life forms to collect over a very long period of time as well.

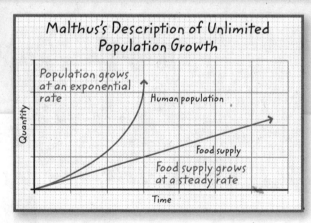

A Struggle for Survival Exists

After his journey Darwin read an essay about population growth by economist Thomas Malthus. The essay helped Darwin understand how the environment could influence which organisms survive and which organisms die. All populations are affected by factors that limit population growth, such as disease, predation, and competition for food. Darwin reasoned that the survivors probably have traits that help them survive, and that some of these traits could be passed on from parent to offspring.

Visualize It!

10 Infer What can you infer from the two red growth lines on this graph?

_____

_____

Natural Selection

What are the four parts of natural selection?

Darwin proposed that most evolution happens through the natural selection of advantageous traits. **Natural selection** is the process by which organisms that inherit advantageous traits tend to reproduce more successfully than the other organisms do.

Overproduction

When a plant or animal reproduces, it usually makes more offspring than the environment can support. For example, a female jaguar may have up to four pups. Only some of them will survive to adulthood, and a smaller number of them will successfully reproduce.

11 Infer A fish may have hundreds of offspring at a time, and only a small number will survive. What characteristics of fish might allow them to survive?

_____

_____

_____

Not all of these jaguar cubs will survive to reproduce.

Variation exists in the jaw size between these two jaguars. This variation will get passed on to the next generation.

Genetic Variation

Within a species there are natural differences, or **variations**, in traits. For example, the jaw size of the two jaguar skulls to the left is different. This difference results from a difference in the genetic material of the jaguars. Genetic variations can be passed on from parent to offspring. Sometimes a mutation occurs that changes genetic material.

As each new generation is produced, new genetic differences may be introduced into a population. In this way, genetic variations can add up in a population. The more genetic variation a population has, the more likely it is that some individuals might have traits that will be advantageous if the environment changes.

Selection

Individuals try to get the resources they need to survive. These resources include food, water, space and, in most cases, mates for reproduction. About 11,000 years ago jaguars faced a shortage of food because the climate changed and many species died. A genetic variation in jaw size became important for survival. Jaguars with larger jaws could eat hard-shelled reptiles when other prey were hard to find.

Darwin reasoned that individuals with a particular trait, like a large jaw, are more likely to survive long enough to reproduce. As a result, the trait is "selected," or becomes more common in the next generation of offspring.

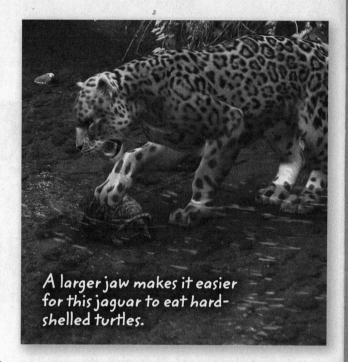

A larger jaw makes it easier for this jaguar to eat hard-shelled turtles.

12 Summarize How did large jaws and teeth become typical traits of jaguars?

_____

_____

_____

Adaptation

An inherited trait that helps an organism survive and reproduce in its environment is an **adaptation**. A larger jaw size helped jaguars survive when food was hard to find. As the process of natural selection repeats from generation to generation, these adaptations become more common in the population, and new adaptations may arise. Over time, the population becomes better adapted to the environment.

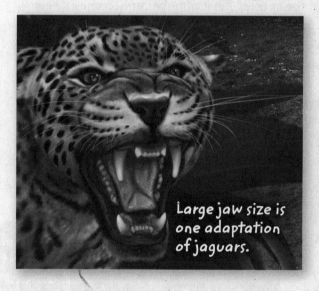

Large jaw size is one adaptation of jaguars.

13 Explain In the table below, explain how each part of natural selection works.

Principle of natural selection	How it works
overproduction	
genetic variation	
selection	
adaptation	

Well-adapted

How do species change over time?

Life first appeared on Earth nearly 4 billion years ago. Since then, many species—such as dinosaurs—appeared, survived for a time, and then died. An incredible diversity of life exists because species have changed over time, or evolved.

Sometimes a population changes so much that it can no longer reproduce with the rest of the species. That population becomes a new species. An early form of a species, called an *ancestor*, may give rise to many new *descendent* species over time.

The skin of this frog looks like a dead leaf.

14 Apply How does this frog's color help it survive?

_____

_____

_____

Species Change in Response to Their Environment

Adaptations are genetic variations that help a species survive and reproduce in a particular environment. Some adaptations, such as a butterfly's long tongue, are physical. Other adaptations, such as a bird's mating ritual, are behaviors that help it find food, protect itself, or reproduce. The frog above is adapted to its environment because it can hide from predators.

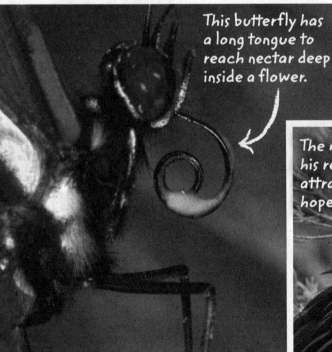

This butterfly has a long tongue to reach nectar deep inside a flower.

The male frigate bird uses his red throat pouch to attract a female and hopefully reproduce.

A Venus flytrap is well-adapted to catch prey!

This dinosaur went extinct about 65 million years ago.

Why is adaptation important for survival?

The traits that help an organism survive depend on both the needs of the species and environmental factors. For example, a snake that lives in tall, green grass may benefit from being green. In this environment, a green snake will be able to hide from predators more easily than a brown snake will. Therefore, green snakes will survive and reproduce more than brown snakes will. But being brown may be more beneficial if the snake lives on a forest floor that has a large amount of dead leaves. On a forest floor, a brown snake will probably survive and reproduce more than a green snake will.

Visualize It!

15 Summarize Examine the four photos of adaptations. Describe how each of the adaptations below helps the species survive and/or reproduce.

Species Not Adapted to the Environment May Go Extinct

What happens when the environment that a species has adapted to changes? The environmental change could be gradual, or it could happen suddenly. Changes in environmental conditions can affect the survival of individuals with a particular trait. The species may be able to survive at first. But, if no individuals were born with traits that help them to survive and reproduce in the changed environment, the species will become extinct.

Extinction is when all of the members of a species have died. Competition, new predators, and the loss of habitat are environmental pressures that can limit the growth of populations and could lead to extinction. The fossil record is a record of the things that have lived in a particular location. It shows that many species, like the dinosaur above, have gone extinct in the course of the history of life on Earth.

Organism	Adaptation	Role in survival or reproduction
Venus flytrap	trap helps catch prey	
frog	skin looks like a dead leaf	
bird	male has large red throat pouch	
butterfly	long tongue to reach inside flower	

Visual Summary

To complete this summary, circle the correct word. Then use the key below to check your answers. You can use this page to review the main concepts of the lesson.

Darwin's theory of natural selection was influenced by his own observations and the work of other scientists.

16 During natural / artificial selection, breeders choose the traits that are passed on to the next generation.

Evolution is Change Over Time

The theory of evolution by natural selection states that organisms with advantageous traits produce more offspring.

17 Natural selection can only act on acquired traits / inherited variation.

Species that are not adapted to their environment may go extinct.

18 Dinosaurs are an example of organisms that have undergone variation / extinction.

Answers: 16 artificial; 17 inherited variation; 18 extinction

19 Infer How does the environment influence natural selection?

Lesson Review

Vocabulary

Use a term from the lesson to complete the sentences below.

1 _____ is the natural difference between members of a species.

2 Owners of cattle herds who only choose to breed cows that produce the most milk are engaging in _____ selection.

3 A trait that improves an individual's ability to survive and reproduce in a specific environment is called a(n) _____

Key Concepts

4 Summarize Describe what Darwin observed during his voyage on the HMS *Beagle*.

_____
_____
_____
_____

5 Explain How does the environment impact a species's survival?

_____
_____
_____
_____

6 Compare Why are only inherited traits, not acquired ones, necessary for the process of natural selection?

_____
_____
_____
_____

7 Describe How are fish adapted to their environment?

_____
_____
_____

Critical Thinking

Use the diagram to answer the following question.

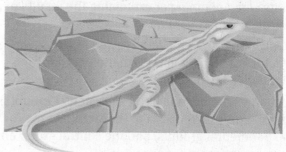

8 Apply How is each of these lizards adapted to its environment?

_____
_____
_____
_____
_____
_____
_____

9 Infer How can natural selection account for the long snout of an anteater?

_____
_____
_____
_____
_____
_____
_____

Scientific Debate

Not all scientific knowledge is gained through experimentation. It is also the result of a great deal of debate and confirmation.

Sunshine State Standards

SC6.N.1.3 Explain the difference between an experiment and other types of scientific investigation, and explain the relative benefits and limitations of each.

SC.7.N.1.3 Distinguish between an experiment (which must involve the identification and control of variables) and other forms of scientific investigation and explain that not all scientific knowledge is derived from experimentation.

LA.6.2.2.3 The student will organize information to show understanding (e.g., representing main ideas within text through charting, mapping, paraphrasing, summarizing, or comparing/contrasting).

Tutorial

As you prepare for a debate, look for information from the following sources.

Controlled Experiments Consider the following points when planning or examining the results of a controlled experiment.

- Only one factor should be tested at a time. A factor is anything in the experiment that can influence the outcome.
- Samples are divided into experimental group(s) and a control group. All of the factors of the experimental group(s) and the control group are the same except for one variable.
- A variable is a factor that can be changed. If there are multiple variables, only one variable should be changed at a time.

Independent Studies The results of a different group may provide stronger support for your argument than your own results. And using someone else's results helps to avoid the claim that your results are biased. Bias is the tendency to think about something from only one point of view. The claim of bias can be used to argue against your point.

Comparison with Similar Objects or Events If you cannot gather data from an experiment to help support your position, finding a similar object or event might help. The better your example is understood, the stronger your argument will be.

Read the passage below and answer the questions.

Many people want to protect endangered species but do not agree on the best methods to use. Incubating, or heating eggs to ensure hatching, is commonly used with bird eggs. It was logical to apply the same technique to turtle eggs. The Barbour's map turtle is found in Florida, Georgia, and Alabama. To help more turtles hatch, people would gather eggs and incubate them. However, debate really began when mostly female turtles hatched. Were efforts to help the turtles really harming them? Scientists learned that incubating eggs at 25°C (77°F) produces males and at 30°C (86°F) produces females. As a result, conservation programs have stopped artificially heating the eggs.

1 What is the variable described in the article about Barbour's map turtles?

_____

2 Write a list of factors that were likely kept the same between the sample groups described in the article.

_____

_____

_____

3 What argument could people have used who first suggested incubating the turtle eggs?

_____

_____

_____

© Houghton Mifflin Harcourt Publishing Company • Image Credits: (bl) ©David A. Northcott/Corbis

You Try It!

Fossils from the Burgess Shale Formation in Canada include many strange creatures that lived over 500 million years ago. The fossils are special because the soft parts of the creatures were preserved. Examine the fossil of the creature *Marrella* and the reconstruction of what it might have looked like.

Fossil

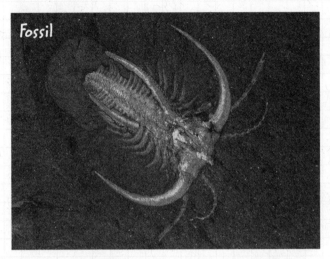

Reconstruction

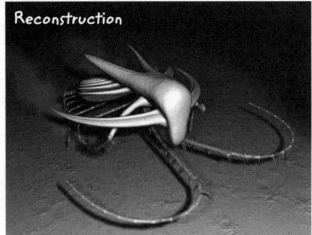

1 Recognizing Relationships Find four features on the reconstruction that you can also identify in the fossil. Write a brief description of each feature.

_____
_____
_____
_____
_____
_____

2 Applying Concepts *Marrella* is extinct. How do you think *Marrella* behaved when it was alive? What did it eat? How did it move? On what do you base your argument?

_____
_____
_____
_____
_____
_____
_____
_____

3 Communicating Ideas Share your description with a classmate. Discuss and debate your positions. Complete the table to show the points on which you agree and disagree.

Agree	Disagree

Take It Home

Research more about the creatures of the Burgess Shale Formation. Find at least one other fossil creature and its reconstruction. What do you think the creature was like?

Evidence of Evolution

ESSENTIAL QUESTION

What evidence supports the theory of evolution?

By the end of this lesson, you should be able to describe the evidence that supports the theory of evolution by natural selection.

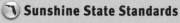

Sunshine State Standards

SC.7.N.1.5 Describe the methods used in the pursuit of a scientific explanation as seen in different fields of science such as biology, geology, and physics.

SC.7.L.15.1 Recognize that fossil evidence is consistent with the scientific theory of evolution that living things evolved from earlier species.

LA.6.4.2.2 The student will record information (e.g., observations, notes, lists, charts, legends) related to a topic, including visual aids to organize and record information and include a list of sources used.

Fossils show us what a dinosaur looks like. This dinosaur lived millions of years ago!

Engage Your Brain

1 Predict Check T or F to show whether you think each statement is true or false.

T	F	
☑	☐	Fossils provide evidence of organisms that lived in the past.
☑	☐	The wing of a bat has similar bones to those in a human arm.
☑	☐	DNA can tell us how closely related two organisms are.
☑	☐	Whales are descended from land-dwelling mammals.

2 Infer This is a Petoskey stone, which is made up of tiny coral fossils. What can you infer if you find a coral fossil on land?

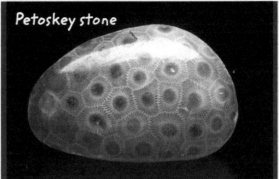

Petoskey stone

The fossil comes from a land and sea animal, or washed up onto shore.

Active Reading

3 Synthesize You can often define an unknown word if you understand the parts of the word. Use the words below to make an educated guess about the meaning of the word *fossil record*.

Word	Meaning
fossil	the remains or trace of once-living organisms
record	an account that preserves information about facts or events

Vocabulary Terms

- fossil
- fossil record

4 Apply As you learn the definition of each vocabulary term in this lesson, create your own definition or sketch to help you remember the meaning of the term.

fossil record:

Fossil Hunt

How do fossils form?

Evidence that organisms have changed over time can be found in amber, ice, or sedimentary rock. Sedimentary rock is formed when particles of sand or soil are deposited in horizontal layers. Often this occurs as mud or silt hardens. After one rock layer forms, newer rock layers form on top of it. So, older layers are found below or underneath younger rock layers. The most basic principle of dating such rocks and the remains of organisms inside is "the deeper it is, the older it is."

Amber fossils form when small creatures are trapped in tree sap and the sap hardens.

5 Examine What features of the organism are preserved in amber?

_____

_____

_____

This flying dinosaur is an example of a cast fossil.

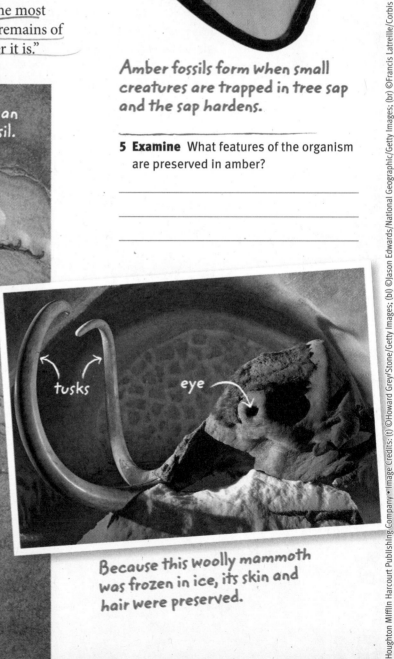

tusks

eye

Because this woolly mammoth was frozen in ice, its skin and hair were preserved.

Many Fossils Form in Sedimentary Rock

Rock layers preserve evidence of organisms that were once alive. The remains or imprints of once-living organisms are called **fossils**. Fossils commonly form when a dead organism is covered by a layer of sediment or mud. Over time, more sediment settles on top of the organism. Minerals in the sediment may seep into the organism and replace the body's material with minerals that harden over time. This process produces a cast fossil. Many familiar fossils are casts of hard parts, such as shells and bones. If the organism rots away completely after being covered, it may leave an imprint of itself in the rock. Despite all of the fossils that have been found, it is rare for an organism to become a fossil. Most often, the dead organism is recycled back into the biological world by scavengers, decomposers, or the process of weathering.

 **Active Reading**

6 Identify As you read, underline the steps that describe how a cast fossil forms.

How do fossils show change over time?

All of the fossils that have been discovered make up the **fossil record**. The fossil record provides evidence about the order in which species have existed through time, and how they have changed over time. By examining the fossil record, scientists can learn about the history of life on Earth.

Despite all the fossils that have been found, there are gaps in the fossil record. These gaps represent chunks of geologic time for which a fossil has not been discovered. Also, the transition between two groups of organisms may not be well understood. Fossils that help fill in these gaps are *transitional fossils*. The illustration on the right is based on a transitional fossil.

Fossils found in newer layers of Earth's crust tend to have physical or molecular similarities to present-day organisms. These similarities indicate that the fossilized organisms were close relatives of the present-day organisms. Fossils from older layers are less similar to present-day organisms than fossils from newer layers are. Most older fossils are of earlier life-forms such as dinosaurs, which don't exist anymore.

Visualize It!

A transitional form between fish and four-legged land vertebrates may be this creature called *Tiktaalik roseae*.

7 Identify Describe the environment in which this organism lives.

_____

_____

_____

8 Infer How is this organism like both a fish and a four-legged vertebrate, such as an amphibian?

_____

_____

_____

© Houghton Mifflin Harcourt Publishing Company • Image Credits: ©Zina Deretsky, National Science Foundation

More clues . . .

What other evidence supports evolution?

Many fields of study provide evidence that modern species and extinct species share an ancestor. A *common ancestor* is the most recent species from which two different species have evolved. Structural data, DNA, developmental patterns, and fossils all support the theory that populations change over time. Sometimes these populations become new species. Biologists observe that all living organisms have some traits in common and inherit traits in similar ways. Evidence of when and where those ancestors lived and what they looked like is found in the fossil record.

Active Reading

9 List What is a common ancestor?

_____

_____

_____

Common Structures

Scientists have found that related organisms share structural traits. Structures reduced in size or function may have been complete and functional in the organism's ancestor. For example, snakes have traces of leglike structures that are not used for movement. These unused structures are evidence that snakes share a common ancestor with animals like lizards and dogs.

Scientists also consider similar structures with different functions. The arm of a human, the front leg of a cat, and the wing of a bat do not look alike and are not used in the same way. But as you can see, they are similar in structure. The bones of a human arm are similar in structure to the bones in the front limbs of a cat and a bat. These similarities suggest that cats, bats, and humans had a common ancestor. Over millions of years, changes occurred. Now, these bones perform different functions in each type of animal.

front limb of a bat

front limb of a cat

Visualize It!

10 Relate Do you see any similarities between the bones of the bat and cat limbs and the bones of the human arm? If so, use the colors of the bat and cat bones to color similar bones in the human arm. If you don't have colored pencils, label the bones with the correct color names.

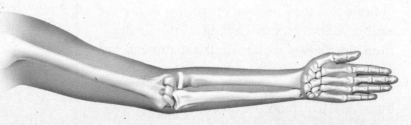

Similar DNA

The genetic information stored in an organism's DNA determines the organism's traits. Because an organism's DNA stays almost exactly the same throughout its entire lifetime, scientists can compare the DNA from many organisms. The greater the number of similarities between the molecules of any two species, the more recently the two species most likely shared a common ancestor.

Recall that DNA determines which amino acids make up a protein. Scientists have compared the amino acids that make up cytochrome c proteins in many species. Cytochrome c is involved in cellular respiration. Organisms that have fewer amino acid differences are more likely to be closely related.

Frogs also have cytochrome c proteins, but they're a little different from yours.

Cytochrome C Comparison	
Organism	Number of amino acid differences from human cytochrome c
Chimpanzee	0
Rhesus monkey	1
Whale	10
Turtle	15
Bullfrog	18
Lamprey	20

Source: M.Dayhoff, *Atlas of Protein Sequence and Structure*

Visualize It!

11 Infer The number of amino acids in human cytochrome c differs between humans and the species at left. Which two species do you infer are the least closely related to humans?

_____

_____

_____

_____

Developmental Similarities

The study of development is called *embryology.* Embryos undergo many physical and functional changes as they grow and develop. If organisms develop in similar ways, they also likely share a common ancestor.

Scientists have compared the development of different species to look for similar patterns and structures. Scientists think that such similarities come from an ancestor that the species have in common. For example, at some time during development, all animals with backbones have a tail. This observation suggests that they shared a common ancestor.

These embryos are at a similar stage of development.

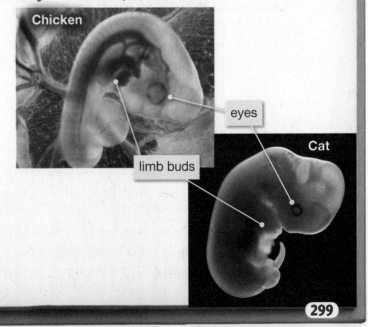

Chicken

eyes

Cat

limb buds

How do we know organisms are related?

Scientists examine organisms carefully for clues about their ancestors. In a well-studied example, scientists looked at the characteristics of whales that made them different from other ocean animals. Unlike fish and sharks, whales breathe air, give birth to live young, and produce milk. Fossil and DNA evidence support the hypothesis that modern whales evolved from hoofed mammals that lived on land.

Fossil Evidence

Scientists have examined fossils of extinct species that have features in between whales and land mammals. These features are called *transitional characters.* None of these species are directly related to modern whales. But their skeletons suggest how a gradual transition from land mammal to aquatic whale could have happened.

Ⓐ Pakicetus 52 million years ago
- whale-shaped skull and teeth adapted for hunting fish
- ran on four legs
- ear bones in between those of land and aquatic mammals

Ⓑ Ambulocetus natans 50 million years ago
- name means "the walking whale that swims"
- hind limbs that were adapted for swimming
- a fish eater that lived on water and on land

Ⓒ Dorudon About 40 million years ago
- lived in warm seas and propelled itself with a long tail
- tiny hind legs could not be used for swimming
- pelvis and hind limbs not connected to spine, could not support weight for walking

Unused Structures

Most modern whales have pelvic bones and some have leg bones. These bones do not help the animal move.

Molecular Evidence

The DNA of whales is very similar to the DNA of hoofed mammals. Below are some DNA fragments of a gene that makes a type of milk protein.

Hippopotamus   TCC TGGCA GTCCA GTGGT
Humpback whale   CCC TGGCA GTGCA GTGCT

12 Identify Circle the pairs of nitrogen bases (G, T, C, or A) that differ between the hippopotamus and humpback whale DNA.

13 Infer How do you think these bones are involved in a whale's movement?

_____

_____

_____

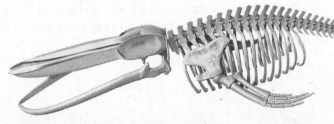

Modern Whale   *Present day*
- no hind limbs, front limbs are flippers
- some whales have tiny hip bones left over from their hoofed-mammal ancestors
- breathe air with lungs like other mammals do

14 Analyze Examine the four skeletons. Indicate which species appears to be best adapted for swimming underwater for a long time. Which characters allow the animal to behave this way?

_____

_____

_____

_____

_____

_____

Visual Summary

To complete this summary, circle the correct word. Then use the key below to check your answers. You can use this page to review the main concepts of the lesson.

Evidence of Evolution

Fossil evidence shows that life on Earth has changed over time.

15 The remains of once-living organisms are called (fossils) / ancestors.

Scientists use evidence from many fields of research to study the common ancestors of living organisms.

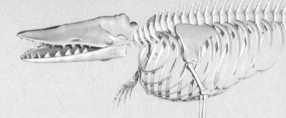

Evolutionary theory is also supported by structural, genetic, and developmental evidence.

16 (Similarities) / Differences in internal structures support evidence of common ancestry.

17 The (tiny leg bones) / large dorsal fins of modern whales are an example of unused structures.

Answers: 15 fossils, 16 similarities, 17 tiny leg bones

---

18 Summarize How does the fossil record provide evidence of the diversity of life?

Lesson Review

Vocabulary

1 Which word means "the remains or imprints of once-living organisms found in layers of rock?"

_____

2 Which word means "the history of life in the geologic past as indicated by the imprints or remains of living things?"

_____

Key Concepts

3 Identify What are two types of evidence that suggest that evolution has occurred?

_____

_____

_____

4 Explain How do fossils provide evidence that evolution has taken place?

_____

_____

_____

5 Apply What is the significance of the similar number and arrangement of bones in a human arm and a bat wing?

_____

_____

_____

_____

Critical Thinking

6 Imagine If you were a scientist examining the DNA sequence of two unknown organisms that you hypothesize share a common ancestor, what evidence would you expect to find?

_____

_____

_____

_____

Use this table to answer the following questions.

Cytochrome C Comparison	
Organism	Number of amino acid differences from human cytochrome c
Chimpanzee	0
Turtle	15
Tuna	21

Source: M. Dayhoff, *Atlas of Protein Sequence and Structure*

7 Identify What do the data suggest about how related turtles are to humans compared to tuna and chimpanzees?

_____

_____

_____

_____

8 Infer If there are no differences between the amino acid sequences in the cytochrome c protein of humans and chimpanzees, why aren't we the same species?

_____

_____

_____

_____

_____

9 Apply Explain why the pattern of differences that exists from earlier to later fossils in the fossil record supports the idea that evolution has taken place on Earth.

_____

_____

_____

_____

_____

My Notes

Unit 5 **Summary**

Life over Time

is described by

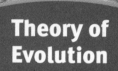

Evidence of Evolution

supports the

Theory of Evolution

---

1 Interpret The Graphic Organizer above shows that life over time is described by evidence of evolution. Name two types of evidence that support evolution.

_____

_____

_____

_____

2 Explain Did the finches that Darwin observed on the Galápagos Islands show evidence of evolution? Explain.

_____

_____

_____

_____

_____

_____

3 Compare How is natural selection different from evolution?

_____

_____

_____

_____

_____

_____

4 Explain The fossil record reveals changes over time in the environment. Why might a scientist studying evolution be interested in how the environment has changed over time?

_____

_____

_____

_____

Name _____

Multiple Choice

Identify the choice that best completes the statement or answers the question.

1 While exploring a rock formation, Hiroto finds a rock that has footprints pressed into it. A geologist tells Hiroto that the rock is millions of years old. Which of these statements is **correct** about Hiroto's find?

   A. It is not a fossil, because footprints are not fossils.

   B. It is not a fossil, because only whole organisms are fossils.

   C. It is a fossil only if Hiroto finds actual parts of the organism in rocks nearby.

   D. It is a fossil because footprints of organisms from million of years ago are considered to be fossils.

2 The diagram below shows a model of the proposed relationships between some groups of ancient and modern mammals. Branch points represent when two species diverged from the proposed common ancestor.

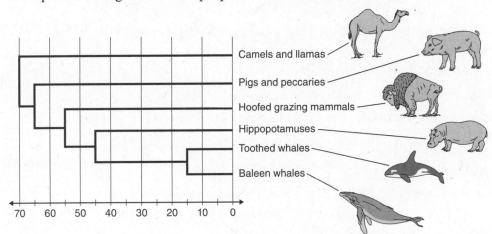

Which of these organisms is **most closely** related to whales?

   F. bison

   G. camel

   H. hippo

   I. pig

3 Which of these conditions is **least likely** to cause a species to become extinct due to environmental changes?

   A. less genetic variation

   B. more genetic variation

   C. specific food preferences

   D. more competition for food

4 The diagram below shows a portion of the fossil record in sedimentary rock. Different rock layers and fossils are clearly visible.

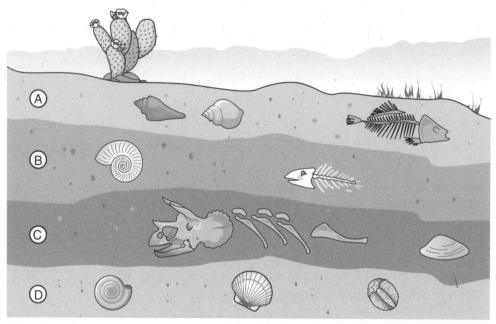

Which of these statements is **true** of the fossils and rock layers shown in the diagram?

F. Layer B contains the second-oldest fossils.

G. Layer A contains the most recently formed fossils.

H. The fossils in layer B are older than those in layer D.

I. The fossils in layer D are the most recently formed.

5 When farmers want two desirable traits in cows, they often breed individuals that have those traits in the hopes that the offspring will have both desirable traits. What is this practice called?

A. variation

B. adaptation

C. natural selection

D. artificial selection

6   Ronald observes a sparrow's nest in a shrub outside his home. The table below describes his findings.

Week	Observations
1	Six eggs were laid in the nest.
3	Five eggs hatched, and one egg did not hatch.
4	One of the chicks disappeared.
7	Three of the chicks learned to fly, and another one disappeared.

What part of natural selection did Ronald observe?

F.   adaptation

G.   overproduction

H.   selection

I.   variation

7   Environmental changes may lead to the evolution of a species. Polar bears live in the Arctic. Ice in the Arctic is melting fast, reducing the range where the polar bear can live. If polar bears do not have adaptations that allow them to survive these changes, what may happen to them?

A.   They may become extinct.

B.   They may overpopulate.

C.   They may change the environment.

D.   They may become another species.

8   Juan is studying fossils. His teacher wrote the following statements on the board and asked the students to put them in the correct order to describe how fossils are formed.

1. Minerals seep into the organism's body and replace it with stone.
2. The organism completely decomposes, leaving behind an imprint.
3. An organism dies and its body is covered with a layer of sediment.
4. Time passes, and sediment layers continue to build up on the organism.

Which is the correct order of events for fossil formation?

F.   3, 4, 1, 2

G.   2, 3, 4, 1

H.   1, 3, 2, 4

I.   3, 2, 1, 4

© Houghton Mifflin Harcourt Publishing Company

9 When Charles Darwin observed finches on the Galápagos Islands, he noted differences in the shapes of the birds' beaks. He observed that finches that ate insects had longer, narrower beaks than finches that crushed and ate seeds. Which finch shown below is **most likely** adapted to eating seeds?

A.

B.

C.

D.

10 At the zoo, Anya observes that the red kangaroos are of several sizes and colors. What characteristic of populations is Anya observing?

F. adaptation

G. evolution

H. selection

I. variation

11 Fossils enable scientists to piece together what ancient organisms looked like. Which of these answers **best** describes how fossils are classified?

A. by features of the organism that can be observed in the fossil

B. by the type of rock in which they are found

C. by the size of the fossils

D. by similarities in their DNA and in the minerals they contain

12 A species of rodent lives in a moist forest. Over time, the climate becomes drier and more desert-like. Which of these adaptations is most likely to improve the chances that the species will survive as its environment changes?

F. being able to eat plants that survive in the changed environment

G. being able to eat only one type of berry

H. living above ground in damp areas

I. having dark hair and small ears

Reproduction and Heredity

Big Idea 16

Heredity and Reproduction

What do you think?

Every organism—including oranges and dogs—that reproduces shares traits with its offspring. How are qualities passed on from generation to generation?

CITIZEN SCIENCE
Pass It On

Heredity was a mystery that scientists worked to crack over hundreds of years. The modern field of genetics is vital to the understanding of hereditary diseases. The study of genetics can also predict which traits will be passed from parent to offspring.

1856–1863

Many people consider Gregor Mendel to be the Father of Modern Genetics. His famous pea plant experiments, conducted from 1856–1863, helped to illustrate and establish the laws of inheritance.

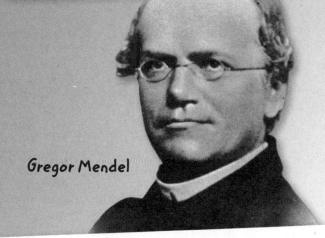

Gregor Mendel

Can you predict the traits Mendel might have examined in pea plants? What traits might a fruit or vegetable plant inherit from a parent plant?

_____

_____

_____

_____

_____

Pairs of chromosomes, viewed under a microscope

Fruit fly

DNA samples

1882
Walther Flemming discovered chromosomes while observing the process of cell division. He didn't know it, but chromosomes pass characteristics from parents to offspring.

1908
Thomas Hunt Morgan was the first to actually realize that chromosomes carry traits. Morgan's fruit fly studies established that genes are located on chromosomes. Studies using fruit flies are still happening.

2003
Our DNA carries information about all of our traits. In fact, the human genome is made up of 20,000–25,000 genes! In 2003, the Human Genome Project successfully mapped the first human genome.

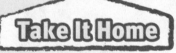

Take It Home **Making Trait Predictions**

① Think About It

Different factors influence appearance. Family members may look similar in some ways but different in others. What factors influence a person's appearance?

_____
_____
_____

② Ask Some Questions

Can you spot any physical characteristics, like bent or straight pinky fingers, that people in your family share?

_____
_____
_____

③ Make A Plan

Consider the characteristics that are most distinctive in your family. How can you trace the way these characteristics have been passed through the family? Design an investigation of hereditary characteristics in your family.

_____
_____
_____

Describe how these characteristics might be the same or different as they are passed on to offspring. What factors might influence this? Make notes here, and illustrate your descriptions on a separate sheet of paper.

_____
_____

Mitosis

ESSENTIAL QUESTION

How do cells divide?

By the end of this lesson, you should be able to relate the process of mitosis to its functions in single-celled and multicellular organisms.

A human skin cell divides, producing two new cells that are identical to the original cell.

🔄 Sunshine State Standards

SC.7.L.16.3 Compare and contrast the general processes of sexual reproduction requiring meiosis and asexual reproduction requiring mitosis.

LA.6.4.2.2 The student will record information (e.g., observations, notes, lists, charts, legends) related to a topic, including visual aids to organize and record information and include a list of sources used.

Engage Your Brain

1 Predict Check T or F to show whether you think each statement is true or false.

T	F	
☐	☐	Single-celled organisms can reproduce by cell division.
☐	☐	The only function of cell division is reproduction.
☐	☐	In multicellular organisms, cell division can help repair injured areas.
☐	☐	Cell division produces two cells that are different from each other.

2 Infer An old sequoia tree weighs many tons and has billions of cells. These trees start out as tiny seeds. Predict how these trees get so large.

_____

_____

_____

_____

Active Reading

3 Synthesize You can often define an unknown word if you know the meaning of its word parts. Use the word parts and sentence below to make an educated guess about the meaning of the word *cytokinesis*.

Word part	Meaning
cyto-	hollow vessel
-kinesis	division

Example sentence
When a dividing cell undergoes <u>cytokinesis</u>, two cells are produced.

Vocabulary Terms

- DNA
- chromosomes
- cell cycle
- interphase
- mitosis
- cytokinesis

4 Apply As you learn the definition of each vocabulary term in this lesson, write your own definition or make a sketch to help you remember the meaning of the term.

cytokinesis:

_____

_____

_____

Splitsville!

Why do cells divide?

Cell division happens in all organisms. Cell division takes place for different reasons. For example, single-celled organisms reproduce through cell division. In multicellular organisms, cell division is involved in growth, development, and repair, as well as reproduction.

Reproduction

Cell division is important for asexual reproduction, which involves only one parent organism. In single-celled organisms, the parent divides in two, producing two identical offspring. In single-celled and some multicellular organisms, offspring result when a parent organism buds, producing offspring. In multicellular organisms, reproduction by cell division can include plant structures such as runners and plantlets.

Growth and Repair

One characteristic of all living things is that they grow. You are probably bigger this year than you were last year. Your body is made up of cells. Although cells themselves grow, most growth in multicellular organisms happens because cell division produces new cells.

Cell division also produces cells for repair. If you cut your hand or break a bone, the damaged cells are replaced by new cells that form during cell division.

 Visualize It!

5 Apply Take a look at the photos below. Underneath each photo, describe the role of cell division in what is taking place.

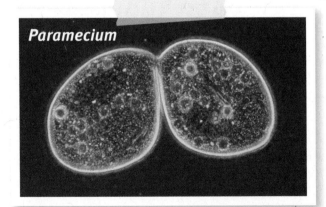

Paramecium

Starfish

Role of cell division:

_____

_____

Role of cell division:

_____

_____

What happens to genetic material during cell division?

The genetic material in cells is called DNA (deoxyribonucleic acid). A **DNA** molecule contains the information that determines the traits that a living thing inherits and needs to live. It contains instructions for an organism's growth, development, and activities. In eukaryotes, DNA is found in the nucleus.

During most of a cell's life cycle, DNA, along with proteins, exists in a complex material called *chromatin* (KROH•muh•tin). Before cell division, DNA is duplicated, or copied. Then, in an early stage of cell division, the chromatin is compacted into visible structures called **chromosomes** (KROH•muh•sohmz). A duplicated chromosome consists of two identical structures called *chromatids* (KROH•muh•tidz). The chromatids are held together by a *centromere* (SEN•truh•mir).

© Houghton Mifflin Harcourt Publishing Company • Image Credits: (cl) ©Andrew Syred/Photo Researchers, Inc.; (bl) ©Biophoto Associates/Photo Researchers, Inc.

Active Reading

6 Describe What happens to DNA before cell division?

_____

_____

_____

_____

Chromosome
A duplicated chromosome has two chromatids, which are held together by a centromere.

Centromere

Chromatid

A chromosome is made of compacted chromatin.

Chromatin
Chromatin is made up of DNA and proteins.

Protein

DNA

DNA
DNA is found in the nucleus of a eukaryotic cell.

Visualize It!

7 Analyze What happens to chromatin in the early stages of cell division?

_____

_____

_____

Around and Around

What are the stages of the cell cycle?

The life cycle of an organism includes birth, growth, reproduction, and death. The life cycle of a eukaryotic cell, called the **cell cycle,** can be divided into three stages: interphase, mitosis, and cytokinesis. During the cell cycle, a parent cell divides into two new cells. The new cells are identical to the parent.

Active Reading

8 Identify As you read, underline the main characteristics of each stage of the cell cycle.

Interphase

The part of the cell cycle during which the cell is not dividing is called **interphase** (IN•ter•fayz). A lot of activity takes place in this stage of the cell's life. The cell grows to about twice the size it was when it was first produced. It also produces various organelles. The cell engages in normal life activities, such as transporting materials into the cell and getting rid of wastes.

Changes that occur during interphase prepare a cell for division. Before a cell can divide, DNA must be duplicated. This ensures that, after cell division, each new cell gets an exact copy of the genetic material in the original cell.

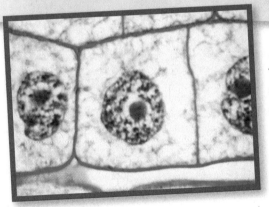

During interphase, the cell carries out normal life activities.

INTERPHASE

Active Reading

9 Describe What happens during interphase?

_____

_____

_____

_____

_____

Mitosis

In eukaryotic cells, **mitosis** (my•TOH•sis) is the part of the cell cycle during which the nucleus divides. Prokaryotes do not undergo mitosis because they do not have a nucleus. Mitosis results in two nuclei that are identical to the original nucleus. So, the two new cells formed after cell division have the same genetic material. During mitosis, chromosomes condense from chromatin. When viewed with a microscope, chromosomes are visible inside the nucleus. At the end of mitosis, the cell has two identical sets of chromosomes in two separate nuclei.

During mitosis, the cell's nucleus divides into two identical nuclei.

MITOSIS

Prophase
Metaphase
Anaphase
Telophase

CYTOKINESIS

Cytokinesis

Cytokinesis (sy•toh•kuh•NEE•sis) is the division of the parent cell's cytoplasm. Cytokinesis begins during the last step of mitosis. During cytokinesis, the cell membrane pinches inward between the new nuclei. Eventually, it pinches all the way, forming two complete cells.

In a cell that has a cell wall, such as a plant cell, a cell plate forms. The cell plate becomes cell membranes that separate the new cells. New cell walls form where the plate was.

During cytokinesis, the cytoplasm divides and two new cells are produced.

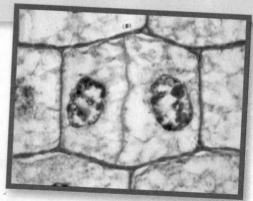

Visualize It!

10 Interpret Based on this diagram, in what stage does a cell spend most of its time?

_____

_____

Phasing Out

What are the phases of mitosis?

Mitosis has four phases: prophase (PROH•fayz), metaphase (MET•uh•fayz), anaphase (AN•uh•fayz), and telophase (TEE•luh•fayz). By the end of these phases, the cell will have two identical nuclei and cytokinesis will begin.

Active Reading

11 Identify As you read, underline the major events that take place in each phase of mitosis.

Prophase

During prophase, the chromatin in the nucleus of a cell condenses and becomes visible under a microscope. Each chromosome consists of two chromatids held together by a centromere. The membrane around the nucleus breaks down.

Metaphase

During metaphase, chromosomes line up in the middle of the cell. Centromeres of the chromosomes are the same distance from each side of the cell.

Anaphase

During anaphase, the chromatids separate. They are pulled to opposite sides of the cell. Each side of the cell ends up with a complete set of chromosomes.

During interphase, DNA is duplicated.

Prophase

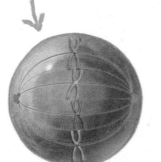

Metaphase

Anaphase

Think Outside the Book (Inquiry)

12 Model With a small group, write a play that acts out the steps of mitosis. Trade your play with another group, and perform the play for your classmates.

Both new cells start the cycle again.

After mitosis, cytokinesis results in two new cells.

Telophase

Telophase

The last phase of mitosis is telophase. A new nuclear membrane forms around each group of chromosomes. So, the cell now has two identical nuclei. The chromosomes become less condensed. Cytokinesis begins during this phase.

13 Apply Use the table below to draw a picture for each step of the cell cycle.

Step	Drawing
Interphase	
Mitosis: Prophase	
Mitosis: Metaphase	
Mitosis: Anaphase	
Mitosis: Telophase	
Cytokinesis	

Visual Summary

To complete this summary, fill in the blanks with the correct word or phrase. Then, use the key below to check your answers. You can use this page to review the main concepts of the lesson.

During the cell cycle, cells divide to produce two identical cells.

14 Three reasons that cells divide are

_____

_____

_____

DNA is duplicated before cell division.

15 Loose chromatin is compacted into

_____ ,

each of which has two

_____ that are

held together by a centromere.

Mitosis

The cell cycle is the life cycle of a cell.

16 They lack nuclei, so prokaryotes do not undergo _____

17 The cell produces organelles during _____

18 _____ results in the formation of two new cells.

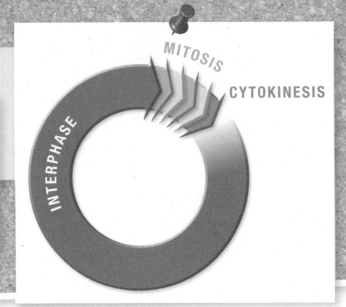

INTERPHASE · MITOSIS · CYTOKINESIS

Answers: 14 reproduction, growth, repair; 15 chromosomes, chromatids; 16 mitosis; 17 interphase; 18 Cytokinesis

---

19 Summarize Briefly describe the four phases of mitosis.

Lesson Review

Vocabulary

Fill in the blanks with the term that best completes the following sentences.

1 _____ provides the information for cell growth and function.

2 The cell spends most of its time in the _____ stage of the cell cycle.

3 After _____ , the nucleus of the parent cell has divided into two new nuclei.

4 A _____ is the condensed, visible form of chromatin.

Key Concepts

5 Relate What happens in a cell during interphase?

_____

_____

_____

_____

6 Compare Describe the functions of cell division in single-celled and multicellular organisms.

_____

_____

_____

_____

7 Explain Why is it important for DNA to be duplicated before mitosis?

_____

_____

_____

_____

Critical Thinking

Use the figures below to answer the questions that follow.

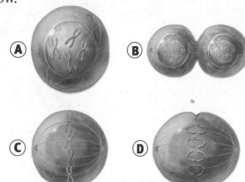

8 Sequence Starting with prophase, what is the correct order of the four diagrams above?

_____

9 Identify What phase is shown in each of the diagrams above?

_____

_____

_____

_____

10 Describe What is happening to the cell in diagram B?

_____

_____

_____

_____

11 Predict What would happen if the cell went through mitosis but not cytokinesis?

_____

_____

_____

_____

_____

_____

Lesson 2
Meiosis

ESSENTIAL QUESTION

How do cells divide for sexual reproduction?

By the end of this lesson, you should be able to describe the process of meiosis and its role in sexual reproduction.

Sunshine State Standards

SC.7.L.16.3 Compare and contrast the general processes of sexual reproduction requiring meiosis and asexual reproduction requiring mitosis.

LA.6.4.2.2 The student will record information (e.g., observations, notes, lists, charts, legends) related to a topic, including visual aids to organize and record information and include a list of sources used.

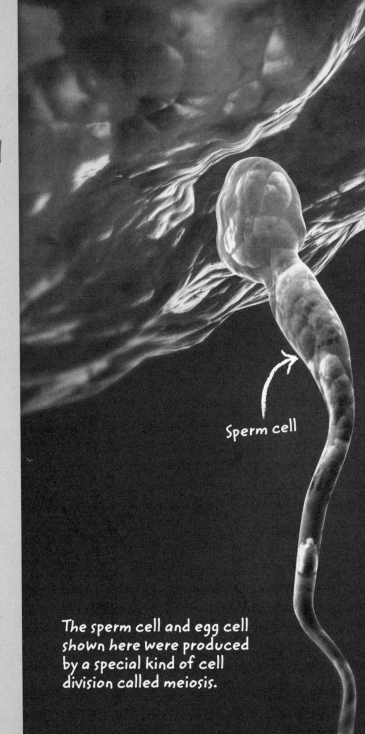

Egg cell

Sperm cell

The sperm cell and egg cell shown here were produced by a special kind of cell division called meiosis.

Engage Your Brain

1 Predict Check T or F to show whether you think each statement is true or false.

T	F	
☐	☐	The offspring of sexual reproduction have fewer chromosomes than their parents have.
☐	☐	During sexual reproduction, two cells combine to form a new organism.
☐	☐	Sex cells are produced by cell division.
☐	☐	Sex cells have half the normal number of chromosomes.

2 Calculate Organisms have a set number of chromosomes. For example, humans have 46 chromosomes in body cells and half that number (23) in sex cells. In the table below, fill in the number of chromosomes for different organisms.

Organism	Full set of chromosomes	Half set of chromosomes
Human	46	23
Fruit fly		4
Chicken		39
Salamander	24	
Potato	48	

Active Reading

3 Synthesize You can often define an unknown word if you know the meaning of its word parts. Use the word parts and the sentence below to make an educated guess about the meaning of the term *homologous*.

Word part	Meaning
homo-	same
-logos	word, structure

Example sentence
Homologous chromosomes are a pair of chromosomes that look similar and have the same genes.

homologous:

_____

_____

_____

Vocabulary Terms
- homologous chromosomes
- meiosis

4 Apply As you learn the definition of each vocabulary term in this lesson, write your own definition or make a sketch to help you remember the meaning of the term.

Number Off!

How do sex cells differ from body cells?

Before sexual reproduction can take place, each parent produces sex cells. *Sex cells* have half of the genetic information that body cells have. Thus, when the genetic information from two parents combines, the offspring have a full set of genetic information. The offspring will have the same total number of chromosomes as each of its parents.

Active Reading **5 Relate** Describe sex cells.

This photo shows the 23 chromosome pairs in a human male. Body cells contain all of these chromosomes. Sex cells contain one chromosome from each pair.

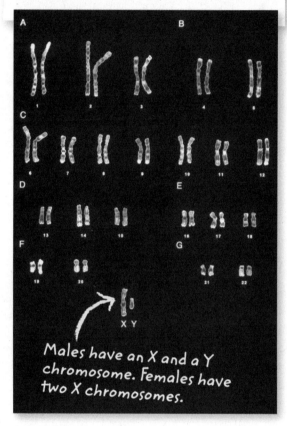

Males have an X and a Y chromosome. Females have two X chromosomes.

Chromosome Number

In body cells, most chromosomes are found in pairs that have the same structure and size. These **homologous chromosomes** (huh•MAHL•uh•guhs KROH•muh•sohmz) carry the same genes. A homologous chromosome pair may have different versions of the genes they carry. One chromosome pair is made up of *sex chromosomes.* Sex chromosomes control the development of sexual characteristics. In humans, these chromosomes are called X and Y chromosomes. Cells with a pair of every chromosome are called *diploid* (DIP•loyd). Many organisms, including humans, have diploid body cells.

Visualize It! (Inquiry)

6 Predict The cell shown is a body cell that has two pairs of homologous chromosomes. Use the space to the right to draw a sex cell for the same organism.

Body cell   Sex cell

Why do organisms need sex cells?

Most human body cells contain 46 chromosomes. Think about what would happen if two body cells were to combine. The resulting cell would have twice the normal number of chromosomes. A sex cell is needed to keep this from happening.

Sex cells are also known as *gametes* (GAM•eetz). Gametes contain half the usual number of chromosomes—one chromosome from each homologous pair and one sex chromosome. Cells that contain half the usual number of chromosomes are known as *haploid* (HAP•loyd).

Gametes are found in the reproductive organs of plants and animals. An egg is a gamete that forms in female reproductive organs. The gamete that forms in male reproductive organs is called a sperm cell.

How are sex cells made?

You know that body cells divide by the process of mitosis. Mitosis produces two new cells, each containing exact copies of the chromosomes in the parent cell. Each new cell has a full set of chromosomes. But to produce sex cells, a different kind of cell division is needed.

Meiosis

A human egg and a human sperm cell each have 23 chromosomes. When an egg is joined with, or *fertilized* by, a sperm cell, a new diploid cell is formed. This new cell has 46 chromosomes, or 23 pairs of chromosomes. One set is from the mother, and the other set is from the father. The newly formed diploid cell may develop into an offspring. **Meiosis** (my•OH•sis) is the type of cell division that produces haploid sex cells such as eggs and sperm cells.

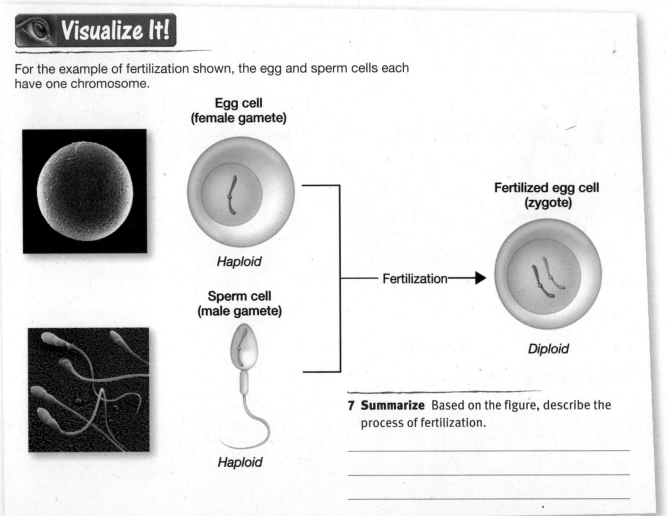

Visualize It!

For the example of fertilization shown, the egg and sperm cells each have one chromosome.

Egg cell (female gamete)

Haploid

Sperm cell (male gamete)

Haploid

→ Fertilization →

Fertilized egg cell (zygote)

Diploid

7 Summarize Based on the figure, describe the process of fertilization.

_____

_____

_____

One Step at a Time

What are the stages of meiosis?

Meiosis results in the formation of four haploid cells. Each haploid cell has half the number of chromosomes found in the original cell. Meiosis has two parts: meiosis I and meiosis II.

Meiosis I

Remember that homologous chromosomes have the same genes, but they are not exact copies of each other. Before meiosis I begins, each chromosome is duplicated, or copied. Each half of a duplicated chromosome is called a *chromatid* (KROH•muh•tid). Chromatids are connected to each other by *centromeres* (SEN•truh•mirz). Duplicated chromosomes are drawn in an **X** shape. Each side of the **X** represents a chromatid, and the point where they touch is the centromere.

During meiosis I, pairs of homologous chromosomes and sex chromosomes split apart into two new cells. These cells each have one-half of the chromosome pairs and their duplicate chromatids. The steps of meiosis I are shown below.

Active Reading

8 Sequence As you read, underline what happens to chromosomes during meiosis.

Duplicated homologous chromosomes

Half of a homologous chromosome pair

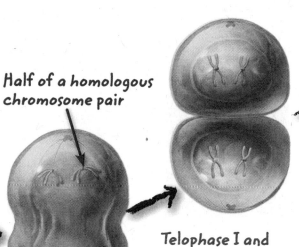

Prophase I
The chromosomes are copied before meiosis begins. The duplicated chromosomes, each made up of two chromatids, pair up.

Metaphase I
After the nuclear membrane breaks down, the chromosome pairs line up in the middle of the cell.

Anaphase I
The chromosomes separate from their partners, and then move to opposite ends of the cell.

Telophase I and cytokinesis
The nuclear membranes re-form, and the cell divides into two cells. The chromatids are still joined.

9 Contrast How does meiosis II differ from meiosis I?

_____

_____

_____

_____

Centromere

Chromatid

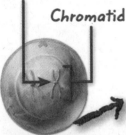

Telophase II and cytokinesis
The nuclear membranes re-form and the cells divide. Four new haploid cells are formed. Each has half the usual number of chromosomes.

Anaphase II
The chromatids are pulled apart and move to opposite sides of the cell.

Metaphase II
The chromosomes line up in the middle of each cell.

Prophase II
The chromosomes are not copied again before meiosis II. The nuclear membrane breaks down.

Think Outside the Book

10 Summarize Work with a partner to make a poster that describes all the steps of meiosis.

Meiosis II

Meiosis II involves both of the new cells formed during meiosis I. The chromosomes of these cells are not copied before meiosis II begins. Both of the cells divide during meiosis II. The steps of meiosis II are shown above.

Meiosis II results in four haploid sex cells. In male organisms, these cells develop into sperm cells. In female organisms, these cells become eggs. In females of some species, three of the cells are broken down and only one haploid cell becomes an egg.

11 Identify At the end of meiosis II, how many cells have formed?

_____

How does meiosis compare to mitosis?

The processes of meiosis and mitosis are similar in many ways. However, they also have several very important differences.

- Only cells that will become sex cells go through meiosis. All other cells divide by mitosis.
- During meiosis, chromosomes are copied once, and then the nucleus divides twice. During mitosis, the chromosomes are copied once, and then the nucleus divides once.
- The cells produced by meiosis contain only half of the genetic material of the parent cell—one chromosome from each homologous pair and one sex chromosome. The cells produced by mitosis contain exactly the same genetic material as the parent—a full set of homologous chromosomes and a pair of sex chromosomes.

Single chromosome   Single chromosome

Cell produced by meiosis (haploid)

Chromosome pair   Chromosome pair

Cell produced by mitosis (diploid)

12 Summarize Using the table below, compare meiosis and mitosis.

Characteristic	Meiosis	Mitosis
Number of nuclear divisions		
Number of cells produced		
Number of chromosomes in new cells (diploid or haploid)		
Type of cell produced (body cell or sex cell)		
Steps of the process		

Down Syndrome

HEALTH WATCH

Down syndrome is a genetic disease. It is usually caused by an error during meiosis. During meiosis, the chromatids of chromosome 21 do not separate. So, a sex cell gets two copies of chromosome 21 instead of one copy. When this sex cell joins with a normal egg or sperm, the fertilized egg has three copies of chromosome 21 instead of two copies.

Beating the Odds

Down syndrome causes a number of health problems and learning difficulties, but many people with Down syndrome have fulfilling lives.

1 2 3 4 5

6 7

11 12

One Too Many
Someone who has Down syndrome has three copies of chromosome 21 instead of two copies.

18

19 20 21 22

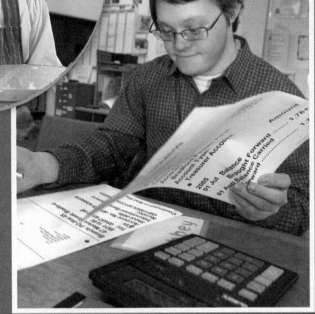

Extend

Inquiry

13 Identify What type of error in meiosis causes Down syndrome?

14 Investigate Research the characteristics of Down syndrome. How can some of the difficulties caused by the disorder be overcome?

15 Recommend Research the Special Olympics. Then make an informative brochure, poster, or oral presentation that describes how the Special Olympics gives people with Down syndrome and other disabilities the chance to compete in sports.

Visual Summary

To complete this summary, fill in the blanks with the correct word or phrase. Then use the key below to check your answers. You can use this page to review the main concepts of the lesson.

Meiosis

Meiosis produces haploid cells that can become sex cells.

16 List the steps of meiosis I.

_____

_____

_____

_____

17 List the steps of meiosis II.

_____

_____

_____

_____

Sex cells have half as many chromosomes as body cells.

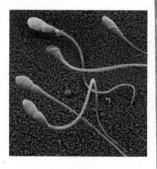

18 Sex cells produced by males are called _____, and sex cells produced by females are called _____

Mitosis and meiosis have similarities and differences.

Single chromosome

Single chromosome

Chromosome pair

Chromosome pair

Cell produced by meiosis (haploid)

Cell produced by mitosis (diploid)

19 During _____, chromosomes are copied once and the nucleus divides twice.

20 During _____, chromosomes are copied once and the nucleus divides once.

Answers: 16 prophase I, metaphase I, anaphase I, telophase I and cytokinesis; 17 prophase II, metaphase II, anaphase II, telophase II and cytokinesis; 18 sperm cells, eggs; 19 meiosis; 20 mitosis

21 Summarize Briefly describe what happens during meiosis I and meiosis II.

Lesson Review

Vocabulary

Fill in the blanks with the term that best completes the following sentences.

1 _____ chromosomes are found in body cells but not sex cells.

2 The process of _____ produces haploid cells.

Key Concepts

3 Compare How does the number of chromosomes in sex cells compare with the number of chromosomes in body cells?

_____

_____

_____

4 Identify What is the function of meiosis?

_____

_____

_____

5 List Identify the steps of meiosis.

_____

_____

_____

_____

_____

_____

6 Compare How are mitosis and meiosis alike and different?

_____

_____

_____

_____

_____

_____

_____

Critical Thinking

Use the figure to answer the following questions.

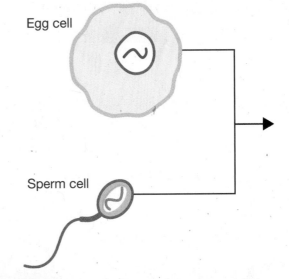

Egg cell

Sperm cell

7 Identify By what process did these cells form?

_____

8 Identify How many chromosomes does a body cell for the organism shown have?

_____

9 Predict Draw a picture of the cell that would form if the sperm cell fused with the egg cell. What is this cell called?

10 Synthesize What would happen if meiosis did not occur?

_____

_____

_____

_____

Sexual and Asexual Reproduction

ESSENTIAL QUESTION

How do organisms reproduce?

By the end of this lesson, you should be able to describe asexual and sexual reproduction and list the advantages and disadvantages of each.

Female wolf spiders carry their young on their backs for a short period of time after the young hatch.

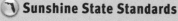

🜋 Sunshine State Standards

SC.7.L.16.3 Compare and contrast the general processes of sexual reproduction requiring meiosis and asexual reproduction requiring mitosis.

LA.6.4.2.2 The student will record information (e.g., observations, notes, lists, charts, legends) related to a topic, including visual aids to organize and record information and include a list of sources used.

Engage Your Brain

1 Predict Check T or F to show whether you think each statement is true or false.

T F

☐ ☐ Reproduction requires two parents.

☐ ☐ Some organisms reproduce by cell division.

☐ ☐ New plants can grow from parts of a parent plant, such as roots and stems.

☐ ☐ Offspring of two parents always look like one of their parents.

2 Describe How is the young wolf in the photo below similar to its mother?

_____

_____

_____

Active Reading

3 Synthesize You can often define an unknown word if you know the meaning of its word parts. Use the word parts and sentence below to make an educated guess about the meaning of the word *reproduction*.

Word part	Meaning
re-	again
produce	to make
-ion	act or process

Example sentence
Flowers are plant organs that are used for reproduction.

reproduction:

_____

_____

Vocabulary Terms

- asexual reproduction
- sexual reproduction
- fertilization

4 Apply As you learn the definition of each vocabulary term in this lesson, write your own definition or make a sketch to help you remember the meaning of the term.

One Becomes Two

What is asexual reproduction?

An individual organism does not live forever. The survival of any species depends on the ability to reproduce. Reproduction lets genetic information be passed on to new organisms. Reproduction involves various kinds of cell division.

Most single-celled organisms and some multicellular organisms reproduce asexually. In **asexual reproduction** (ay•SEHK•shoo•uhl ree•pruh•DUHK•shuhn), one organism produces one or more new organisms that are identical to itself. These organisms live independently of the original organism. The organism that produces the new organism or organisms is called a *parent*. Each new organism is called an *offspring*. The parent passes on all of its genetic information to the offspring. So, the offspring produced by asexual reproduction are genetically identical to their parents. They may differ only if a genetic mutation happens.

Active Reading

5 Relate Describe the genetic makeup of the offspring of asexual reproduction.

_____

_____

_____

Dandelions usually reproduce asexually. The dandelions in this field may all be genetically identical!

Think Outside the Book (Inquiry)

6 Summarize Research five organisms that reproduce asexually. Make informative flash cards that describe how each organism reproduces asexually. When you have finished, trade flashcards with a classmate to learn about five more organisms.

How do organisms reproduce asexually?

Organisms reproduce asexually in many ways. In prokaryotes, which include bacteria and archaea, asexual reproduction happens by cell division. In eukaryotes, which include single-celled and multicellular organisms, asexual reproduction is a more involved process. It often involves a type of cell division called *mitosis* (my•TOH•sis). Mitosis produces genetically identical cells.

Binary Fission

Binary fission (BY•nuh•ree FISH•uhn) is the form of asexual reproduction in prokaryotes. It is a type of cell division. During binary fission, the parent organism splits in two, producing two new cells. Genetically, the new cells are exactly like the parent cell.

Budding

During *budding,* an organism develops tiny buds on its body. A bud grows until it forms a new full-sized organism that is genetically identical to the parent. Budding is the result of mitosis. Eukaryotes such as single-celled yeasts and multicellular hydras reproduce by budding.

Spores

A *spore* is a specialized cell that can survive harsh conditions. Both prokaryotes and eukaryotes can form spores. Spores are produced asexually by one parent. Spores are light and can be carried by the wind. In the right conditions, a spore develops into an organism, such as a fungus.

Vegetative Reproduction

Some plants are able to reproduce asexually by *vegetative reproduction.* Mitosis makes vegetative reproduction possible. New plants may grow from stems, roots, or leaves. Runners are aboveground stems from which a new plant can grow. Tubers are underground stems from which new plants can grow. Plantlets are tiny plants that grow along the edges of a plant's leaves. They drop off the plant and grow on their own.

Visualize It!

7 Infer Pick one of the pictures below. Describe how the type of asexual reproduction can help the organism reproduce quickly.

_____

_____

_____

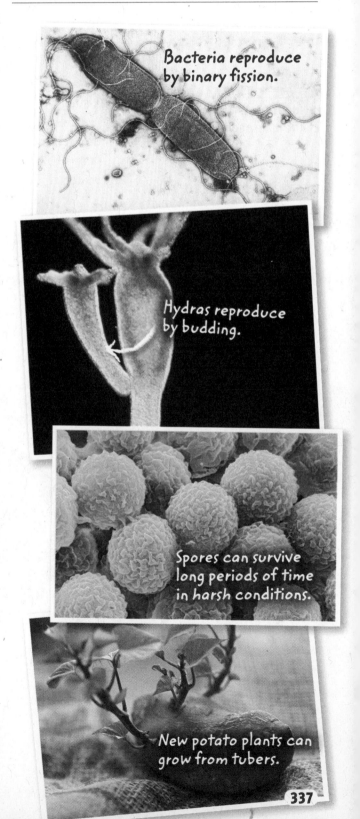

Bacteria reproduce by binary fission.

Hydras reproduce by budding.

Spores can survive long periods of time in harsh conditions.

New potato plants can grow from tubers.

Two Make One

What is sexual reproduction?

Most multicellular organisms can reproduce sexually. In **sexual reproduction** (SEHK•shoo•uhl ree•pruh•DUHK•shuhn), two parents each contribute a sex cell to the new organism. Half the genes in the offspring come from each parent. So, the offspring are not identical to either parent. Instead, they have a combination of traits from each parent.

Fertilization

Usually, one parent is male and the other is female. Males produce sex cells called *sperm cells.* Females produce sex cells called *eggs.* Sex cells are produced by a type of cell division called *meiosis* (my•OH•sis). Sex cells have only half of the full set of genetic material found in body cells.

A sperm cell and an egg join together in a process called **fertilization** (fer•tl•i•ZAY•shuhn). When an egg is fertilized by a sperm cell, a new cell is formed. This cell is called a *zygote* (ZY•goht). It has a full set of genetic material. The zygote develops into a new organism. The zygote divides by mitosis, which increases the number of cells. This increase in cells produces growth. You are the size that you are today because of mitosis.

Active Reading

8 Identify As you read, underline the male and female sex cells.

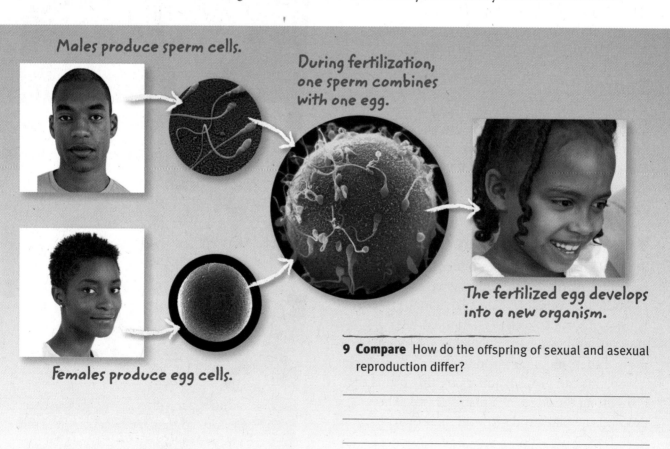

Males produce sperm cells.

During fertilization, one sperm combines with one egg.

The fertilized egg develops into a new organism.

Females produce egg cells.

9 Compare How do the offspring of sexual and asexual reproduction differ?

_____

_____

_____

Odd Reproduction

It may seem like only single-celled organisms undergo asexual reproduction. However, many multicellular organisms reproduce asexually.

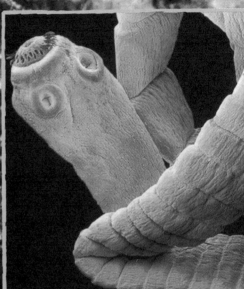

Original arm

Appearing Act
Some organisms, such as aphids, reproduce asexually by *parthenogenesis*. A female produces young without fertilization.

Falling to Pieces
Tapeworms can reproduce asexually by *fragmentation*. Each segment of the worm can become a new organism if it breaks off of the worm.

Newly grown body and arms

Seeing Stars
Organisms such as starfish reproduce asexually by *regeneration*. Even a small part of the starfish can grow into a new organism.

Extend

Inquiry

10 Identify Which types of asexual reproduction involve part of an organism breaking off?

11 Investigate Research the advantages and disadvantages of a type of reproduction shown on this page.

12 Hypothesize A female shark was left alone in an aquarium tank. She was not pregnant when placed in the tank. But scientists were surprised one morning to find a baby shark in the tank. Form a hypothesis about what type of reproduction took place in this scenario.

Added Advantage

What are the advantages of each type of reproduction?

Organisms reproduce asexually, sexually, or both. Each type of reproduction has advantages. For example, sexual reproduction involves complex structures, such as flowers and other organs. These are not needed for asexual reproduction. But the offspring of sexual reproduction may be more likely to survive in certain situations. Read on to find out more about the advantages of each.

13 Compare Use the Venn diagram below to compare asexual and sexual reproduction.

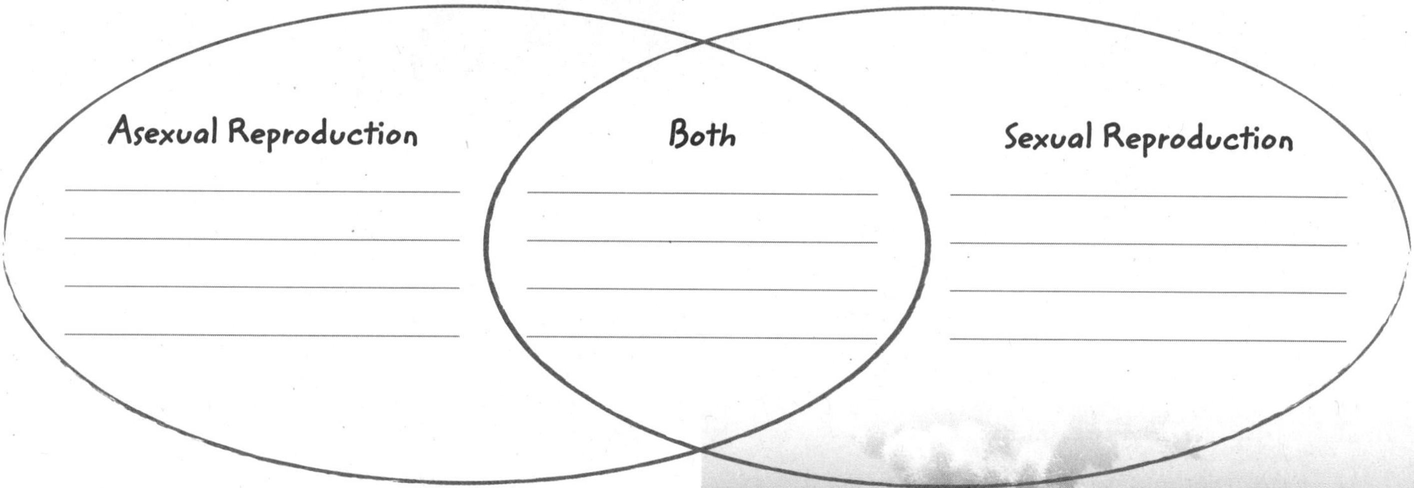

Asexual Reproduction
_____
_____
_____
_____

Both
_____
_____
_____
_____

Sexual Reproduction
_____
_____
_____
_____

Advantages of Asexual Reproduction

Asexual reproduction has many advantages. First, an organism can reproduce very quickly. Offspring are identical to the parent. So, it also ensures that any favorable traits the parent has are passed on to offspring. Also, a parent organism does not need to find a partner to reproduce. Finally, all offspring—not just females—are able to produce more offspring.

14 List Identify four advantages of asexual reproduction.

_____
_____
_____
_____

Cholla cactuses reproduce asexually by vegetative reproduction. They drop off small pieces that grow into new plants.

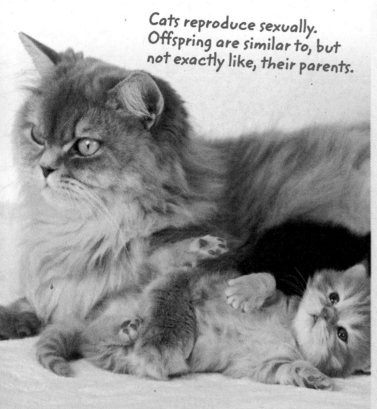

Cats reproduce sexually. Offspring are similar to, but not exactly like, their parents.

Advantages of Sexual Reproduction

Sexual reproduction is not as quick as asexual reproduction. Nor does it produce as many offspring. However, it has advantages. First, it increases genetic variation. Offspring have different traits that improve the chance that at least some offspring will survive. This is especially true if the environment changes. Offspring are not genetically identical to the parents. So, they may have a trait that the parents do not have, making them more likely to survive.

15 Explain How can increased genetic variation help some offspring survive?

_____

_____

_____

_____

_____

Advantages of Using Both Types of Reproduction

Some organisms can use both types of reproduction. For example, when conditions are favorable, many plants and fungi will reproduce asexually. Doing so lets them spread quickly and take over an area. When the environment changes, these organisms will switch to sexual reproduction. This strategy increases the chance that the species will survive. Because of genetic variation, at least some of the offspring may have traits that help them make it through the environmental change.

16 Compare In the table below, place a check mark in the cells that describe a characteristic of asexual or sexual reproduction.

	Quick	Increases chance of survival in changing environments	Produces genetic variation	Doesn't need a partner	Requires complex structures
Asexual reproduction					
Sexual reproduction					

Visual Summary

To complete this summary, circle the correct word that completes each statement. Then use the key below to check your answers. You can use this page to review the main concepts of the lesson.

Reproduction

Asexual reproduction involves one parent.

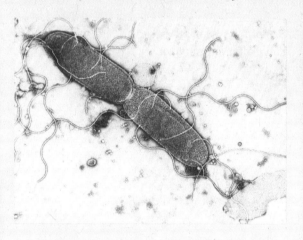

17 The offspring of asexual reproduction are genetically identical / similar to the parent organisms.

18 Prokaryotes reproduce by budding / binary fission.

19 Specialized reproductive structures called runners / spores can survive harsh conditions.

20 A benefit of asexual reproduction is that it is fast / slow.

Sexual reproduction involves two parents.

21 Male organisms produce sex cells called eggs / sperm cells.

22 Male and female sex cells join during fertilization / meiosis.

23 Sexual reproduction increases genetic variation / similarity.

Answers: 17 identical; 18 binary fission; 19 spores; 20 fast; 21 sperm cells; 22 fertilization; 23 variation

24 Explain How can both asexual reproduction and sexual reproduction allow for the survival of a species?

Lesson Review

Vocabulary

Fill in the blanks with the term that best completes the following sentences.

1 After _____ , the zygote develops into a larger organism.

2 An advantage of _____ reproduction is the ability to reproduce quickly.

3 The offspring of _____ reproduction are more likely to survive changes in the environment.

Key Concepts

4 Identify What are some advantages of asexual and sexual reproduction?

_____

_____

_____

_____

_____

_____

5 Compare In sexual reproduction, how do the offspring compare to the parents?

_____

_____

_____

6 Identify List four types of asexual reproduction.

_____

_____

_____

7 Explain Why do some organisms use both types of reproduction?

_____

_____

_____

_____

_____

Critical Thinking

Use the graph to answer the following questions.

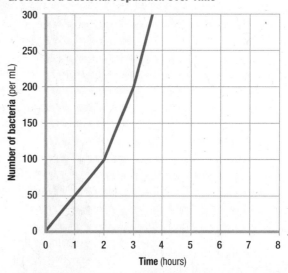

Growth of a Bacterial Population Over Time

8 Infer What type of reproduction is most likely taking place?

_____

_____

9 Analyze Which advantage of reproduction does the graph show? Explain.

_____

_____

_____

_____

10 Predict How might the graph change if the environmental conditions of the bacteria suddenly change? Explain.

_____

_____

_____

_____

_____

_____

Heredity

ESSENTIAL QUESTION

How are traits inherited?

By the end of this lesson, you should be able to analyze the inheritance of traits in individuals.

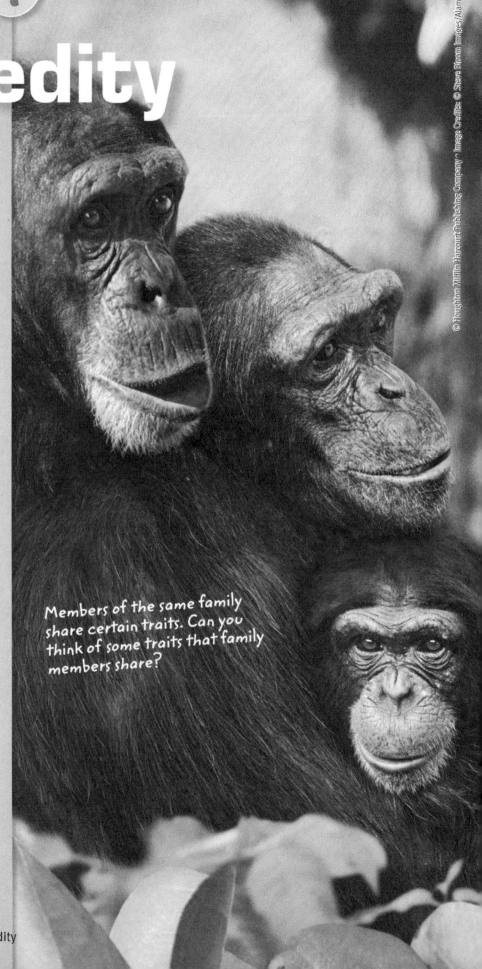

Members of the same family share certain traits. Can you think of some traits that family members share?

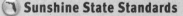
Sunshine State Standards

SC.7.L.16.1 Understand and explain that every organism requires a set of instructions that specifies its traits, that this hereditary information (DNA) contains genes located in the chromosomes of each cell, and that heredity is the passage of these instructions from one generation to another.

HE.6.C.1.4 Recognize how heredity can affect personal health.

LA.6.4.2.2 The student will record information (e.g., observations, notes, lists, charts, legends) related to a topic, including visual aids to organize and record information and include a list of sources used.

Engage Your Brain

1 Predict Check T or F to show whether you think each statement is true of false.

T   F

☐   ☐   Siblings look similar because they each have some traits of their parents.

☐   ☐   Siblings always have the same hair color.

☐   ☐   Siblings have the same DNA.

2 Describe Do you know any identical twins? How are they similar? How are they different?

_____

_____

_____

_____

_____

Active Reading

3 Infer Use context clues to write your own definition for the words *exhibit* and *investigate*.

Example sentence
You may <u>exhibit</u> a certain trait, such as brown eye color.

exhibit:

_____

_____

Example sentence
Gregor Mendel began to <u>investigate</u> the characteristics of pea plants.

investigate:

_____

_____

Vocabulary Terms

- **heredity**
- **gene**
- **allele**
- **genotype**
- **phenotype**
- **dominant**
- **recessive**
- **incomplete dominance**
- **codominance**

4 Identify This list contains the key terms you'll learn in this lesson. As you read, circle the definition of each term.

Give Peas a Chance

What is heredity?

Imagine a puppy. The puppy has long floppy ears like his mother has, and the puppy has dark brown fur like his father has. How did the puppy get these traits? The traits are a result of information stored in the puppy's genetic material. The passing of genetic material from parents to offspring is called **heredity**.

What did Gregor Mendel discover about heredity?

The first major experiments investigating heredity were performed by a monk named Gregor Mendel. Mendel lived in Austria in the 1800s. Before Mendel became a monk, he attended a university and studied science and mathematics. This training served him well when he began to study the inheritance of traits among the pea plants in the monastery's garden. Mendel studied seven different characteristics of pea plants: plant height, flower and pod position, seed shape, seed color, pod shape, pod color, and flower color. A *characteristic* is a feature that has different forms in a population. Mendel studied each pea plant characteristic separately, always starting with plants that were true-breeding for that characteristic. A true-breeding plant is one that will always produce offspring with a certain trait when allowed to self-pollinate. Each of the characteristics that Mendel studied had two different forms. For example, the color of a pea could be green or yellow. These different forms are called *traits*.

Characteristics of Pea Plants		
Characteristic	**Traits**	
Seed color		
Seed shape		
Pod color		
Flower position		

5 Apply Is flower color a characteristic or a trait?

Traits Depend on Inherited Factors

In his experiments with seed pod color, Mendel took two sets of plants, one true-breeding for plants that produce yellow seed pods and the other true-breeding for plants that produce green seed pods. Instead of letting the plants self-pollinate as they do naturally, he paired one plant from each set. He did this by fertilizing one plant with the pollen of another plant. Mendel called the plants that resulted from this cross the first generation. All of the plants from this first generation produced green seed pods. Mendel called this trait the *dominant* trait. Because the yellow trait seemed to recede, or fade away, he called it the *recessive* trait.

Then Mendel let the first-generation plants self-pollinate. He called the offspring that resulted from this self-pollination the second generation. About three-fourths of the second-generation plants had green seed pods, but about one-fourth had yellow pods. So the trait that seemed to disappear in the first generation reappeared in the second generation. Mendel hypothesized that each plant must have two heritable "factors" for each trait, one from each parent. Some traits, such as yellow seed pod color, could only be observed if a plant received two factors—one from each parent—for yellow pod color. A plant with one yellow factor and one green factor would produce green pods because producing green pods is a dominant trait. However, this plant could still pass on the yellow factor to the next generation of plants.

6 Identify As you read, underline Mendel's hypothesis about how traits are passed from parents to offspring.

7 Apply Which pod color is recessive?

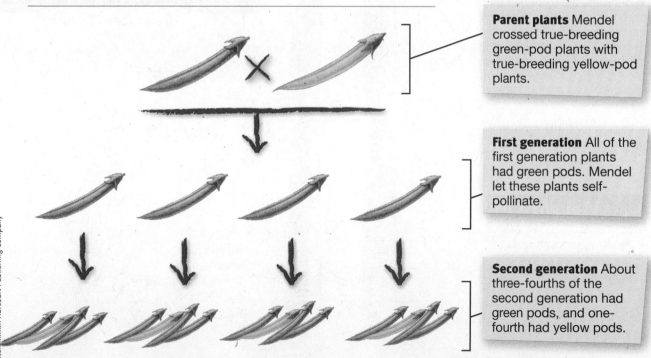

Parent plants Mendel crossed true-breeding green-pod plants with true-breeding yellow-pod plants.

First generation All of the first generation plants had green pods. Mendel let these plants self-pollinate.

Second generation About three-fourths of the second generation had green pods, and one-fourth had yellow pods.

It's in your genes!

→ Genes are made up of DNA.

How are traits inherited?

Mendel's experiments and conclusions have been the basis for much of the scientific thought about heredity. His ideas can be further explained by our modern understanding of the genetic material DNA. What Mendel called "factors" are actually segments of DNA known as genes!

Genes Are Passed from Parents to Offspring

Genes are segments of DNA found in chromosomes that give instructions for producing a certain characteristic. Humans, like many other organisms, inherit their genes from their parents. Each parent gives one set of genes to the offspring. The offspring then has two versions, or forms, of the same gene for every characteristic—one version from each parent. The different versions of a gene are known as **alleles** (uh•LEELZ). Genes are often represented by letter symbols. Dominant alleles are shown with a capital letter, and recessive alleles are shown with a lowercase version of the same letter. An organism with two dominant or two recessive alleles is said to be *homozygous* for that gene. An organism that has one dominant and one recessive allele is *heterozygous*.

Humans have 23 pairs of chromosomes.

In humans, cells contain pairs of chromosomes. One chromosome of each pair comes from each of two parents. Each chromosome contains sites where specific genes are located.

A gene occupies a specific location on both chromosomes in a pair.

Visualize It!

8 Apply Circle a gene pair for which this person is heterozygous.

Alleles are alternate forms of the same gene.

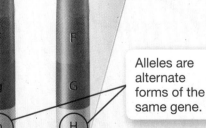

© Houghton Mifflin Harcourt Publishing Company • Image Credits: (cr) ©L. Willatt/Photo Researchers, Inc.

This girl has dimples.

This girl does not have dimples.

9 Apply The girls in this photograph have different types of hair. Is hair type a genotype or a phenotype?

Genes Influence Traits

The alternate forms of genes, called alleles, determine the traits of all living organisms. The combination of alleles that you inherited from your parents is your **genotype** (JEEN•uh•typ). Your observable traits make up your **phenotype** (FEEN•uh•typ). The phenotypes of some traits follow patterns similar to the ones that Mendel discovered in pea plants. That is, some traits are dominant over others. For example, consider the gene responsible for producing dimples, or creases in the cheeks. This gene comes in two alleles: one for dimples and one for no dimples. If you have even one copy of the allele for dimples, you will have dimples. This happens because the allele for producing dimples is dominant. The **dominant** allele contributes to the phenotype if one or two copies are present in the genotype. The no-dimples allele is recessive. The **recessive** allele contributes to the phenotype only when two copies of it are present. If one chromosome in the pair contains a dominant allele and the other contains a recessive allele, the phenotype will be determined by the dominant allele. If you do not have dimples, it is because you inherited two no-dimples alleles—one from each parent. This characteristic shows *complete dominance,* because one trait is completely dominant over another. However, not all characteristics follow this pattern.

🦅 **Active Reading**

11 Identify What is the phenotype of an individual with one allele for dimples and one allele for no dimples?

_____

_____

Think Outside the Book Inquiry

10 Imagine Write a short story about a world in which you could change your DNA and your traits. What would be the advantages? What would be the disadvantages?

© Houghton Mifflin Harcourt Publishing Company • Image Credits: (t) ©Stockbyte/Getty Images

Many Genes Can Influence a Single Trait

Some characteristics, such as the color of your skin, hair, and eyes, are the result of several genes acting together. Different combinations of alleles can result in different shades of eye color. Because there is not always a one-to-one relationship between a trait and a gene, many traits do not have simple patterns of inheritance.

A Single Gene Can Influence Many Traits

Sometimes, one gene influences more than one trait. For example, a single gene causes the tiger shown below to have white fur. If you look closely, you will see that the tiger also has blue eyes. The gene that affects fur color also influences eye color.

Many genetic disorders in humans are linked to a single gene but affect many traits. For example, the genetic disorder sickle cell anemia occurs in individuals who have two recessive alleles for a certain gene. This gene carries instructions for producing a protein in red blood cells. When a person has sickle cell anemia alleles, the body makes a different protein. This protein causes red blood cells to be sickle or crescent shaped when oxygen levels are low. Sickle-shaped blood cells can stick in blood vessels, sometimes blocking the flow of blood. These blood cells are also more likely to damage the spleen. With fewer healthy red blood cells, the body may not be able to deliver oxygen to the body's organs. All of the traits associated with sickle cell anemia are due to a single gene.

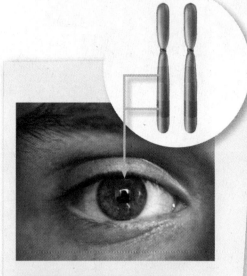

Visualize It!

12 Identify How many genes are responsible for eye color in this example?

_____

_____

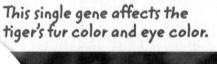
This single gene affects the tiger's fur color and eye color.

The Environment Can Influence Traits

Sometimes, the environment influences an organism's phenotype. For example, the arctic fox has a gene that is responsible for coat color. This gene is affected by light. In the winter, there are fewer hours of daylight, and the hairs that make up the arctic fox's coat grow in white. In the summer, when there are more daylight hours, the hairs in the coat grow in brown. In this case, both genes and the environment contribute to the organism's phenotype. The environment can influence human characteristics as well. For example, your genes may make it possible for you to grow to be tall, but you need a healthy diet to reach your full height potential.

Traits that are learned in one's environment are not inherited. For example, your ability to read and write is an acquired trait—a skill you learned. You were not born knowing how to ride a bike, and if you have children, they will not be born knowing how to do it either. They will have to learn the skill just as you did.

**Active Reading**

13 Identify Give an example of an acquired trait.

_____

_____

In the summer, the arctic fox has a brown coat.

In the winter, the arctic fox has a white coat.

14 Predict What advantage does white fur give the arctic fox in winter?

_____

_____

_____

Bending the Rules

What are the exceptions to complete dominance?

The characteristics that Mendel chose to study demonstrated complete dominance, meaning that heterozygous individuals show the dominant trait. Some human traits, such as freckles and dimples, follow the pattern of complete dominance, too. However, other traits do not. For traits that show incomplete dominance or codominance, one trait is not completely dominant over another.

Incomplete Dominance

In **incomplete dominance**, each allele in a heterozygous individual influences the phenotype. The result is a phenotype that is a blend of the phenotypes of the parents. One example of incomplete dominance is found in the snapdragon flower, shown below. When a true-breeding red snapdragon is crossed with a true-breeding white snapdragon, all the offspring are pink snapdragons. Both alleles of the gene have some influence. Hair texture is an example of incomplete dominance in humans. A person with one straight-hair allele and one curly-hair allele will have wavy hair.

Active Reading

15 Identify As you read, underline examples of incomplete dominance and codominance.

Visualize It!

16 Analyze How can you tell that these snapdragons do not follow the pattern of complete dominance?

_____

_____

_____

_____

Pink snapdragons are produced by a cross between a red snapdragon and a white snapdragon.

Codominance

For a trait that shows **codominance**, both of the alleles in a heterozygous individual contribute to the phenotype. Instead of having a blend of the two phenotypes, heterozygous individuals have both of the traits associated with their two alleles. An example of codominance is shown in the genes that determine human blood types. There are three alleles that play a role in determining a person's blood type: *A, B,* and *O.* The alleles are responsible for producing small particles on the surface of red blood cells called antigens. The *A* allele produces red blood cells coated with A antigens. The *B* allele produces red blood cells coated with B antigens. The *O* allele does not produce antigens. The *A* and *B* alleles are codominant. So, someone with one *A* allele and one *B* allele will have blood cells that are coated with A antigens and B antigens. This person would have type AB blood.

Think Outside the Book Inquiry

17 Research Blood type is an important factor when people give or receive blood. Research the meanings of the phrases "universal donor" and "universal recipient." What are the genotypes of each blood type?

Active Reading **18 Identify** What antigens coat the red blood cells of a person with type AB blood?

_____

Visualize It!

19 Predict The color of these imaginary fish is controlled by a single gene. Sketch or describe their offspring if the phenotypes follow the pattern of complete dominance, incomplete dominance, or codominance.

Complete dominance (Blue is dominant to yellow.)	Incomplete dominance	Codominance

© Houghton Mifflin Harcourt Publishing Company

Visual Summary

To complete this summary, circle the correct word or phrase. Then use the key below to check your answers. You can use this page to review the main concepts of the lesson.

Heredity

Gregor Mendel studied patterns of heredity in pea plants.

20 Traits that seemed to disappear in Mendel's first-generation crosses were dominant / recessive traits.

Inherited genes influence the traits of an individual.

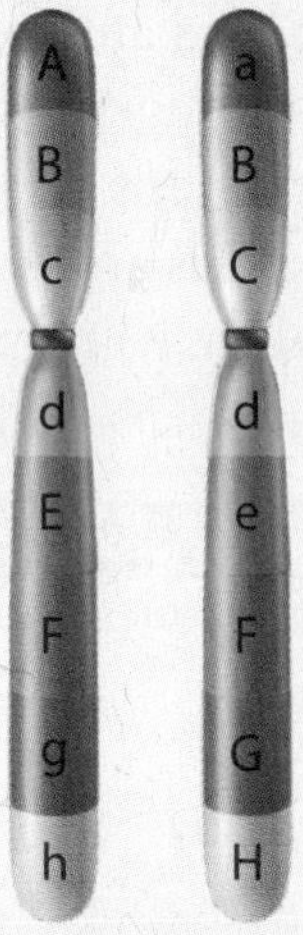

21 An individual with the genotype BB is heterozygous / homozygous.

Phenotypes can follow complete dominance, incomplete dominance, or codominance.

22 When these imaginary fish cross, their offspring are all green. This is an example of codominance / incomplete dominance.

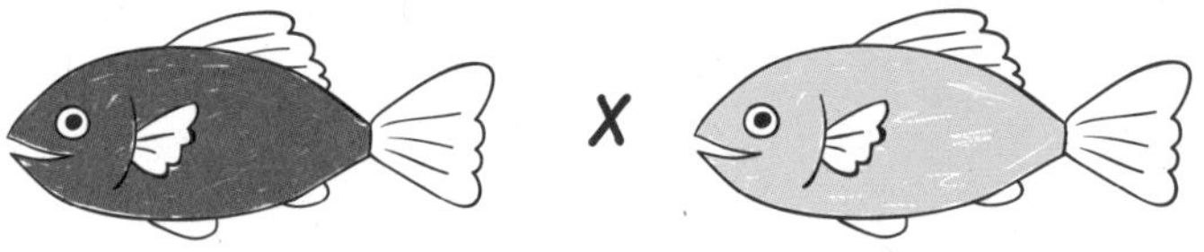

Answers: 20 recessive; 21 homozygous; 22 incomplete dominance

23 Apply If a child has blonde hair and both of her parents have brown hair, what does that tell you about the allele for blonde hair?

Lesson Review

Vocabulary

Draw a line to connect the following terms to their definitions.

1 heredity   **A** an organism's appearance or other detectable characteristic

2 gene

3 phenotype   **B** a section of DNA that contains instructions for a particular characteristic

C the passing of genetic material from parent to offspring

Key Concepts

4 Describe What did Mendel discover about genetic factors in pea plants?

_____

_____

_____

_____

_____

_____

_____

5 Describe What is the role of DNA in determining an organism's traits?

_____

_____

_____

_____

6 Apply Imagine that a brown horse and a white horse cross to produce an offspring whose coat is made up of some brown hairs and some white hairs. Which pattern of dominance is this an example of?

_____

_____

7 Identify Give an example of a trait that is controlled by more than one gene.

_____

_____

Use this diagram to answer the following questions.

8 Identify What is the genotype at the Q gene?

_____

9 Apply For which genes is this individual heterozygous?

_____

_____

Critical Thinking

10 Describe Marfan syndrome is a genetic disorder caused by a dominant allele. Describe how Marfan syndrome is inherited.

_____

_____

_____

11 Describe Jenny, Jenny's mom, and Jenny's grandfather are all good basketball players. Give an example of an inherited trait and an acquired trait that could contribute to their skill at basketball.

_____

_____

_____

_____

_____

Interpreting Tables

Visual displays, such as diagrams, tables, or graphs, are useful ways to show data collected in an experiment. A table is the most direct way to communicate this information. Tables are also used to summarize important trends in scientific data. Making a table may seem easy. However, if tables are not clearly organized, people will have trouble reading them. Below are a few strategies to help you improve your skills in interpreting scientific tables.

Sunshine State Standards

MA.6.A.3.6 Construct and analyze tables, graphs, and equations to describe linear functions and other simple relations using both common language and algebraic notation.

LA.6.2.2.3 The student will organize information to show understanding (e.g., representing main ideas within text through charting, mapping, paraphrasing, summarizing, or comparing/contrasting).

Tutorial

Use the following instructions to study the parts of a table about heredity in Brittanies and to analyze the data shown in the table.

Offspring from Cross of Black Solid and Liver Tricolor Brittanies		
Color	**Pattern**	**Number of Offspring**
orange and white	solid	1
black and white	solid	1
	tricolor	3
liver and white	solid	1
	tricolor	3

Reading the Title
Every table should have an informative title. By reading the title of the table to the left, we know that the table contains data about the offspring of a cross between a black solid Brittany and a liver tricolor Brittany.

Summarizing the Title
Sometimes it is helpful to write a sentence to summarize a table's title. For example, you could write, "This table shows how puppies that are the offspring of a black solid Brittany and a liver tricolor Brittany might look."

Analyzing the Headings
Row and column headings describe the data in the cells. Headings often appear different from the data in the cells, such as being larger, bold, or being shaded. The row headings in the table to the left organize three kinds of data: the coat color of the puppies, the coat pattern of the puppies, and the number of puppies that have each combination of coat color and pattern.

Describing the Data
In complete sentences, record the information that you read in the table. For example, you could write, "There are five different kinds of offspring. Tricolor puppies are most common, and puppies with a solid coat pattern are least common. There are twice as many tricolor puppies as solid puppies."

Analyzing the Data
Now that you have seen how the table is organized, you can begin to look for trends in the data. Which combinations are most common? Which combinations are least common?

You Try It!

The table below shows the characteristics of Guinea pig offspring. Look at the table, and answer the questions that follow.

Characteristics of Guinea Pig Offspring from Controlled Breeding			
Hair Color	Coat Texture	Hair Length	Number of Guinea Pigs
black	rough	short	27
		long	9
	smooth	short	9
		long	3
white	rough	short	9
		long	3
	smooth	short	3
		long	1

1 Summarizing the Title Circle the title of the table. Write a one-sentence description of the information shown in the table.

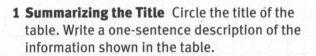

2 Analyzing the Headings Shade the column headings in the table. What information do they show? How many combinations of hair color, coat texture, and hair length are shown?

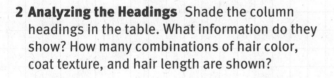

3 Analyzing the Data Circle the most common type of Guinea pig. Box the least common type of Guinea pig. Write sentences to describe the characteristics of each.

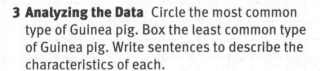

4 Applying Mathematics Calculate the total number of Guinea pig offspring. Write this total at the bottom of the table. What percentage of the total number of Guinea pigs has short hair? What percentage of the total number of Guinea pigs has long hair?

5 Observing Trends Based on your data from Step 4, which characteristic is dominant in Guinea pigs: long hair or short hair?

6 Applying Concepts What is one advantage of displaying data in tables? What is one advantage of describing data in writing?

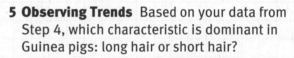

Take It Home

With an adult, practice making tables. You can categorize anything that interests you. Make sure your table has a title and clearly and accurately organizes your data using headings. If possible, share your table with your class.

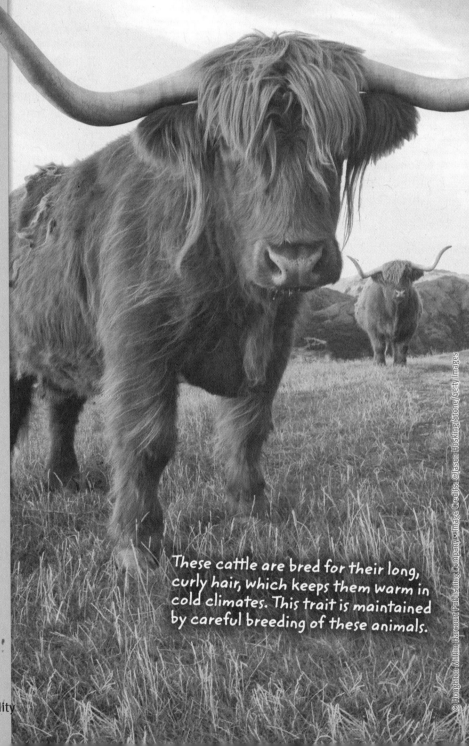

Lesson 5

Punnett Squares and Pedigrees

ESSENTIAL QUESTION

How are patterns of inheritance studied?

By the end of this lesson, you should be able to explain how patterns of heredity can be predicted by Punnett squares and pedigrees.

Sunshine State Standards

SC.7.L.16.2 Determine the probabilities for genotype and phenotype combinations using Punnett Squares and pedigrees.

MA.6.A.3.6 Construct and analyze tables, graphs, and equations to describe linear functions and other simple relations using both common language and algebraic notation.

LA.6.4.2.2 The student will record information (e.g., observations, notes, lists, charts, legends) related to a topic, including visual aids to organize and record information, as appropriate, and attribute sources of information.

HE.6.C.1.4 Recognize how heredity can affect personal health.

These cattle are bred for their long, curly hair, which keeps them warm in cold climates. This trait is maintained by careful breeding of these animals.

Engage Your Brain

1 Infer Why do you think that children look like their parents?

_____

_____

_____

_____

_____

_____

_____

2 Apply Color or label each circle with the color that results when the two paints mix. As you read the lesson, think about how this grid is similar to and different from a Punnett square.

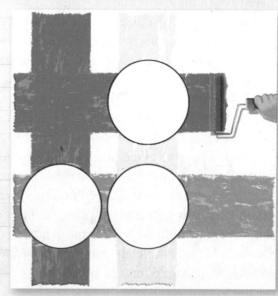

Active Reading

3 Apply Use context clues to write your own definition for the words *occur* and *outcome*.

Example sentence
Tools can be used to predict the likelihood that a particular genetic combination will <u>occur</u>.

occur:

_____

_____

Example sentence
A Punnett square can be used to predict the <u>outcome</u> of a genetic cross.

outcome:

_____

_____

Vocabulary Terms

- **Punnett square**
- **probability**
- **ratio**
- **pedigree**

4 Apply As you learn the definition of each vocabulary term in this lesson, create your own definition or sketch to help you remember the meaning of the term.

Squared Away

How are Punnett squares used to predict patterns of heredity?

When Gregor Mendel studied pea plants, he noticed that traits are inherited in patterns. One tool for understanding the patterns of heredity is a diagram called a *Punnett square*. A **Punnett square** is a graphic used to predict the possible genotypes of offspring in a given cross. Each parent has two alleles for a particular gene. An offspring receives one allele from each parent. A Punnett square shows all of the possible allele combinations in the offspring.

The Punnett square below shows how alleles are expected to be distributed in a cross between a pea plant with purple flowers and a pea plant with white flowers. The top of the Punnett square shows one parent's alleles for this trait (*F* and *F*). The left side of the Punnett square shows the other parent's alleles (*f* and *f*). Each compartment within the Punnett square shows an allele combination in potential offspring. You can see that in this cross, all offspring would have the same genotype (*Ff*). Because purple flower color is completely dominant to white flower color, all of the offspring would have purple flowers.

Active Reading

5 Identify In a Punnett square, where are the parents' alleles written?

In their genes &
combinations of
their offsprings

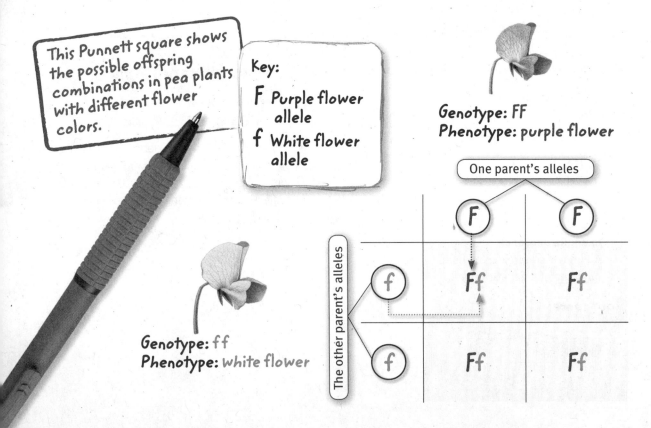

This Punnett square shows the possible offspring combinations in pea plants with different flower colors.

Key:
F Purple flower allele
f White flower allele

Genotype: FF
Phenotype: purple flower

One parent's alleles

Genotype: ff
Phenotype: white flower

The other parent's alleles

	F	F
f	Ff	Ff
f	Ff	Ff

6 Apply Fill in the genotypes and phenotypes of the parents and offspring in this Punnett square. Sketch the resulting offspring possibilities in the white boxes below. (Hint: Assume complete dominance.)

Key:

R Round pea allele

r Wrinkled pea allele

Genotype: _R_____

Phenotype: _r_____

	R	r
R	RR Genotype: _____ Phenotype: _____	Rr Genotype: _____ Phenotype: _____
r	Rr Genotype: _____ Phenotype: _____	rr Genotype: _____ Phenotype: _____

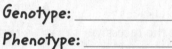

Genotype: _R_____

Phenotype: _r_____

7 Analyze What does each compartment of the Punnett square represent?

_____

_____

_____

_____

How can a Punnett square be used to make predictions about offspring?

A Punnett square does not tell you what the exact results of a certain cross will be. A Punnett square only helps you find the probability that a certain genotype will occur. **Probability** is the mathematical chance of a specific outcome in relation to the total number of possible outcomes.

Probability can be expressed in the form of a **ratio** (RAY•shee•oh), an expression that compares two quantities. A ratio written as 1:4 is read as "one to four." The ratios obtained from a Punnett square tell you the probability that any one offspring will get certain alleles. Another way of expressing probability is as a *percentage*. A percentage is like a ratio that compares a number to 100. A percentage states the number of times a certain outcome might happen out of a hundred chances.

1:4 is the ratio of red squares to total squares.

![calculator icon] **Do the Math** **Sample Problem**

In guinea pigs, the dominant *B* allele is responsible for black fur, while the recessive *b* allele is responsible for brown fur. Use the Punnett square to find the probability of this cross resulting in offspring with brown fur.

	B	b
b	Bb	bb
b	Bb	bb

Identify

A. What do you know?

Parent genotypes are Bb and bb. Possible offspring genotypes are Bb and bb.

B. What do you want to find out?

Probability of the cross resulting in offspring with brown fur

Plan

C. Count the total number of offspring allele combinations: 4

D. Count the number of allele combinations that will result in offspring with brown fur: 2

Solve

E. Write the probability of offspring with brown fur as a ratio: 2:4

F. Rewrite the ratio to express the probability out of 100 offspring by multiplying each side of the ratio by the same number (such as 25):   50:100

G. Convert the ratio to a percentage: 50%

Answer: 50% chance of offspring with brown fur

8 Calculate This Punnett square shows a cross between two *Bb* guinea pigs. What is the probability of the cross resulting in offspring with black fur?

	B	b
B	 BB	Bb
b	Bb	bb

Identify

A. What do you know?

B. What do you want to find out?

Plan

C. Count the total number of offspring allele combinations:

D. Count the number of allele combinations that will result in offspring with black fur:

Solve

E. Write the probability of offspring with black fur as a ratio:

F. Rewrite the ratio to express the probability out of 100 offspring by multiplying each side of the ratio by the same number:

G. Convert the ratio to a percentage:

Answer:

9 Graph In the cross above, what is the ratio of each of the possible genotypes? Show your results by filling in the pie chart at the right. Fill in the key with color or shading to show which pieces of the chart represent the different genotypes.

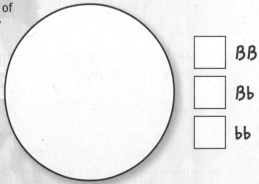

☐ BB
☐ Bb
☐ bb

How can a pedigree trace a trait through generations?

A pedigree is another tool used to study patterns of inheritance. A **pedigree** traces the occurrence of a trait through generations of a family. Pedigrees can be created to trace any inherited trait—even hair color!

Pedigrees can be useful in tracing a special class of inherited disorders known as *sex-linked disorders*. Sex-linked disorders are associated with an allele on a sex chromosome. Many sex-linked disorders, such as hemophilia and colorblindness, are caused by an allele on the X chromosome. Women have two X chromosomes, so a woman can have one allele for colorblindness without being colorblind. A woman who is heterozygous for this trait is called a *carrier*, because she can carry or pass on the trait to her offspring. Men have just one X chromosome. In men, this single chromosome determines if the trait is present.

The pedigree below traces a disease called *cystic fibrosis*. Cystic fibrosis causes serious lung problems. Carriers of the disease have one recessive allele. They do not have cystic fibrosis, but they are able to pass the recessive allele on to their children. If a child receives a recessive allele from each parent, then the child will have cystic fibrosis. Other genetic conditions follow a similar pattern.

Think Outside the Book Inquiry

10 **Design** Create a pedigree chart that traces the occurrence of dimples in your family or in the family of a friend. Collect information for as many family members as you can.

Visualize It!

Pedigree for Cystic Fibrosis

Generation

I   1   2

II   1   2   3   4   5   6

III   1   2   3   4

IV   1   2   3

☐ Males   ◯ Females

Vertical lines connect children to their parents.

☐ or ◯ A solid square or circle indicates that the person has a certain trait.

◧ or ◑ A half-filled square or circle indicates that the person is a carrier of the trait.

11 Analyze Does anyone in the third generation have cystic fibrosis? Explain.

_____

_____

_____

12 Calculate What is the probability that the child of two carriers will have cystic fibrosis?

_____

_____

_____

Saving the European Mouflon

The European mouflon is an endangered species of sheep. Scientists at the University of Teramo in Italy used genetic tools and techniques to show how the population of mouflon could be preserved.

Maintaining Genetic Diversity

When a very small population of animals interbreeds, there is a greater risk that harmful genetic conditions can appear in the animals. This is one issue that scientists face when trying to preserve endangered species. One way to lower this risk is to be sure that genetically-similar animals do not breed.

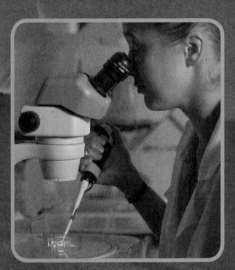

Genetics to the Rescue!

Researchers combined the sperm and egg of genetically-dissimilar European mouflons in a laboratory. The resulting embryo was implanted into a mother sheep. By controlling the combination of genetic material, scientists hope to lower the risk of inherited disorders.

Extend

Inquiry

13 Explain Why are small populations difficult to preserve?

14 Research Research another population of animals that has been part of a captive breeding program.

15 Describe Describe these animals and the results of the breeding program by doing one of the following:
- make a poster
- write a song
- write a short story
- draw a graphic novel

Visual Summary

To complete this summary, fill in the blanks with the correct word or phrase. Then use the key below to check your answers. You can use this page to review the main concepts of the lesson.

Predicting Patterns of Inheritance

Punnett squares can be used to make predictions about possible offspring.

	F	F
f	Ff	Ff
f	Ff	Ff

16 A Punnett square shows combinations of different _____ received from each parent.

Pedigrees trace a trait through generations.

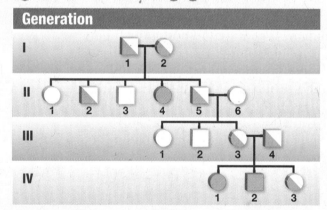

17 An allele responsible for a _____ is found on a sex chromosome.

18 Compare How is a heterozygous individual represented in the Punnett square and pedigree shown above?

Lesson Review

Vocabulary

Circle the term that best completes the following sentences.

1 A *Punnett square / ratio* is a tool that can be used to predict the genotypes of potential offspring in a given cross.

2 The results from a Punnett square can be used to find the *pedigree / probability* that a certain allele combination will occur in offspring.

3 A mathematical expression that compares one number to another is called a *pedigree / ratio*.

Key Concepts

Use this diagram to answer the following questions.

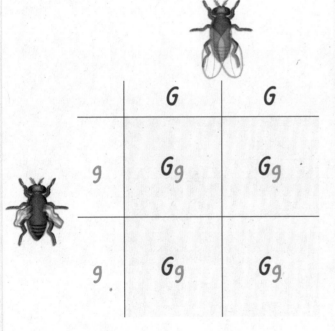

4 Analyze What is gene G responsible for in these fruit flies?

_____

_____

5 Analyze What is the ratio of heterozygous offspring to total offspring in the Punnett square?

6 Define What is a sex-linked disorder?

_____

_____

_____

_____

Critical Thinking

7 Infer Imagine a pedigree that traces an inherited disorder found in individuals with two recessive alleles for gene D. The pedigree shows three siblings with the genotypes *DD, Dd,* and *dd.* Did the parents of these three children have the disorder? Explain.

_____

_____

_____

_____

8 Explain A *Bb* guinea pig crosses with a *Bb* guinea pig, and four offspring are produced. All of the offspring are black. Explain how this could happen.

_____

_____

_____

_____

9 Synthesize You are creating a pedigree to trace freckles, a recessive trait, in a friend's family. You find out which of her family members have freckles and which do not. When you complete the pedigree, what can you learn about members of your friend's family that you could not tell just by looking at them?

_____

_____

_____

_____

My Notes

Unit 6 **Summary**

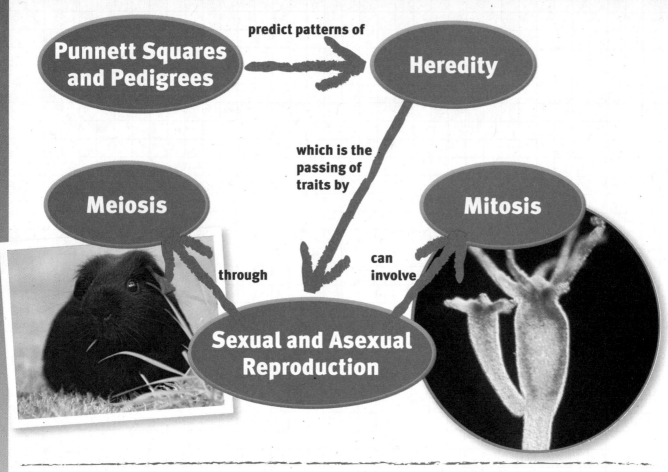

Punnett Squares and Pedigrees → predict patterns of → **Heredity**

which is the passing of traits by

Meiosis

Mitosis

through

can involve

Sexual and Asexual Reproduction

1 Interpret The Graphic Organizer above shows that Punnett squares are used to make predictions about heredity. Are Punnett squares more useful for predicting the results of sexual or asexual reproduction? Explain.

_____

_____

_____

_____

_____

_____

_____

_____

_____

2 Compare How are meiosis and mitosis similar? How are they different?

_____

_____

_____

_____

_____

_____

_____

3 Relate Compare the phenotype and genotype of a parent to the phenotype and genotype of its offspring produced by asexual reproduction.

_____

_____

_____

_____

Benchmark Review

Name _____

Multiple Choice

Identify the choice that best completes the statement or answers the question.

1 Cassie draws flashcards for each phase of mitosis and cytokinesis. Before she can label the backs of the flashcards, Cassie drops them onto the floor. The flashcards get mixed up as shown below.

    1   2   3   4   5

In what order should Cassie place the cards to show mitosis from start to finish?

- **A.** $1 \rightarrow 2 \rightarrow 3 \rightarrow 4 \rightarrow 5$
- **B.** $2 \rightarrow 4 \rightarrow 5 \rightarrow 1 \rightarrow 3$
- **C.** $3 \rightarrow 1 \rightarrow 5 \rightarrow 2 \rightarrow 4$
- **D.** $4 \rightarrow 2 \rightarrow 1 \rightarrow 5 \rightarrow 3$

2 Brandy knows that chromosomes behave differently in meiosis and mitosis. What do chromosomes do in meiosis but **not** in mitosis?

- **F.** Each chromosome makes an exact copy of itself.
- **G.** The homologous chromosomes form pairs.
- **H.** Chromosomes line up in the middle of the cell.
- **I.** Chromosomes condense, becoming visible under a microscope.

3 Noriko is studying a plant species she found in a forest. She collects leaf samples from a large parent plant, and from the smaller offspring that are growing next to it. After running some tests, she finds that the offspring are genetically identical to the parent plant. Which of these statements is **true** about Noriko's find?

- **A.** The offspring were produced sexually, and two parents were required.
- **B.** The offspring were produced asexually, and two parents were required.
- **C.** The offspring were produced sexually, and only one parent was required.
- **D.** The offspring were produced asexually, and only one parent was required.

4 Examine the Punnett square below.

	B	**B**
B	*BB*	*BB*
b	*Bb*	*Bb*

Which of the following choices gives the alleles of the parents shown here?

F. *BB* and *BB*

G. *BB* and *Bb*

H. *Bb* and *Bb*

I. *Bb* and *bb*

5 The diagram below shows the results of crossing a pea plant with round seeds and a pea plant with wrinkled seeds.

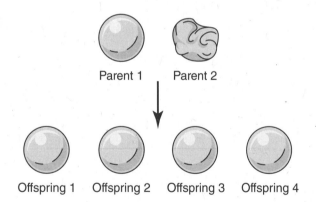

What can be determined from the results of the experiment?

A. Round shape and wrinkled shape are both recessive traits.

B. Round shape and wrinkled shape are both dominant traits.

C. Round shape is a dominant trait, and wrinkled shape is a recessive trait.

D. Round shape is a recessive trait, and wrinkled shape is a dominant trait.

6 Delia is teaching her sister about important molecules in the body. She tells her sister that one molecule provides a set of instructions that determines characteristics, such as eye color or hair color. Which molecule is Delia describing?

    F.   DNA

    G. glucose

    H. gamete

    I.   spore

7 Lucinda decides to investigate what would happen if there is an error at different stages of the cell cycle. She examines interphase, mitosis, and cytokinesis. Which of these statements describes what is **most likely** to happen if DNA is not duplicated during interphase?

    A. The new cells would be more numerous.

    B. The new cells would have too many chromosomes.

    C. The new cells would have too many nuclei.

    D. The new cells would have too few chromosomes.

8 Which of the following choices correctly pairs a type of cell with how it could be produced?

    F.   egg cell—meiosis in males

    G. sperm cell—mitosis in males

    H. body cell—mitosis in females

    I.   body cell—meiosis in females

9 A species of rabbit can have brown fur or white fur. One rabbit with two alleles for brown fur (*BB*) has brown fur. A second rabbit with two alleles for white fur (*bb*) has white fur. Which statement is true about the alleles *B* and *b*?

    A. They are on two different genes.

    B. They result in the same phenotype.

    C. They are two different versions of the same gene.

    D. They provide identical instructions for a characteristic.

Benchmark Review

10 Dante drew this pedigree for a recessive trait.

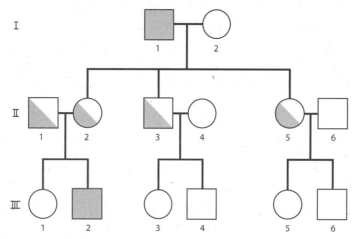

Which of the following statements correctly describes individual 2 in generation II?

F. She has the recessive trait.

G. She is a carrier of the recessive trait.

H. Both of her parents have the recessive trait.

I. Both of her children have the recessive trait.

11 Alpha-1 is a hereditary disorder that affects the lungs. In order for the disease to develop, a child must inherit one recessive allele from each parent. Suppose Caryn's mother has Alpha-1 and her father carries only one recessive allele. Which of the following statements **best** describes Caryn's situation?

A. Caryn has no chance of developing Alpha-1.

B. Caryn has no chance of being a carrier for Alpha-1.

C. Caryn has a 50 percent chance of developing Alpha-1.

D. Caryn has a 100 percent chance of developing Alpha-1.

12 Leah cuts a small stem from an azalea plant and gives it to John. John takes the cutting home and plants it in his garden. In a few months, the small stem has grown into a full-sized, new plant. Which of these choices correctly describes this situation?

F. Leah's plant reproduced by budding, and is genetically different than the plant in John's garden.

G. Leah's plant reproduced by binary fission, and is genetically different than the plant in John's garden.

H. Leah's plant reproduced by spore formation, and is genetically identical to the plant in John's garden.

I. Leah's plant reproduced by vegetative reproduction, and is genetically identical to the plant in John's garden.

UNIT 7

DNA and Modern Genetics

© Houghton Mifflin Harcourt Publishing Company • Image Credits: (bkgd) ©Tek Image/Photo Researchers, Inc.; (br) ©David R. Frazier Photolibrary, Inc./Alamy

Big Idea 16

Heredity and Reproduction

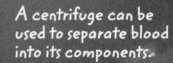

A centrifuge can be used to separate blood into its components.

What do you think?

Not all clues are large! Biological evidence gathered at crime scenes can tell forensic scientists many things. How do detectives in forensics labs use genetics to interpret evidence?

Unit 7
DNA and Modern Genetics

CITIZEN SCIENCE
Solved with Forensics

Modern crime labs use genetics, the study of how traits are inherited, to interpret evidence found at the scene of a crime. In the following scenario, a bike has been stolen and you will use genetic evidence to figure out what happened.

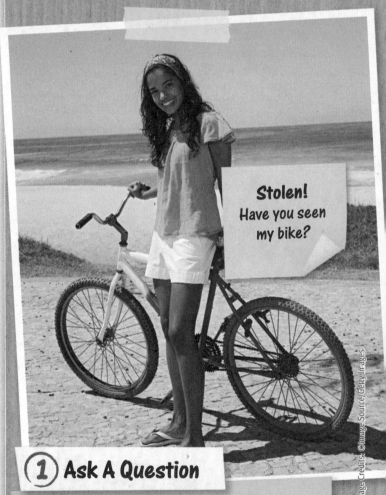

Stolen!
Have you seen my bike?

① Ask A Question

What should a detective at a crime scene look for?

Determine what types of evidence a detective could find at a crime scene. Consider that some evidence might be microscopic! In this case, you have found an empty juice box and a lock of hair.

② Think About It

List some of the traits (like fingerprints) that are unique to every individual.

_____

_____

_____

_____

What biological evidence might be found on the juice box and lock of hair left behind at the crime scene? What could they tell you about the crime?

_____

_____

_____

_____

_____

③ Apply Your Knowledge

A The hair sample you gathered is in a sealed bag. Why is it important to protect samples?

_____

_____

_____

B When lab technicians analyze DNA, it doesn't have a name on it. How can you match your sample to an individual and solve the crime?

_____

_____

_____

_____

C Can forensics determine for sure that the person identified by the evidence committed the crime? Explain.

_____

_____

Take It Home

Find out how DNA forensics is applied in our justice system. How accurate is it? Has it been used to reverse any court decisions or overturn any convictions?

DNA Structure and Function

ESSENTIAL QUESTION

What is DNA?

By the end of this lesson, you should be able to describe the structure and main functions of DNA.

Sunshine State Standards

SC.7.N.1.1 Define a problem from the seventh grade curriculum, use appropriate reference materials to support scientific understanding, plan and carry out scientific investigation of various types, such as systematic observations or experiments, identify variables, collect and organize data, interpret data in charts, tables, and graphics, analyze information, make predictions, and defend conclusions.

SC.7.N.1.5 Describe the methods used in the pursuit of a scientific explanation as seen in different fields of science such as biology, geology, and physics.

SC.7.L.16.1 Understand and explain that every organism requires a set of instructions that specifies its traits, that this hereditary information (DNA) contains genes located in the chromosomes of each cell, and that heredity is the passage of these instructions from one generation to another.

HE.7.C.1.4 Recognize how heredity can affect personal health.

LA.6.4.2.2 The student will record information (e.g., observations, notes, lists, charts, legends) related to a topic, including visual aids to organize and record information and include a list of sources used.

This bacterium was treated with a special chemical, causing a twisted maze of DNA to burst from the cell.

Engage Your Brain

1 Predict Check T or F to show whether you think each statement is true or false.

T   F

☐   ☐   DNA is found in the cells of all living things.

☐   ☐   All DNA mutations are harmful.

☐   ☐   The cell can make copies of its DNA.

2 Describe DNA is sometimes called the *blueprint of life*. Why do you think that is?

_____

_____

_____

_____

_____

_____

Active Reading

3 Synthesize Many English words have their roots in other languages. Use the Latin words below to make an educated guess about the meanings of the words *replication* and *mutation*.

Latin word	Meaning
mutare	to change
replicare	to repeat

Example sentence
DNA can undergo <u>mutation</u>.

mutation:

_____

_____

Example sentence
Before cell division, DNA <u>replication</u> occurs.

replication:

_____

_____

Vocabulary Terms

- DNA
- nucleotide
- replication
- mutation
- RNA
- ribosome

4 Identify This list contains the key terms you'll learn in this lesson. As you read, circle the definition of each term.

Cracking the
CODE
ATTAGCGATCACTAAATTAGC

Active Reading

5 Identify As you read, underline the meaning of the word *code*.

What is DNA?

The genetic material of a cell contains information needed for the cell's growth and other activities. It also determines the inherited characteristics of an organism. The genetic material in cells is contained in a molecule called deoxyribonucleic (dee•OK•see•ry•boh•noo•KLAY•ik) acid, or **DNA** for short. You could compare the information in DNA to the books in your local library. You might find a book describing how to bake a cake or complete your favorite video game. The books, however, don't actually do any of those things—you do. Similarly, the "books" that make up the DNA "library" carry the information that a cell needs to function, grow, and divide. However, DNA doesn't do any of those things. Proteins do most of the work of a cell and also make up much of the structure of a cell.

Scientists describe DNA as containing a code. A *code* is a set of rules and symbols used to carry information. For example, your computer uses a code of ones and zeroes that is translated into numbers, letters, and graphics on a computer screen. To understand how DNA functions as a code, you first need to learn about the structure of the DNA molecule.

DNA Timeline

Review this timeline to learn about some of the important scientific contributions to our understanding of DNA.

1875	1900	1925

1869 Friedrich Miescher identifies a substance that will later be known as DNA.

1919 Phoebus Levene publishes a paper on nucleic acids. His research helps scientists determine that DNA is made up of sugars, phosphate groups, and four nitrogen-containing bases: adenine, thymine, guanine, and cytosine. Bases are often referred to by their first letter: A, T, C, or G. Each base has a different shape.

6 Analyze In this model, what do *P, S,* and *A bases* represent?

_____

_____

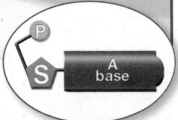

How was DNA discovered?

The discovery of the structure and function of DNA did not happen overnight. Many scientists from all over the world contributed to our current understanding of this important molecule. Some scientists discovered the chemicals that make up DNA. Others learned how these chemicals fit together. Still others determined the three-dimensional structure of the DNA molecule. The timeline below shows some of the key steps in this process of discovery.

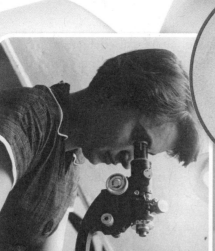

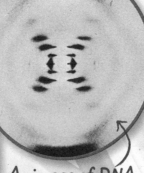

An image of DNA produced by using x-rays.

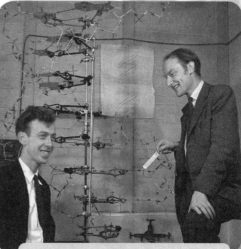

1951 Rosalind Franklin and Maurice Wilkins make images of DNA using x-rays. When an x-ray passes through the molecule, the ray bends and creates a pattern that is captured on film.

1953 James Watson and Francis Crick use Chargaff's rules and the x-ray images of DNA to conclude that DNA looks like a long, twisted ladder. They build a large-scale model of DNA using simple materials from their laboratory.

1950

1975

1950 Erwin Chargaff observes that the amount of guanine always equals the amount of cytosine, and the amount of adenine equals the amount of thymine. His findings are now known as *Chargaff's rules*.

1952 Alfred Hershey and Martha Chase perform experiments with viruses to confirm that DNA, not proteins, carries genetic information.

Unraveling DNA

DNA is found in the nucleus of eukaryotic cells.

What does DNA look like?

The chemical components that make up DNA are too small to be observed directly. But experiments and imaging techniques have helped scientists to infer the shape of DNA and the arrangement of its parts.

The Shape of DNA Is a Double Helix

The structure of DNA is a twisted ladder shape called a *double helix*. The two sides of the ladder, often referred to as the DNA backbone, are made of alternating sugars and phosphate groups. The rungs of the ladder are made of a pair of bases, each attached to one of the sugars in the backbone.

Active Reading **8 Describe** Where are phosphate groups found in a DNA molecule?

_____

_____

The DNA molecule has a double-helix shape.

Visualize It!

9 Compare Explain how the double-helix structure of DNA is like a spiral staircase.

_____

_____

_____

_____

_____

DNA Is Made Up of Nucleotides

A base, a sugar, and a phosphate group make a building block of DNA known as a **nucleotide**. These repeating chemical units join together to form the DNA molecule. There are four different nucleotides in DNA, identified by their bases: adenine (A), thymine (T), cytosine (C), and guanine (G). Because of differences in size and shape, adenine always pairs with thymine (A-T) and cytosine always pairs with guanine (C-G). These paired, or *complementary,* bases fit together like two pieces of a puzzle.

The order of the nucleotides in DNA is a code that carries information. The DNA code is read like a book. *Genes* are segments of DNA that relate to a certain trait. Each gene has a starting point and an ending point, with the DNA code being read in one direction. The bases A, T, C, and G form the alphabet of the code. The code stores information about which proteins the cells should build. The types of proteins your body makes help to determine your traits.

10 Apply Place boxes around the bases that pair with each other.

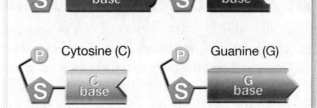

Adenine (A) Thymine (T) Cytosine (C) Guanine (G)

11 Devise The bases are often referred to simply by their initials—A, T, C, and G. The phrase "all tigers can growl" may help you remember them. Think of another phrase that uses words starting with A, T, C, and G that could help you remember the bases. Write your phrase below.

_____

_____

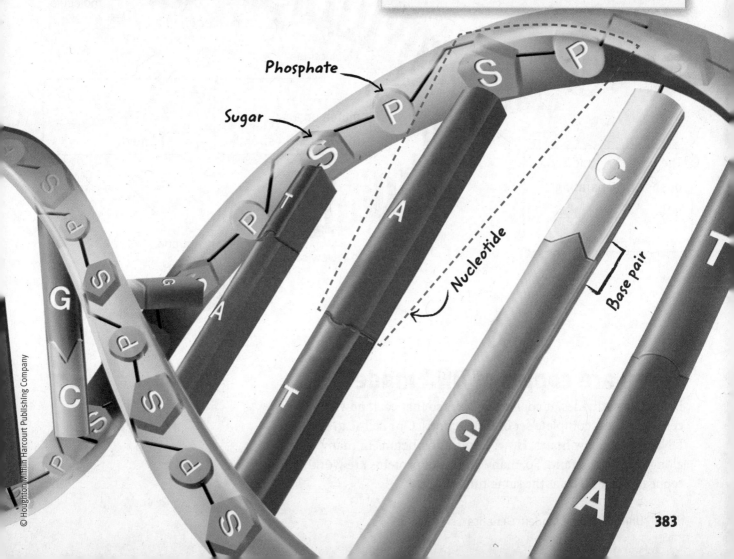

Phosphate

Sugar

Nucleotide

Base pair

Replication and

How are copies of DNA made?

The cell is able to make copies of DNA molecules through a process known as **replication**. During replication, the two strands of DNA separate, almost like two threads in a string being unwound. The bases on each side of the molecule are used as a pattern for a new strand. As the bases on the original molecule are exposed, complementary nucleotides are added. For example, an exposed base containing adenine attaches to a nucleotide containing thymine. When replication is complete, there are two identical DNA molecules. Each new DNA molecule is made of one strand of old DNA and one strand of new DNA.

Visualize It!

12 Apply Fill in the blanks to complete the labels on this model of replicating DNA.

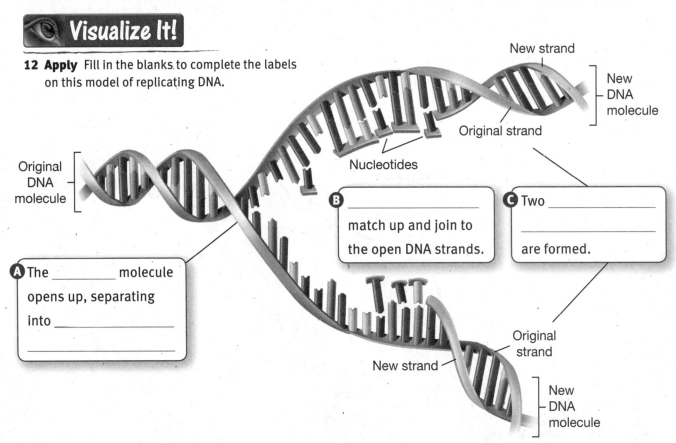

New strand

New DNA molecule

Original strand

Nucleotides

Original DNA molecule

B _____ match up and join to the open DNA strands.

C Two _____ _____ are formed.

A The _____ molecule opens up, separating into _____ _____

Original strand

New strand

New DNA molecule

When are copies of DNA made?

Before a cell divides, it copies the DNA so that each new daughter cell will have a complete set of instructions. Our cells can replicate DNA in just a few hours. How? Replication begins in many places along the DNA strand. So, many groups of proteins are working to replicate your DNA at the same time.

Mutation

What are mutations?

Changes in the number, type, or order of bases on a piece of DNA are known as **mutations**. Sometimes, a base is left out. This kind of change is known as a *deletion*. Or, an extra base might be added. This kind of change is an *insertion*. The most common mutation happens when one base replaces another. This kind of change is known as a *substitution*.

How do mutations happen? Given the large number of bases in an organism's DNA, it is not surprising that random errors can occur during replication. However, DNA can also be damaged by physical or chemical agents called *mutagens*. Ultraviolet light and the chemicals in cigarette smoke are examples of mutagens.

Cells make proteins that can fix errors in DNA. But sometimes a mistake isn't corrected, and it becomes part of the genetic code. Mutations to DNA may be beneficial, neutral, or harmful. A *genetic disorder* results from mutations that harm the normal function of a cell. Some of these disorders, such as Tay-Sachs disease and sickle-cell anemia, are *inherited*, or passed on from parent to offspring. Other genetic disorders result from mutations that occur during a person's lifetime. Most cancers fall into this category.

Visualize It!

13 Apply Place a check mark in the box to indicate which type of mutation is being shown.

Original sequence

A

☐ deletion ☐ insertion ☐ substitution

B

☐ deletion ☐ insertion ☐ substitution

C

☐ deletion ☐ insertion ☐ substitution

This snake has albinism, a condition in which the body cannot make the pigments that give color to the skin and eyes.

14 Explain Albinism is an inherited genetic disorder. Explain what is meant by "inherited genetic disorder."

_____

_____

_____

_____

Protein Factory

What is the role of DNA and RNA in building proteins?

Imagine that you are baking cookies. You have a big cookbook that contains the recipe. If you take the book with you into the kitchen, you risk damaging the book and losing important instructions. You only need one page from the book, so you copy the recipe on a piece of paper and leave the cookbook on the shelf. This process is similar to the way that the cell uses DNA to build proteins. First, some of the information in the DNA is copied to a separate molecule called ribonucleic acid, or **RNA.** Then, the copy is used to build proteins. Not all the instructions are needed all the time. In eukaryotes, the DNA is protected inside the cell's nucleus.

Like DNA, RNA has a sugar-phosphate backbone and the bases adenine (A), guanine (G), and cytosine (C). But instead of thymine (T), RNA contains the base uracil (U). Also, the sugar found in RNA is different from the one in DNA. There are three types of RNA: messenger RNA, ribosomal RNA, and transfer RNA. Each type of RNA has a special role in making proteins.

> **Active Reading** 15 **Identify** As you read, number the sentences that describe the steps of transcription.

Transcription: The Information in DNA Is Copied to Messenger RNA

When a cell needs a set of instructions for making a protein, it first makes an RNA copy of the necessary section of DNA. This process is called *transcription.* Transcription involves DNA and messenger RNA (mRNA). Only individual genes are transcribed, not the whole DNA molecule. During transcription, DNA is used as a template to make a complementary strand of mRNA. The DNA opens up where the gene is located. Then RNA bases match up to complementary bases on the DNA template. When transcription is complete, the mRNA is released and the DNA molecule closes.

DNA

RNA

Protein

RNA uses the genetic information stored in DNA to build proteins.

mRNA

Cell nucleus

A During transcription, DNA is used as a template to make a complementary strand of mRNA. In eukaryotes, the mRNA then exits the nucleus.

Translation: The Information in Messenger RNA Is Used to Build Proteins

Once the mRNA has been made, it is fed through a protein assembly line within a ribosome. A **ribosome** is a cell organelle made of ribosomal RNA (rRNA) and protein. As mRNA passes through the ribosome, transfer RNA (tRNA) molecules deliver amino acids to the ribosome. Each group of three bases on the mRNA strand codes for one amino acid. So the genetic code determines the order in which amino acids are brought to the ribosome. The amino acids join together to form a protein. The process of making proteins from RNA is called *translation*.

B A ribosome attaches to an mRNA strand at the beginning of a gene.

tRNA

Amino acid

Ribosome

C A tRNA molecule enters the ribosome. Three bases on the tRNA match up to 3 complementary bases on the mRNA strand. The bases on the mRNA strand determine which tRNA and amino acid move into the ribosome.

Chain of amino acids

Chain of amino acids is released

D The tRNA transfers its amino acid to a growing chain. Then, the tRNA is released. The ribosome moves down the mRNA and the process repeats.

E Once the ribosome reaches the end of the gene, the chain of amino acids is released.

16 Apply Fill in the table below by placing check marks in the appropriate boxes and writing the product of transcription and translation.

Process	What molecules are involved?				What is the product?
Transcription	☐ DNA	☐ mRNA	☐ tRNA	☐ ribosome	
Translation	☐ DNA	☐ mRNA	☐ tRNA	☐ ribosome	

Visual Summary

To complete this summary, fill in the blanks with the correct word or phrase. Then use the key below to check your answers. You can use this page to review the main concepts of the lesson.

DNA has a double-helix shape and is made up of nucleotides.

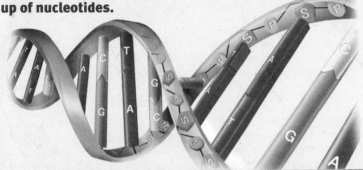

17 The four bases in DNA nucleotides are

_____

_____

_____

_____

The cell can make copies of DNA.

18 DNA replication happens before cells _____

DNA and RNA are involved in making proteins.

20 The two processes involved in making proteins from the DNA code are

DNA can mutate.

19 Three types of DNA mutations are _____

_____

_____

Answers: **17** adenine, guanine, cytosine, and thymine; **18** divide; **19** insertion, deletion, and substitution; **20** transcription, translation

21 Explain How could a mutation in the DNA affect what proteins are made by the cell?

Lesson Review

Vocabulary

In your own words, define the following terms.

1 A(n) _____ of DNA consists of a sugar, a phosphate, and a nitrogen-containing base.

2 A(n) _____ is a change in the base sequence of a DNA molecule.

Key Concepts

Draw a line to connect the following scientists to their contributions to our understanding of DNA.

3 Erwin Chargaff

4 Rosalind Franklin and Maurice Wilkins

5 James Watson and Francis Crick

A took x-ray images of DNA molecule

B proposed a double-helix model of DNA

C found that the amount of adenine equals the amount of thymine and that the amount of guanine equals the amount of cytosine

6 Identify How does the structure of RNA differ from the structure of DNA?

_____
_____
_____
_____

7 Identify When does DNA replication occur?

_____
_____

8 Describe Name the three types of RNA and list their roles in making proteins.

_____
_____
_____
_____
_____
_____
_____

9 Identify What can cause DNA mutations?

_____
_____
_____

Critical Thinking

Use this diagram to answer the following questions.

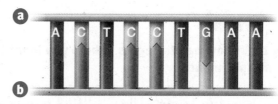

10 Describe What is the sequence of bases on DNA strand *b*, from left to right?

11 Apply This segment of DNA is transcribed to form a complementary strand of mRNA. The mRNA then undergoes translation. How many amino acids would the RNA code for?

_____

12 Infer After many cell divisions, a segment of DNA has more base pairs than it originally did. Explain what has happened.

_____
_____
_____

13 Explain Why must DNA replicate?

_____
_____
_____
_____
_____
_____

Think Science

Identifying Variables

When you are analyzing or designing a scientific experiment, it is important to identify the variables in the experiment. Usually, an experiment is designed to discover how changing one variable affects another variable. In a scientific investigation, the independent variable is the factor that is purposely changed. The dependent variable is the factor that changes in response to the independent variable.

Sunshine State Standards

SC.7.N.1.4 Identify test variables (independent variables) and outcome variables (dependent variables) in an experiment.

MA.6.A.3.6 Construct and analyze tables, graphs, and equations to describe linear functions and other simple relations using both common language and algebraic notation.

LA.6.2.2.3 The student will organize information to show understanding (e.g., representing main ideas within text through charting, mapping, paraphrasing, summarizing, or comparing/contrasting).

Tutorial

Use the following strategies to help you identify the variables in an experiment.

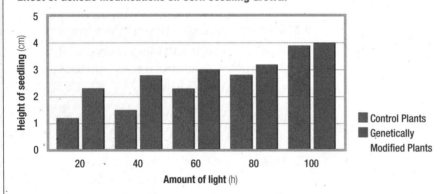

Summary: We genetically modified corn plants to increase growth in low-light conditions.

Effect of Genetic Modifications on Corn Seedling Growth

Height of seedling (cm) vs Amount of light (h)

■ Control Plants
■ Genetically Modified Plants

Reading a Summary
The published results of an experiment usually include a brief summary. You should be able to identify the variables from it. In the summary to the left, the independent variable is the DNA of the corn plants, and the dependent variable is the height of the plants.

Analyzing a Graph Making a graph can be a very effective way to show the relationship between variables. For a line graph, the independent variable is usually shown on the *x*-axis, or the horizontal axis. The dependent variable is usually shown on the *y*-axis, or the vertical axis.

Describing the Data When you read a graph, describing the information in complete sentences can help you to identify the variables. For example, you could write, "In the first 80 hours, the genetically modified corn plants grew much more quickly than the control plants grew. But by 100 hours, both kinds of plants were about the same height. This shows that the effect of the independent variable was greatest during the first 80 hours of plant growth."

Identifying the Effects of Variables Look closely at the graph. Notice that the genetically modified seedlings grew more quickly than the control seedlings, but the effects were greatest in the early part of the experiment. A variable's effect is not always constant throughout an experiment.

© Houghton Mifflin Harcourt Publishing Company • Image Credits: (b) ©Chris Knapton/Photo Researchers, Inc.

You Try It!

The passage below describes the process of gel electrophoresis.
Use the description to answer the question that follows.

> During gel electrophoresis, DNA is broken into separate fragments.
> These fragments are added to a gel. When an electric current is
> applied to the gel, the fragments travel different distances through
> the gel. The size of the DNA fragments determines how far they
> travel. Smaller fragments travel farther than larger fragments do.
> Scientists can use these data to identify unknown samples of DNA.

1 Reading a Summary Identify the variables described in
the passage.

_____

_____

**The graph below shows the results of DNA
analysis using gel electrophoresis. Look at the
graph, and answer the questions that follow.**

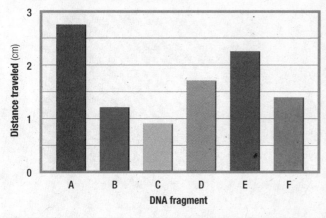

Distance Traveled by DNA Fragments

4 Applying Mathematics Calculate the average
distance that the DNA fragments traveled. How
much farther than the average distance did the
smallest DNA fragment travel?

2 Analyzing a Graph Which variables are shown
in the graph? Circle the axis that shows the
dependent variable.

_____

_____

3 Analyzing the Data What is the relationship
between the size of the DNA fragments and the
distance they traveled? Circle the DNA fragment
that is the smallest.

_____

_____

5 Applying Concepts Why is it important to limit
the number of variables in an experiment?

_____

_____

_____

_____

_____

Take It Home

**With an adult, plan and conduct a simple
experiment that includes an independent
variable and a dependent variable. Record
your results and graph your data if possible.
Then share your results with the class.**

Biotechnology

ESSENTIAL QUESTION

How does biotechnology impact our world?

By the end of this lesson, you should be able to explain how biotechnology impacts human life and the world around us.

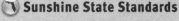

Sunshine State Standards

SC.7.L.16.4 Recognize and explore the impact of biotechnology (cloning, genetic engineering, artificial selection) on the individual, society and the environment.

LA.6.4.2.2 The student will record information (e.g., observations, notes, lists, charts, legends) related to a topic, including visual aids to organize and record information and include a list of sources used.

These glowing bands contain fragments of DNA that have been treated with a special chemical. This chemical glows under ultraviolet light, allowing scientists to see the DNA.

© Houghton Mifflin Harcourt Publishing Company • Image Credits: ©Sinclair Stammers/Photo Researchers, Inc.

1 Predict Fill in the blanks with the word or phrase you think correctly completes the following sentences.

A medical researcher might study DNA in order to learn _____

_____

_____

A crime scene investigator might study DNA in order to learn _____

_____

_____

2 Apply *GMO* stands for "genetically modified organism." Write a caption to accompany the following photo.

_____

_____

_____

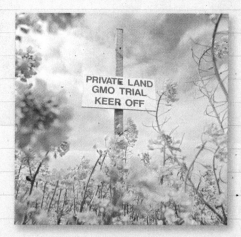

Active Reading

3 Apply Use context clues to write your own definition for the words *inserted* and *technique*.

Example sentence
Using special technologies, a gene from one organism can be <u>inserted</u> into the DNA of another.

inserted:

_____

_____

Example sentence
Cloning is a <u>technique</u> in which the genetic information of an organism is copied.

technique:

_____

_____

Vocabulary Terms

- biotechnology
- artificial selection
- genetic engineering
- clone

4 Apply As you learn the definition of each vocabulary term in this lesson, create your own definition or sketch to help you remember the meaning of the term.

Protective clothing keeps this geneticist safe as he works with infectious particles.

This scientist works inside of a greenhouse. He breeds potato plants.

5 Research Research careers in biotechnology. Choose a career that you might like to have and share it with your class. You may choose to present your findings in one of the following ways:
- a poster
- a computer presentation
- a play
- a short essay

What is biotechnology?

A forensic scientist makes copies of DNA from a crime scene. A botanist breeds flowers for their bright red blooms. A geneticist works to place a human gene into the DNA of bacteria. What do these processes have in common? They are all examples of biotechnology. **Biotechnology** is the use and application of living things and biological processes. In the past 40 years, new technologies have allowed scientists to directly change DNA. But biotechnology is not a new scientific field. For thousands of years, humans have been breeding plants and animals and using bacteria and yeast to ferment foods. These, too, are examples of biotechnology.

Active Reading **6 Identify** Name three examples of biotechnology.

_____

_____

_____

© Houghton Mifflin Harcourt Publishing Company • Image Credits: (l) ©Patrick Landmann/Photo Researchers, Inc.; (r) ©Scott Bauer/U.S. Department of Agriculture/Photo Researchers, Inc

Different dog breeds are produced by artificial selection.

What are some applications of biotechnology?

Biotechnology processes fall into some broad categories. Artificial selection, genetic engineering, and cloning are some of the most common techniques.

Artificial Selection

For thousands of years, humans have been carefully selecting and breeding certain plants and animals that have desirable traits. Over many generations, horses have gotten faster, pigs have gotten leaner, and corn has become sweeter. **Artificial selection** is the process of selecting and breeding organisms that have certain desired traits. Artificial selection is also known as *selective breeding*.

Artificial selection can be successful as long as the desirable traits are controlled by genes. Animal and plant breeders select for alleles, which are different versions of a gene. The alleles being selected must already be present in the population. People do not change DNA during artificial selection. Instead, they cause certain alleles to become more common in a population. The different dog breeds are a good example of artificial selection. All dogs share a common ancestor, the wolf. However, thousands of years of selection by humans have produced dogs with a variety of characteristics.

These vegetables have been developed through artificial selection. Their common ancestor is the mustard plant.

kale

broccoli

cabbage

cauliflower

Brussels sprouts

7 Infer Why might farmers use artificial selection to develop different types of vegetables?

_____

_____

_____

_____

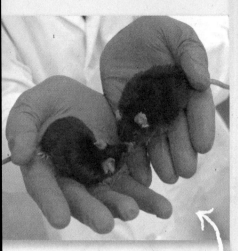

Scientists have disabled a gene in the mouse on the right. As a result, this mouse cannot control how much food it eats.

Genetic Engineering

Within the past 40 years, it has become possible to directly change the DNA of an organism. **Genetic engineering** is the process in which a piece of DNA is modified for use in research, medicine, agriculture, or industry. The DNA that is engineered often codes for a certain trait of interest. Scientists can isolate a segment of DNA, change it in some way, and return it to the organism. Or, scientists can take a segment of DNA from one species and transfer it to the DNA of an organism from another species.

Active Reading **8 Describe** For what purposes can genetic engineering be used?

_____

_____

_____

These genetically modified plant cells produce tiny, biodegradable plastic pellets. The pellets are then collected to make plastic products.

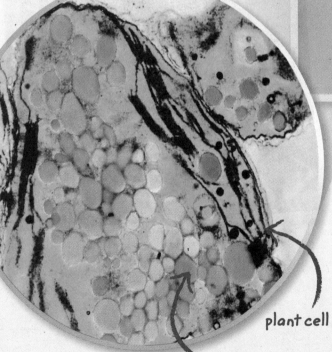

plant cell

plastic pellets

9 Infer Traditional plastics are made from petroleum, a nonrenewable resource. What benefit could plastic made by plants have over traditional plastic?

_____

_____

_____

_____

_____

Cloning

A **clone** is an organism, cell, or piece of genetic material that is genetically identical to the one from which it was derived. Cloning has been used to make copies of small traces of DNA found at crime scenes or on ancient artifacts. Also, cloning can be used to copy segments of DNA for genetic engineering.

In 1996, scientists cloned the DNA from one sheep's body cell to produce another sheep named Dolly. The ability to clone a sheep, which is a mammal, raised many concerns about the future uses of cloning, because humans are also mammals. It is important that people understand the science of genetics. Only then can we make informed decisions about how and when the technology should be used.

Dolly was cloned from a body cell of an adult sheep.

---

10 Apply Review each of the examples of biotechnology below. Then classify each as artificial selection, genetic engineering, or cloning.

	Scientists have introduced a gene to the DNA of these fish that causes the fish to glow.	☐ artificial selection ☐ genetic engineering ☐ cloning
	A scientist is gathering DNA from clothing found at a crime scene. Then many copies of the DNA sample will be made. This will allow the scientist to better study the DNA. Then the scientist might be able to confirm the identity of the person at the crime scene.	☐ artificial selection ☐ genetic engineering ☐ cloning
	Wild carrots have thin, white roots. Over time, carrot farmers have selected carrots that have thick, bright orange roots.	☐ artificial selection ☐ genetic engineering ☐ cloning
	Diabetes can be treated in some people with injections that contain the hormone insulin. The gene responsible for producing insulin in humans has been inserted into the DNA of bacteria. These bacteria then produce the human insulin that is used in the injection.	☐ artificial selection ☐ genetic engineering ☐ cloning

Feel the IMPACT!

How does biotechnology impact our world?

Scientists are aware that there are many ethical, legal, and social issues that arise from the ability to use and change living things. Biotechnology can impact both our society and our environment. We must decide how and when it is acceptable to use biotechnology. The examples that follow show some concerns that might be raised during a classroom debate about biotechnology.

---

11 Evaluate Read the first two examples of biotechnology and what students had to say about their effects on individuals, society, and the environment. Then complete Example 3 by filling in questions or possible effects of the technology.

Example 1

A Glowing Mosquito?

This is the larva of a genetically engineered mosquito. Its DNA includes a gene from a glowing jellyfish that causes the engineered mosquito to glow. Scientists hope to use this same technology to modify the mosquito's genome in other ways. For example, it is thought that the DNA of the mosquito could be changed so that the mosquito could not spread malaria.

Effects on Individuals and Society

"If the mosquito could be engineered so that it does not spread malaria, many lives could be saved."

Effects on Environment

"Mosquitoes are a food source for birds and fish. Are there health risks to animals that eat genetically modified mosquitoes?"

Think Outside the Book (Inquiry)

12 Debate As a class, choose a current event that involves biotechnology. Then hold a debate to present the benefits and risks of this technology.

© Houghton Mifflin Harcourt Publishing Company • Image Credits: ©Sinclair Stammers/Photo Researchers, Inc.

© Houghton Mifflin Harcourt Publishing Company • Image Credits: (bkgd) ©Mauro Fermariello/Photo Researchers, Inc.; (tr) ©Tom McHugh/Photo Researchers, Inc.; (br) ©Chris Knapton/Photo Researchers, Inc.

Example 2

Cloning the Gaur

The gaur is an endangered species. In 2001, a gaur was successfully cloned. The clone, named Noah, died of a bacterial infection 2 days after birth.

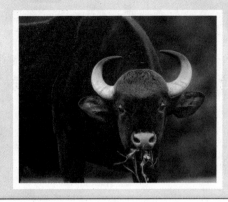

Effects on Individuals and Society

"How will we decide when it is appropriate to clone other types of organisms?"

Effects on Environment

"Cloning could help increase small populations of endangered species like the gaur and save them from extinction."

Example 3

Tough Plants!

Much of the corn and soybeans grown in the United States is genetically engineered. The plants have bacterial genes that make them more resistant to plant-eating insects.

Effects on Individuals and Society

Effects on Environment

Visual Summary

To complete this summary, circle the correct word or phrase. Then use the key below to check your answers. You can use this page to review the main concepts of the lesson.

Biotechnology

Biotechnology is the use of living things and biological processes.

13 Modern biotechnology techniques can change an organism's DNA / environment.

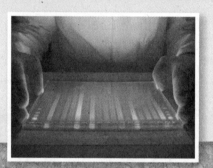

Aritifical selection, genetic engineering, and cloning are three types of biotechnology.

14 The DNA of the mouse on the right has been modified through a technique called cloning / genetic engineering.

Biotechnology impacts individuals, society, and the environment.

15 Creating a clone / gene of an endangered species could impact the environment.

Answers: 13 DNA, 14 genetic engineering; 15 clone

16 **Compare** Both artificial selection and genetic engineering produce organisms that have traits that are different from the original organism. Explain how these two techniques differ.

Lesson Review

Vocabulary

In your own words, define the following terms.

1 biotechnology

_____

_____

_____

2 artificial selection

_____

_____

_____

_____

3 clone

_____

_____

_____

Key Concepts

4 Identify Wheat has been bred by farmers for thousands of years to improve its ability to be ground into flour. This is an example of what kind of biotechnology?

A artificial selection

B genetic engineering

C cloning

D PCR

5 Identify Which of the following statements correctly describes why society must carefully consider the use of biotechnology?

A Biotechnology is a relatively new scientific field.

B Biotechnology can impact individuals and the environment.

C The methods of genetic engineering are not well understood.

D Artificial selection is an example of biotechnology.

Critical Thinking

Use this graph to answer the following questions.

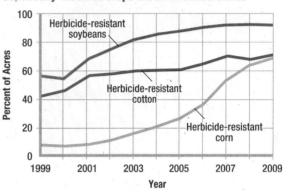

Genetically-modified Crops Grown in United States

Source: *USDA, 2009*

6 Analyze In 2003, what percentage of soybean crops in the United States were genetically engineered to be herbicide resistant?

_____

7 Analyze From 1999 to 2009, which genetically engineered crop had the greatest increase in acreage?

_____

_____

8 Synthesize Some salmon have been genetically engineered to grow more quickly. The salmon are raised in pens set in rivers or in the sea. Describe how these salmon might impact society and the environment.

_____

_____

_____

_____

_____

_____

_____

_____

_____

My Notes

Unit 7 Summary

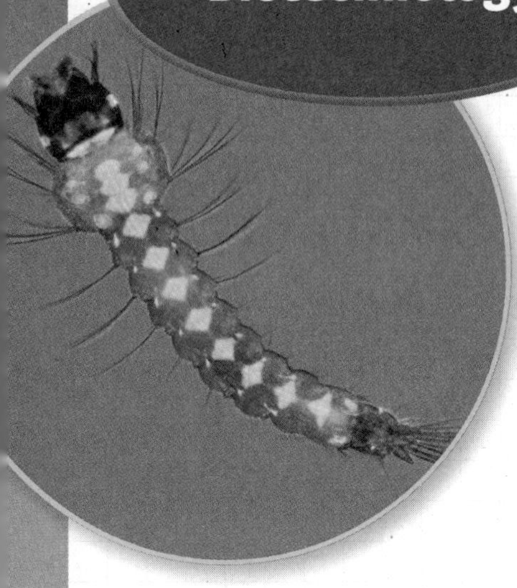

Biotechnology

relies on an understanding of

DNA Structure and Function

contributes to the field of

Modern Genetics

---

1 Interpret The Graphic Organizer above shows that biotechnology relies on an understanding of the structure and function of DNA. Explain.

_____

_____

_____

_____

_____

_____

_____

2 Compare How are DNA replication and DNA cloning similar? How are they different?

_____

_____

_____

_____

3 Predict The variety of traits seen in house cats is due in part to artificial selection. Explain how mutations could contribute to the artificial selection of cats.

_____

_____

_____

_____

_____

Benchmark Review

Name _____

Multiple Choice
Identify the choice that best completes the statement or answers the question.

1 Terrie is creating a model of DNA. Which of these shapes illustrates how her model should look?

A.

C.

B.

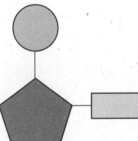

D.

2 Scientists must carefully weigh the risks and benefits of biotechnology. Which of these **best** describes a risk to society that scientists might consider when genetically engineering a crop?

F. how the plant reproduces

G. the sequence of bases in the plant's DNA

H. what kinds of soil the plant will need in order to grow

I. whether the plant will produce a substance that can cause an allergic reaction in humans

3 The diagram below shows an original sequence of DNA, and then a mutated sequence of DNA.

Original sequence

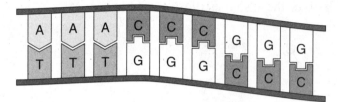

New sequence

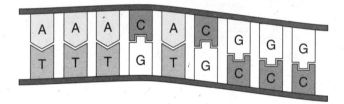

Which type of mutation took place?

A. deletion

B. insertion

C. substitution

D. translation

4 Sickle cell anemia is an inherited disorder. Which of the following is **a true** statement about sickle cell anemia?

F. It is never inherited from a parent.

G. The mutation occurs during a person's lifetime.

H. It is an infectious disease.

I. It is caused by a change in the bases in DNA.

5 Alice is studying biological molecules. She isolated a molecule and identified the nucleotide bases adenine, cytosine, guanine, and thymine. Which molecule did Alice isolate?

A. DNA

B. mRNA

C. rRNA

D. tRNA

6 Cloning is one type of biotechnology. Which of these choices is an example of cloning?

    F.   Certain chickens are bred for their distinctive feather color.

    G.   Several copies of a fruit fly gene are produced in a laboratory.

    H.   Plants with red flowers are bred with plants with blue flowers.

    I.   Yeast cells are placed under an ultraviolet lamp, causing their DNA to mutate.

7 Luis wants to interview someone who has a career in biotechnology. Which of the following **best** describes a career in biotechnology?

    A.   Athena uses a sophisticated telescope to observe stars.

    B.   Zach tracks the number of fish that inhabit a certain coastal area.

    C.   Vincent modifies the DNA of bacteria to study the function of their genes.

    D.   Lindsey writes computer programs that model the three-dimensional structure of chemical compounds.

8 Dylan is listing the substances that make up DNA. Which of these substances should he list as a nucleotide base found in DNA?

    F.   adenine

    G.   phosphate

    H.   sugar

    I.   uracil

9 A scientist transfers a fragment of genetic material from one organism to another organism of a different species. What is this process called?

    A.   artificial selection

    B.   selective breeding

    C.   genetic engineering

    D.   asexual reproduction

10 The two mice pictured below were created by cloning.

What do the mice have in common that allows scientists to call them clones?

F. their diet

G. when they were born

H. their genetic material

I. the number of siblings they have

11 Rachel is analyzing a DNA sample to identify its base pairs. Her results show that 40% of the sample is adenine. Which other base makes up 40% of the sample?

A. cytosine

B. guanine

C. thymine

D. uracil

12 The following sequence of letters represents the order of bases in a single strand of DNA.

C-T-T-A-G-G-C-T-T-A-C-C-A

Which of these sequences would be the complementary strand that forms during replication?

F. G-A-A-T-C-C-G-A-A-T-G-G-T

G. C-T-T-A-G-G-C-T-T-A-C-C-A

H. T-C-C-G-A-A-T-C-C-G-T-T-G

I. A-G-G-C-T-T-A-G-G-C-A-A-C

Ecology

Fish and sponges
in a coral reef

Big Idea 17

Interdependence

What do you think?

Ecosystems consist of living things that depend on
each other to survive. How might these fish depend
on a coral reef? How might this bird depend on a
dragonfly population?

Eastern bluebirds
feed on insects.

Sharing Spaces

Florida provides living space for many kinds of birds. Ospreys are large birds of prey that eat mostly fish. They often nest on telephone poles and other man-made structures. Yellow-rumped warblers are small birds that live in trees and eat insects and berries.

1 Ask A Question

How can organisms affect each other and a whole ecosystem?

An ecosystem is made up of all the living and nonliving things in an environment. Ospreys and yellow-rumped warblers are part of the same ecosystem. With your teacher and your classmates, brainstorm ways in which ospreys and yellow-rumped warblers might affect each other.

Yellow-rumped warbler

Osprey nest

② Think About It

Look at the photos of the ospreys in their environment. List at least two resources they need to survive and explain how the ospreys get them.

_____
_____
_____

What are two ways nonliving things could affect yellow-rumped warblers?

_____
_____
_____

③ Apply Your Knowledge

A List the ways in which yellow-rumped warblers and ospreys share resources.

_____
_____
_____

B Yellow-rumped warblers live in Florida during the winter only. How might the warblers affect other organisms in the ecosystem if they stayed in Florida all year?

_____
_____
_____
_____

C Describe a situation that could negatively affect both the osprey population and the yellow-rumped warbler population.

_____
_____
_____

Take It Home

Are ecologists looking for people to report observations in your community? Contact a university near your community to see if you can help gather information about plants, flowers, birds, or invasive species. Then, share your results with your class.

Introduction to Ecology

ESSENTIAL QUESTION

What parts make up an ecosystem?

By the end of this lesson, you should be able to analyze the components of an ecosystem.

This rainforest is an ecosystem. Hornbills are organisms in the ecosystem that use the trees for shelter.

Sunshine State Standards

LA.6.4.2.2 The student will record information (e.g., observations, notes, lists, charts, legends) related to a topic, including visual aids to organize and record information and include a list of sources used.

Engage Your Brain

1 Describe In your own words, write a list of living or nonliving things that are in your community.

_____

_____

_____

_____

_____

_____

_____

_____

_____

2 Relate Below, write a photo caption that compares the ecosystem shown above and the ecosystem shown on the previous page.

_____

_____

_____

_____

 Active Reading

3 Synthesize You can often define an unknown word or term if you know the meaning of its word parts. Use the word parts and sentence below to make an educated guess about the meaning of the term *abiotic factor*.

Word part	Meaning
a-	without
bio-	life

Example sentence

In an ecosystem, rocks are an example of an abiotic factor.

Vocabulary Terms

- ecology
- biotic factor
- abiotic factor
- population
- species
- community
- ecosystem
- habitat
- niche

4 Apply As you learn the definition of each vocabulary term in this lesson, create your own definition or sketch to help you remember the meaning of the term.

abiotic factor:

_____

_____

The Web of Life

How are all living things connected?

The web of life connects all organisms to each other and to the environment. Organisms need energy and matter for life. Interactions between organisms allow the exchange of energy and matter to occur. **Ecology** is the study of how organisms interact with one another and with the environment.

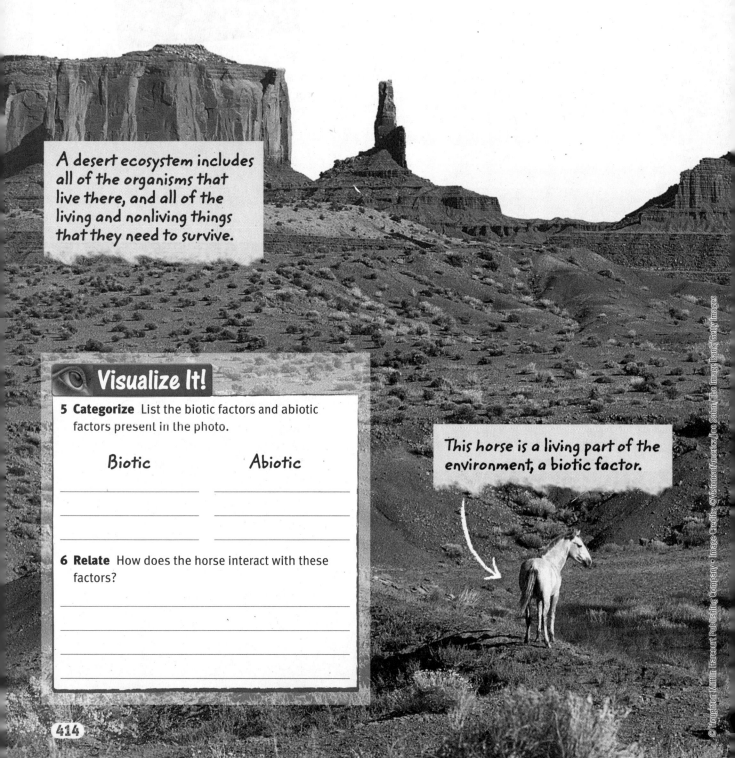

A desert ecosystem includes all of the organisms that live there, and all of the living and nonliving things that they need to survive.

This horse is a living part of the environment, a biotic factor.

Visualize It!

5 Categorize List the biotic factors and abiotic factors present in the photo.

Biotic	Abiotic
_____	_____
_____	_____
_____	_____

6 Relate How does the horse interact with these factors?

_____

_____

_____

_____

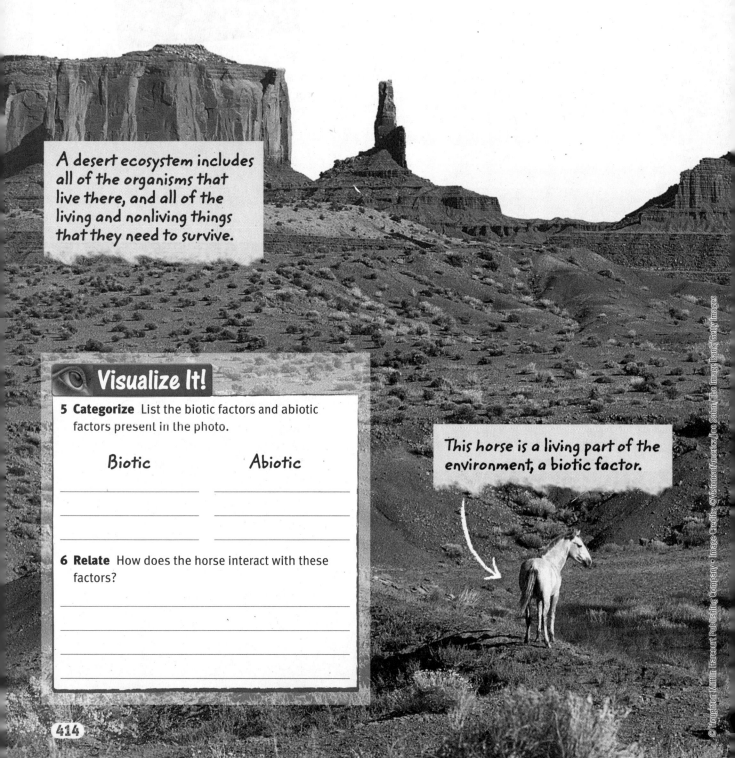

Through the Living Environment

Biodiversity is the variation of living organisms, from tiny bacteria to huge whales. Each individual organism has a role to play in the flow of energy and matter. In this way, organisms are connected to all other organisms. Relationships among organisms affect each one's growth and survival. A **biotic factor** is a living part of the environment. Organisms, and how they interact, are examples of biotic factors.

Through the Nonliving Environment

All organisms rely on the nonliving environment for survival. An **abiotic factor** is a nonliving part of an environment, such as water, nutrients, soil, sunlight, rainfall, or temperature. Some of these are resources that organisms need to grow and survive. For example, plants use sunlight, water, and soil nutrients to make food. Similarly, some organisms rely on soil or rocks for shelter.

Abiotic factors determine where organisms can survive. The ranges of organisms that can live in an environment are limited by basic requirements in the abiotic environment. In a terrestrial environment, temperature and rainfall are important abiotic factors. In aquatic environments, temperature, salinity, and oxygen content are important abiotic factors. Changes in these basic abiotic factors cause changes in where organisms can live and how many can live there.

Active Reading **7 Infer** How does the environment determine where an organism can survive? Explain your answer.

_____

_____

_____

_____

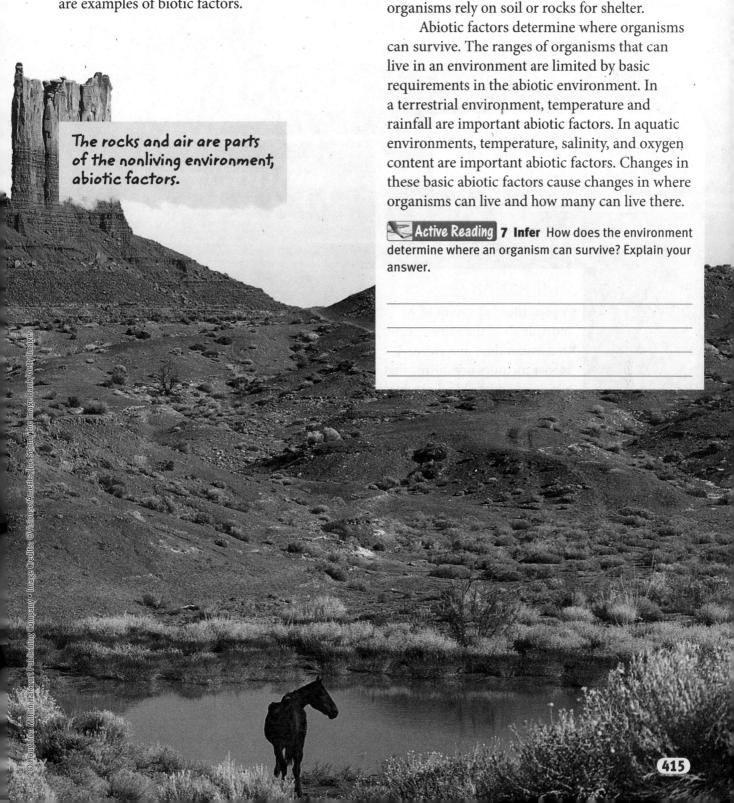

The rocks and air are parts of the nonliving environment, abiotic factors.

Stay Organized!

What are all the levels of organization in the environment?

The environment can be organized into different levels. These levels range from a single organism to all of the organisms and their surroundings in an area. The levels of organization get more complex as more of the environment is considered.

Active Reading **8 Identify** As you read, underline the characteristics of each of the following levels of organization.

Populations

A **population** is a group of individuals of the same species that live in the same place. A **species** includes organisms that are closely related and can mate to produce fertile offspring. The alligators that live in the Everglades are a population. Individuals within a population often compete with each other for food, shelter, and mates.

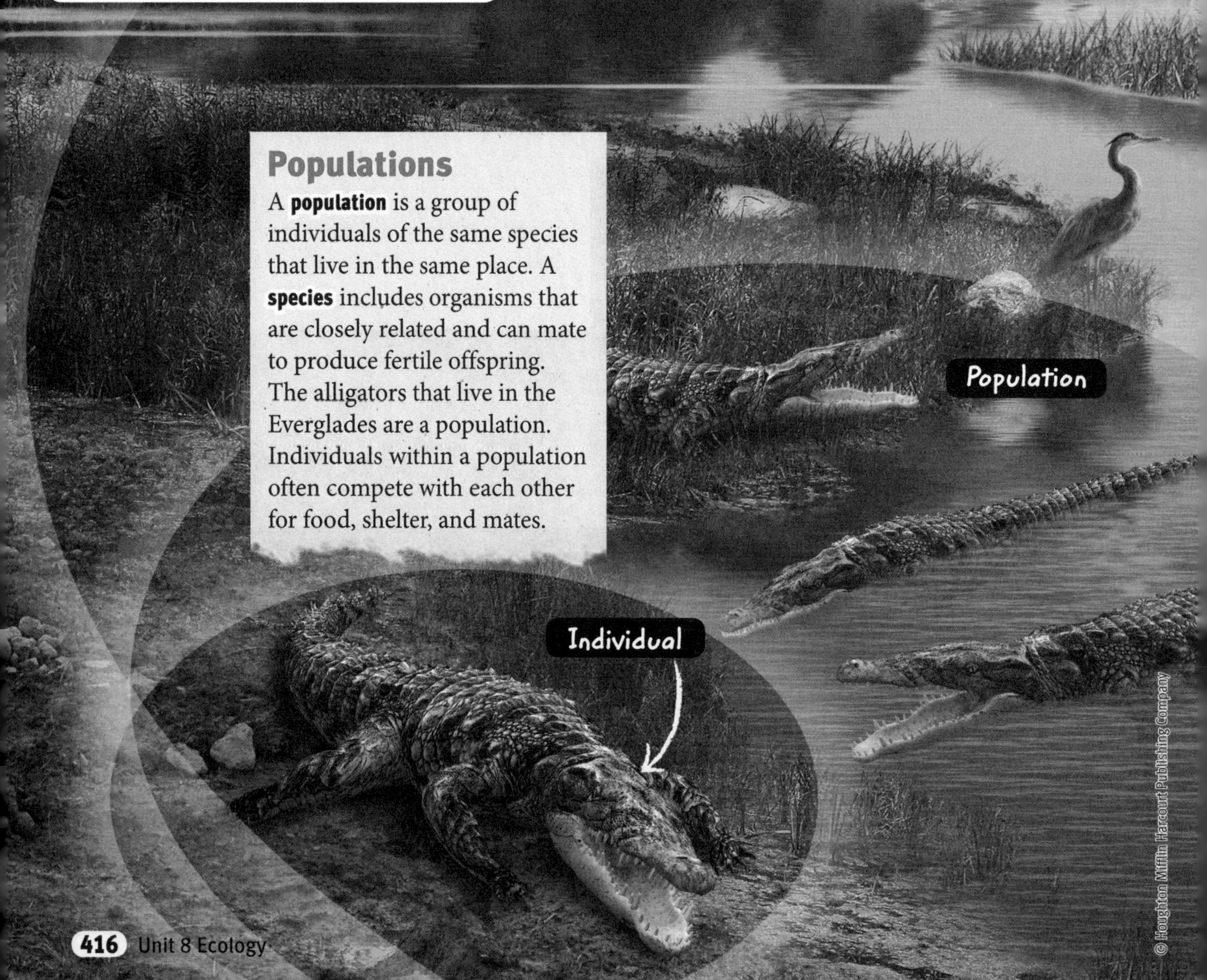

Population

Individual

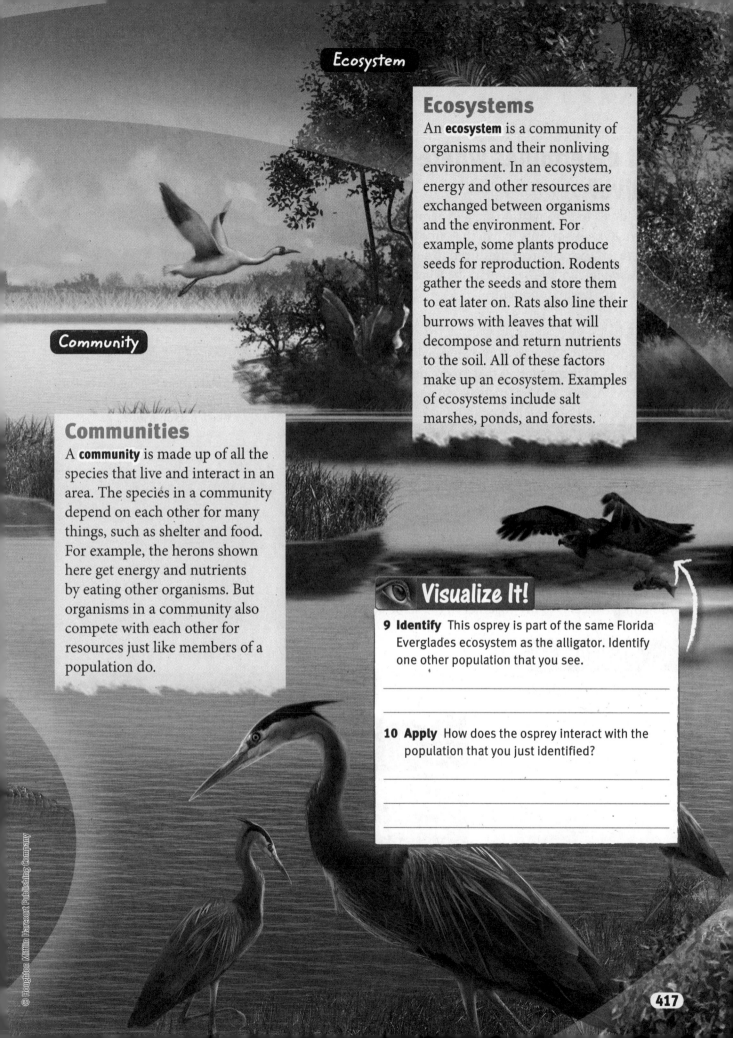

Ecosystems

An **ecosystem** is a community of organisms and their nonliving environment. In an ecosystem, energy and other resources are exchanged between organisms and the environment. For example, some plants produce seeds for reproduction. Rodents gather the seeds and store them to eat later on. Rats also line their burrows with leaves that will decompose and return nutrients to the soil. All of these factors make up an ecosystem. Examples of ecosystems include salt marshes, ponds, and forests.

Community

Communities

A **community** is made up of all the species that live and interact in an area. The species in a community depend on each other for many things, such as shelter and food. For example, the herons shown here get energy and nutrients by eating other organisms. But organisms in a community also compete with each other for resources just like members of a population do.

Visualize It!

9 Identify This osprey is part of the same Florida Everglades ecosystem as the alligator. Identify one other population that you see.

_____

_____

10 Apply How does the osprey interact with the population that you just identified?

_____

_____

_____

Home Sweet Home

What determines where a population can live?

All individuals in a population are a dynamic part of their ecosystem. Organisms that live in the same area play different roles in order to get the resources they need to survive. Ecologists use the terms *habitat* and *niche* to describe where an organism lives and its role in the environment.

Habitat

Habitat is the place where an organism usually lives. The habitat must provide all the resources that an organism needs to grow and survive. Abiotic factors, such as temperature, often determine whether a species can live in a certain place. Biotic factors, such as other organisms that live in the area, also play a role. For example, the habitat of a shark must include populations of fish it can eat.

Niche

Each population in an ecosystem plays a specific role. A population's **niche** is the role the population plays in the ecosystem, like how it gets food and interacts with other populations.

In general, two populations cannot occupy exactly the same niche. Small differences in habitats, roles, and adaptations can allow similar species to live together in the same ecosystem.

Active Reading

11 Relate How is a habitat is like a person's address and a niche is like a person's job?

_____

_____

_____

_____

_____

_____

_____

Visualize It!

12 Infer What do you think is the prairie dog's niche?

_____

_____

_____

_____

_____

Prairie dogs dig burrows in grassy plains. They eat plants and are hunted by predators like owls and foxes.

Lizard Invasion

Green anole lizards (*Anolis carolinensis*) have been part of the South Florida ecosystem for many years. Recently a closely related lizard, the brown anole (*Anolis sagrei*), has invaded the natural habitat of the green anole. How do they avoid competing with each other for resources?

Home Base

The green anole lives on perches on the whole tree. Brown anoles mainly live on ground branches. If green and brown anoles are in the same tree, green anoles move up to avoid the ground perches. In this way they can avoid occupying the same habitat as the brown anole.

Competition Arrives

Although brown and green anoles have shifted their habitat in order to coexist, they do not live together peacefully. Brown anoles also interfere with the green anoles by eating their young.

Extend

Inquiry

13 **Describe** How do the anoles separate themselves to avoid competition? Draw a picture of a tree with both green and brown anoles on it.

14 **Research** What are other examples of two species dividing a niche or habitat?

15 **Relate** Infer what would happen if the habitats or niches of these species overlapped. Present your findings in a format such as a short story or a soap opera or play.

Visual Summary

To complete this summary, circle the correct word. Then use the key below to check your answers. You can use this page to review the main concepts of the lesson.

Ecology and Ecosystems

Ecology is the study of the biotic and abiotic factors in an ecosystem, and the relationships between them.

16 In a desert ecosystem, sand is an example of a biotic / abiotic factor, and cacti are an example of a biotic / abiotic factor.

Every organism has a habitat and a niche.

17 Certain types of fish live in desert ponds where they feed on other organisms from the water. In this example, the lake is a habitat / niche and filter-feeding behavior is part of a habitat / niche.

The environment can be organized into different levels, including populations, communities, and ecosystems.

18 Populations of cacti, together with sand and rocks, are included in a desert community / ecosystem.

Answers: 16 abiotic, biotic; 17 habitat, niche; 18 ecosystem

19 Predict In the desert ecosystem shown above, name a biotic factor and describe the effect on the horses if it were removed from the ecosystem.

Lesson Review

Vocabulary

1 Explain how the meanings of the terms *biotic factor* and *abiotic factor* differ. _____

_____

_____

2 In your own words, write a definition for *ecology*. _____

_____

_____

_____

3 Explain how the meanings of the terms *habitat* and *niche* differ. _____

_____

_____

_____

Key Concepts

4 List What are two ways that organisms are connected to the nonliving environment?

_____

_____

_____

5 Explain How can the environment be organized into levels from simple to complex?

_____

_____

_____

_____

6 Infer How do the populations in a community depend on each other?

_____

_____

_____

_____

7 Identify What factors determine whether a species can be present in a place?

_____

_____

_____

_____

Critical Thinking

Use this graph to answer the following question.

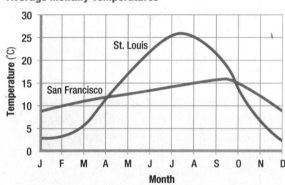

Average Monthly Temperatures

8 Calculate What is the average temperature difference in July between the two cities?

_____

9 Predict What might happen in a tropical rainforest biome if the area received very little rain for an extended period of time?

_____

_____

_____

_____

10 Infer Owls and hawks both eat rodents. They are also found in the same habitats. Since no two populations can occupy exactly the same niche, how can owls and hawks coexist?

_____

_____

_____

_____

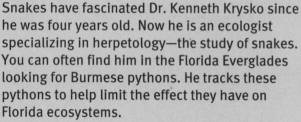

Kenneth Krysko

ECOLOGIST

Snakes have fascinated Dr. Kenneth Krysko since he was four years old. Now he is an ecologist specializing in herpetology—the study of snakes. You can often find him in the Florida Everglades looking for Burmese pythons. He tracks these pythons to help limit the effect they have on Florida ecosystems.

Burmese pythons can grow to be 6 meters long. They are native to southeast Asia and were illegally brought to Florida as pets. Many owners released them into the wild when the snakes grew too large. The snakes breed well in Florida's subtropical climate. And they eat just about any animal they can swallow, including many native species. Dr. Krysko tracks down these invasive pythons. Through wildlife management, molecular genetics, and other areas of study, he works with other scientists to search for ways to reduce the python population.

Dr. Krysko studies many other invasive species, that is, nonnative species that can do harm in Florida ecosystems. He shares what he learns, including ways to identify and deal with invasive species with other ecologists. Along with invasion ecology, he has done research in reproduction and conservation biology. Dr. Krysko also works as a collections manager in the herpetology division at the Florida Museum of Natural History.

Dr. Krysko works to get a handle on what to do about the invasive pythons.

JOB BOARD

Park Naturalist

What You'll Do: Teach visitors at state and national parks about the park's ecology, geology, and landscape. Lead field trips, prepare and deliver lectures with slides, and create educational programs for park visitors. You may participate in research projects and track organisms in the park.

Where You Might Work: State and national parks

Education: An advanced degree in science and teacher certification

Other Job Requirements: You need to be good at communicating and teaching. Having photography and writing skills helps you prepare interesting educational materials.

Conservation Warden

What You'll Do: Patrol an area to enforce rules, and work with communities and groups to help educate the public about conservation and ecology.

Where You Might Work: Indoors and outdoors in state and national parks and ecologically sensitive areas

Education: A two-year associate's degree or at least 60 fully accredited college-level credits

Other Job Requirements: To work in the wild, good wilderness skills, map-reading, hiking, and excellent hearing are useful.

PEOPLE IN SCIENCE NEWS

Phil McCRORY

Saved by a Hair!

Phil McCrory, a hairdresser in Huntsville, Alabama, asked a brilliant question when he saw an otter whose fur was drenched with oil from the Exxon Valdez oil spill. If the otter's fur soaked up oil, why wouldn't human hair do the same? McCrory gathered hair from the floor of his salon and performed his own experiments. He stuffed hair into a pair of pantyhose and tied the ankles together. McCrory floated this bundle in his son's wading pool and poured used motor oil into the center of the ring. When he pulled the ring closed, not a drop of oil remained in the water! McCrory's discovery was tested as an alternative method for cleaning up oil spills. Many people donated their hair to be used for cleanup efforts. Although the method worked well, the engineers conducting the research concluded that hair is not as useful as other oil-absorbing materials for cleaning up large-scale spills.

Roles in Energy Transfer

ESSENTIAL QUESTION

How does energy flow through an ecosystem?

By the end of this lesson, you should be able to relate the roles of organisms to the transfer of energy in food chains and food webs.

Energy is transferred from the sun to producers, such as kelp. It flows through the rest of the ecosystem.

This goldfish also needs energy to live. How do you think it gets this energy? From the sun like kelp do?

Sunshine State Standards

SC.7.L.17.1 Explain and illustrate the roles of and relationships among producers, consumers, and decomposers in the process of energy transfer in a food web.

LA.6.4.2.2 The student will record information (e.g., observations, notes, lists, charts, legends) related to a topic, including visual aids to organize and record information and include a list of sources used.

Engage Your Brain

1 Describe Most organisms on Earth get energy from the sun. How is energy flowing through the ecosystem pictured on the opposite page?

_____
_____
_____
_____
_____

2 Predict List two of your favorite foods. Then, explain how the sun's energy helped make those foods available to you.

_____
_____
_____
_____
_____

Active Reading

3 Synthesize You can often define an unknown word if you know the meaning of its word parts. Use the word parts and sentences below to make an educated guess about the meaning of the words _herbivore_ and _carnivore_.

Word part	Meaning
-vore	to eat
herbi-	plant
carni-	meat

Example sentence
A koala bear is an <u>herbivore</u> that eats eucalyptus leaves.

herbivore:

_____
_____
_____

Example sentence
A great white shark is a <u>carnivore</u> that eats fish and other marine animals.

carnivore:

_____
_____
_____

Vocabulary Terms

- producer
- decomposer
- consumer
- herbivore
- carnivore
- omnivore
- food chain
- food web

4 Apply As you learn the definition of each vocabulary term in this lesson, create your own definition or sketch to help you remember the meaning of the term.

Get Energized!

How do organisms get energy?

Energy is all around you. Chemical energy is stored in the bonds of molecules and holds molecules together. The energy from food is chemical energy in the bonds of food molecules. All living things need a source of chemical energy to survive.

Active Reading 6 **Identify** As you read, underline examples of producers, decomposers, and consumers.

Think Outside the Book

5 **Apply** Record what you eat at your next meal. Where do you think these items come from, before they reach the market?

Producers Convert Energy Into Food

A **producer**, also called an autotroph, uses energy to make food. Most producers use sunlight to make food in a process called photosynthesis. The sun powers most life on Earth. In photosynthesis, producers use light energy to make food from water, carbon dioxide, and nutrients found in water and soil. The food contains chemical energy and can be used immediately or stored for later use. All green plants, such as grasses and trees, are producers. Algae and some bacteria are also producers. The food that these producers make supplies the energy for other living things in an ecosystem.

Decomposers Break Down Matter

An organism that gets energy and nutrients by breaking down the remains of other organisms is a **decomposer**. Fungi, such as the mushrooms on this log, and some bacteria are decomposers. Decomposers are nature's recyclers. By converting dead organisms and animal and plant waste into materials such as water and nutrients, decomposers help move matter through ecosystems. Decomposers make these simple materials available to other organisms.

This plant is a producer. Producers make food using light energy from the sun.

These mushrooms are decomposers. They break down the remains of plants and animals.

Consumers Eat Other Organisms

A **consumer** is an organism that eats other organisms. Consumers use the energy and nutrients stored in other living organisms because they cannot make their own food. A consumer that eats only plants, such as a grasshopper or bison, is called an **herbivore**. A **carnivore**, such as a badger or this wolf, eats other animals. An **omnivore** eats both plants and animals. A *scavenger* is a specialized consumer that feeds on dead organisms. Scavengers, such as the turkey vulture, eat the leftovers of the meals of other animals or eat dead animals.

This wolf is a consumer. It eats other organisms to get energy.

Consumers

Visualize It!

7 List Beside each image, place a check mark next to the word that matches the type of consumer the animal is.

Name: Moose
What I eat: grasses, fruits

What am I?
- ☑ herbivore
- ☐ omnivore
- ☐ carnivore

Name: Hedgehog
What I eat: leaves, earthworms, insects

What am I?
- ☐ herbivore
- ☑ omnivore
- ☐ carnivore

Name: Komodo dragon
What I eat: insects, birds, mammals

What am I?
- ☐ herbivore
- ☐ omnivore
- ☑ carnivore

8 Infer Explain how carnivores might be affected if the main plant species in a community were to disappear.

_____
_____
_____

Energy Transfer

How is energy transferred among organisms?

Organisms change energy from the environment or from their food into other types of energy. Some of this energy is used for the organism's activities, such as breathing or moving. Some of the energy is saved within the organism to use later. If an organism is eaten or decomposes, the consumer or decomposer takes in the energy stored in the original organism. Only chemical energy that an organism has stored in its tissues is available to consumers. In this way, energy is transferred from organism to organism.

Active Reading **9 Infer** When a grasshopper eats grass, only some of the energy from the grass is stored in the grasshopper's body. How does the grasshopper use the rest of the energy?

_____

_____

This tree gets its energy from the sun.

This ant eats plants like the mesquite tree, and other insects.

10 Identify By what process does this tree get its energy?

_____

_____

11 Apply What type of energy is this ant consuming?

_____

_____

Energy Flows Through a Food Chain

A **food chain** is the path of energy transfer from producers to consumers. Energy moves from one organism to the next in one direction. The arrows in a food chain represent the transfer of energy, as one organism is eaten by another. Arrows represent the flow of energy from the body of the consumed organism to the body of the consumer of that organism.

Producers form the base of food chains. Producers transfer energy to the first, or primary, consumer in the food chain. The next, or secondary, consumer in the food chain consumes the primary consumer. A tertiary consumer eats the secondary consumer. Finally, decomposers recycle matter back to the soil.

This hawk eats the lizard. It is at the top of the food chain.

Visualize It!

The photographs below show a typical desert food chain. Answer the following four questions from left to right based on your understanding of how energy flows in a food chain.

13 Predict If nothing ever eats this hawk, what might eventually happen to the energy that is stored in its body?

_____

_____

This lizard eats mostly insects.

12 Apply What does the arrow between the ant and the lizard represent?

_____

_____

World Wide Webs

How do food webs show energy connections?

Few organisms eat just one kind of food. So, the energy and nutrient connections in nature are more complicated than a simple food chain. A **food web** is the feeding relationships among organisms in an ecosystem. Food webs are made up of many food chains.

The next page shows a coastal food web. Most of the organisms in this food web live in the water. The web also includes some birds that live on land and eat fish. Tiny algae called phytoplankton form the base of this food web. Like plants on land, phytoplankton are producers. Tiny consumers called zooplankton eat phytoplankton. Larger animals, such as fish and squid, eat zooplankton. At the top of each chain are top predators, animals that eat other animals but are rarely eaten. In this food web, the killer whale is a top predator. Notice how many different energy paths lead from phytoplankton to the killer whale.

Active Reading

14 Identify Underline the type of organism that typically forms the base of the food web.

Visualize It!

15 Apply Complete the statements to the right with the correct organism names from the food web.

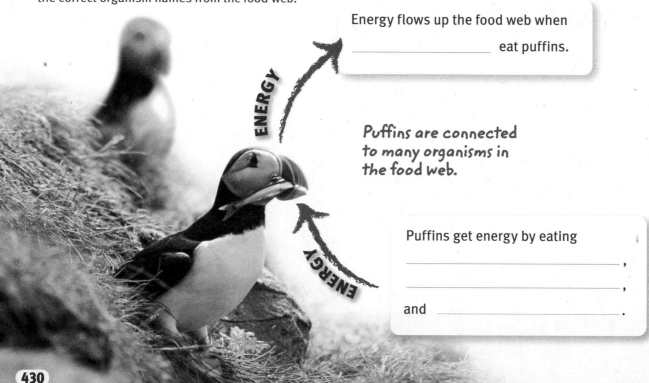

Energy flows up the food web when
_____ eat puffins.

Puffins are connected to many organisms in the food web.

Puffins get energy by eating
_____ ,
_____ ,
and _____ .

Food Web

The top predator is shown at the top of the food web. What is the top predator in this food web?

Killer whale

Seal

Gull

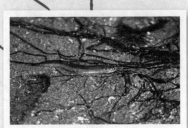

Cod

Herring

Squid

Sand lance

Consumers can eat producers and other consumers.

Zooplankton

Phytoplankton

Producers, such as these phytoplankton, form the base of the food web.

Puffin

How are organisms connected by food webs?

All living organisms are connected by global food webs. Global food webs include webs that begin on land and webs that begin in the water. Many organisms have feeding relationships that connect land- and water-based food webs. For example, algae might be eaten by a fish, which might then be eaten by a bird.

Food webs that start on land may also move into the water. Many insects that eat plants on land lay their eggs in the water. Some fish eat these eggs and the insect larvae that hatch from them. Because the global food webs are connected, removing even one organism can affect many organisms in other ecosystems.

Visualize It!

Imagine how these organisms would be affected if herring disappeared from the food web. Answer the questions starting at the bottom of the page.

■ Puffin

■ Squid

Herring

16 Identify Put a check mark next to the organisms that eat herring.

■ Gull

18 Infer Gulls don't eat herring but they are still connected by the food web. How might gull populations be affected?

_____
_____
_____
_____

■ Cod

17 Predict With no herring to eat, how might the eating habits of cod change?

_____
_____
_____
_____
_____
_____
_____
_____

Why It Matters

Dangerous Competition

EYE ON THE ENVIRONMENT

Sometimes species are introduced into a new area. These invasive species often compete with native species for energy resources, such as sunlight and food.

Full Coverage
The kudzu plant was introduced to stop soil erosion, but in the process it outgrew all the native plants, preventing them from getting sunlight. Sometimes it completely covers houses or cars!

Destructive Zebras
The zebra mussel is one of the most destructive invasive species in the United States. They eat by filtering tiny organisms out of the water, often leaving nothing for the native mussel species.

Across the Grass
The walking catfish can actually move across land to get from one pond to another! As a result, sometimes the catfish competes with native species for food.

Extend

Inquiry

19 Relate Describe how the competition between invasive and native species might affect a food web.

20 Describe Give an example of competition for a food resource that may occur in an ecosystem near you.

21 Illustrate Provide an illustration of your example of competition in a sketch or a short story. Be sure to include the important aspects of food webs that you learned in the lesson.

433

Visual Summary

To complete this summary, circle the correct word. Then use the key below to check your answers. You can use this page to review the main concepts of the lesson.

Energy Transfer
in Ecosystems

Organisms get energy in different ways.

- Producers make their own food.
- Consumers eat other living organisms.
- Decomposers break down dead organisms.

22 Herbivores, carnivores, and omnivores are three types of producers / ~~consumers~~ / decomposers.

Food chains and food webs describe the flow of energy in an ecosystem.

23 All food chains start with ~~producers~~ / consumers / decomposers.

Answers: 22 consumers; 23 producers

24 Predict Describe the effects on global food webs if the sun's energy could no longer reach Earth.

Food Web

Lesson Review

Vocabulary

Fill in the blanks with the term that best completes the following sentences.

1 _____ is the primary source of energy for most ecosystems.

2 A _____ eats mostly dead matter.

3 A _____ contains many food chains.

4 _____ is the process by which light energy from the sun is converted to food.

Key Concepts

5 Describe What are the roles of producers, consumers, and decomposers in an ecosystem?

_____

_____

_____

_____

6 Apply What types of organisms typically make up the base, middle, and top of a food web?

_____

_____

_____

_____

_____

_____

7 Describe Identify the two types of global food webs and describe how they are connected.

_____

_____

_____

_____

_____

Use the figure to answer the following questions.

8 Apply Describe the flow of energy in this food chain. Be sure to use the names of the organisms and what role they serve in the food chain (producer, consumer, or decomposer). If an organism is a consumer, identify whether it is an herbivore, carnivore, or omnivore.

_____

_____

_____

_____

9 Apply What do the arrows represent in the figure above?

_____

_____

Critical Thinking

10 Predict Give an example of a decomposer, and explain what would happen if decomposers were absent from a forest ecosystem.

_____

_____

_____

11 Predict How would a food web be affected if a species disappeared from an ecosystem?

_____

_____

_____

_____

_____

Interactions in Communities

These birds, called tickbirds, eat ticks and flies on a rhinoceros. This behavior helps the rhino. The ticks are also parasites that sometimes drink the rhino's blood!

ESSENTIAL QUESTION

How do organisms interact?

By the end of this lesson, you should be able to predict the effects of different interactions in communities.

Sunshine State Standards

SC.7.N.1.1 Define a problem from the seventh grade curriculum, use appropriate reference materials to support scientific understanding, plan and carry out scientific investigation of various types, such as systematic observations or experiments, identify variables, collect and organize data, interpret data in charts, tables, and graphics, analyze information, make predictions, and defend conclusions.

SC.7.L.17.2 Compare and contrast the relationships among organisms such as mutualism, predation, parasitism, competition, and commensalism.

LA.6.4.2.2 The student will record information (e.g., observations, notes, lists, charts, legends) related to a topic, including visual aids to organize and record information and include a list of sources used.

LA.6.2.2.3 The student will organize information to show understanding (e.g., representing main ideas within text through charting, mapping, paraphrasing, summarizing, or comparing/contrasting).

Engage Your Brain

1 Predict Check T or F to show whether you think each statement is true or false.

T   F

☐   ☐   Different animals can compete for the same food.

☐   ☐   Parasites help the organisms that they feed on.

☐   ☐   Some organisms rely on each other for necessities such as food or shelter.

☐   ☐   Organisms can defend themselves against predators that try to eat them.

2 Explain Draw an interaction between two living things that you might observe while on a picnic. Write a caption to go with your sketch.

Active Reading

3 Synthesize You can often define an unknown word if you know the meaning of its word parts. Use the word parts and sentence below to make an educated guess about the meaning of the word *symbiosis*.

Word part	Meaning
bio-	life
sym-	together

Example sentence

The relationship between a sunflower and the insect that pollinates it is an example of symbiosis.

symbiosis:

_____

_____

_____

Vocabulary Terms

- predator
- prey
- symbiosis
- mutualism
- commensalism
- parasitism
- competition

4 Apply As you learn the meaning of each vocabulary term in this lesson, create your own definition or sketch to help you remember the meaning of the term.

Feeding Frenzy!

How do predator and prey interact?

Every organism lives with and affects other organisms. Many organisms must feed on other organisms in order to get the energy and nutrients they need to survive. These feeding relationships establish structure in a community.

Predators Eat Prey

In a predator–prey relationship, an animal eats another animal for energy and nutrients. The **predator** eats another animal. The **prey** is an animal that is eaten by a predator. An animal can be both predator and prey. For example, if a warthog eats a lizard, and is, in turn, eaten by a lion, the warthog is both predator and prey.

Predators and prey have adaptations that help them survive. Some predators have talons, claws, or sharp teeth, which provide them with deadly weapons. Spiders, which are small predators, use their webs to trap unsuspecting prey. Camouflage (CAM•ah•flaj) can also help a predator or prey to blend in with its environment. A tiger's stripes help it to blend in with tall grasses so that it can ambush its prey, and the wings of some moths look just like tree bark, which makes them difficult for predators to see. Some animals defend themselves with chemicals. For example, skunks and bombardier beetles spray predators with irritating chemicals.

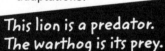
Active Reading

5 Identify As you read, underline examples of predator–prey adaptations.

This lion is a predator. The warthog is its prey.

Adaptations of Predators and Prey

Most organisms wouldn't last a day without their adaptations. This bald eagle's vision and sharp talons allow it to find and catch prey.

sharp talons

Predators and Prey Populations Are Connected

Predators rely on prey for food, so the sizes of predator and prey populations are linked together very closely. If one population grows or shrinks, the other population is affected. For example, when there are a lot of warthogs to eat, the lion population may grow because the food supply is plentiful. As the lion population grows, it requires more and more food, so more and more warthogs are hunted by the lions. The increased predation may cause the warthog population to shrink. If the warthog population shrinks enough, the lion population may shrink due to a shortage in food supply. If the lion population shrinks, the warthog population may grow due to a lack of predators.

This lion is hunting down the antelope. If most of the antelope are killed, the lions will have less food to eat.

6 Compare Fill in the Venn diagram to compare and contrast predators and prey.

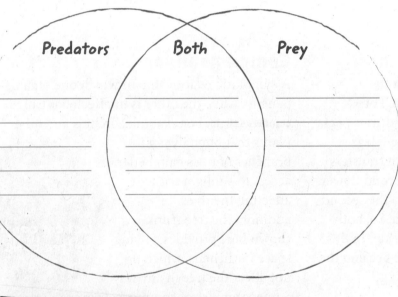

Predators   Both   Prey

Think Outside the Book

7 Apply Choose a predator and think about what it eats and how it hunts. Then do one of the following:

- Write a nomination for the predator to be "Predator of the Year."
- Draw the predator and label the adaptations that help it hunt.

Don't be surprised if this "leaf" walks away—it's actually an insect.

Visualize It!

8 Analyze How might this insect's appearance help keep it from getting eaten?

_____

_____

_____

_____

_____

Living Together

What are the types of symbiotic relationships?

A close long-term relationship between different species in a community is called **symbiosis** (sim•bee•OH•sis). In symbiosis, the organisms in the relationship can benefit from, be unaffected by, or be harmed by the relationship. Often, one organism lives in or on the other organism. Symbiotic relationships are classified as mutualism, commensalism, or parasitism.

 **Active Reading** 9 **Identify** As you read, underline examples of symbiotic relationships.

Mutualism

A symbiotic relationship in which both organisms benefit is called **mutualism**. For example, when the bee in the photo drinks nectar from a flower, it gets pollen on its hind legs. When the bee visits another flower, it transfers pollen from the first flower to the second flower. In this interaction, the bee is fed and the second flower is pollinated for reproduction. So, both organisms benefit from the relationship. In this example, the mutualism benefits the bee and the two parent plants that are reproducing.

Bees pollinate flowers. This is an example of mutualism.

Commensalism

A symbiotic relationship in which one organism benefits while the other is unaffected is called **commensalism.** For example, orchids and other plants that often live in the branches of trees gain better access to sunlight without affecting the trees. In addition, the tree trunk shown here provides a living space for lichens, which do not affect the tree in any way. Some examples of commensalism involve protection. For example, certain shrimp live among the spines of the fire urchin. The fire urchin's spines are poisonous but not to the shrimp. By living among the urchin's spines, the shrimp are protected from predators. In this relationship, the shrimp benefits and the fire urchin is unaffected.

Lichens can live on tree bark.

10 **Compare** How does commensalism differ from mutualism?

_____

_____

_____

_____

© Houghton Mifflin Harcourt Publishing Company • Image Credits: (l) ©Jason Hosking/Getty Images; (r) ©Kathy Wright/Alamy

12 Predict Observe and take notes about how the organisms in your area interact with one another. Imagine what would happen if one of these organisms disappeared. Write down three effects that you can think of.

parasite

host

Parasitism

A symbiotic relationship in which one organism benefits and another is harmed is called **parasitism** (PAR•uh•sih•tiz•uhm). The organism that benefits is the *parasite*. The organism that is harmed is the *host*. The parasite gets food from its host, which weakens the host. Some parasites, such as ticks, live on the host's surface and feed on its blood. These parasites can cause diseases such as Lyme disease. Other parasites, such as tapeworms, live within the host's body. They can weaken their host so much that the host dies.

11 Summarize Using the key, complete the table to show how organisms are affected by symbiotic relationships.

Symbiosis	Species 1	Species 2
Mutualism	+	
	+	0
Parasitism		

Key + organism benefits
0 organism not affected
— organism harmed

Let the Games Begin!

Why does competition occur in communities?

In a team game, two groups compete against each other with the same goal in mind—to win the game. In a biological community, organisms compete for resources. **Competition** occurs when organisms fight for the same limited resource. Organisms compete for resources such as food, water, sunlight, shelter, and mates. If an organism doesn't get all the resources it needs, it could die.

Sometimes competition happens among individuals of the same species. For example, different groups of lions compete with each other for living space. Males within these groups also compete with each other for mates.

Competition can also happen among individuals of different species. Lions mainly eat large animals, such as zebras. They compete for zebras with leopards and cheetahs. When zebras are scarce, competition increases among animals that eat zebras. As a result, lions may steal food or compete with other predators for smaller animals.

Active Reading

13 Identify Underline each example of competition.

14 Predict In the table below, fill in the missing cause and effect of two examples of competition in a community.

Cause	Effect
A population of lions grows too large to share their current territory.	
	Several male hyenas compete to mate with the females present in their area.

Many organisms rely on the same water source.

Think Outside the Book

15 Apply With a classmate, discuss how competition might affect the organisms in this photo.

442

© Houghton Mifflin Harcourt Publishing Company • Image Credits: ©Martin Harvey/Corbis

Strange Relationships

Glow worms? Blind salamanders? Even creepy crawlers in this extreme cave community interact in ways that help them meet their needs. How do these interactions differ from ones in your own community?

Guano Buffet

Cave swiftlets venture out of the cave daily to feed. The food they eat is recycled as bird dung, or guano, which piles up beneath the nests. The guano feeds many cave dwellers, such as insects. As a result, these insects never have to leave the cave!

A Blind Hunter

Caves are very dark and, over generations, these salamanders have lost the use of their eyes for seeing. Instead of looking for food, they track prey by following water movements.

Sticky Traps

Bioluminescent glow worms make lines of sticky beads to attract prey. Once a prey is stuck, the worm pulls in the line to feast.

Extend

Inquiry

16 Identify Name the type of relationship illustrated in two of the examples shown above.

17 Research Name some organisms in your community and the interactions they have.

18 Create Illustrate two of the interactions you just described by doing one of the following:
- make a poster
- write a song
- write a play
- draw a graphic novel

Visual Summary

To complete this summary, fill in the blanks with the correct word or phrase. Then, use the key below to check your answers. You can use this page to review the main concepts of the lesson.

Organisms interact in feeding relationships.

19 Predators eat

_____

_____

Organisms interact in symbiosis—very close relationships between two species.

Mutualism:

Commensalism:

Parasitism:

20 A parasite gets nourishment from its

_____

Interactions
in Communities

Organisms interact in competition.

21 Organisms compete for resources such as

_____

_____

_____

_____

Competition can occur between:

Members of the same species • Members of different species

Answers: 19 prey; 20 host; 21 food, mates, shelter, and water.

_____

22 Synthesize Explain how interactions can be both beneficial and harmful to the organisms in a community.

Lesson Review

Vocabulary

Fill in the blank with the term that best completes the following sentences.

1 A _____ is an animal that kills and eats another animal, known as prey.

2 A long-term relationship between two different species within a community is called

_____

3 _____ occurs when organisms fight for limited resources.

Key Concepts

Fill in the table below.

Example	Type of symbiosis
4 Identify Tiny organisms called mites live in human eyelashes and feed on dead skin, without harming humans.	
5 Identify Certain bacteria live in human intestines, where they get food and also help humans break down their food.	

6 Describe Think of an animal, and list two resources that it might compete for in its community. Then describe what adaptations the animal has to compete for these resources.

_____

_____

_____

_____

_____

_____

7 Explain What is the relationship between the size of a predator population and the size of a prey population?

_____

_____

_____

Critical Thinking

Use this graph to answer the following question.

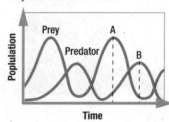

Predator and Prey Populations Over Time

8 Analyze At which point (A or B) on this graph would you expect competition within the predator population to be the highest?

_____

9 Infer Think of a resource, and predict what happens to the resource when competition for it increases.

_____

_____

_____

10 Apply Identify a community near where you live, such as a forest, a pond, or your own backyard. Think about the interactions of the organisms in this community. Describe an interaction and identify it as predation, mutualism, commensalism, parasitism, or competition.

_____

_____

_____

_____

_____

Sunshine State Standards

SC.7.L.17.3 Describe and investigate various limiting factors in the local ecosystem and their impact on native populations, including food, shelter, water, space, disease, parasitism, predation, and nesting sites.

Florida Populations

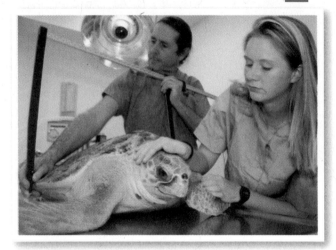

This injured sea turtle is being treated at the Turtle Hospital in Marathon, Florida.

Sea Turtles

Every summer, Florida becomes home to about 50,000 new residents who are famous for their hard shells and amazing swimming skills. Five species of sea turtles, including the loggerhead and leatherback turtles, make nests on the beaches of Florida in May. Two months later, their eggs hatch. The newborn turtles, or hatchlings, emerge from their nests and make their way to the water. The turtles stay in the Gulf Stream for a few years. Hatchlings are vulnerable to fish and seabirds, but even adult sea turtles must watch out for sharks. While their hard shells protect them from most predators, many turtles are injured every year through contact with human beings. Outboard motors can damage a turtle's shell. Fishing nets can trap turtles and drown them. Humans also hunt female turtles for their meat. Human development and construction threaten the habitats of sea turtles. Laws are in place to help protect the declining sea turtle population.

Social Studies Connection

Loggerhead turtles, the most common sea turtle in Florida, usually nest along the east coast of Florida. The hatchling loggerheads migrate to the Gulf Stream. The table shows data collected from a tracking device placed on a loggerhead turtle. Plot the points on the map to see the route the turtle followed.

Tracking Data for Loggerhead Turtle Migration		
Date	**Latitude (°N)**	**Longitude (°W)**
February 6	33	79
February 13	36	74
February 17	38	67
February 23	42	59
March 10	40	49

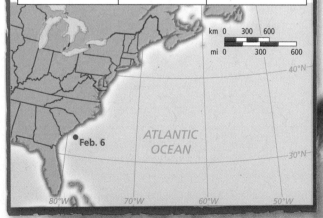

Wild iguana

Iguanas on the Loose!

You don't have to go to a zoo or a pet store to see an iguana. Sometimes you can find them in the middle of town! Iguanas are not native to Florida. People originally brought iguanas to Florida as pets. Over time, many were released or escaped, and iguanas now live and reproduce in the wild.

Iguana trappers have been used to capture iguanas, but this reptile population has become harder to control. Florida's subtropical climate is a favorable ecosystem for iguanas. Wild adult iguanas are large and powerful. They do not have many natural predators—alligators, dogs, raccoons, and some birds of prey are the only species that seem to threaten them.

Iguanas pose hazards to humans in several ways. Iguanas can cause structural damage to buildings by burrowing into their foundations. In addition, their wastes contain the salmonella bacteria, which pose a health risk to humans.

Iguanas do not respond well to sudden drops in temperature. At low temperatures, an iguana's metabolism slows down and the iguana appears frozen. However, once the weather warms up, it returns to its regular state. During a cold snap, it seems like it's raining iguanas in Florida as these "frozen" reptiles fall out of trees. Because hundreds of thousands of iguanas live in Florida, you could get caught in an iguana storm!

Managing Deer

They are about the size of a medium-sized dog, but otherwise look like a deer. Tiny Key deer are unique to one of Florida's ecosystems. And they very nearly disappeared! In the 1930s, the Key deer population was very low. Poaching and hunting meant that only about 50 Key deer were alive. With careful wildlife and habitat management, the current Key deer population is now at 300, but is still considered endangered. A larger population of Key deer means a healthier Florida ecosystem. The endangered Florida panther is a predator of Key deer. So when the Key deer population shrinks, the panther population is also threatened.

Key deer

Take It Home

You are part of a campaign to protect endangered animals of Florida like the leatherback sea turtle, Key deer, or Florida panther. Research one of these animals and create a profile page or blog post about it. Include links to websites for more information on your endangered animal.

Florida's Ecosystems

ESSENTIAL QUESTION

How do limiting factors affect Florida's ecosystems?

By the end of this lesson, you should be able to explain how limiting factors affect the native populations in Florida's ecosystems.

Human activity near beaches may keep animals such as this leatherback sea turtle from reproducing.

🐢 Sunshine State Standards

SC.7.N.1.1 Define a problem from the seventh grade curriculum, use appropriate reference materials to support scientific understanding, plan and carry out scientific investigation of various types, such as systematic observations or experiments, identify variables, collect and organize data, interpret data in charts, tables, and graphics, analyze information, make predictions, and defend conclusions.

SC.7.L.17.3 Describe and investigate various limiting factors in the local ecosystem and their impact on native populations, including food, shelter, water, space, disease, parasitism, predation, and nesting sites.

LA.6.4.2.2 The student will record information (e.g., observations, notes, lists, charts, legends) related to a topic, including visual aids to organize and record information and include a list of sources used.

Engage Your Brain

1 Predict Check T or F to show whether you think each statement is true or false.

T F

☐ ☐ Florida has many different land and water ecosystems.

☐ ☐ The plants and animals in Florida's ecosystems do not change.

☐ ☐ Populations can be limited by a nonliving factor, such as water.

☐ ☐ Coral reefs along the coast of Florida are home to many different animals.

2 Model Make a sketch of an ecosystem that you have visited or are familiar with. Label the plants and animals you know.

Active Reading

3 Synthesize Learning where a word comes from can help you understand what it means. Use the origin of the word *estuary* to guess the meaning of the term.

Word origin	Meaning
aestus	tide

Example sentence

The estuaries that form where the Mississippi River meets the Gulf of Mexico are rich in life.

estuary:

_____

_____

_____

_____

Vocabulary Terms

- limiting factor
- native species
- introduced species
- wetland
- coral reef
- estuary

4 Apply As you learn the definition of each vocabulary term in this lesson, make a sketch that shows the meaning of the term or an example of that term. Write your own definition of the term next to your sketch.

Pushing THE LIMIT

What limits the size of populations?

Active Reading **5 Identify** As you read, underline the limiting factors that might affect organisms in an ecosystem.

Populations of organisms don't grow forever. When the environment cannot support more individuals, a population will stop growing. A **limiting factor** is an environmental factor that keeps a population from reaching its full potential size. Imagine a habitat that has enough water to support 1,000 armadillos but only enough food for 500. Only 500 armadillos can live in the habitat. In this example, food is the limiting factor.

Limiting Factors

Both living and nonliving environmental factors can limit the size of a population. The amount of food often limits the size of populations. If there are too many individuals, some will starve. If there were more food, populations likely would grow. Water, light, nutrients, shelter, and living space also can limit populations. So can predators, parasites, and diseases.

One factor limits a population at a time. Suppose the area that had only enough food for 500 armadillos suddenly had enough food for 2,000 armadillos, but only enough water for 1,000 armadillos. The population still couldn't grow to 2,000 armadillos. Water would keep the population at 1,000 armadillos. In this case, water is the limiting factor.

Birds, such as these wood storks, need space for nests. If there aren't enough nesting sites, bird populations won't grow.

6 Predict For each limiting factor listed below, choose an animal or plant and predict how that limiting factor might affect the population of the organism:

Limiting factor	How does the limiting factor affect a population?
Space	
Food	
Light	

The Burmese python is an introduced species from Asia that is now found in the Everglades.

What are introduced species?

Species that naturally live in an ecosystem are called **native species**. On the other hand, **introduced species** are species that have been brought to an ecosystem by human actions. Some introduced species were brought to new places on purpose. Others traveled in vehicles or on other animals. Escaped or released pets can also start new populations in the wild.

Many introduced species are successful because they do not have predators, parasites, or diseases in the new habitat. Some introduced species may be better competitors for resources than native species. Introduced species may eat native species. As a result, introduced species often are limiting factors.

Many species have been introduced to Florida. For example, Burmese pythons from Asia are now found in the Everglades. Many of these pythons were pets. In the wild, they eat many native animals, such as wading birds, deer, and even alligators! By eating these animals, pythons compete with native predators for food.

Little blue herons are just one of the many native species that Burmese pythons eat.

---

7 Cause and Effect Use the diagram below to describe how the Burmese python affects Florida's ecosystems.

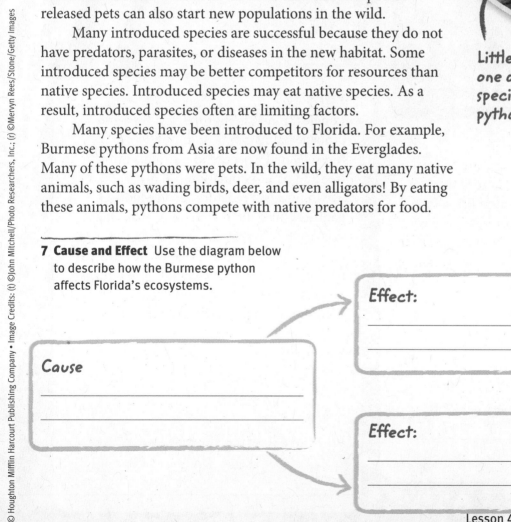

Effect:
_____
_____

Cause
_____
_____

Effect:
_____
_____

Land, HO!

What are Florida's land ecosystems?

Many species live in Florida's land ecosystems—forests, prairies, beaches, and dunes. Some native species are found nowhere else on Earth. Introduced plants and animals can threaten native species. Different factors limit populations in these ecosystems.

Active Reading

8 Summarize After you read each heading, list organisms and limiting factors in the land ecosystems described.

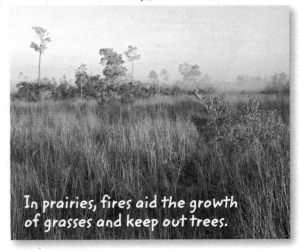
In prairies, fires aid the growth of grasses and keep out trees.

Prairies

Plants such as grasses, sedges, and rushes dominate Florida's prairies. Fire is an important limiting factor on prairies. Fires keep trees from growing. Fires also cause new growth in grasses. Herbivores, which are animals that eat plants, can limit plant populations on prairies.

Who lives here?

_____

_____

What are limiting factors here?

_____

_____

Forests

Longleaf pines, mangroves, cypress, and cabbage palms can be found in Florida's forests. Light, space, and nutrients limit tree and plant populations. Many animals live in forests. Predators such as Florida panthers limit the populations of animals such as deer. Fire is also a limiting factor in forests. Although some species are harmed by fire, other species rely on it. Fire returns nutrients to the soil. A few species, such as sand pines, release seeds only after a fire.

Who lives here?

_____

_____

What are limiting factors here?

_____

_____

In forests, such as this cypress forest, light can be a limiting factor.

Dunes are threatened by human activity.

Dunes

Blowing sand forms dunes along beaches. Low-growing plants that can survive being sprayed with salt water grow here. They hold sand in place, allowing other plants to grow. Steep slopes limit plant growth. Big trees can't grow on dunes. Sand doesn't provide enough support for roots. Dunes are important for nesting birds. Development can limit the space and resources available to organisms. It also damages the plants that hold sand in place.

Who lives here?

_____

_____

What are limiting factors here?

_____

_____

On beaches, many animals live in tunnels in the sand.

Beaches

Beaches are found where land meets water. Most beaches in Florida are sandy. Animals, such as clams and crabs, live under the sand. Birds eat these animals and organisms that wash up on the beach. So, birds can limit populations of some animals. Beaches are nesting sites for sea turtles and birds. Development can decrease the space available for nests.

Who lives here?

_____

_____

What are limiting factors here?

_____

_____

9 Infer Why are fires important to prairies but not important to dunes?

_____

_____

_____

_____

_____

Gator COUNTRY

What are Florida's freshwater ecosystems?

Active Reading **10 Identify** As you read, underline factors that limit populations in Florida's freshwater ecosystems.

Freshwater ecosystems are very important in Florida. They include lakes, ponds, rivers, streams, and wetlands. Water is a limiting factor in many of these ecosystems. Freshwater ecosystems have different water depths, speeds of water flow, and types of organisms. They provide food and drinking water for people. People also use them for activities such as boating and swimming.

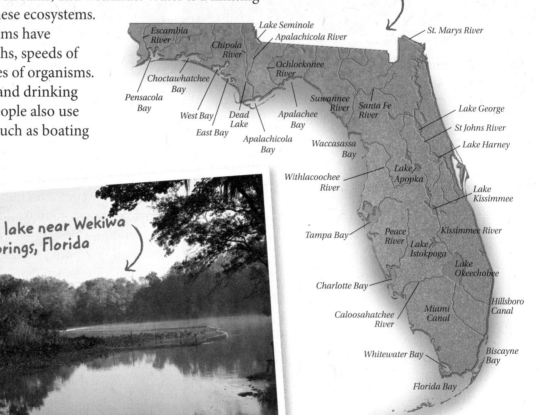

Florida has many rivers, canals, and lakes.

A lake near Wekiwa Springs, Florida

Lakes and Ponds

Lakes and ponds are standing bodies of water. So, water flows very little if at all. Some plants float on top of the water. Other plants grow in shallow areas, where they can get light and air. If the amount of oxygen in lakes and ponds is low, it can limit populations. When there is enough oxygen, ponds and lakes support many kinds of fish. Introduced fish, such as walking catfish, and introduced plants, such as water hyacinth, can be found in many lakes and ponds in Florida.

Rivers and Streams

Rivers and streams have flowing water. They carry nutrients that are important to the ecosystems that they flow into. Rivers and streams are home to many organisms, including the endangered manatee. Shelter is often a limiting factor in rivers and streams. Rocks provide hiding places from predators. Rocks also shelter organisms from currents that would sweep them away.

Wetlands

The Florida Everglades are wetlands. A **wetland** is an area where land is covered by water for at least part of the year. Water flows slowly in wetlands. Many birds, fish, reptiles, and mammals live in wetlands. Wetland plants help remove wastes and pollution from water. Nutrients limit plant populations. Low oxygen levels and drying up of wetlands can limit fish. Animals and trees rely on *hammocks,* which are areas that are dry most of the year.

Think Outside the Book (Inquiry)

11 Apply With a partner, work together to make lists of the animals and plants in a local freshwater ecosystem. Then, identify how water moves through the ecosystem.

Development limits space and can pollute wetlands.

Sawgrass covers the Everglades. Cypress trees dominate other wetlands.

The Everglades are home to many bird species, including osprey, great blue herons, and white ibis.

Hammocks provide dry spots for alligators and other animals.

Visualize It!

12 Infer How do the organisms in this image rely on water to survive?

_____

_____

_____

_____

_____

Just Add SALT!

What are Florida's marine ecosystems?

The marine, or saltwater, ecosystems of Florida include coral reefs, estuaries (ES•choo•ehr•eez), salt marshes, and mangrove swamps. Florida's marine ecosystems support many species. They provide food and recreation for people. Florida's marine ecosystems are at risk from development and pollution. Both can limit populations.

 **Active Reading**

13 Identify As you read, underline the limiting factors in the ecosystem described.

Coral Reefs

One of the most diverse marine ecosystems is the coral reef. A **coral reef** grows in waters that are warm, shallow, and clear. Coral reefs are made up of the skeletons of tiny animals called *corals*. Tiny protists live inside coral bodies and give coral reefs their color. These protists use light to produce food, which corals can use. Because they need light to grow, water depth and sunlight limit the growth of the protists and coral in reefs.

Reefs are home to many kinds of fish, sea turtles, and other animals such as crabs, shrimps, anemones, urchins, and starfish. A reef may be home to thousands of species. So, space is often a limiting factor. High temperatures and polluted water from land can also limit populations of corals and other reef animals.

Visualize It!

14 Analyze What limiting factors do you see in this coral reef ecosystem?

_____

_____

_____

_____

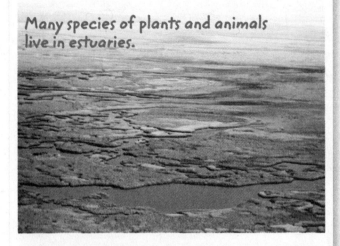

Many species of plants and animals live in estuaries.

Grasses dominate salt marshes.

Mangrove populations are limited by nutrients, water, and temperature.

Estuaries

Many streams and rivers flow into the ocean, forming estuaries. An **estuary** is an area where fresh water mixes with salt water. Both grasses and seagrasses grow in estuaries. Many fish lay eggs here, and plants provide shelter for young fish. Birds, turtles, alligators, and many other animals live in estuaries.

Many organisms rely on the nutrients provided by estuaries. So, nutrients are a limiting factor. Populations also are limited by water movement and salt levels in the water. Some species need high salt levels whereas other species, such as alligators, need lower levels.

Salt Marshes

Salt marshes are found along the coast. Grasses and other plants, such as sedges and rushes, live in these areas. Salt marshes are occasionally flooded by tides. This flooding can limit plant populations. Plants do not grow where water is too deep or the ground is wet for too long. Salt levels and nutrients can also limit plants and animals in salt marshes. If oxygen levels in water get too low, they limit the populations of fish and other species.

Mangrove Swamps

Mangrove swamps are found in areas that are flooded by tides and also receive freshwater runoff. They are dominated by mangrove trees. Mangroves need nutrients to survive. Mangroves cannot survive low temperatures. So, temperature also limits mangrove populations.

Mangrove roots often reach below the water. They shelter small fish from predators. For organisms that live in mangrove swamps, the amount of time the area is wet or dry is a limiting factor. Salt levels also limit populations in mangrove swamps.

15 Compare What limiting factors do estuaries, salt marshes, and mangrove swamps have in common?

_____

_____

_____

Visual Summary

To complete this summary, fill in the blanks with the correct word or phrase. Then, use the key below to check your answers. You can use this page to review the main concepts of the lesson.

Florida's Ecosystems

Populations are limited by living and nonliving factors.

16 The Burmese python is a(n) ________________ species in the Florida Everglades.

Florida's land ecosystems include forests, prairies, dunes, and beaches.

17 In forests, sunlight is a(n) ________________ for plants on the forest floor.

Freshwater ecosystems include lakes, ponds, rivers, streams, and wetlands.

18 The Florida Everglades are an example of a(n) ________________.

Marine habitats include coral reefs, estuaries, salt marshes, and mangrove swamps.

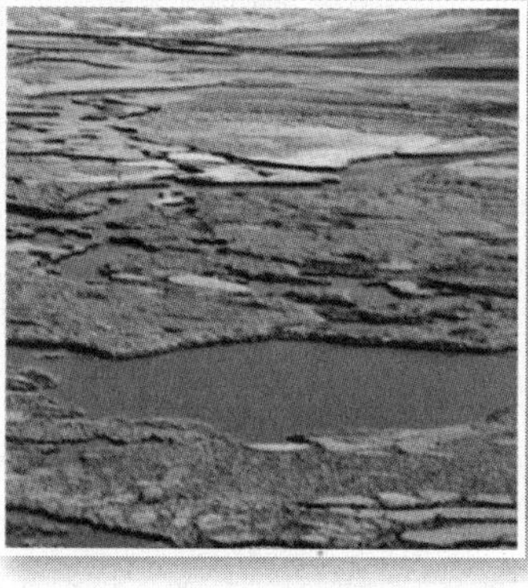

19 A(n) ________________ is an area where fresh water meets salt water.

Answers: 16 introduced; 17 limiting factor; 18 wetland; 19 estuary

20 **Predict** What might happen to a native fish species if an introduced fish species that ate the same food was released in a pond?

Lesson Review

Vocabulary

Fill in the blanks with the terms that best complete the following sentence.

1 A(n) _____ is a species that naturally lives in an ecosystem.

2 A(n) _____ is an ecosystem that is covered with water for at least part of the year.

3 A(n) _____ is an ecosystem found in warm, clear salt water.

4 _____ keep populations from reaching their full potential size.

Key Concepts

5 Identify A population of birds has nesting sites for 500 birds and food for 400 birds. What is the limiting factor for this population? Explain your answer.

_____

_____

_____

_____

6 Predict Imagine a new species of bird was introduced to the same area as a population of native birds. What effects might the introduced species have on the native species?

_____

_____

_____

_____

_____

7 Explain What characteristics of estuaries make them good places for fish to lay their eggs?

_____

_____

_____

_____

_____

Critical Thinking

8 Apply Choose an ecosystem near you. List three organisms in the ecosystem and describe limiting factors for each of them.

_____

_____

_____

_____

_____

The graphs below show how the size of a gull population is affected by nesting sites and crabs, which gulls eat. Use the graphs to answer the questions that follow.

Limiting Factors That May Affect Gull Populations

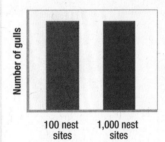
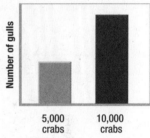

9 Analyze What factor limits the gull population, nesting sites or crabs? Explain.

_____

_____

_____

10 Predict What do you think would happen to the gull population if there were only 10 nest sites? Why?

_____

_____

_____

_____

_____

_____

My Notes

Unit 8 Summary

```
            Introduction
             to Ecology

include feeding
relationships that lead to

Interactions in                    Roles in Energy
  Communities      →                   Transfer

            depend on

              Florida's
             Ecosystems
```

1 Interpret The Graphic Organizer above shows that Florida's ecosystems depend on the transfer of energy. Give an example of an energy transfer in a Florida ecosystem.

_____

_____

_____

_____

_____

_____

2 Explain Do organisms compete for abiotic resources? Explain.

_____

_____

_____

3 Describe Name a feeding relationship within one of Florida's land ecosystems.

_____

_____

_____

4 Synthesize How could introduced species disrupt existing feeding relationships?

_____

_____

_____

_____

_____

_____

Name _____

Multiple Choice

Identify the choice that best completes the statement or answers the question.

1 Mangrove swamps are found along the southern coasts of Florida. A mangrove swamp contains an ecosystem of many organisms living among the large roots of the mangrove trees. This food web shows some of the relationships in that ecosystem.

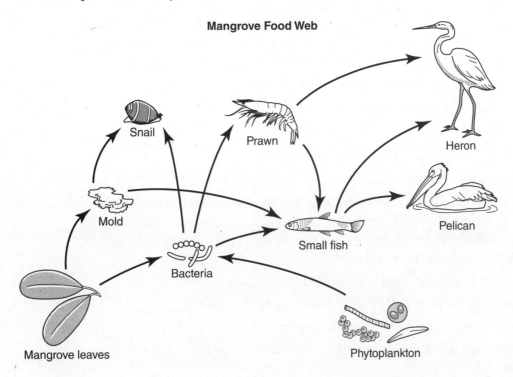

Mangrove Food Web

According to the food web, which organism is a producer in the mangrove swamp?

A. crab

B. mold

C. pelican

D. phytoplankton

2 Ecosystems have producers, decomposers, and consumers. Carnivores and scavengers are both types of consumers in an ecosystem. Which of the following is a characteristic of scavengers that makes them different from carnivores?

F. Scavengers eat only plant materials.

G. Scavengers are omnivores that always eat live animals.

H. Scavengers are omnivores that eat dead plants and animals.

I. Scavengers are able to produce their own food when no other food is available.

3 Remoras are small fish that attach to sharks but do not harm them. When sharks tear prey apart, remoras eat the leftovers. What relationship do remoras have with sharks?

A. mutualism

B. parasitism

C. commensalism

D. predator-prey

4 Ecological environments can be divided into different levels of organization. From the following choices, identify the correct order from largest to smallest.

F. ecosystem, population, community, individual

G. community, ecosystem, population, individual

H. ecosystem, community, population, individual

I. individual, population, community, ecosystem

5 Cogongrass, a nonnative species of grass, grows in many areas of Florida. Its roots can spread quickly underground. Cogongrass thrives where fires allow it to spread. Which of the following is a negative effect that cogongrass could have on other organisms in its habitat?

A. It provides places for animals in the habitat to hide.

B. It provides a new source of food for animals in the habitat.

C. It replaces native plants that animals depend on for food or shelter.

D. It contributes nutrients to the soil in the habitat so that soil organisms can grow.

6 Honeybees are important pollinators of flowers. Mites that live in the bodies of bees can attack honeybee colonies. Some birds, amphibians, and insects eat honeybees. Which of the following relationships is **not** included in the description above?

F. parasitism

G. mutualism

H. commensalism

I. predator-prey

7 Earth's environments include both biotic and abiotic factors that living things need to survive. Large mangrove ecosystems are found along the coastlines in Florida. The figure shows a mangrove ecosystem that has both biotic and abiotic factors.

Which of the following are **both** abiotic factors in the mangrove ecosystem?

- **A.** water and pelican
- **B.** sun and rocks
- **C.** pelican and crab
- **D.** snail and water

8 Two types of global food webs show the feeding relationships of organisms. What distinguishes one type of global web from the other?

- **F.** whether or not the food web includes tertiary consumers
- **G.** whether the producers in the food web are located on land or in water
- **H.** whether the web includes animals that migrate during the year
- **I.** whether the ecosystem described by the web is localized or very broad

9 The Florida panther used to live in forests, prairies, and swamps over most of the southeastern United States. Now it lives only in the southern tip of Florida, south of the Caloosahatchee River. Based on this information, what is the **most likely** cause of the decline of the Florida panther population?

A. the unintentional introduction of a larger predator

B. the break-up of the panther's natural habitat by human settlement

C. the weakening of species due to inbreeding

D. competition for territory between panthers

10 Devon noticed that it has rained much more this year than it did in each of the previous 10 years. How might this increase in rainfall affect populations in the area?

F. Populations for whom water is a limiting factor will increase in size.

G. Populations for whom water is a limiting factor will decrease in size.

H. Populations for whom water is not a limiting factor will increase in size.

I. Populations for whom water is not a limiting factor will decrease in size.

11 The interiors of some plants have tunnels and holes that ants can live in. These plants may also produce food on their leaves that ants like to eat. Which of the following is **not** a likely reason that some plants are adapted to attract ants?

A. Ants could pollinate the plant's flowers.

B. Ants could farm aphids, which eat the plant's sap.

C. Ants could attack invaders that might eat the plant.

D. Ants could die, adding nutrients to the soil below the plant.

12 A company is planning to build a new factory that uses freshwater pumped from a river to cool its machines while they operate. The company plans on constructing the new factory near an estuary. The freshwater used by the factory will be cooled back to outside temperatures, and then released into the estuary. Which limiting factor in the estuary would be **most** affected by the building of this new factory?

F. sunlight penetration

G. salt levels in the water

H. nutrient levels in the soil

I. temperature of the water

UNIT 9
Cycling of Matter and Energy

Big Idea 18

Matter and Energy Transformations

Mangroves

Roseate Spoonbill

What do you think?

Mangroves and Roseate Spoonbills are both found in Florida. How do organisms like these get and use matter and energy?

Cycling of Matter and Energy

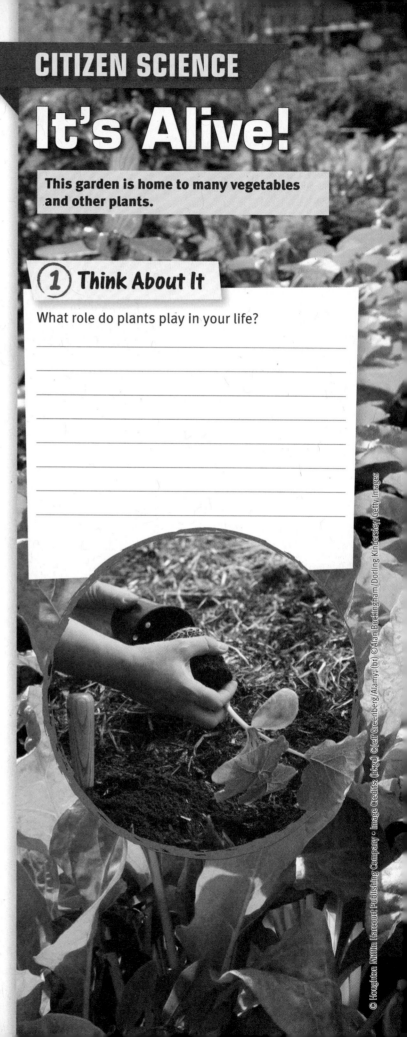

CITIZEN SCIENCE

It's Alive!

This garden is home to many vegetables and other plants.

1 Think About It

What role do plants play in your life?

_____
_____
_____
_____
_____
_____
_____

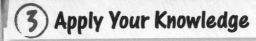

② Ask a Question

How do plants use matter and energy?

As a class, design a plan for a garden plot or window box garden in which the class can grow a variety of plants. Remember that plants have different growing periods and requirements.

Sketch It!

Draw your plan to show where each plant will be placed.

③ Apply Your Knowledge

A What do your plants need in order to grow?

_____
_____
_____

B Which of the things you listed above are examples of matter? Which are examples of energy?

_____
_____
_____
_____

C Create and care for your classroom garden and observe the plant growth.

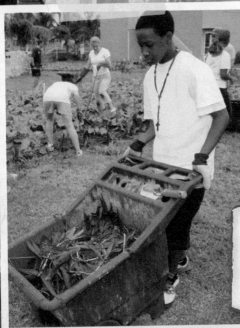

Take It Home

Describe an area in your community that is used for growing food. If there is no such area, initiate a plan to use an area that you think could be used.

Photosynthesis and Cellular Respiration

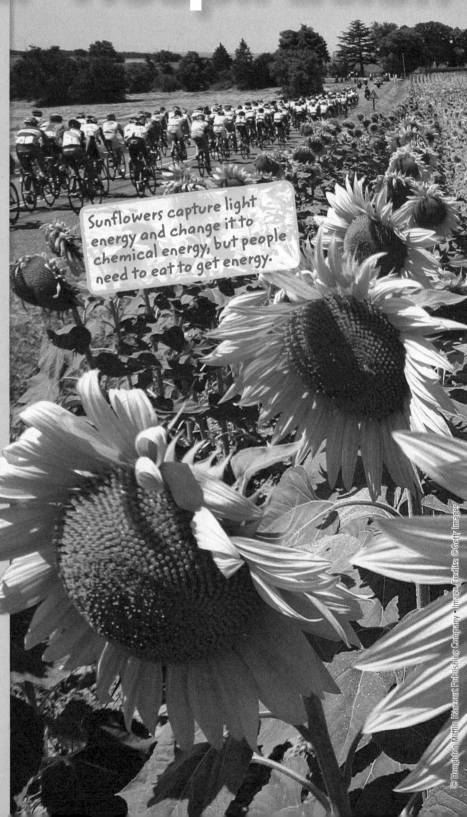

Sunflowers capture light energy and change it to chemical energy, but people need to eat to get energy.

ESSENTIAL QUESTION

How do cells get and use energy?

By the end of this lesson, you should be able to explain how cells capture and release energy.

Sunshine State Standards

SC.8.N.1.1 Define a problem from the eighth grade curriculum using appropriate reference materials to support scientific understanding, plan and carry out scientific investigations of various types, such as systematic observations or experiments, identify variables, collect and organize data, interpret data in charts, tables, and graphics, analyze information, make predictions, and defend conclusions.

SC.8.L.18.1 Describe and investigate the process of photosynthesis, such as the roles of light, carbon dioxide, water and chlorophyll; production of food; release of oxygen.

SC.8.L.18.2 Describe and investigate how cellular respiration breaks down food to provide energy and releases carbon dioxide.

LA.6.4.2.2 The student will record information (e.g., observations, notes, lists, charts, legends) related to a topic, including visual aids to organize and record information and include a list of sources used.

Engage Your Brain

1 Predict Check T or F to show whether you think each of the following statements is true or false.

T	F	
☐	☐	All living things must eat other living things for food.
☐	☐	Plants can make their own food.
☐	☐	Plants don't need oxygen, only carbon dioxide.
☐	☐	Animals eat plants or other animals that eat plants.
☐	☐	Many living things need oxygen to release energy from food.

2 Infer Look at the photo. Describe the differences between the plants. What do you think caused these differences?

_____

_____

_____

_____

_____

_____

_____

Active Reading

3 Synthesize You can often define an unknown word if you know the meaning of its word parts. Use the word parts and sentence below to make an educated guess about the meaning of the term *chlorophyll*.

Word part	Meaning
chloro-	green
-phyll	leaf

Example sentence
Chlorophyll is a pigment that captures light energy.

chlorophyll:

_____

_____

_____

Vocabulary Terms

- photosynthesis
- chlorophyll
- cellular respiration

4 Apply As you learn the definition of each vocabulary term in this lesson, write your own definition or make a sketch to help you remember the meaning of the term.

Energize!

How do the cells in an organism function?

Active Reading **5 Identify** As you read, underline sources of energy for living things.

How do you get the energy to run around and play soccer or basketball? How does a tree get the energy to grow? All living things, from the tiniest single-celled bacterium to the largest tree, need energy. Cells must capture and use energy or they will die. Cells get energy from food. Some living things can make their own food. Many living things get their food by eating other living things.

Your cells use energy all the time, whether you are active or not.

Cells Need Energy

Growing, moving, and other cell functions use energy. Without energy, a living thing cannot replace cells, build body parts, or reproduce. Even when a living thing is not very active, it needs energy. Cells constantly use energy to move materials into and out of the cell. They need energy to make different chemicals. And they need energy to get rid of wastes. A cell could not survive for long if it did not have the energy for all of these functions.

Active Reading **6 Relate** Why do living things need energy at all times?

_____

_____

_____

© Houghton Mifflin Harcourt Publishing Company • Image Credits: (t) ©Ty Allison/Getty Images; (inset) ©rubberball/Getty Images

Cells Get Energy from Food

The cells of all living things need chemical energy. Food contains chemical energy. Food gives living things the energy and raw materials needed to carry out life processes. When cells break down food, the energy of the chemical bonds in food is released. This energy can be used or stored by the cell. The atoms and molecules in food can be used as building blocks for the cell.

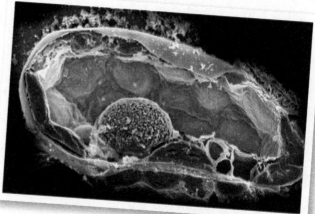

Plant cells make their own food using energy from the sun.

Living things get food in different ways. In fact, they can be grouped based on how they get food. Some living things, such as plants and many single-celled organisms, are called *producers* (proh•DOO•suhrz). Producers can make their own food. Most producers use energy from the sun. They capture and store light energy from the sun as chemical energy in food. A small number of producers, such as those that live in the deepest parts of the ocean, use chemicals to make their own food. Producers use most of the food they produce for energy. The unused food is stored in their bodies.

Many living things, such as people and other animals, are *consumers* (kun•SOO•muhrz). Consumers must eat, or consume, other living things to get food. Consumers may eat producers or other consumers. The cells of consumers break down food to release the energy it contains. A special group of consumers is made up of *decomposers* (dee•cum•POH•zhurhz). Decomposers break down dead organisms or the wastes of other organisms. Fungi and many bacteria are decomposers.

7 Compare Use the Venn diagram below to describe how producers and consumers get energy.

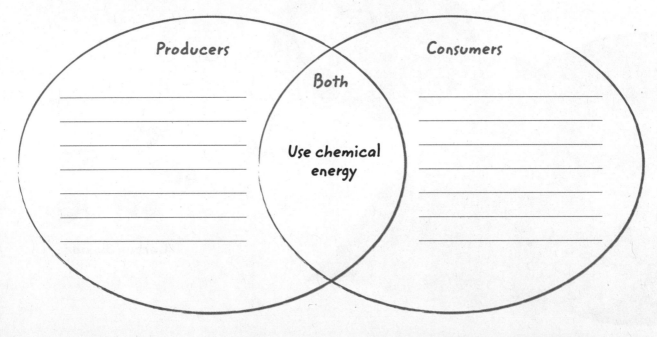

Producers

Both

Consumers

Use chemical energy

Cooking with Chloroplasts

How do plant cells make food?

Nearly all life on Earth gets energy from the sun. Plants make food with the energy from the sun. So, plants use energy from the sun directly. Animals use energy from the sun indirectly when they eat a plant or another animal.

In a process called **photosynthesis** (foh•toh•SYN•thuh•sys), plants use energy from sunlight, carbon dioxide, and water to make sugars. Plants capture light energy from the sun and change it to chemical energy in sugars. These sugars are made from water and carbon dioxide. In addition to sugars, photosynthesis also produces oxygen gas. The oxygen gas is given off into the air.

Active Reading

8 Identify What is the source of energy for nearly all life on Earth?

The sun

Visualize It!

Photosynthesis In many plants, photosynthesis takes place in the leaf. Chlorophyll, which is located in chloroplasts, captures light energy from the sun. This light energy is converted to chemical energy in sugars.

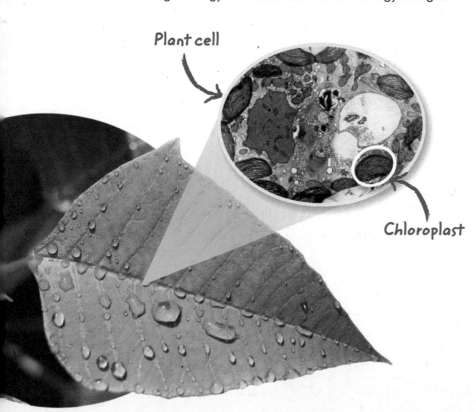

Plant cell

Chloroplast

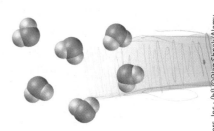

Water

Carbon dioxide

Capturing Light Energy

Energy from sunlight powers the process of photosynthesis. The light energy is converted to chemical energy, which is stored in the bonds of the sugar molecules made during photosynthesis.

Photosynthesis takes place in organelles called *chloroplasts* (KLOHR•oh•plahstz). These organelles are found only in the cells of plants and other organisms that undergo photosynthesis. They are not found in animal or fungal cells. Chloroplasts contain a green pigment called **chlorophyll** (KLOHR•oh•fill). Chlorophyll captures energy from sunlight. This energy is used to combine carbon dioxide (CO_2) and water (H_2O), forming the sugar glucose ($C_6H_{12}O_6$) and oxygen gas (O_2). Photosynthesis is a series of reactions summarized by the following chemical equation:

$$6CO_2 + 6 H_2O + \text{light energy} \rightarrow C_6H_{12}O_6 + 6O_2$$

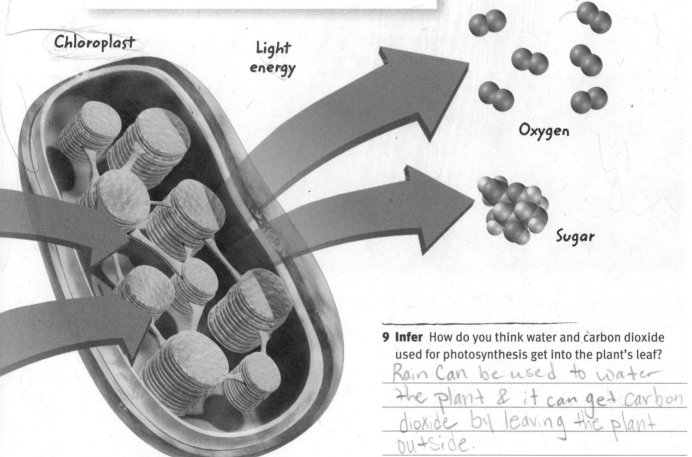

Chloroplast

Light energy

Oxygen

Sugar

9 Infer How do you think water and carbon dioxide used for photosynthesis get into the plant's leaf?

Rain Can be used to water the plant & it can get carbon dioxide by leaving the plant outside.

Storing Chemical Energy

Glucose (GLOO•kohs) is a sugar that stores chemical energy. It is the food that plants make. Plant cells break down glucose for energy. Excess sugars are stored in the body of the plant. They are often stored as starch in the roots and stem of the plant. When another organism eats the plant, the organism can use these stored sugars for energy.

Mighty Mitochondria

How do cells get energy from food?

When sugar is broken down, energy is released. It is stored in a molecule called *adenosine triphosphate (ATP)*. ATP powers many of the chemical reactions that enable cells to survive. The process of breaking down food to produce ATP is called **cellular respiration** (SELL•yoo•lahr ress•puh•RAY•shuhn).

 **Active Reading**

10 Identify As you read, underline the starting materials and products of cellular respiration.

Mitochondria are found in both plant cells and animal cells.

Mitochondrion

Visualize It!

Cellular Respiration During cellular respiration, cells use oxygen gas to break down sugars and release energy.

Oxygen

Using Oxygen

Cellular respiration takes place in the cytoplasm and cell membranes of prokaryotic cells. In eukaryotic cells, cellular respiration takes place in organelles called *mitochondria* (singular, *mitochondrion*). Mitochondria are found in both plant and animal cells. The starting materials of cellular respiration are glucose and oxygen.

In eukaryotes, the first stage of cellular respiration takes place in the cytoplasm. Glucose is broken down into two 3-carbon molecules. This releases a small amount of energy. The next stage takes place in the mitochondria. This stage requires oxygen. Oxygen enters the cell and travels into the mitochondria. As the 3-carbon molecules are broken down, energy is captured and stored in ATP.

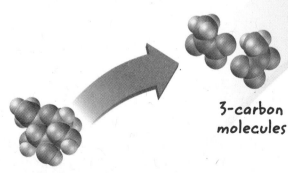

3-carbon molecules

Sugar from photosynthesis

© Houghton Mifflin Harcourt Publishing Company • Image Credits: (tl) ©Medford Taylor/National Geographic/Getty Images; (inset) ©Thomas Deerinck, NCMIR/Photo Researchers, Inc.

Releasing Energy

The products of cellular respiration are chemical energy (ATP), carbon dioxide, and water. The carbon dioxide formed during cellular respiration is released by the cell. In many animals, the carbon dioxide is carried to the lungs and exhaled during breathing.

Some of the energy produced during cellular respiration is released as heat. However, much of the energy produced during cellular respiration is transferred to ATP. ATP can be carried throughout the body. When ATP is broken down, the energy released is used for cellular activities. The steps of cellular respiration can be summarized by the following equation:

$$C_6H_{12}O_6 + 6O_2 \rightarrow 6CO_2 + 6H_2O + \text{chemical energy (ATP)}$$

Think Outside the Book Inquiry

11 **Identify** With a partner, write a creative story or play that describes the process of cellular respiration.

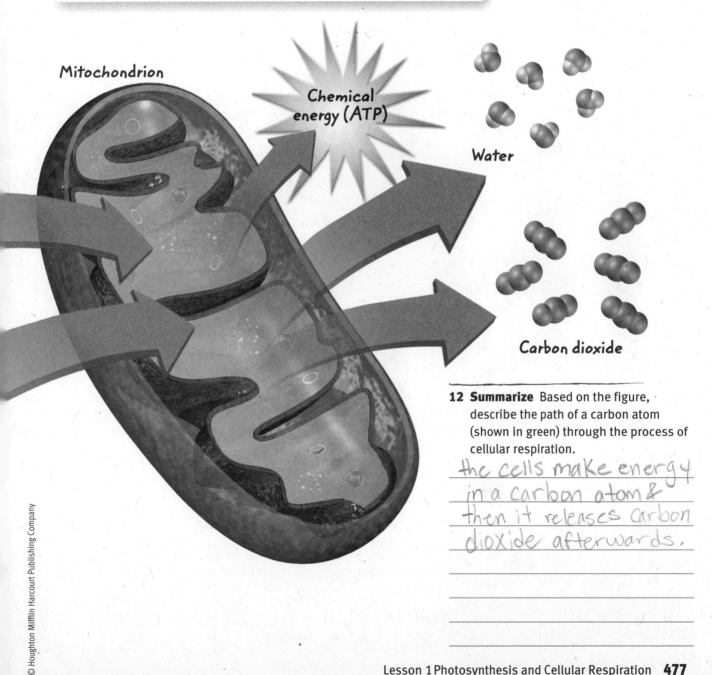

Mitochondrion

Chemical energy (ATP)

Water

Carbon dioxide

12 **Summarize** Based on the figure, describe the path of a carbon atom (shown in green) through the process of cellular respiration.

the cells make energy in a carbon atom & then it releases carbon dioxide afterwards.

Merry-Go-Round!

How are photosynthesis and cellular respiration connected?

Most of the oxygen in the atmosphere was made during photosynthesis. Nearly all organisms use this oxygen during cellular respiration. They produce carbon dioxide and release it into the environment. In turn, plants use the carbon dioxide to make sugars. So, photosynthesis and respiration are linked, each depending on the products of the other.

A _____
energy

🔍 Visualize It!

13 Synthesize Fill in the missing labels, and draw in the missing molecules.

D _____

Used in

Produces

Chloroplast
(in plant cells)

Oxygen

Carbon
dioxide

B _____

Produces

Used in

Mitochondrion
(in plant and
animal cells)

14 Summarize How are the starting materials and products of cellular respiration and photosynthesis related?

C _____
energy

_____

_____

_____

Why It Matters

Out of Air

When there isn't enough oxygen, living things can get energy by anaerobic respiration (AN•uh•roh•bick ress•puh•RAY•shuhn). *Anaerobic* means "without oxygen." Like cellular respiration, anaerobic respiration produces ATP. However, it does not produce as much ATP as cellular respiration.

Rising to the Top

Fermentation is a type of anaerobic respiration. Many yeasts rely on fermentation for energy. Carbon dioxide is a product of fermentation. Carbon dioxide causes bread to rise, and gives it air pockets.

Feel the Burn!

The body uses anaerobic respiration during hard exercise, such as sprinting. This produces lactic acid, which can cause muscles to ache after exercise.

Extend

Inquiry

15 Compare What products do both cellular and anaerobic respiration have in common?

16 Research Blood delivers oxygen to the body. If this is the case, why does the body rely on anaerobic respiration during hard exercise? Research the reasons why the body switches between cellular and anaerobic respiration.

17 Compare Research and compare cellular respiration and fermentation. How are they similar? How do they differ? Summarize your results by doing one of the following:
- make a poster
- write a brochure
- draw a comic strip
- make a table

Visual Summary

To complete this summary, check the box that indicates true or false. Then, use the key below to check your answers. You can use this page to review the main concepts of the lesson.

Cells get and use energy

Living things need energy to survive.

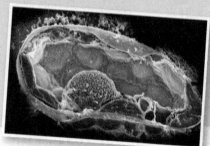

Plants make their own food.

	T	F	
18	☐	☐	Organisms get energy from food.
19	☐	☐	A producer eats other organisms.

	T	F	
20	☐	☐	Photosynthesis is the process by which plants make their own food.
21	☐	☐	Chlorophyll captures light energy during photosynthesis.

Cells release energy from food during cellular respiration.

	T	F	
22	☐	☐	Carbon dioxide is required for cellular respiration.
23	☐	☐	Cellular respiration takes place in chloroplasts.

Photosynthesis and cellular respiration are interrelated.

	T	F	
24	☐	☐	The products of photosynthesis are the starting materials of cellular respiration.

Answers: 18 T; 19 F; 20 T; 21 T; 22 F; 23 F; 24 T

25 Identify Describe how the cells in your body get energy and then use that energy.

Lesson Review

Vocabulary

Fill in the blank with the term that best completes the following sentences.

1 _____ takes place in organelles called *chloroplasts*.

2 Light energy is captured by the green pigment _____

3 Cells use oxygen to release energy during _____

Key Concepts

Use the figure to answer the following questions.

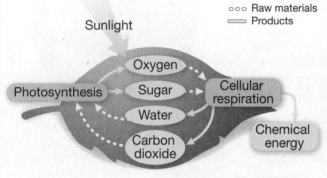

4 Identify What are the starting materials and products of photosynthesis and cellular respiration?

_____
_____
_____
_____
_____

5 Relate What does the diagram above reveal about the connections between photosynthesis and cellular respiration?

_____
_____
_____
_____

6 Contrast How do plants and animals get their energy in different ways?

_____
_____
_____
_____
_____

Critical Thinking

7 Infer Does your body get all its energy from the sun? Explain.

_____
_____
_____
_____
_____
_____

8 Synthesize Could cellular respiration happen without photosynthesis? Explain your reasoning.

_____
_____
_____
_____
_____
_____

9 Apply Plants don't move around, so why do they need energy?

_____
_____
_____
_____
_____
_____
_____

Interpreting Circle Graphs

Scientists display data in tables and graphs in order to organize it and show relationships. A *circle graph*, also called a *pie graph*, is used to show and compare the pieces of a whole.

Sunshine State Standards

MA.6.A.3.6 Construct and analyze tables, graphs, and equations to describe linear functions and other simple relations using both common language and algebraic notation.

LA.6.2.2.3 The student will organize information to show understanding (e.g., representing main ideas within text through charting, mapping, paraphrasing, summarizing, or comparing/contrasting).

Tutorial

In a circle graph, the entire circle represents the whole, and each piece is called a *sector*. Follow the instructions below to learn how to interpret a circle graph.

1 Evaluating Data Data on circle graphs may be given in one of two ways: as values (such as dollars, days, or numbers of items) or as percentages of the whole.

2 Changing Percentage to Value The word *percent* means "per hundred," so 25% means 25 per 100, or 25/100. To find the total volume represented by a sector, such as the volume of fresh water in surface water, multiply the whole value by the percent of the sector, and then divide by 100.

$$35{,}030{,}000 \text{ km}^3 \times \frac{0.3}{100} = 105{,}090 \text{ km}^3 \text{ of Earth's}$$
$$\text{fresh water is in surface water.}$$

Distribution of Fresh Water (in values)

■ Icecaps and Glaciers 24,065,610 km³
■ Ground Water 10,544,030 km³
■ Surface Water 105,090 km³
■ Other 315,270 km³

Source: Gleick, P. H., 1996: Water resources. In Encyclopedia of Climate and Weather, ed. by S. H. Schneider, Oxford University Press, New York, vol. 2, pp.817-823

3 Changing Value to Ratio The sum of the sectors, 35,030,000 km³, is the whole, or total value. Divide the value of a sector, such as the icecaps and glaciers sector, by the value of the whole. Simplify this fraction to express it as a ratio.

$$\frac{24{,}065{,}610 \text{ km}^3}{35{,}030{,}000 \text{ km}^3} \approx \frac{25}{35} = \frac{5}{7}$$

About $\frac{5}{7}$ of Earth's fresh water is in icecaps and glaciers. This ratio can be expressed as $\frac{5}{7}$, 5:7, or 5 to 7.

4 Changing Value to Percentage The whole circle graph is 100%. To find the percentage of a sector, such as the world's fresh water that is found as groundwater, divide the value of the sector by the value of the whole, and then multiply by 100%.

$$\frac{10{,}544{,}030 \text{ km}^3}{35{,}030{,}000 \text{ km}^3} \times 100\% = 30.1\% \text{ of Earth's fresh water is groundwater.}$$

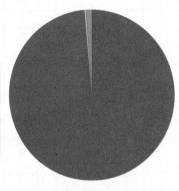

Distribution of Fresh Water (in percentages)

■ Icecaps and Glaciers 68.7%
■ Ground Water 30.1%
■ Surface Water 0.3%
■ Other 0.9%

Source: Gleick, P. H., 1996: Water resources. In Encyclopedia of Climate and Weather, ed. by S. H. Schneider, Oxford University Press, New York, vol. 2, pp.817-823

You Try It!

Use the circle graphs below to answer the following questions.

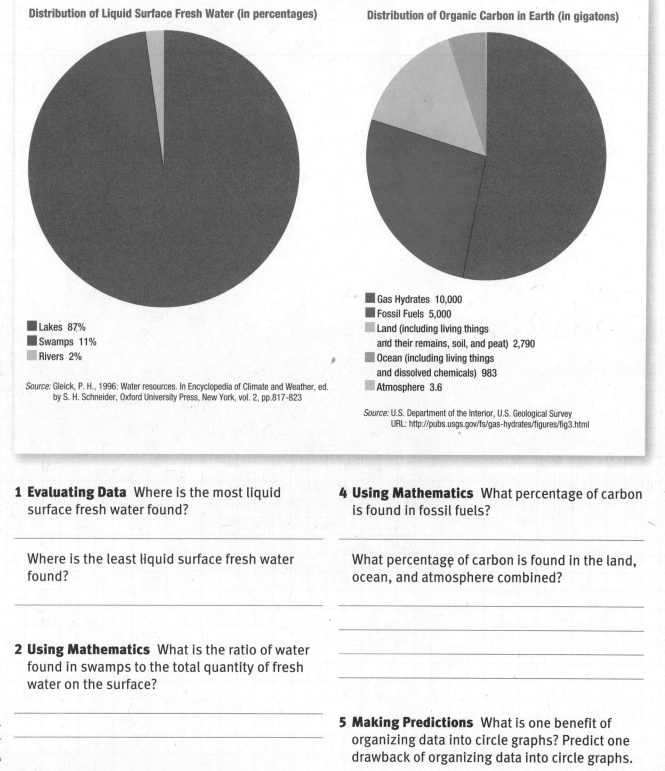

Distribution of Liquid Surface Fresh Water (in percentages)

- Lakes 87%
- Swamps 11%
- Rivers 2%

Source: Gleick, P. H., 1996: Water resources. In Encyclopedia of Climate and Weather, ed. by S. H. Schneider, Oxford University Press, New York, vol. 2, pp.817-823

Distribution of Organic Carbon in Earth (in gigatons)

- Gas Hydrates 10,000
- Fossil Fuels 5,000
- Land (including living things and their remains, soil, and peat) 2,790
- Ocean (including living things and dissolved chemicals) 983
- Atmosphere 3.6

Source: U.S. Department of the Interior, U.S. Geological Survey
URL: http://pubs.usgs.gov/fs/gas-hydrates/figures/fig3.html

1 Evaluating Data Where is the most liquid surface fresh water found?

Where is the least liquid surface fresh water found?

2 Using Mathematics What is the ratio of water found in swamps to the total quantity of fresh water on the surface?

3 Using Mathematics If there is a total volume of 105,090 km³ of liquid surface fresh water, what volume is found in swamps?

4 Using Mathematics What percentage of carbon is found in fossil fuels?

What percentage of carbon is found in the land, ocean, and atmosphere combined?

5 Making Predictions What is one benefit of organizing data into circle graphs? Predict one drawback of organizing data into circle graphs.

Energy and Matter in Ecosystems

ESSENTIAL QUESTION

How do energy and matter move through ecosystems?

By the end of this lesson, you should be able to explain how the energy and matter in ecosystems are connected by the carbon cycle.

Living things get energy from food. Plants can make their own food, but people have to eat other organisms.

🌀 Sunshine State Standards

SC.6.N.3.2 Recognize and explain that a scientific law is a description of a specific relationship under given conditions in the natural world. Thus, scientific laws are different from societal laws.

SC.6.N.3.3 Give several examples of scientific laws.

SC.7.N.3.1 Recognize and explain the difference between theories and laws and give several examples of scientific theories and the evidence that supports them.

SC.8.N.3.1 Select models useful in relating the results of their own investigations.

SC.8.L.18.3 Construct a scientific model of the carbon cycle to show how matter and energy are continuously transferred within and between organisms and their physical environment.

SC.8.L.18.4 Cite evidence that living systems follow the Laws of Conservation of Mass and Energy.

LA.6.4.2.2 The student will record information (e.g., observations, notes, lists, charts, legends) related to a topic, including visual aids to organize and record information and include a list of sources used.

Engage Your Brain

1 Predict Organisms get energy from food. Underline the organisms in the list below that get food by eating other organisms.

Lizard	Butterfly
Pine tree	Cactus
Grass	Mountain lion
Salamander	Scrub jay
Turtle	Moss

2 Diagram Choose a nearby ecosystem, and draw a diagram below of the flow of energy from the sun to the organisms in the ecosystem.

Active Reading

3 Apply Many scientific words, such as *law*, also have everyday meanings. In everyday use, a *law* is a rule that is enforced by the government. In contrast, a scientific *law* describes a natural principle. It describes what happens in nature, but it does not explain how it happens. For example, Newton's laws of motion describe how objects move under certain conditions

In science, theories are well-supported and widely accepted explanations of how things happen. How is a theory different from a law?

_____

_____

Would you expect the law of conservation of energy to explain how energy is conserved in nature? Why or why not?

_____

_____

_____

Vocabulary Terms

- energy
- matter
- law of conservation of energy
- law of conservation of mass
- energy pyramid
- carbon cycle

4 Apply As you learn the definition of each vocabulary term in this lesson, create your own definition or sketch to help remember the meaning of the term.

Soak Up the Sun

5 Identify As you read, underline the characteristics of producers and consumers.

How do organisms get energy and matter?

The ability to do work is called **energy.** Energy comes in many forms, including the chemical energy in food and light energy and heat energy from the sun. **Matter** is anything that has mass and takes up space. All organisms need energy and matter to survive, grow, and reproduce.

The Sun

The sun is the original source of energy in most ecosystems. Some organisms, called *producers,* make their own food. Plants and algae are producers that use water, carbon dioxide, and energy from sunlight to make sugars. In a few ecosystems, producers use chemical energy instead of light energy to make food. *Consumers* are organisms that cannot make their own food. Consumers eat producers or other consumers to get energy.

Food

Organisms need energy and matter to build their bodies. Producers get energy from the sun. They get matter for making food and building their bodies from soil and air. The food that consumers eat provides both energy and building materials. Carbon, nitrogen, and phosphorus are some of the important building materials consumers get from food.

Roots help trees get matter, such as water and nutrients, from the soil.

6 Infer Use this table to identify where producers and consumers get energy and matter.

Type of organism	How they get energy	How they get matter
Producers		
Consumers		

What happens to energy and matter in ecosystems?

Organisms need energy and matter for many functions, such as moving, growing, and reproducing. Energy and matter are constantly moving through ecosystems. Producers use carbon dioxide and water to make sugars. They collect materials from their environment to build their bodies. Consumers eat other organisms to get food that they use for energy. As one organism eats another, some energy is lost as heat. Matter is returned to the physical environment as wastes or when organisms die.

Energy and Matter Are Conserved

The **law of conservation of energy** states that energy cannot be created or destroyed. Energy changes forms. Producers change light energy from the sun to chemical energy in sugars. When sugars are used, some energy is given off as heat. Much of the energy in sugars is changed to another form of chemical energy that cells can use for life functions. The **law of conservation of mass** states that mass cannot be created or destroyed. Instead, matter moves through the environment in different forms.

Energy and Matter Leave Ecosystems

Ecosystems do not have clear boundaries, so energy and matter can leave them. Matter and energy can leave an ecosystem when organisms move. For example, some birds feed on fish in the ocean. When birds fly back to land, they take the matter and energy from the fish out of the ocean. Matter and energy can leave ecosystems by drifting down rivers or by being blown by the wind. Even though the matter and energy leave an ecosystem, they are never destroyed.

Visualize It!

7 Analyze How might energy and matter leave the ecosystem shown in the picture above?

_____

_____

_____

_____

_____

8 Compare Use the Venn diagram below to relate how energy and matter move through ecosystems.

Energy

_____

_____

_____

_____

Both

Energy and matter are conserved.

Matter

_____

_____

_____

_____

Cycle *and* Flow

How does energy move through an ecosystem?

Energy enters most ecosystems as sunlight, which producers use to make food. Primary consumers, such as herbivores, get energy by eating producers. Secondary consumers, such as carnivores, get energy by eating primary consumers, and so on up the food chain. An organism uses most of the energy it takes in for life processes. However, some energy is lost to the environment as heat. A small amount of energy is stored in an organism's body. Only this stored energy can be used by a consumer that eats the organism.

An **energy pyramid** is a tool that can be used to trace the flow of energy through an ecosystem. The pyramid's shape shows that there is less energy and fewer organisms at each level. At each step in the food chain, energy is lost. Because less energy is available, fewer organisms can be supported at higher levels. The bottom level—the producers—has the largest population and the most energy. The other levels are consumers. At the highest level, consumers will have the smallest population because of the limited amount of energy available to them.

Visualize It!

9 Analyze Describe how energy flows through each level in this energy pyramid. Is all the matter and energy from one level transferred to the next level?

_____
_____
_____
_____
_____
_____
_____
_____
_____
_____

Tertiary consumers

The amount of energy available and population size decrease as you go up the energy pyramid.

Secondary consumers

Primary consumers

Producers

How does matter move through an ecosystem?

Producers use matter from the physical environment as building materials for their bodies. Primary consumers use the matter in producers to build their bodies. Secondary consumers use the matter in primary consumers to build their bodies. In this way, matter flows from producers through to consumers. Water, carbon, nitrogen, phosphorus, and oxygen all cycle through ecosystems.

Consumers don't use all the food they eat. Some of the matter in food is turned into waste products. *Decomposers*, such as bacteria or fungi, break down waste products and dead organisms to return matter to the physical environment. Producers can then use this matter to build their bodies, starting the cycle of matter again.

Active Reading **10 Identify** What is the role of decomposition in cycling matter?

_____

_____

_____

Visualize It!

11 Analyze Describe how matter is moving through this ecosystem.

_____

_____

_____

_____

The Carbon Cycle

Carbon is an important building block of organisms. Carbon is found in sugars, which store the chemical energy that organisms need to live. Carbon also is found in the atmosphere (as carbon dioxide gas), in bodies of water, in rocks and soils, in organisms, and in fossil fuels. Energy and matter move through organisms and between organisms and the physical environment in the **carbon cycle**.

Active Reading **12 List** Identify five places where carbon may be found.

_____

_____

Respiration

Photosythesis

Photosynthesis

During photosynthesis, producers in the water and on land take in light energy from the sun and use carbon dioxide and water to make sugars. These sugars contain carbon and store chemical energy. Oxygen gas is also a product of photosynthesis.

Respiration

Cellular respiration occurs in producers and consumers on land and in water. During respiration, sugars are broken down to release energy. The process uses oxygen gas. Carbon dioxide, water, and heat are released.

carbon in organisms

carbon dioxide dissolved in water

Visualize It!

13 Relate Briefly describe how carbon enters and exits a consumer, such as the sheep shown in this diagram.

_____

_____

_____

_____

_____

Combustion

Combustion is the burning of once living materials, including wood and fossil fuels. This releases carbon dioxide, water, heat energy, and other materials into the environment. It may also produce pollution.

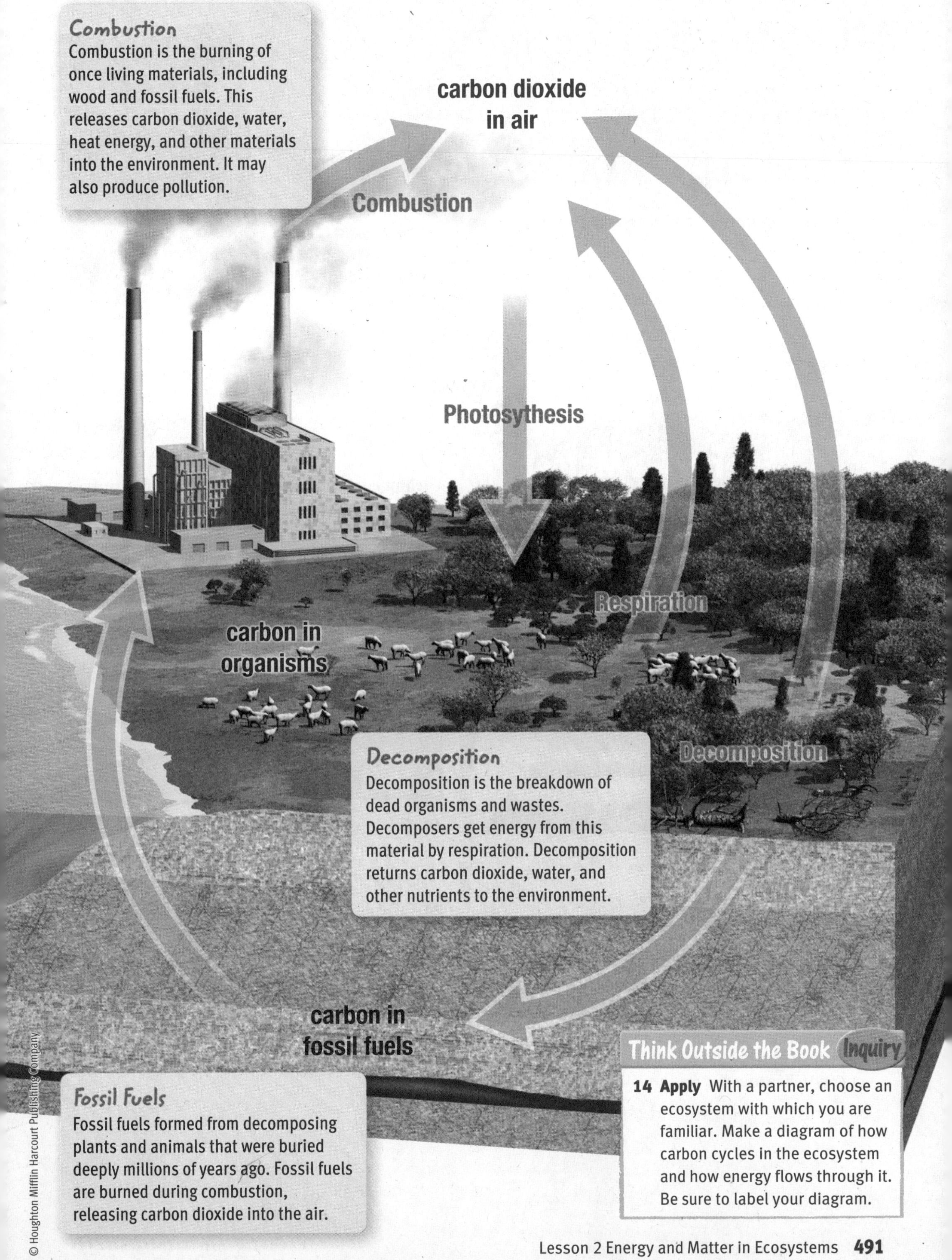

carbon dioxide in air

Combustion

Photosythesis

Respiration

carbon in organisms

Decomposition

Decomposition

Decomposition is the breakdown of dead organisms and wastes. Decomposers get energy from this material by respiration. Decomposition returns carbon dioxide, water, and other nutrients to the environment.

carbon in fossil fuels

Fossil Fuels

Fossil fuels formed from decomposing plants and animals that were buried deeply millions of years ago. Fossil fuels are burned during combustion, releasing carbon dioxide into the air.

Think Outside the Book (Inquiry)

14 Apply With a partner, choose an ecosystem with which you are familiar. Make a diagram of how carbon cycles in the ecosystem and how energy flows through it. Be sure to label your diagram.

Visual Summary

To complete this summary, fill in the blanks with the correct word or phrase. Then use the key below to check your answers. You can use this page to review the main concepts of the lesson.

Organisms get energy from different sources.

15 Many _____
get energy from sunlight.

16 _____ get
energy from other organisms.

Organisms need energy and matter to survive, grow, and reproduce.

17 Energy and matter can neither be _____

nor _____

Energy and Matter in Ecosystems

As energy flows through a food chain, some energy is lost to the environment.

18 Where in an energy pyramid is the most energy?

_____

Carbon cycles through organisms, into the physical environment, and back again.

19 Dead organisms that were buried turned into _____ after millions of years.

20 Carbon from this material reenters the atmosphere by _____

Answers: 15 producers; 16 Consumers; 17 created, destroyed;18 the bottom level; 19 fossil fuels; 20 combustion

21 **Explain** If energy and matter cannot be destroyed, what happens to energy and matter when an organism is eaten?

Lesson Review

Vocabulary

Fill in the blanks with the term that best completes the following sentences.

1 _____ comes in many forms, including food and heat.

2 Anything that takes up space is called _____

3 A(n) _____ traces the flow of matter and energy in ecosystems.

Key Concepts

For each example, identify the organism as a producer, consumer, or decomposer.

Example	Type of organism
4 Identify A whale shark eats algae.	
5 Identify Algae use sunlight to make sugars.	
6 Identify Fungi break down a log.	

7 Identify What process in the carbon cycle takes carbon out of the air?

_____

8 Compare How are the law of conservation of energy and the law of conservation of mass similar?

_____

_____

_____

_____

9 Identify In an ecosystem, which would have a larger population, producers or primary consumers? Explain.

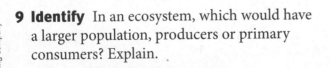

_____

_____

_____

Critical Thinking

Use this graph to answer the following questions.

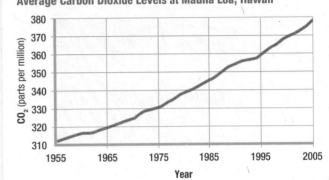

Average Carbon Dioxide Levels at Mauna Loa, Hawaii

Source: *NOAA 2004*

10 Analyze What process of the carbon cycle is likely causing the increase in carbon dioxide levels shown in the graph above?

_____

11 Identify What is the most likely source of the carbon dioxide shown in the graph above?

_____

12 Evaluate If people planted huge numbers of trees and other plants, how might the carbon dioxide levels in the graph above change? Explain.

_____

_____

_____

_____

_____

13 Synthesize Mountain lions are tertiary consumers. How might the removal of mountain lions affect the flow of matter and energy in the rest of the energy pyramid?

_____

_____

_____

_____

_____

My Notes

Unit 9 **Summary**

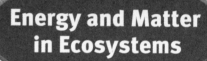

Cycling of Matter and Energy

involves

which depend on

Photosynthesis and Cellular Respiration

Energy and Matter in Ecosystems

1 Interpret As shown in the Graphic Organizer above, energy and matter in ecoystems are interdependent with the processes of photosynthesis and cellular respiration. Explain this relationship.

_____

_____

_____

_____

_____

_____

_____

2 Identify Why is the carbon cycle important to the cycling of matter and energy?

_____

_____

_____

_____

_____

_____

3 Apply How are energy and matter important to the survival of an organism?

_____

_____

_____

_____

_____

_____

4 Predict What might happen if plants and other photosynthetic organisms disappeared from an ecosystem?

_____

_____

_____

_____

_____

_____

_____

_____

Name _____

Multiple Choice
Identify the choice that best completes the statement or answers the question.

1 One of the largest cypress trees in Florida has a tree trunk with a diameter of about 3.5 m. What is the source of **most** of the carbon in the cypress tree's trunk?

    A. The tree created carbon during photosynthesis.

    B. The tree used carbon that it had stored in seeds.

    C. The tree took in carbon dioxide molecules from the atmosphere.

    D. The tree took in carbon dioxide molecules from the soil.

2 There is a connection between photosynthesis and cellular respiration. The products from one provide the raw materials for the other. This image shows the relationship between the two processes.

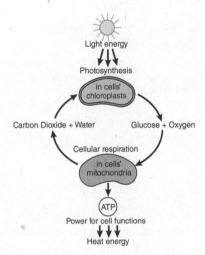

What products of photosynthesis are starting materials for cellular respiration?

    F. glucose and oxygen

    G. heat energy and ATP

    H. carbon dioxide and water

    I. light energy and chlorophyll

3 A freshwater marsh is a type of ecosystem. Grasses, fish, wading birds, frogs, and alligators live together in freshwater marshes. Pieces of decaying material sink to the bottom of the marsh. In which of these places can carbon be found in the marsh?

    A. in the atmosphere and water only

    B. in living things only

    C. in living things and decaying materials only

    D. in the atmosphere, water, living things, and decaying materials

4   Green plants produce their own food during photosynthesis. This image
shows the process of photosynthesis.

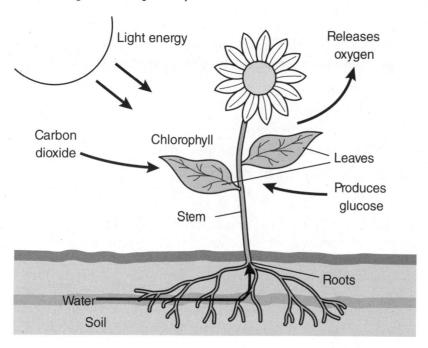

Which of these substances is also a product of photosynthesis?

F.   carbon dioxide

G.   chlorophyll

H.   oxygen

I.   water

5   Jamal is running a race this afternoon. He eats a big breakfast to make sure
that he can reach the finish line, since food provides the energy his cells need
to complete any activity. What form of energy is stored in food?

A.   chemical energy

B.   kinetic energy

C.   light energy

D.   mechanical energy

6   Plant cells produce their own food. They also must get energy from this food,
which they use for cell activities, growth, and reproduction. What is the name
of the process in which plant cells use oxygen to get energy from food?

F.   photosynthesis

G.   cellular respiration

H.   fermentation

I.   mitochondrion

7 Kristine goes to her neighborhood health club to exercise. The process of
cellular respiration makes it possible for Kristine to run on the treadmill and
to lift weights. What do her cells do during cellular respiration?

    A. convert kinetic energy into chemical energy

    B. absorb light energy through the chlorophyll in their chloroplasts

    C. break down glucose to convert energy in the form of ATP

    D. combine water and carbon dioxide to produce oxygen and glucose

8 There is a relationship between breathing and cellular respiration. Breathing
involves taking in oxygen and releasing carbon dioxide. How is oxygen related
to the process of cellular respiration?

    F. Cellular respiration uses ATP to release the energy stored in oxygen.

    G. Cellular respiration uses oxygen to release the energy stored in food.

    H. Cellular respiration uses oxygen to produce food in the form of sugars.

    I. Cellular respiration uses carbon to produce energy in the form of oxygen.

9 Worms break down dead plants in the soil, and in the process they release
nutrients back into the soil. Which property of nutrients shows that they are a
type of matter?

    A. Nutrients are colorful.

    B. Nutrients can do work.

    C. Nutrients contain energy.

    D. Nutrients have mass.

10 A coral reef is damaged during a hurricane. The waves and currents move
broken pieces of coral onto the beach. What happened to the matter in the
broken pieces of coral?

    F. It has remained part of the coral reef ecosystem.

    G. It was removed from the environment.

    H. It became part of the beach ecosystem.

    I. It was lost due to the energy in the waves.

11 An alligator lives in a swamp with deer, birds, fish, trees, and other plants. The alligator eats a bird that eats seeds and plants. What is the original source of the energy that the alligator gets from eating the bird?

A. the flowing water in the swamp

B. the energy that the bird creates

C. the sunlight that the plants absorb

D. the heat from the air in the swamp

12 Carbon exists in many forms on Earth. The diagram below shows part of the carbon cycle.

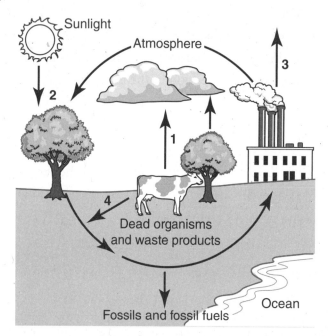

The process labeled "1" on the diagram indicates carbon moving from the cow into the atmosphere. What is happening in this process?

F. The cow releases energy and stores carbon.

G. The cow decomposes and releases carbon.

H. The cow converts carbon dioxide into sugars.

I. The cow breaks down sugars and releases carbon dioxide.

Look It Up!

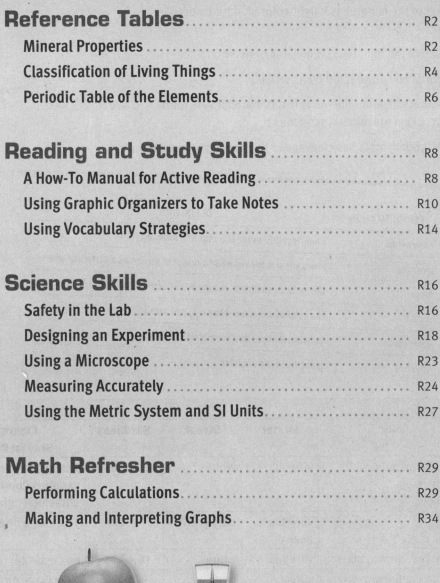

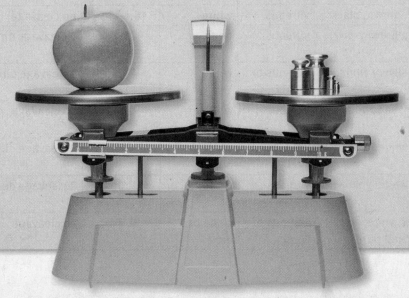

Reference Tables

Mineral Properties

Here are five steps to take in mineral identification:

1 Determine the color of the mineral. Is it light-colored, dark-colored, or a specific color?

2 Determine the luster of the mineral. Is it metallic or non-metallic?

3 Determine the color of any powder left by its streak.

4 Determine the hardness of your mineral. Is it soft, hard, or very hard? Using a glass plate, see if the mineral scratches it.

5 Determine whether your sample has cleavage or any special properties.

TERMS TO KNOW	DEFINITION
adamantine	a non-metallic luster like that of a diamond
cleavage	how a mineral breaks when subject to stress on a particular plane
luster	the state or quality of shining by reflecting light
streak	the color of a mineral when it is powdered
submetallic	between metallic and nonmetallic in luster
vitreous	glass-like type of luster

Silicate Minerals					
Mineral	**Color**	**Luster**	**Streak**	**Hardness**	**Cleavage and Special Properties**
Beryl	deep green, pink, white, bluish green, or yellow	vitreous	white	7.5–8	1 cleavage direction; some varieties fluoresce in ultraviolet light
Chlorite	green	vitreous to pearly	pale green	2–2.5	1 cleavage direction
Garnet	green, red, brown, black	vitreous	white	6.5–7.5	no cleavage
Hornblende	dark green, brown, or black	vitreous	none	5–6	2 cleavage directions
Muscovite	colorless, silvery white, or brown	vitreous or pearly	white	2–2.5	1 cleavage direction
Olivine	olive green, yellow	vitreous	white or none	6.5–7	no cleavage
Orthoclase	colorless, white, pink, or other colors	vitreous	white or none	6	2 cleavage directions
Plagioclase	colorless, white, yellow, pink, green	vitreous	white	6	2 cleavage directions
Quartz	colorless or white; any color when not pure	vitreous or waxy	white or none	7	no cleavage

Nonsilicate Minerals

Mineral	Color	Luster	Streak	Hardness	Cleavage and Special Properties
Native Elements					
Copper	copper-red	metallic	copper-red	2.5–3	no cleavage
Diamond	pale yellow or colorless	adamantine	none	10	4 cleavage directions
Graphite	black to gray	submetallic	black	1–2	1 cleavage direction
Carbonates					
Aragonite	colorless, white, or pale yellow	vitreous	white	3.5–4	2 cleavage directions; reacts with hydrochloric acid
Calcite	colorless or white to tan	vitreous	white	3	3 cleavage directions; reacts with weak acid; double refraction
Halides					
Fluorite	light green, yellow, purple, bluish green, or other colors	vitreous	none	4	4 cleavage directions; some varieties fluoresce
Halite	white	vitreous	white	2.0–2.5	3 cleavage directions
Oxides					
Hematite	reddish brown to black	metallic to earthy	dark red to red-brown	5.6–6.5	no cleavage; magnetic when heated
Magnetite	iron-black	metallic	black	5.5–6.5	no cleavage; magnetic
Sulfates					
Anhydrite	colorless, bluish, or violet	vitreous to pearly	white	3–3.5	3 cleavage directions
Gypsum	white, pink, gray, or colorless	vitreous, pearly, or silky	white	2.0	3 cleavage directions
Sulfides					
Galena	lead-gray	metallic	lead-gray to black	2.5–2.8	3 cleavage directions
Pyrite	brassy yellow	metallic	greenish, brownish, or black	6–6.5	no cleavage

Reference Tables

Classification of Living Things

Domains and Kingdoms

All organisms belong to one of three domains: Domain Archaea, Domain Bacteria, or Domain Eukarya. Some of the groups within these domains are shown below. (Remember that genus names are italicized.)

Domain Archaea

The organisms in this domain are single-celled prokaryotes, many of which live in extreme environments.

Archaea		
Group	**Example**	**Characteristics**
Methanogens	*Methanococcus*	produce methane gas; can't live in oxygen
Thermophiles	*Sulpholobus*	require sulphur; can't live in oxygen
Halophiles	*Halococcus*	live in very salty environments; most can live in oxygen

Domain Bacteria

Organisms in this domain are single-celled prokaryotes and are found in almost every environment on Earth.

Bacteria		
Group	**Example**	**Characteristics**
Bacilli	*Escherichia*	rod shaped; some fix nitrogen; some cause disease
Cocci	*Streptococcus*	spherical shaped; cause diseases; can form spores
Spirilla	*Treponema*	spiral shaped; cause diseases, such as syphilis

Domain Eukarya

Organisms in this domain are single-celled or multicellular eukaryotes.

Kingdom Protista Many protists resemble fungi, plants, or animals, but are smaller and simpler in structure. Most are single-celled.

Protists		
Group	**Example**	**Characteristics**
Sarcodines	*Amoeba*	radiolarians; single-celled consumers
Ciliates	*Paramecium*	single-celled consumers
Flagellates	*Trypanosoma*	single-celled parasites
Sporozoans	*Plasmodium*	single-celled parasites
Euglenas	*Euglena*	single celled; photosynthesize
Diatoms	*Pinnularia*	most are single celled; photosynthesize
Dinoflagellates	*Gymnodinium*	single celled; some photosynthesize
Algae	*Volvox*	single celled or multicellular; photosynthesize
Slime molds	*Physarum*	single celled or multicellular; consumers or decomposers
Water molds	powdery mildew	single celled or multicellular; parasites or decomposers

Kingdom Fungi Most fungi are multicellular. Their cells have thick cell walls. Fungi absorb food from their environment.

Fungi		
Group	**Examples**	**Characteristics**
Bread molds	black bread mold	decomposers
Sac fungi	yeast; morels	saclike; parasites and decomposers
Club fungi	mushrooms; rusts; smuts	club shaped; parasites and decomposers
Chytrids	chytrid frog fungus	usually aquatic; can be decomposers or parasites

Kingdom Plantae Plants are multicellular and have cell walls made of cellulose. Plants make their own food through photosynthesis. Plants are classified into divisions instead of phyla.

Plants		
Group	**Examples**	**Characteristics**
Bryophytes	mosses, peat moss	no vascular tissue; reproduce by spores
Anthocerotophytes	hornworts	no vascular tissue; reproduce using horn-like structures
Hepatophytes	liverworts	no vascular tissue; live in moist environments
Lycophytes	*Lycopodium*; ground pine	grow in wooded areas; reproduce by spores
Pterophytes	horsetails; ferns	seedless, vascular tissue; reproduce by spores
Conifers	pines; spruces; firs	needlelike leaves; reproduce by seeds made in cones
Cycads	*Zamia*	slow-growing; reproduce by seeds made in large cones
Ginkgoes	*Ginkgo*	only one living species; reproduce by seeds
Angiosperms	all flowering plants	reproduce by seeds made in flowers; fruit

Kingdom Animalia Animals are multicellular. Their cells do not have cell walls. Most animals have specialized tissues and complex organ systems. Animals get food by eating other organisms.

Animals		
Group	**Examples**	**Characteristics**
Sponges	glass sponges	no symmetry or true segmentation; aquatic
Cnidarians	jellyfish; coral	radial symmetry; aquatic
Flatworms	planaria; tapeworms; flukes	bilateral symmetry; organ systems
Roundworms	*Trichina*; hookworms	bilateral symmetry; organ systems
Annelids	earthworms; leeches	bilateral symmetry; organ systems
Mollusks	snails; octopuses	bilateral symmetry; organ systems
Echinoderms	sea stars; sand dollars	radial symmetry; organ systems
Arthropods	insects; spiders; lobsters	bilateral symmetry; organ systems
Chordates	fish; amphibians; reptiles; birds; mammals	bilateral symmetry; complex organ systems

Reference Tables

Periodic Table of the Elements

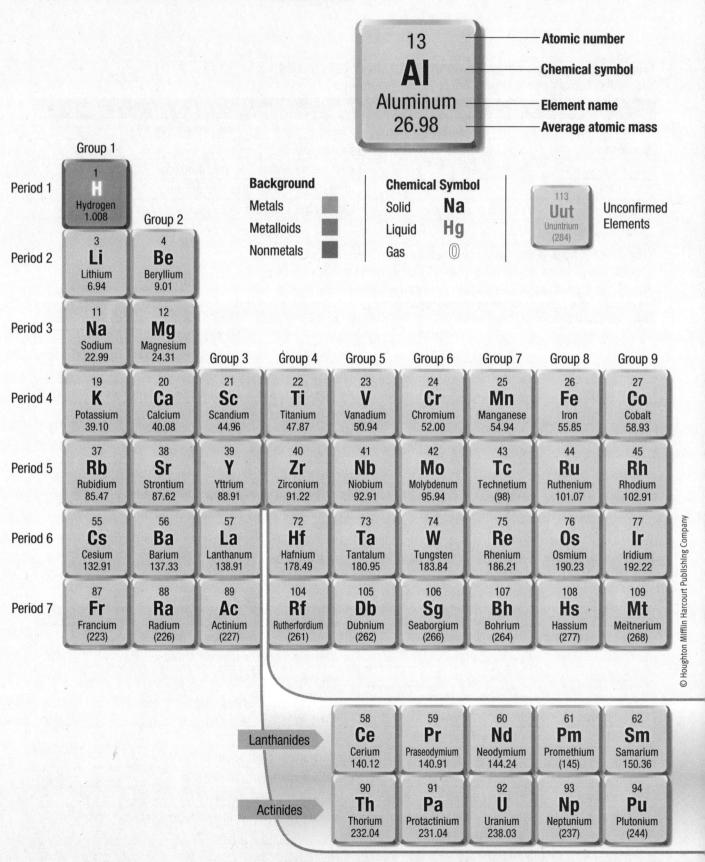

13
Al
Aluminum
26.98

- Atomic number
- Chemical symbol
- Element name
- Average atomic mass

Background
- Metals
- Metalloids
- Nonmetals

Chemical Symbol
- Solid **Na**
- Liquid **Hg**
- Gas Ⓞ

113
Uut
Ununtrium
(284)

Unconfirmed Elements

Group 1

| Period 1 | 1
H
Hydrogen
1.008 |

Group 2

| Period 2 | 3
Li
Lithium
6.94 | 4
Be
Beryllium
9.01 |

| Period 3 | 11
Na
Sodium
22.99 | 12
Mg
Magnesium
24.31 |

	Group 3	Group 4	Group 5	Group 6	Group 7	Group 8	Group 9
Period 4	21 **Sc** Scandium 44.96	22 **Ti** Titanium 47.87	23 **V** Vanadium 50.94	24 **Cr** Chromium 52.00	25 **Mn** Manganese 54.94	26 **Fe** Iron 55.85	27 **Co** Cobalt 58.93
Period 5	39 **Y** Yttrium 88.91	40 **Zr** Zirconium 91.22	41 **Nb** Niobium 92.91	42 **Mo** Molybdenum 95.94	43 **Tc** Technetium (98)	44 **Ru** Ruthenium 101.07	45 **Rh** Rhodium 102.91
Period 6	57 **La** Lanthanum 138.91	72 **Hf** Hafnium 178.49	73 **Ta** Tantalum 180.95	74 **W** Tungsten 183.84	75 **Re** Rhenium 186.21	76 **Os** Osmium 190.23	77 **Ir** Iridium 192.22
Period 7	89 **Ac** Actinium (227)	104 **Rf** Rutherfordium (261)	105 **Db** Dubnium (262)	106 **Sg** Seaborgium (266)	107 **Bh** Bohrium (264)	108 **Hs** Hassium (277)	109 **Mt** Meitnerium (268)

Period 4 Group 1-2: 19 **K** Potassium 39.10 | 20 **Ca** Calcium 40.08
Period 5 Group 1-2: 37 **Rb** Rubidium 85.47 | 38 **Sr** Strontium 87.62
Period 6 Group 1-2: 55 **Cs** Cesium 132.91 | 56 **Ba** Barium 137.33
Period 7 Group 1-2: 87 **Fr** Francium (223) | 88 **Ra** Radium (226)

Lanthanides

| 58
Ce
Cerium
140.12 | 59
Pr
Praseodymium
140.91 | 60
Nd
Neodymium
144.24 | 61
Pm
Promethium
(145) | 62
Sm
Samarium
150.36 |

Actinides

| 90
Th
Thorium
232.04 | 91
Pa
Protactinium
231.04 | 92
U
Uranium
238.03 | 93
Np
Neptunium
(237) | 94
Pu
Plutonium
(244) |

© Houghton Mifflin Harcourt Publishing Company

Group 18

2					
He					
Helium					
4.003					

Group 13	Group 14	Group 15	Group 16	Group 17
5	6	7	8	9
B	**C**	**N**	**O**	**F**
Boron	Carbon	Nitrogen	Oxygen	Fluorine
10.81	12.01	14.01	16.00	19.00

10
Ne
Neon
20.18

Group 10	Group 11	Group 12	Group 13	Group 14	Group 15	Group 16	Group 17	Group 18
			13	14	15	16	17	18
			Al	**Si**	**P**	**S**	**Cl**	**Ar**
			Aluminum	Silicon	Phosphorus	Sulfur	Chlorine	Argon
			26.98	28.09	30.97	32.07	35.45	39.95
28	29	30	31	32	33	34	35	36
Ni	**Cu**	**Zn**	**Ga**	**Ge**	**As**	**Se**	**Br**	**Kr**
Nickel	Copper	Zinc	Gallium	Germanium	Arsenic	Selenium	Bromine	Krypton
58.69	63.55	65.41	69.72	72.64	74.92	78.96	79.90	83.80
46	47	48	49	50	51	52	53	54
Pd	**Ag**	**Cd**	**In**	**Sn**	**Sb**	**Te**	**I**	**Xe**
Palladium	Silver	Cadmium	Indium	Tin	Antimony	Tellurium	Iodine	Xenon
106.42	107.87	112.41	114.82	118.71	121.76	127.6	126.9	131.29
78	79	80	81	82	83	84	85	86
Pt	**Au**	**Hg**	**Tl**	**Pb**	**Bi**	**Po**	**At**	**Rn**
Platinum	Gold	Mercury	Thallium	Lead	Bismuth	Polonium	Astatine	Radon
195.08	196.97	200.59	204.38	207.2	208.98	(209)	(210)	(222)
110	111	112	113	114	115	116		118
Ds	**Rg**	**Cn**	**Uut**	**Uuq**	**Uup**	**Uuh**		**Uuo**
Darmstadtium	Roentgenium	Copernicium	Ununtrium	Ununquadium	Ununpentium	Ununhexium		Ununoctium
(271)	(272)	(285)	(284)	(289)	(288)	(292)		(294)

63	64	65	66	67	68	69	70	71
Eu	**Gd**	**Tb**	**Dy**	**Ho**	**Er**	**Tm**	**Yb**	**Lu**
Europium	Gadolinium	Terbium	Dysprosium	Holmium	Erbium	Thulium	Ytterbium	Lutetium
151.96	157,25	158.93	162.5	164.93	167.26	168.93	173.04	174.97
95	96	97	98	99	100	101	102	103
Am	**Cm**	**Bk**	**Cf**	**Es**	**Fm**	**Md**	**No**	**Lr**
Americium	Curium	Berkelium	Californium	Einsteinium	Fermium	Mendelevium	Nobelium	Lawrencium
(243)	(247)	(247)	(251)	(252)	(257)	(258)	(259)	(262)

Reading and Study Skills

A How-To Manual for Active Reading

This book belongs to you, and you are invited to write in it. In fact, the book won't be complete until you do. Sometimes you'll answer a question or follow directions to mark up the text. Other times you'll write down your own thoughts. And when you're done reading and writing in the book, the book will be ready to help you review what you learned and prepare for the Sunshine State Benchmark tests.

Active Reading Annotations

Before you read, you'll often come upon an Active Reading prompt that asks you to underline certain words or number the steps in a process. Here's an example.

Marking the text this way is called **annotating,** and your marks

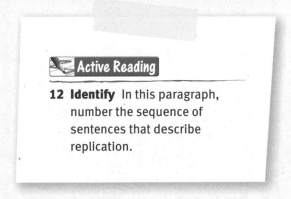

Active Reading

12 Identify In this paragraph, number the sequence of sentences that describe replication.

are called **annotations.** Annotating the text can help you identify important concepts while you read.

There are other ways that you can annotate the text. You can draw an asterisk (*) by vocabulary terms, mark unfamiliar or confusing terms and information with a question mark (?), and mark main ideas with a double underline. And you can even invent your own marks to annotate the text!

Other Annotating Opportunities

Keep your pencil, pen, or highlighter nearby as you read, so you can make a note or highlight an important point at any time. Here are a few ideas to get you started.

• Notice the headings in red and blue. The blue headings are questions that point to the main idea of what you're reading. The red headings are answers to the questions in the blue ones. Together these headings outline the content of the lesson. After reading a lesson, you could write your own answers to the questions.

- Notice the bold-faced words that are highlighted in yellow. They are highlighted so that you can easily find them again on the page where they are defined. As you read or as you review, challenge yourself to write your own sentence using the bold-faced term.

- Make a note in the margin at any time. You might
  - Ask a "What if" question
  - Comment on what you read
  - Make a connection to something you read elsewhere
  - Make a logical conclusion from the text

Use your own language and abbreviations. Invent a code, such as using circles and boxes around words to remind you of their importance or relation to each other. Your annotations will help you remember your questions for class discussions, and when you go back to the lesson later, you may be able to fill in what you didn't understand the first time you read it. Like a scientist in the field or in a lab, you will be recording your questions and observations for analysis later.

Active Reading Questions

After you read, you'll often come upon Active Reading questions that ask you to think about what you've just read. You'll write your answer underneath the question. Here's an example.

 Active Reading

8 Describe Where are phosphate groups found in a DNA molecule?

_____

_____

This type of question helps you sum up what you've just read and pull out the most important ideas from the passage. In this case the question asks you to **describe** the structure of a DNA molecule that you have just read about. Other times you may be asked to do such things as **apply** a concept, **compare** two concepts, **summarize** a process, or **identify a cause-and-effect** relationship. You'll be strengthening those critical thinking skills that you'll use often in learning about science.

Reading and Study Skills

Using Graphic Organizers to Take Notes

Graphic organizers help you remember information as you read it for the first time and as you study it later. There are dozens of graphic organizers to choose from, so the first trick is to choose the one that's best suited to your purpose. Following are some graphic organizers to use for different purposes.

To remember lots of information	To relate a central idea to subordinate details	To describe a process	To make a comparison
• Arrange data in a Content Frame • Use Combination Notes to describe a concept in words and pictures	• Show relationships with a Mind Map or a Main Idea Web • Sum up relationships among many things with a Concept Map	• Use a Process Diagram to explain a procedure • Show a chain of events and results in a Cause-and-Effect Chart	• Compare two or more closely related things in a Venn Diagram

Content Frame

1 Make a four-column chart.

2 Fill the first column with categories (e.g., snail, ant, earthworm) and the first row with descriptive information (e.g., group, characteristic, appearance).

3 Fill the chart with details that belong in each row and column.

4 When you finish, you'll have a study aid that helps you compare one category to another.

Invertebrates

NAME	GROUP	CHARACTERISTICS	DRAWING
snail	mollusks	mangle	
ant	arthropods	six legs, exoskeleton	
earthworm	segmented worms	segmented body, circulatory and digestive systems	
heartworm	roundworms	digestive system	
sea star	echinoderms	spiny skin, tube feet	
jellyfish	cnidarians	stinging cells	

Combination Notes

1 Make a two-column chart.

2 Write descriptive words and definitions in the first column.

3 Draw a simple sketch that helps you remember the meaning of the term in the second column.

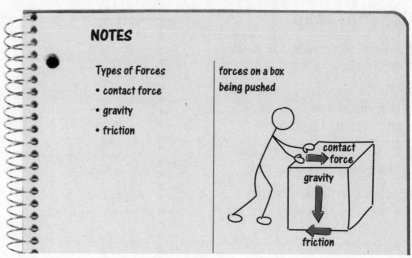

Mind Map

1 Draw an oval, and inside it write a topic to analyze.

2 Draw two or more arms extending from the oval. Each arm represents a main idea about the topic.

3 Draw lines from the arms on which to write details about each of the main ideas.

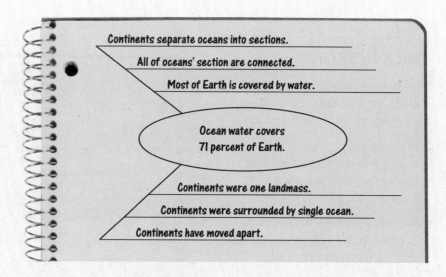

Main Idea Web

1 Make a box and write a concept you want to remember inside it.

2 Draw boxes around the central box, and label each one with a category of information about the concept (e.g., definition, formula, descriptive details)

3 Fill in the boxes with relevant details as you read.

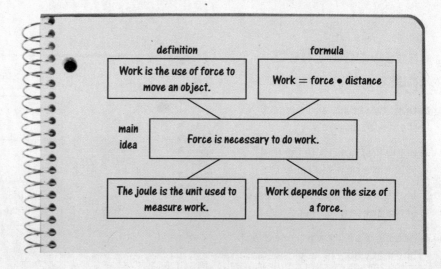

Reading and Study Skills

Concept Map

1 Draw a large oval, and inside it write a major concept.

2 Draw an arrow from the concept to a smaller oval, in which you write a related concept.

3 On the arrow, write a verb that connects the two concepts.

4 Continue in this way, adding ovals and arrows in a branching structure, until you have explained as much as you can about the main concept.

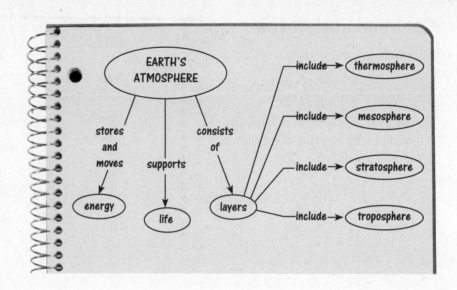

Venn Diagram

1 Draw two overlapping circles or ovals—one for each topic you are comparing—and label each one.

2 In the part of each circle that does not overlap with the other, list the characteristics that are unique to each topic.

3 In the space where the two circles overlap, list the characteristics that the two topics have in common.

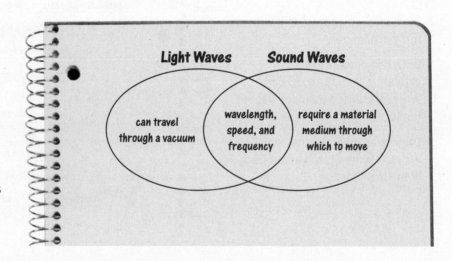

Cause-and-Effect Chart

1 Draw two boxes and connect them with an arrow.

2 In the first box, write the first event in a series (a cause).

3 In the second box, write a result of the cause (the effect).

4 Add more boxes when one event has many effects, or vice versa.

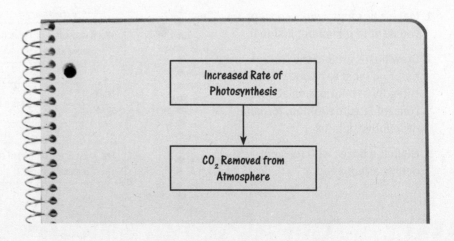

© Houghton Mifflin Harcourt Publishing Company • Image Credits:

Process Diagram

A process can be a never-ending cycle. As you can see in this technology design process, engineers may backtrack and repeat steps, they may skip steps entirely, or they may repeat the entire process before a useable design is achieved.

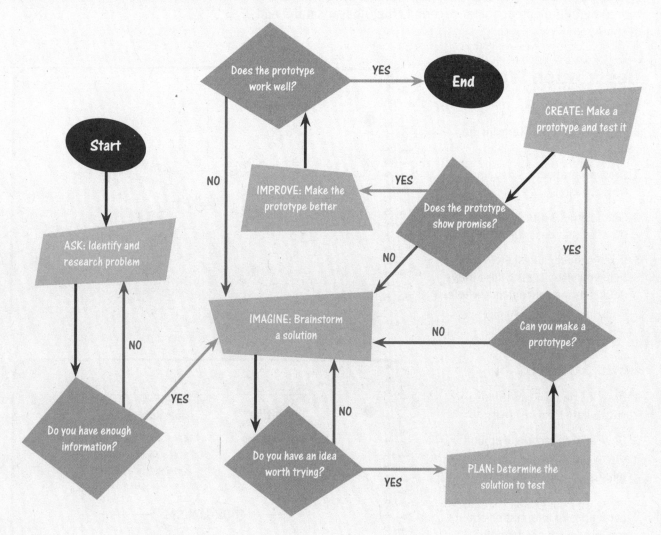

Reading and Study Skills

Using Vocabulary Strategies

Important science terms are highlighted where they are first defined in this book. One way to remember these terms is to take notes and make sketches when you come to them. Use the strategies on this page and the next for this purpose. You will also find a formal definition of each science term in the Glossary at the end of the book.

Description Wheel

1 Draw a small circle.

2 Write a vocabulary term inside the circle.

3 Draw several arms extending from the circle.

4 On the arms, write words and phrases that describe the term.

5 If you choose, add sketches that help you visualize the descriptive details or the concept as a whole.

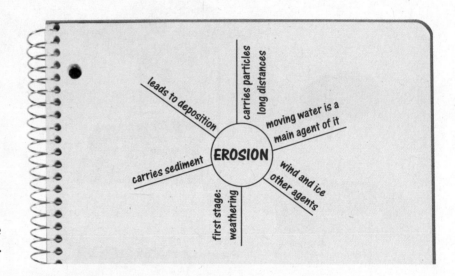

Four Square

1 Draw a small oval and write a vocabulary term inside it.

2 Draw a large rectangle around the oval, and divide the rectangle into four smaller squares.

3 Label the smaller squares with categories of information about the term, such as: definition, characteristics, examples, non-examples, appearance, and root words.

4 Fill the squares with descriptive words and drawings that will help you remember the overall meaning of the term and its essential details.

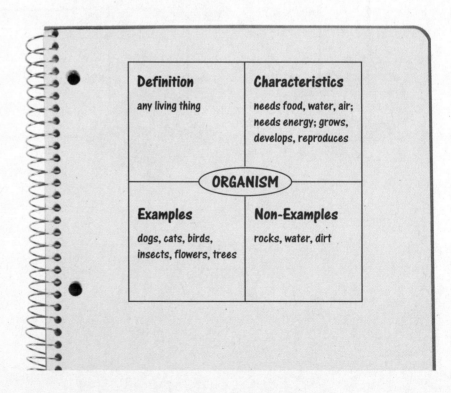

Frame Game

1 Draw a small rectangle, and write a vocabulary term inside it.

2 Draw a larger rectangle around the smaller one. Connect the corners of the larger rectangle to the corners of the smaller one, creating four spaces that frame the word.

3 In each of the four parts of the frame, draw or write details that help define the term. Consider including a definition, essential characteristics, an equation, examples, and a sentence using the term.

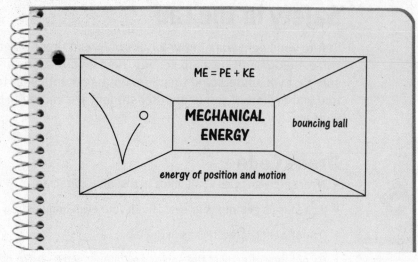

Magnet Word

1 Draw horseshoe magnet, and write a vocabulary term inside it.

2 Add lines that extend from the sides of the magnet.

3 Brainstorm words and phrases that come to mind when you think about the term.

4 On the lines, write the words and phrases that describe something essential about the term.

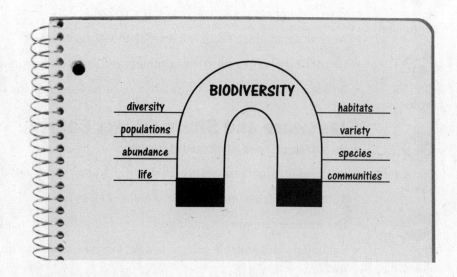

Word Triangle

1 Draw a triangle, and add lines to divide it into three parts.

2 Write a term and its definition in the bottom section of the triangle.

3 In the middle section, write a sentence in which the term is used correctly.

4 In the top section, draw a small picture to illustrate the term.

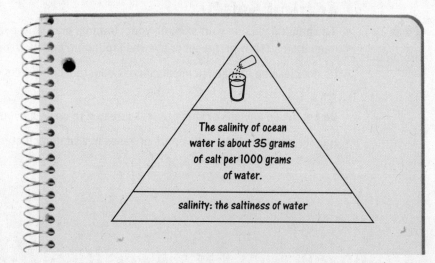

Science Skills

Safety in the Lab

Before you begin work in the laboratory, read these safety rules twice. Before starting a lab activity, read all directions and make sure that you understand them. Do not begin until your teacher has told you to start. If you or another student are injured in any way, tell your teacher immediately.

Dress Code

Eye Protection

Hand Protection

Clothing Protection

- Wear safety goggles at all times in the lab as directed.
- If chemicals get into your eyes, flush your eyes immediately.
- Do not wear contact lenses in the lab.
- Do not look directly at the sun or any intense light source or laser.
- Do not cut an object while holding the object in your hand.
- Wear appropriate protective gloves as directed.
- Wear an apron or lab coat at all times in the lab as directed.
- Tie back long hair, secure loose clothing, and remove loose jewelry.
- Do not wear open-toed shoes, sandals, or canvas shoes in the lab.

Glassware and Sharp Object Safety

Glassware Safety

Sharp Objects Safety

- Do not use chipped or cracked glassware.
- Use heat-resistant glassware for heating or storing hot materials.
- Notify your teacher immediately if a piece of glass breaks.
- Use extreme care when handling all sharp and pointed instruments.
- Cut objects on a suitable surface, always in a direction away from your body.

Chemical Safety

Chemical Safety

- If a chemical gets on your skin, on your clothing, or in your eyes, rinse it immediately (shower, faucet or eyewash fountain) and alert your teacher.
- Do not clean up spilled chemicals unless your teacher directs you to do so.
- Do not inhale any gas or vapor unless directed to do so by your teacher.
- Handle materials that emit vapors or gases in a well-ventilated area.

Electrical
Safety

Electrical Safety

- Do not use equipment with frayed electrical cords or loose plugs.

- Do not use electrical equipment near water or when clothing or hands are wet.

- Hold the plug housing when you plug in or unplug equipment.

Heating
Safety

Heating and Fire Safety

- Be aware of any source of flames, sparks, or heat (such as flames, heating coils, or hot plates) before working with any flammable substances.
- Know the location of lab fire extinguishers and fire-safety blankets.
- Know your school's fire-evacuation routes.
- If your clothing catches on fire, walk to the lab shower to put out the fire.
- Never leave a hot plate unattended while it is turned on or while it is cooling.
- Use tongs or appropriate insulated holders when handling heated objects.
- Allow all equipment to cool before storing it.

Wafting

Plant
Safety

Animal
Safety

Plant and Animal Safety

- Do not eat any part of a plant.
- Do not pick any wild plants unless your teacher instructs you to do so.
- Handle animals only as your teacher directs.
- Treat animals carefully and respectfully.
- Wash your hands thoroughly after handling any plant or animal.

Proper
Waste
Disposal

Cleanup

- Clean all work surfaces and protective equipment as directed by your teacher.
- Dispose of hazardous materials or sharp objects only as directed by your teacher.
- Keep your hands away from your face while you are working on any activity.
- Wash your hands thoroughly before you leave the lab or after any activity.

Hygienic
Care

Science Skills

Designing an Experiment

An **experiment** is an organized procedure to study something under controlled conditions. Use the following steps of the scientific method when designing or conducting an experiment.

1 Identify a Research Problem

Every day you make **observations** by using your senses to gather information. Careful observations lead to good **questions,** and good questions can lead you to a purpose, or problem, for an experiment.

Imagine, for example, that you pass a pond every day on your way to school, and you notice green scum beginning to form on top of it. You wonder what it is and why it seems to be growing. You list your questions, and then you do a little preliminary research to find out what is already known.

You talk to others about your observations, learn that the scum is algae, and look for relvant information in books, journals, and online. You are especially interested in the data and conclusions from earlier experiments. Finally, you write the problem that you want to investigate. Your notes might look like these.

Area of Interest	Research Questions	Research Problem
Algae growth in lakes and ponds	• How do algae grow? • How do people measure algae? • What kind of fertilizer would affect the growth of algae? • Can fertilizer and algae be used safely in a lab? How?	How does fertilizer affect the presence of algae in a pond?

2 Make a Prediction

A **prediction** is a statement of what you expect will happen in your experiment. Before making a prediction, you need to decide in a general way what you will do in your procedure. You may state your prediction in an if-then format.

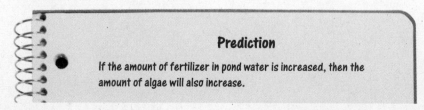

Prediction

If the amount of fertilizer in pond water is increased, then the amount of algae will also increase.

3 Form a Hypothesis

Many experiments are designed to test a hypothesis. A **hypothesis** is a tentative explanation for an expected result. You have predicted that additional fertilizer will cause additional algae growth in pond water; your hypothesis goes beyond your prediction to explain why fertilizer has that effect.

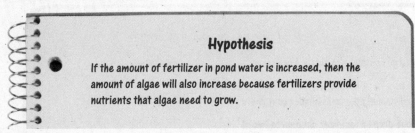

Hypothesis

If the amount of fertilizer in pond water is increased, then the amount of algae will also increase because fertilizers provide nutrients that algae need to grow.

4 Identify Variables to Test the Hypothesis

The next step is to design an experiment to test the hypothesis. The experiment may or may not support the hypothesis. Either way, the information that results from the experiment may be useful for future investigations.

Experimental Group and Control Group

An experiment to determine how two factors are related has a control group and an experimental group. The two groups are the same, except that the experimenter changes a single factor in the experimental group and does not change it in the control group.

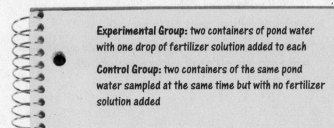

Experimental Group: two containers of pond water with one drop of fertilizer solution added to each

Control Group: two containers of the same pond water sampled at the same time but with no fertilizer solution added

Variables and Constants

In a controlled experiment, a **variable** is any factor that can change. **Constants** are all of the variables that are kept the same in both the experimental group and the control group.

The **independent variable** is the factor that is manipulated or changed in order to test the effect of the change on another variable. The **dependent variable** is the factor that the experimenter measures to gather data about the effect.

Independent Variable	Dependent Variable	Constants
Amount of fertilizer in pond water	Amount of algae that grow	• Where and when the pond water is obtained • The type of container used • Light and temperature conditions where the water is stored

Science Skills

5 Write a Procedure

Write each step of your procedure. Start each step with a verb, or action word, and keep the steps short. Your procedure should be clear enough for someone else to use as instructions for repeating your experiment.

Procedure

1. Put on your gloves. Use the large container to obtain a sample of pond water.

2. Divide the water sample equally among the four smaller containers.

3. Use the eyedropper to add one drop of fertilizer solution to two of the containers.

4. Use the masking tape and the marker to label the containers with your initials, the date, and the identifiers "Jar 1 with Fertilizer," "Jar 2 with Fertilizer," "Jar 1 without Fertilizer," and "Jar 2 without Fertilizer."

5. Cover the containers with clear plastic wrap. Use the scissors to punch ten holes in each of the covers.

6. Place all four containers on a window ledge. Make sure that they all receive the same amount of light.

7. Observe the containers every day for one week.

8. Use the ruler to measure the diameter of the largest clump of algae in each container, and record your measurements daily.

6 Experiment and Collect Data

Once you have all of your materials and your procedure has been approved, you can begin to experiment and collect data. Record both quantitative data (measurements) and qualitative data (observations), as shown below.

Fertilizer and Algae Growth

Date and Time	Experimental Group		Control Group		Observations
	Jar 1 with Fertilizer (diameter of algae in mm)	Jar 2 with Fertilizer (diameter of algae in mm)	Jar 1 without Fertilizer (diameter of algae in mm)	Jar 2 without Fertilizer (diameter of algae in mm)	
5/3 4:00 P.M.	0	0	0	0	condensation in all containers
5/4 4:00 P.M.	0	3	0	0	tiny green blobs in jar 2 with fertilizer
5/5 4:15 P.M.	4	5	0	3	green blobs in jars 1 and 2 with fertilizer and jar 2 without fertilizer
5/6 4:00 P.M.	5	6	0	4	water light green in jar 2 with fertilizer
5/7 4:00 P.M.	8	10	0	6	water light green in jars 1 and 2 with fertilizer and jar 2 without fertilizer
5/8 3:30 P.M.	10	18	0	6	cover off jar 2 with fertilizer
5/9 3:30 P.M.	14	23	0	8	drew sketches of each container

Drawings of Samples Viewed Under Microscope on 5/9 at 100x

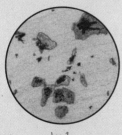
Jar 1 with Fertilizer

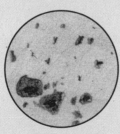
Jar 2 with Fertilizer

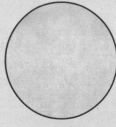
Jar 1 without Fertilizer

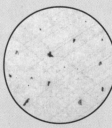
Jar 2 without Fertilizer

Science Skills

7 Analyze Data

After you have completed your experiments, made your observations, and collected your data, you must analyze all the information you have gathered. Tables, statistics, and graphs are often used in this step to organize and analyze the data.

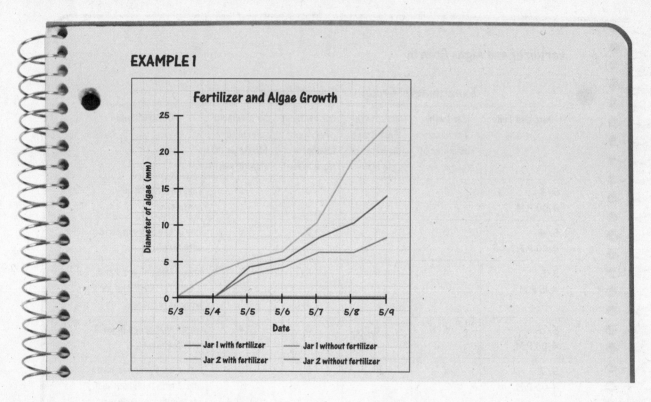

EXAMPLE 1

Fertilizer and Algae Growth

- Jar 1 with fertilizer
- Jar 2 with fertilizer
- Jar 1 without fertilizer
- Jar 2 without fertilizer

8 Make Conclusions

To draw conclusions from your experiment, first write your results. Then compare your results with your hypothesis. Do your results support your hypothesis?

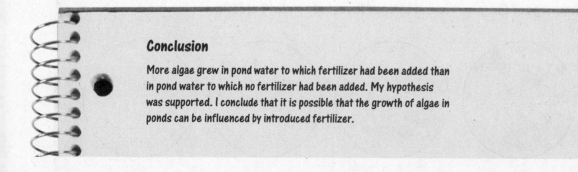

Conclusion

More algae grew in pond water to which fertilizer had been added than in pond water to which no fertilizer had been added. My hypothesis was supported. I conclude that it is possible that the growth of algae in ponds can be influenced by introduced fertilizer.

Using a Microscope

Scientists use microscopes to see very small objects that cannot easily be seen with the eye alone. A microscope magnifies the image of an object so that small details may be observed. A microscope that you may use can magnify an object 400 times—the object will appear 400 times larger than its actual size.

Eyepiece Objects are viewed through the eyepiece. The eyepiece contains a lens that commonly magnifies an image ten times.

Body The body separates the lens in the eyepiece from the objective lenses below.

Coarse Adjustment This knob is used to focus the image of an object when it is viewed through the low-power lens.

Nosepiece The nosepiece holds the objective lenses above the stage and rotates so that all lenses may be used.

Fine Adjustment This knob is used to focus the image of an object when it is viewed through the high-power lens.

High-Power Objective Lens This is the largest lens on the nosepiece. It magnifies an image approximately 40 times.

Low-Power Objective Lens This is the smallest lens on the nosepiece. It magnifies images about 10 times.

Stage The stage supports the object being viewed.

Arm The arm supports the body above the stage. Always carry a microscope by the arm and base.

Diaphragm The diaphragm is used to adjust the amount of light passing through the slide and into an objective lens.

Stage Clip The stage clip holds a slide in place on the stage.

Mirror or Light Source Some microscopes use light that is reflected through the stage by a mirror. Other microscopes have their own light sources.

Base The base supports the microscope.

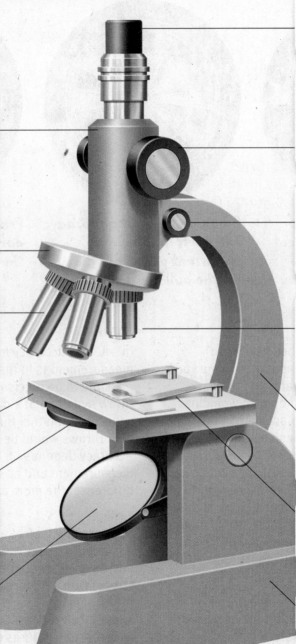

Science Skills

Measuring Accurately

Precision and Accuracy

When you do a scientific investigation, it is important that your methods, observations, and data be both precise and accurate.

Low precision: The darts did not land in a consistent place on the dartboard.

Precision, but not accuracy: The darts landed in a consistent place, but did not hit the bull's eye.

Precision and accuracy: The darts landed consistently on the bull's eye.

Precision

In science, *precision* describes how close measurements are to one another. Imagine you threw five darts at a dart board, and the darts landed all over the board. The result would have low precision because the placement of the five darts on the board is not consistent. Another indicator of precision is the care taken to make sure that methods and observations are as exact and consistent as possible. Every time a particular experiment is done, the same procedure should be used. Precision is necessary because experiments are repeated several times and if the procedure changes, the results might change.

Example

Suppose you are measuring temperatures over a two-week period. Your precision will be greater if you measure each temperature at the same place, at the same time of day, and with the same thermometer than if you change any of these factors from one day to the next.

Accuracy

In science, *accuracy* indicates how close a measurement is to the expected result. It is possible to be precise but not accurate. If you threw five darts at a dart board and they landed very close together but not where you aimed, your throws would be precise but not accurate. Accuracy depends on the difference between a measurement and an actual value. The smaller the difference, the more accurate the measurement.

Example

Suppose you look at a stream and estimate that it is about 1 meter wide at a particular place. You decide to check your estimate by measuring the stream with a meter stick, and you determine that the stream is 1.32 meters wide. However, because it is difficult to measure the width of a stream with a meter stick, it turns out that your measurement was not very accurate. The stream is actually 1.14 meters wide. Therefore, even though your estimate of about 1 meter was less precise than your measurement, your estimate was actually more accurate.

Graduated Cylinders

How to Measure the Volume of a Liquid with a Graduated Cylinder

- Be sure that the graduated cylinder is on a flat surface so that your measurement will be accurate.

- When reading the scale on a graduated cylinder, be sure to have your eyes at the level of the surface of the liquid.

- The surface of the liquid will be curved in the graduated cylinder. Read the volume of the liquid at the bottom of the curve, or meniscus (muh-NIHS-kuhs).

- You can use a graduated cylinder to find the volume of a solid object by measuring the increase in a liquid's level after you add the object to the cylinder.

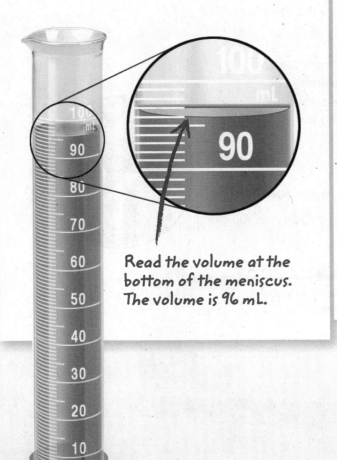

Read the volume at the bottom of the meniscus. The volume is 96 mL.

Metric Rulers

How to Measure the Length of a Leaf with a Metric Ruler

1 Lay a ruler flat on top of the leaf so that the 1-centimeter mark lines up with one end. Make sure the ruler and the leaf do not move between the time you line them up and the time you take the measurement.

2 Look straight down on the ruler so that you can see exactly how the marks line up with the other end of the leaf.

3 Estimate the length by which the leaf extends beyond a marking. For example, the leaf below extends about halfway between the 4.2-centimeter and 4.3-centimeter marks, so the apparent measurement is about 4.25 centimeters.

4 Remember to subtract 1 centimeter from your apparent measurement, since you started at the 1-centimeter mark on the ruler and not at the end. The leaf is about 3.25 centimeters long (4.25 cm − 1 cm = 3.25 cm).

Science Skills

Triple Beam Balance

This balance has a pan and three beams with sliding masses, called riders. At one end of the beams is a pointer that indicates whether the mass on the pan is equal to the masses shown on the beams.

How to Measure the Mass of an Object

1 Make sure the balance is zeroed before measuring the mass of an object. The balance is zeroed if the pointer is at zero when nothing is on the pan and the riders are at their zero points. Use the adjustment knob at the base of the balance to zero it.

2 Place the object to be measured on the pan.

3 Move the riders one notch at a time away from the pan. Begin with the largest rider. If moving the largest rider one notch brings the pointer below zero, begin measuring the mass of the object with the next smaller rider.

4 Change the positions of the riders until they balance the mass on the pan and the pointer is at zero. Then add the readings from the three beams to determine the mass of the object.

300 g	position of largest rider
90 g	position of middle rider
+ 3 g	position of smallest rider
393 g	mass of beaker and water

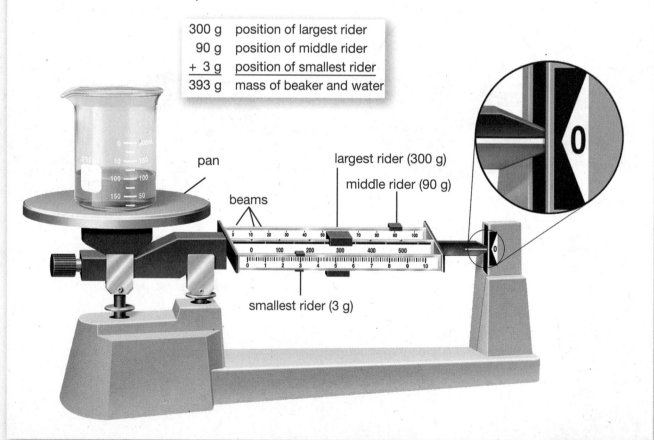

pan

beams

largest rider (300 g)

middle rider (90 g)

smallest rider (3 g)

Using the Metric System and SI Units

Scientists use International System (SI) units for measurements of distance, volume, mass, and temperature. The International System is based on powers of ten and the metric system of measurement.

Basic SI Units		
Quantity	Name	Symbol
length	meter	m
volume	liter	L
mass	gram	g
temperature	kelvin	K

SI Prefixes		
Prefix	Symbol	Power of 10
kilo-	k	1000
hecto-	h	100
deca-	da	10
deci-	d	0.1 or $\frac{1}{10}$
centi-	c	0.01 or $\frac{1}{100}$
milli-	m	0.001 or $\frac{1}{1000}$

Changing Metric Units

You can change from one unit to another in the metric system by multiplying or dividing by a power of 10.

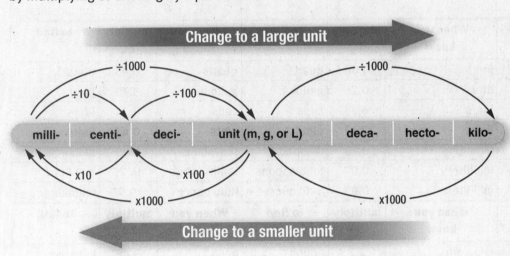

Change to a larger unit

÷1000   ÷10   ÷100   ÷1000

| milli- | centi- | deci- | unit (m, g, or L) | deca- | hecto- | kilo- |

x10   x100   x1000   x1000

Change to a smaller unit

Example

Change 0.64 liters to milliliters.
1 Decide whether to multiply or divide.
2 Select the power of 10.

Change to a smaller unit by multiplying

mL ◄─── x 1000 ─── L

0.64 x 1000 = 640.

ANSWER 0.64 L = 640 mL

Example

Change 23.6 grams to kilograms.
1 Decide whether to multiply or divide.
2 Select the power of 10.

Change to a larger unit by dividing

g ─── ÷ 1000 ──► kg

26.3 ÷ 1000 = 0.0263

ANSWER 23.6 g = 0.0236 kg

Science Skills

Converting Between SI and U.S. Customary Units

Use the chart below when you need to convert between SI units and U.S. customary units.

SI Unit	From SI to U.S. Customary			From U.S. Customary to SI		
Length	**When you know**	**multiply by**	**to find**	**When you know**	**multiply by**	**to find**
kilometer (km) = 1000 m	kilometers	0.62	miles	miles	1.61	kilometers
meter (m) = 100 cm	meters	3.28	feet	feet	0.3048	meters
centimeter (cm) = 10 mm	centimeters	0.39	inches	inches	2.54	centimeters
millimeter (mm) = 0.1 cm	millimeters	0.04	inches	inches	25.4	millimeters
Area	**When you know**	**multiply by**	**to find**	**When you know**	**multiply by**	**to find**
square kilometer (km²)	square kilometers	0.39	square miles	square miles	2.59	square kilometers
square meter (m²)	square meters	1.2	square yards	square yards	0.84	square meters
square centimeter (cm²)	square centimeters	0.155	square inches	square inches	6.45	square centimeters
Volume	**When you know**	**multiply by**	**to find**	**When you know**	**multiply by**	**to find**
liter (L) = 1000 mL	liters	1.06	quarts	quarts	0.95	liters
	liters	0.26	gallons	gallons	3.79	liters
	liters	4.23	cups	cups	0.24	liters
	liters	2.12	pints	pints	0.47	liters
milliliter (mL) = 0.001 L	milliliters	0.20	teaspoons	teaspoons	4.93	milliliters
	milliliters	0.07	tablespoons	tablespoons	14.79	milliliters
	milliliters	0.03	fluid ounces	fluid ounces	29.57	milliliters
Mass	**When you know**	**multiply by**	**to find**	**When you know**	**multiply by**	**to find**
kilogram (kg) = 1000 g	kilograms	2.2	pounds	pounds	0.45	kilograms
gram (g) = 1000 mg	grams	0.035	ounces	ounces	28.35	grams

Temperature Conversions

Even though the kelvin is the SI base unit of temperature, the degree Celsius will be the unit you use most often in your science studies. The formulas below show the relationships between temperatures in degrees Fahrenheit (°F), degrees Celsius (°C), and kelvins (K).

$$°C = \frac{5}{9} \ (°F - 32) \qquad °F = \frac{9}{5} \ °C + 32 \qquad K = °C + 273$$

Examples of Temperature Conversions		
Condition	**Degrees Celsius**	**Degrees Fahrenheit**
Freezing point of water	0	32
Cool day	10	50
Mild day	20	68
Warm day	30	86
Normal body temperature	37	98.6
Very hot day	40	104
Boiling point of water	100	212

Math Refresher

Performing Calculations

Science requires an understanding of many math concepts. The following pages will help you review some important math skills.

Mean

The mean is the sum of all values in a data set divided by the total number of values in the data set. The mean is also called the *average*.

Example

Find the mean of the following set of numbers: 5, 4, 7, and 8.

Step 1　Find the sum.

5 + 4 + 7 + 8 = 24

Step 1　Divide the sum by the number of numbers in your set. Because there are four numbers in this example, divide the sum by 4.

24 ÷ 4 = 6

Answer The average, or mean, is 6.

Median

The median of a data set is the middle value when the values are written in numerical order. If a data set has an even number of values, the median is the mean of the two middle values.

Example

To find the median of a set of measurements, arrange the values in order from least to greatest. The median is the middle value.

13 mm　14 mm　16 mm　21 mm　23 mm

Answer The median is 16 mm.

Mode

The mode of a data set is the value that occurs most often.

Example

To find the mode of a set of measurements, arrange the values in order from least to greatest and determine the value that occurs most often.

13 mm, 14 mm, 14 mm, 16 mm,
21 mm, 23 mm, 25 mm

Answer The mode is 14 mm.

A data set can have more than one mode or no mode. For example, the following data set has modes of 2 mm and 4 mm:

2 mm　2 mm　3 mm　4 mm　4 mm

The data set below has no mode, because no value occurs more often than any other.

2 mm　3 mm　4 mm　5 mm

Math Refresher

Ratios

A **ratio** is a comparison between numbers, and it is usually written as a fraction.

Example

Find the ratio of thermometers to students if you have 36 thermometers and 48 students in your class.

Step 1 Write the ratio.

$$\frac{36 \text{ thermometers}}{48 \text{ students}}$$

Step 2 Simplify the fraction to its simplest form.

$$\frac{36}{48} = \frac{36 \div 12}{48 \div 12} = \frac{3}{4}$$

The ratio of thermometers to students is 3 to 4 or 3:4.

Proportions

A **proportion** is an equation that states that two ratios are equal.

$$\frac{3}{1} = \frac{12}{4}$$

To solve a proportion, you can use cross-multiplication. If you know three of the quantities in a proportion, you can use cross-multiplication to find the fourth.

Example

Imagine that you are making a scale model of the solar system for your science project. The diameter of Jupiter is 11.2 times the diameter of the Earth. If you are using a plastic-foam ball that has a diameter of 2 cm to represent the Earth, what must the diameter of the ball representing Jupiter be?

$$\frac{11.2}{1} = \frac{x}{2 \text{ cm}}$$

Step 1 Cross-multiply.

$$\frac{11.2}{1} = \frac{x}{2}$$

$$11.2 \times 2 = x \times 1$$

Step 2 Multiply.

$$22.4 = x \times 1$$

$$x = 22.4 \text{ cm}$$

You will need to use a ball that has a diameter of 22.4 cm to represent Jupiter.

Rates

A **rate** is a ratio of two values expressed in different units. A unit rate is a rate with a denominator of 1 unit.

Example

A plant grew 6 centimeters in 2 days. The plant's rate of growth was $\frac{6 \text{ cm}}{2 \text{ days}}$.

To describe the plant's growth in centimeters per day, write a unit rate.

Divide numerator and denominator by 2:

$$\frac{6 \text{ cm}}{2 \text{ days}} = \frac{6 \text{ cm} \div 2}{2 \text{ days} \div 2}$$

Simplify:

$$= \frac{3 \text{ cm}}{1 \text{ day}}$$

Answer The plant's rate of growth is 3 centimeters per day.

Percent

A **percent** is a ratio of a given number to 100. For example, 85% = 85/100. You can use percent to find part of a whole.

Example
What is 85% of 40?

Step 1   Rewrite the percent as a decimal by moving the decimal point two places to the left.

$$0.85$$

Step 2   Multiply the decimal by the number that you are calculating the percentage of.

$$0.85 \times 40 = 34$$

85% of 40 is 34.

Decimals

To **add** or **subtract decimals,** line up the digits vertically so that the decimal points line up. Then, add or subtract the columns from right to left. Carry or borrow numbers as necessary.

Example
Add the following numbers: 3.1415 and 2.96.

Step 1   Line up the digits vertically so that the decimal points line up.

```
  3.1415
+ 2.96
```

Step 2   Add the columns from right to left, and carry when necessary.

```
  3.1415
+ 2.96
━━━━━━
  6.1015
```

The sum is 6.1015.

Fractions

A **fraction** is a ratio of two nonzero whole numbers.

Example
Your class has 24 plants. Your teacher instructs you to put 6 plants in a shady spot. What fraction of the plants in your class will you put in a shady spot?

Step 1   In the denominator, write the total number of parts in the whole.

$$\frac{?}{24}$$

Step 2   In the numerator, write the number of parts of the whole that are being considered.

$$\frac{6}{24}$$

So, $\frac{6}{24}$ of the plants will be in the shade.

Math Refresher

Simplifying Fractions

It is usually best to express a fraction in its simplest form. Expressing a fraction in its simplest form is called **simplifying a fraction**.

Example

Simplify the fraction $\frac{30}{45}$ to its simplest form.

Step 1   Find the largest whole number that will divide evenly into both the numerator and denominator. This number is called the greatest common factor (GCF).

Factors of the numerator 30:
1, 2, 3, 5, 6, 10, 15, 30

Factors of the denominator 45:
1, 3, 5, 9, 15, 45

Step 2   Divide both the numerator and the denominator by the GCF, which in this case is 15.

$$\frac{30}{45} = \frac{30 \div 15}{45 \div 15} = \frac{2}{3}$$

Thus, $\frac{30}{45}$ written in its simplest form is $\frac{2}{3}$.

Adding and Subtracting Fractions

To **add** or **subtract fractions** that have the same denominator, simply add or subtract the numerators.

Examples

$\frac{3}{5} + \frac{1}{5} = ?$ and $\frac{3}{4} - \frac{1}{4} = ?$

Step 1   Add or subtract the numerators.
$$\frac{3}{5} + \frac{1}{5} = \frac{4}{} \text{ and } \frac{3}{4} - \frac{1}{4} = \frac{2}{}$$

Step 2   Write the sum or difference over the denominator.
$$\frac{3}{5} + \frac{1}{5} = \frac{4}{5} \text{ and } \frac{3}{4} - \frac{1}{4} = \frac{2}{4}$$

Step 3   If necessary, write the fraction in its simplest form.
$\frac{4}{5}$ cannot be simplified, and $\frac{2}{4} = \frac{1}{2}$.

To **add** or **subtract fractions** that have **different denominators,** first find the least common denominator (LCD)

Examples

$\frac{1}{2} + \frac{1}{6} = ?$ and $\frac{3}{4} - \frac{2}{3} = ?$

Step 1   Write the equivalent fractions that have a common denominator.
$$\frac{3}{6} + \frac{1}{6} = ? \text{ and } \frac{9}{12} - \frac{8}{12} = ?$$

Step 2   Add or subtract the fractions.
$$\frac{3}{6} + \frac{1}{6} = \frac{4}{6} \text{ and } \frac{9}{12} - \frac{8}{12} = \frac{1}{12}$$

Step 3   If necessary, write the fraction in its simplest form.
$\frac{4}{6} = \frac{2}{3}$, and $\frac{1}{12}$ cannot be simplified.

Multiplying Fractions

To **multiply fractions,** multiply the numerators and the denominators together, and then change the fraction to its simplest form.

Example

$\frac{5}{9} \times \frac{7}{10} = ?$

Step 1   Multiply the numerators and denominators.
$$\frac{5}{9} \times \frac{7}{10} = \frac{5 \times 7}{9 \times 10} = \frac{35}{90}$$

Step 2   Simplify the fraction.
$$\frac{35}{90} = \frac{35 \div 5}{90 \div 5} = \frac{7}{18}$$

Dividing Fractions

To **divide fractions**, first exchange the numerator and the denominator of the divisor (the number you divide by). This number is called the reciprocal of the divisor. Then multiply and simplify if necessary.

Example

$$\frac{5}{8} \div \frac{3}{2} = ?$$

Step 1   Rewrite the divisor as its reciprocal.

$$\frac{3}{2} \rightarrow \frac{2}{3}$$

Step 2   Multiply the fractions.

$$\frac{5}{8} \times \frac{2}{3} = \frac{5 \times 2}{8 \times 3} = \frac{10}{24}$$

Step 3   Simplify the fraction.

$$\frac{10}{24} = \frac{10 \div 2}{24 \div 2} = \frac{5}{12}$$

Using Significant Figures

The **significant figures** in a decimal are the digits that are warranted by the accuracy of a measuring device.

When you perform a calculation with measurements, the number of significant figures to include in the result depends in part on the number of significant figures in the measurements. When you multiply or divide measurements, your answer should have only as many significant figures as the measurement with the fewest significant figures.

Examples

Using a balance and a graduated cylinder filled with water, you determined that a marble has a mass of 8.0 grams and a volume of 3.5 cubic centimeters. To calculate the density of the marble, divide the mass by the volume.

Write the formula for density: $\text{Density} = \frac{\text{mass}}{\text{volume}}$

Substitute measurements: $= \frac{8.0 \text{ g}}{3.5 \text{ cm}^3}$

Use a calculator to divide: $\approx 2.285714286 \text{ g/cm}^3$

Answer   Because the mass and the volume have two significant figures each, give the density to two significant figures. The marble has a density of 2.3 grams per cubic centimeter.

Using Scientific Notation

Scientific notation is a shorthand way to write very large or very small numbers. For example, 73,500,000,000,000,000,000,000 kg is the mass of the Moon. In scientific notation, it is 7.35×10^{22} kg. A value written as a number between 1 and 10, times a power of 10, is in scientific notation.

Examples

You can convert from standard form to scientific notation.

Standard Form	Scientific Notation
720,000	7.2×10^5
5 decimal places left	Exponent is 5.
0.000291	2.91×10^{-4}
4 decimal places right	Exponent is −4.

You can convert from scientific notation to standard form.

Scientific Notation	Standard Form
4.63×10^7	46,300,000
Exponent is 7.	7 decimal places right
1.08×10^{-6}	0.00000108
Exponent is −6.	6 decimal places left

Math Refresher

Making and Interpreting Graphs

Circle Graph

A circle graph, or pie chart, shows how each group of data relates to all of the data. Each part of the circle represents a category of the data. The entire circle represents all of the data. For example, a biologist studying a hardwood forest in Wisconsin found that there were five different types of trees. The data table at right summarizes the biologist's findings.

Wisconsin Hardwood Trees	
Type of tree	**Number found**
Oak	600
Maple	750
Beech	300
Birch	1,200
Hickory	150
Total	3,000

How to Make a Circle Graph

1 To make a circle graph of these data, first find the percentage of each type of tree. Divide the number of trees of each type by the total number of trees, and multiply by 100%.

$$\frac{600 \text{ oak}}{3{,}000 \text{ trees}} \times 100\% = 20\%$$

$$\frac{750 \text{ maple}}{3{,}000 \text{ trees}} \times 100\% = 25\%$$

$$\frac{300 \text{ beech}}{3{,}000 \text{ trees}} \times 100\% = 10\%$$

$$\frac{1{,}200 \text{ birch}}{3{,}000 \text{ trees}} \times 100\% = 40\%$$

$$\frac{150 \text{ hickory}}{3{,}000 \text{ trees}} \times 100\% = 5\%$$

2 Now, determine the size of the wedges that make up the graph. Multiply each percentage by 360°. Remember that a circle contains 360°.

$$20\% \times 360° = 72° \qquad 25\% \times 360° = 90°$$

$$10\% \times 360° = 36° \qquad 40\% \times 360° = 144°$$

$$5\% \times 360° = 18°$$

3 Check that the sum of the percentages is 100 and the sum of the degrees is 360.

$$20\% + 25\% + 10\% + 40\% + 5\% = 100\%$$

$$72° + 90° + 36° + 144° + 18° = 360°$$

4 Use a compass to draw a circle and mark the center of the circle.

5 Then, use a protractor to draw angles of 72°, 90°, 36°, 144°, and 18° in the circle.

6 Finally, label each part of the graph, and choose an appropriate title.

A Community of Wisconsin Hardwood Trees

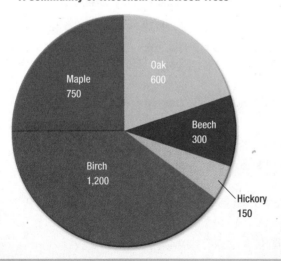

Line Graphs

Line graphs are most often used to demonstrate continuous change. For example, Mr. Smith's students analyzed the population records for their hometown, Appleton, between 1910 and 2010. Examine the data at right.

Because the year and the population change, they are the variables. The population is determined by, or dependent on, the year. Therefore, the population is called the **dependent variable,** and the year is called the **independent variable**. Each year and its population make a **data pair**. To prepare a line graph, you must first organize data pairs into a table like the one at right.

Population of Appleton, 1910–2010	
Year	**Population**
1910	1,800
1930	2,500
1950	3,200
1970	3,900
1990	4,600
2010	5,300

How to Make a Line Graph

1 Place the independent variable along the horizontal (*x*) axis. Place the dependent variable along the vertical (*y*) axis.

2 Label the *x*-axis "Year" and the *y*-axis "Population." Look at your greatest and least values for the population. For the *y*-axis, determine a scale that will provide enough space to show these values. You must use the same scale for the entire length of the axis. Next, find an appropriate scale for the *x*-axis.

3 Choose reasonable starting points for each axis.

4 Plot the data pairs as accurately as possible.

5 Choose a title that accurately represents the data.

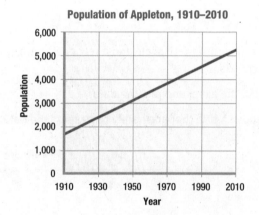

Population of Appleton, 1910–2010

How to Determine Slope

Slope is the ratio of the change in the *y*-value to the change in the *x*-value, or "rise over run."

1 Choose two points on the line graph. For example, the population of Appleton in 2010 was 5,300 people. Therefore, you can define point A as (2010, 5,300). In 1910, the population was 1,800 people. You can define point B as (1910, 1,800).

2 Find the change in the *y*-value.
(*y* at point A) − (*y* at point B) =
5,300 people − 1,800 people =
3,500 people

3 Find the change in the *x*-value.
(*x* at point A) − (*x* at point B) =
2010 − 1910 = 100 years

4 Calculate the slope of the graph by dividing the change in *y* by the change in *x*.

$$slope = \frac{change\ in\ y}{change\ in\ x}$$

$$slope = \frac{3,500\ people}{100\ years}$$

$$slope = 35\ people\ per\ year$$

In this example, the population in Appleton increased by a fixed amount each year. The graph of these data is a straight line. Therefore, the relationship is **linear**. When the graph of a set of data is not a straight line, the relationship is **nonlinear**.

Math Refresher

Bar Graphs

Bar graphs can be used to demonstrate change that is not continuous. These graphs can be used to indicate trends when the data cover a long period of time. A meteorologist gathered the precipitation data shown here for Summerville for April 1–15 and used a bar graph to represent the data.

Precipitation in Summerville, April 1–15			
Date	Precipitation (cm)	Date	Precipitation (cm)
April 1	0.5	April 9	0.25
April 2	1.25	April 10	0.0
April 3	0.0	April 11	1.0
April 4	0.0	April 12	0.0
April 5	0.0	April 13	0.25
April 6	0.0	April 14	0.0
April 7	0.0	April 15	6.50
April 8	1.75		

How to Make a Bar Graph

1 Use an appropriate scale and a reasonable starting point for each axis.

2 Label the axes, and plot the data.

3 Choose a title that accurately represents the data.

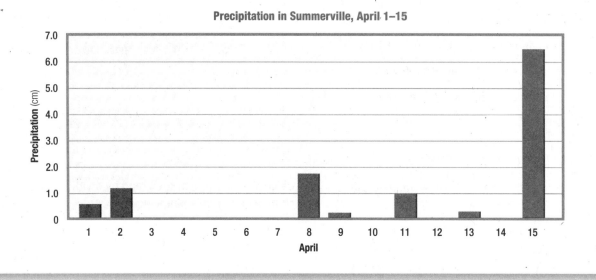

Precipitation in Summerville, April 1–15

Glossary

Sound	Symbol	Example	Respelling	Sound	Symbol	Example	Respelling
ă	a	pat	PAT	ŏ	ah	bottle	BAHT'l
ā	ay	pay	PAY	ō	oh	toe	TOH
âr	air	care	KAIR	ô	aw	caught	KAWT
ä	ah	father	FAH•ther	ôr	ohr	roar	ROHR
är	ar	argue	AR•gyoo	oi	oy	noisy	NOYZ•ee
ch	ch	chase	CHAYS	o͝o	u	book	BUK
ĕ	e	pet	PET	o͞o	oo	boot	BOOT
ĕ (at end of a syllable)	eh	settee lessee	seh•TEE leh•SEE	ou	ow	pound	POWND
ĕr	ehr	merry	MEHR•ee	s	s	center	SEN•ter
ē	ee	beach	BEECH	sh	sh	cache	CASH
g	g	gas	GAS	ŭ	uh	flood	FLUHD
ĭ	i	pit	PIT	ûr	er	bird	BERD
ĭ (at end of a syllable)	ih	guitar	gih•TAR	z	z	xylophone	ZY•luh•fohn
ī	y eye (only for a complete syllable)	pie island	PY EYE•luhnd	z	z	bags	BAGZ
				zh	zh	decision	dih•SIZH•uhn
îr	ir	hear	HIR	ə	uh	around broken focus	uh•ROWND BROH•kuhn FOH•kuhs
j	j	germ	JERM	ər	er	winner	WIN•er
k	k	kick	KIK	th	th	thin they	THIN THAY
ng	ng	thing	THING	w	w	one	WUHN
ngk	ngk	bank	BANGK	wh	hw	whether	HWETH•er

A

abiotic factor an environmental factor that is not associated with the activities of living organisms (415)
factor abiótico un factor ambiental que no está asociado con las actividades de los seres vivos

active transport the movement of chemical substances, usually across the cell membrane, against a concentration gradient; requires cells to use energy (123)
transporte activo el movimiento de sustancias químicas, normalmente a través de la membrana celular, en contra de un gradiente de concentración; requiere que la célula gaste energía

adaptation a characteristic that improves an individual's ability to survive and reproduce in a particular environment (287)
adaptación una característica que mejora la capacidad de un individuo para sobrevivir y reproducirse en un determinado ambiente

allele (uh•LEELZ) one of the alternative forms of a gene that governs a characteristic, such as hair color (348)
alelo una de las formas alternativas de un gene que rige un carácter, como por ejemplo, el color del cabello

alveolus tiny, thin-walled, capillary-rich sac in the lungs where the exchange of oxygen and carbon dioxide takes place; also called *air sac* (190)
alveolo saco diminuto ubicado en los pulmones, de paredes delgadas y rico en capilares, en donde ocurre el intercambio de oxígeno y dióxido de carbono

Animalia a kingdom made up of complex, multicellular organisms that lack cell walls, can usually move around, and quickly respond to their environment (136)
Animalia un reino formado por organismos pluricelulares complejos que no tienen pared celular, normalmente son capaces de moverse y reaccionan rápidamente a su ambiente

antibiotic medicine used to kill bacteria and other microorganisms (266)
antibiótico medicina utilizada para matar bacterias y otros microorganismos

antibody a protein made by B cells that binds to a specific antigen (250)
anticuerpo una proteína producida por las células B que se une a un antígeno específico

antiviral drug a drug that destroys viruses or prevents their growth or replication (266)
medicamento antiviral un medicamento que destruye a los virus o que evita que crezcan o se reproduzcan

Archaea a domain made up of prokaryotes most of which are known to live in extreme environments that are distinguished from other prokaryotes by differences in their genetics and in the makeup of their cell wall (134)
Archaea un dominio compuesto por procariotes la mayoría de los cuales viven en ambientes extremos que se distinguen de otros procariotes por su genética y por la composición de su pared celular

artery a blood vessel that carries blood away from the heart to the body's organs (185)
arteria un vaso sanguíneo que transporta sangre del corazón a los órganos del cuerpo

artificial selection the human practice of breeding animals or plants that have certain desired traits (284, 395)
selección artificial la práctica humana de criar animales o cultivar plantas que tienen ciertos caracteres deseados

asexual reproduction (ay•SEHK•shoo•uhl ree•pruh•DUHK•shuhn) reproduction that does not involve the union of sex cells and in which one parent produces offspring that are genetically identical to the parent (336)
reproducción asexual reproducción que no involucra la unión de células sexuales, en la que un solo progenitor produce descendencia que es genéticamente igual al progenitor

atom the smallest unit of an element that maintains the properties of that element (84)
átomo la unidad más pequeña de un elemento que conserva las propiedades de ese elemento

axon an elongated extension of a neuron that carries impulses away from the cell body (213)
axón una extensión alargada de una neurona que transporta impulsos hacia fuera del cuerpo de la célula

B cell a white blood cell that makes antibodies (250)
célula B un glóbulo blanco de la sangre que fabrica anticuerpos

Bacteria a domain made up of prokaryotes that usually have a cell wall and that usually reproduce by cell division (134)
Bacteria un dominio compuesto por procariotes que por lo general tienen pared celular y se reproducen por división celular

biotechnology (by•oh•tek•NAHL•uh•jee) the use and application of living things and biological processes (394)
biotecnología el uso y la aplicación de seres vivos y procesos biológicos

biotic factor an environmental factor that is associated with or results from the activities of living organisms (415)
factor biótico un factor ambiental que está asociado con las actividades de los seres vivos o que resulta de ellas

blood (BLUHD) the fluid that carries oxygen and nutrients to the body and that is made up of platelets, white blood cells, red blood cells, and plasma (180)
  sangre el líquido que le lleva oxígeno y nutrientes al cuerpo y que está hecho de plaquetas, glóbulos blancos, glóbulos rojos y plasma

brain the organ that is the main control center of the nervous system (210)
  encéfalo el órgano que es el centro principal de control del sistema nervioso

bronchus one of the two main branches of the trachea that lead directly to the lungs; plural, bronchii (190)
  bronquio una de las dos ramificaciones principales de la tráquea que conducen directamente a los pulmones

C

capillary a tiny blood vessel that allows an exchange between blood and cells in tissue (185)
  capilar diminuto vaso sanguíneo que permite el intercambio entre la sangre y las células de los tejidos

carbohydrate a class of molecules that includes sugars, starches, and fiber; contains carbon, hydrogen, and oxygen (87)
  carbohidrato una clase de moléculas entre las que se incluyen azúcares, almidones y fibra; contiene carbono, hidrógeno y oxígeno

carbon cycle the movement of carbon from the nonliving environment into living things and back (490)
  ciclo del carbono el movimiento del carbono del ambiente sin vida a los seres vivos y de los seres vivos al ambiente

cardiovascular system a collection of organs that transport blood throughout the body; the organs in this system include the heart, the arteries, and the veins (180)
  aparato cardiovascular un conjunto de órganos que transportan la sangre a través del cuerpo; los órganos de este sistema incluyen al corazón, las arterias y las venas

carnivore an organism that eats animals (427)
  carnívoro un organismo que se alimenta de animales

cell (SEL) in biology, the smallest unit that can perform all life processes; cells are covered by a membrane and contain DNA and cytoplasm (74)
  célula en biología, la unidad más pequeña que puede realizar todos los procesos vitales; las células están cubiertas por una membrana y tienen ADN y citoplasma

cell cycle the life cycle of a cell (318)
  ciclo celular el ciclo de vida de una célula

cell membrane a phospholipid layer that covers a cell's surface and acts as a barrier between the inside of a cell and the cell's environment (78)
  membrana celular una capa de fosfolípidos que cubre la superficie de la célula y funciona como una barrera entre el interior de la célula y el ambiente de la célula

cellular respiration the process by which cells use oxygen to produce energy from food (120, 476)
  respiración celular el proceso por medio del cual las células utilizan oxígeno para producir energía a partir de los alimentos

cell wall a rigid structure that surrounds the cell membrane and provides support to the cell (98)
  pared celular una estructura rígida que rodea la membrana celular y le brinda soporte a la célula

chlorophyll (KLOHR•oh•fill) a green pigment that captures light energy for photosynthesis (475)
  clorofila un pigmento verde que capta la energía luminosa para la fotosíntesis

chloroplast (KLOHR•oh•plahstz) an organelle found in plant and algae cells where photosynthesis occurs (99)
  cloroplasto un organelo que se encuentra en las células vegetales y en las células de las algas, en el cual se lleva a cabo la fotosíntesis

chromosomes (KROH•muh•sohmz) in a eukaryotic cell, one of the structures in the nucleus that are made up of DNA and protein; in a prokaryotic cell, the main ring of DNA (317)
  cromosoma en una célula eucariótica, una de las estructuras del núcleo que está hecha de ADN y proteína; en una célula procariótica, el anillo principal de ADN

clone (KLOHN) an organism, cell, or piece of genetic material that is genetically identical to one from which it was derived (397)
  clon un organismo, célula o fragmento de material genético que es genéticamente idéntico al organismo, célula o material genético del cual proviene

codominance (koh•DAHM•uh•nuhns) a condition in which two alleles are expressed such that the phenotype of a heterozygous individual is a combination of the phenotypes of the two homozygous parents (353)
  codominancia una condición en la que dos alelos están expresados de modo que el fenotipo de un individuo heterocigoto es una combinación de los fenotipos de los dos padres homocigotos

commensalism a relationship between two organisms in which one organism benefits and the other is unaffected (440)
  comensalismo una relación entre dos organismos en la que uno se beneficia y el otro no es afectado

community all of the populations of species that live in the same habitat and interact with each other (417)
  comunidad todas las poblaciones de especies que viven en el mismo hábitat e interactúan entre sí

competition (kahm•pih•TISH•uhn) ecological relationship in which two or more organisms depend on the same limited resource (442)
  competencia la relación ecológica en la que dos o más organismos dependen del mismo recurso limitado

consumer an organism that eats other organisms or organic matter (427)
consumidor un organismo que se alimenta de otros organismos o de materia orgánica

coral reef a limestone ridge found in tropical climates and composed of coral fragments that are deposited around organic remains (456)
arrecife de coral una cumbre de piedra caliza ubicada en climas tropicales, formada por fragmentos de coral depositados alrededor de restos orgánicos

cytokinesis the division of the cytoplasm of a cell; cytokinesis follows the division of the cell's nucleus by mitosis or meiosis (319)
citocinesis la división del citoplasma de una célula; la citocinesis ocurre después de que el núcleo de la célula se divide por mitosis o meiosis

cytoplasm (SY•tuh•plaz•uhm) the region of the cell within the membrane that includes the fluid, the cytoskeleton, and all of the organelles except the nucleus (78)
citoplasma la región de la célula dentro de la membrana, que incluye el líquido, el citoesqueleto y los organelos, pero no el núcleo

cytoskeleton the cytoplasmic network of protein filaments that plays an essential role in cell movement, shape, and division (95)
citoesqueleto la red citoplásmica de filamentos de proteínas que juega un papel esencial en el movimiento, forma y división de la célula

data (DAY•tuh) information gathered by observation or experimentation that can be used in calculating or reasoning (29)
datos la información recopilada por medio de la observación o experimentación que puede usarse para hacer cálculos o razonar

decomposer an organism that gets energy by breaking down the remains of dead organisms or animal wastes and consuming or absorbing the nutrients (426)
descomponedor un organismo que, para obtener energía, desintegra los restos de organismos muertos o los desechos de animales y consume o absorbe los nutrientes

dendrite (DEN•dryt) branchlike extension of a neuron that receives impulses from neighboring neurons (213)
dendrita la extensión ramificada de una neurona que recibe impulsos de las neuronas vecinas

dependent variable (dih•PEN•duhnt VAIR•ee•uh•buhl) in a scientific investigation, the factor that changes as a result of manipulation of one or more independent variables (29, 42)
variable dependiente en una investigación científica, el factor que cambia como resultado de la manipulación de una o más variables independientes

dichotomous key (di•KOT•uh•muhs KEE) an aid that is used to identify organisms and that consists of the answers to a series of questions (138)
clave dicotómica una ayuda para identificar organismos, que consiste en las respuestas a una serie de preguntas

diffusion the movement of particles from regions of higher concentration to regions of lower concentration (122)
difusión el movimiento de partículas de regiones de mayor concentración a regiones de menor concentración

digestive system the organs that break down food so that it can be used by the body (198)
aparato digestivo los órganos que descomponen la comida de modo que el cuerpo la pueda usar

DNA deoxyribonucleic acid, the material that contains the information that determines inherited characteristics (317, 380)
ADN ácido desoxirribonucleico, el material que contiene la información que determina las características que se heredan

domain in a taxonomic system one of the three broad groups that all living things fall into (134)
dominio en un sistema taxonómico, uno de los tres amplios grupos al que pertenecen todos los seres vivos

dominant (DAHM•uh•nuhnt) describes the allele that is fully expressed when carried by only one of a pair of homologous chromosomes (349)
dominante describe al alelo que contribuye al fenotipo de un individuo cuando una o dos copias del alelo están presentes en el genotipo de ese individuo

ecology the study of the interactions of living organisms with one another and with their environment (414)
ecología el estudio de las interacciones de los seres vivos entre sí mismos y entre sí mismos y su ambiente

ecosystem a community of organisms and their abiotic, or nonliving, environment (417)
ecosistema una comunidad de organismos y su ambiente abiótico o no vivo

egg a sex cell produced by a female (225)
óvulo una célula sexual producida por una hembra

embryo in humans, a developing individual from first division after fertilization through the 10th week of pregnancy (227)
embrión en los seres humanos, un individuo en desarrollo desde la primera división después de la fecundación hasta el final de la décima semana de embarazo

empirical evidence (em•PIR•ih•kuhl EV•ih•duhns) the observations, measurements, and other types of data that people gather and test to support and evaluate scientific explanations (7)
evidencia empírica las observaciones, mediciones y demás tipos de datos que se recopilan y examinan para apoyar y evaluar explicaciones científicas

endocrine system a collection of glands and groups of cells that secrete hormones that regulate growth, development, and homeostasis; includes the pituitary, thyroid, parathyroid, and adrenal glands, the hypothalamus, the pineal body, and the gonads (216)
sistema endocrino un conjunto de glándulas y grupos de células que secretan hormonas las cuales regulan el crecimiento, desarrollo y homeostasis; incluye las glándulas pituitaria, tiroides, paratiroides y suprarrenal, el hipotálamo, el cuerpo pineal y las gónadas

endocytosis (en•doh•sye•TOH•sis) the process by which a cell membrane surrounds a particle and encloses the particle in a vesicle to bring the particle into the cell (124)
endocitosis el proceso por medio del cual la membrana celular rodea una partícula y la encierra en una vesícula para llevarla al interior de la célula

endoplasmic reticulum (ehn•doh•PLAHZ•mick rhett•ICK•yoo•luhm) a system of membranes that is found in a cell's cytoplasm and that assists in the production, processing, and transport of proteins and in the production of lipids (97)
retículo endoplásmico un sistema de membranas que se encuentra en el citoplasma de la célula y que tiene una función en la producción, procesamiento y transporte de proteínas y en la producción de lípidos

energy (EN•er•jee) the capacity to do work (486)
energía la capacidad de realizar un trabajo

energy pyramid a triangular diagram that shows an ecosystem's loss of energy, which results as energy passes through the ecosystem's food chain; each row in the pyramid represents a trophic feeding level in an ecosystem, and the area of a row represents the energy stored in that trophic level (488)
pirámide de energía un diagrama con forma de triángulo que muestra la pérdida de energía que ocurre en un ecosistema a medida que la energía pasa a través de la cadena alimenticia del ecosistema; cada hilera de la pirámide representa un nivel trófico de alimentación en el ecosistema, y el área de la hilera representa la energía almacenada en ese nivel trófico

enzyme (EN•zym) a type of protein that speeds up metabolic reactions in plants and animals without being permanently changed or destroyed (199)
enzima un tipo de proteína que acelera las reacciones metabólicas en las plantas y animales, sin ser modificada permanentemente ni ser destruida

esophagus (ih•SAWF•uh•gus) a long, straight tube that connects the pharynx to the stomach (200)
esófago un conducto largo y recto que conecta la faringe con el estómago

estuary an area where fresh water mixes with salt water from the ocean (457)
estuario un área donde el agua dulce de los ríos se mezcla con el agua salada del océano

Eukarya in a modern taxonomic system, a domain made up of all eukaryotes; this domain aligns with the traditional kingdoms Protista, Fungi, Plantae, and Animalia (135)
Eukarya en un sistema taxonómico moderno, un dominio compuesto por todos los eucariotes; este dominio coincide con los reinos tradicionales Protista, Fungi, Plantae y Animalia

eukaryote (yoo•KAIR•ee•oht) an organism made up of cells that have a nucleus enclosed by a membrane; eukaryotes include protists, animals, plants, and fungi but not archaea or bacteria (79)
eucariote un organismo cuyas células tienen un núcleo contenido en una membrana; entre los eucariotes se encuentran protistas, animales, plantas y hongos, pero no arqueas ni bacterias

evolution the process in which inherited characteristics within a population change over generations such that new species sometimes arise (282)
evolución el proceso por medio del cual las características heredadas dentro de una población cambian con el transcurso de las generaciones de manera tal que a veces surgen nuevas especies

excretory system (EK•skrih•tohr•ee SIS•tuhm) the system that collects and excretes nitrogenous wastes and excess water from the body in the form of urine (203)
aparato excretor el sistema que recolecta y elimina del cuerpo los desperdicios nitrogenados y el exceso de agua en forma de orina

exocytosis (ek•soh•sye•TOH•sis) the process in which a cell releases a particle by enclosing the particle in a vesicle that then moves to the cell surface and fuses with the cell membrane (124)
exocitosis el proceso por medio del cual una célula libera una partícula encerrándola en una vesícula que luego se traslada a la superficie de la célula y se fusiona con la membrana celular

experiment (ik•SPEHR•uh•muhnt) an organized procedure to study something under controlled conditions (28)
experimento un procedimiento organizado que se lleva a cabo bajo condiciones controladas para estudiar algo

extinction the death of every member of a species (289)
extinción la muerte de todos los miembros de una especie

F

fertilization (fer•tl•i•ZAY•shuhn) the union of a male and female gamete to form a zygote (338)
fecundación la unión de un gameto masculino y femenino para formar un cigoto

fetus a developing human from the end of the 10th week of pregnancy until birth (228)
feto un ser humano en desarrollo desde el final de la décima semana del embarazo hasta el nacimiento

food chain the pathway of energy transfer through various stages as a result of the feeding patterns of a series of organisms (429)
cadena alimenticia la vía de transferencia de energía través de varias etapas, que ocurre como resultado de los patrones de alimentación de una serie de organismos

food web a diagram that shows the feeding relationships between organisms in an ecosystem (430)
red alimenticia un diagrama que muestra las relaciones de alimentación entre los organismos de un ecosistema

fossil the trace or remains of an organism that lived long ago, most commonly preserved in sedimentary rock (297)
fósil los indicios o los restos de un organismo que vivió hace mucho tiempo, comúnmente preservados en las rocas sedimentarias

fossil record the history of life in the geologic past as indicated by the traces or remains of living things (297)
registro fósil la historia de la vida en el pasado geológico según la indican los rastros o restos de seres vivos

function the special, normal, or proper activity of an organ or part (110)
función la actividad especial, normal o adecuada de un órgano o parte

Fungi a kingdom made up of nongreen, eukaryotic organisms that reproduce by using spores, and get food by breaking down substances in their surroundings and absorbing the nutrients (136)
Hongos reino compuesto por organismos eucarióticos sin clorofila que se reproducen por medio de esporas y que, para alimentarse, descomponen sustancias del ambiente y absorben sus nutrientes

G

gene one set of instructions for an inherited trait (348)
gene un conjunto de instrucciones para un carácter heredado

genetic engineering a technology in which the genome of a living cell is modified for medical or industrial use (396)
ingeniería genética una tecnología en la que el genoma de una célula viva se modifica con fines médicos o industriales

genotype (JEEN•uh•typ) the entire genetic makeup of an organism; also the combination of genes for one or more specific traits (349)
genotipo la constitución genética completa de un organismo; también, la combinación de genes para uno o más caracteres específicos

genus (JEE•nuhs) the level of classification that comes after family and that contains similar species (132)
género el nivel de clasificación que viene después de la familia y que contiene especies similares

gland (GLAND) a group of cells that make chemicals for use elsewhere in the body (216)
glándula un grupo de células que elaboran sustancias químicas para su utilización en otra parte del cuerpo

Golgi complex (GOHL•ghee COHM•plehkz) a cell organelle that helps make and package materials to be transported out of the cell (97)
aparato de Golgi un organelo celular que ayuda a hacer y a empacar los materiales que serán transportados al exterior de la célula

H

habitat the place where an organism usually lives (418)
hábitat el lugar donde vive normalmente un organismo

herbivore an organism that eats only plants (427)
herbívoro un organismo que sólo come plantas

heredity (huh•RED•ih•tee) the passing of genetic material from parent to offspring (346)
herencia la transmisión de material genético de padres a hijos

homeostasis (hoh•mee•oh•STAY•sis) the maintenance of a constant internal state in a changing environment (118, 160)
homeostasis la capacidad de mantener un estado interno constante en un ambiente en cambio

homologous chromosome (huh•MAHL•uh•guhs KROH•muh•sohmz) chromosomes that have the same sequence of genes and the same structure (326)
cromosoma homólogo cromosomas con la misma secuencia de genes y la misma estructura

hormone a substance that is made in one cell or tissue and that causes a change in another cell or tissue in a different part of the body (216)
hormona una sustancia que es producida en una célula o tejido, la cual causa un cambio en otra célula o tejido ubicado en una parte diferente del cuerpo

hypothesis (hy•PAHTH•eh•sys) a testable idea or explanation that leads to scientific investigation (28)
hipótesis una idea o explicación que conlleva a la investigación científica y que se puede probar

I

immune system the cells and tissues that recognize and attack foreign substances in the body (249)
sistema inmunológico las células y tejidos que reconocen y atacan sustancias extrañas en el cuerpo

immunity the ability to resist or recover from an infectious disease (252)
inmunidad la capacidad de resistir una enfermedad infecciosa o recuperarse de ella

incomplete dominance (in•kuhm•PLEET DAHM•uh•nuhns) a condition in which two alleles are expressed such that the phenotype of a heterozygous individual is an intermediate of the phenotypes of the two homozygous parents (352)
dominancia incompleta una condición en la que dos alelos se expresan de modo que el fenotipo de un individuo heterocigoto es intermedio entre los fenotipos de sus dos padres homocigotos

independent variable (in•dih•PEN•duhnt VAIR•ee•uh•buhl) in a scientific investigation, the factor that is deliberately manipulated (29, 42)
variable independiente en una investigación científica, el factor que se manipula deliberadamente

infectious disease a disease that is caused by a pathogen and that can be spread from one individual to another (261)
enfermedad infecciosa una enfermedad que es causada por un patógeno y que puede transmitirse de un individuo a otro

interphase (IN•ter•fayz) the period of the cell cycle during which activities such as cell growth and protein synthesis occur without visible signs of cell division (318)
interfase el período del ciclo celular durante el cual las actividades como el crecimiento celular y la síntesis de proteínas existen sin signos visibles de división celular

introduced species a species introduced either by accident or on purpose by human actions into places beyond the species's natural range (451)
especie exótica una especie que se ha introducido en lugares ajenos a su área de distribución natural, ya sea por la acción humana o por accidente

J

joint a place where two or more bones meet (170)
articulación un lugar donde se unen dos o más huesos

K

kidney one of the organs that filter water and wastes from the blood, excrete products as urine, and regulate the concentration of certain substances in the blood (204)
riñón uno de los órganos que filtran el agua y los desechos de la sangre, excretan productos como orina y regulan la concentración de ciertas sustancias en la sangre

L

large intestine the broader and shorter portion of the intestine, where water is removed from the mostly digested food to turn the waste into semisolid feces, or stool (201)
intestino grueso la porción más ancha y más corta del intestino, donde el agua se elimina de la mayoría de los alimentos digeridos para convertir los desechos en heces semisólidas o excremento

larynx (LAR•ingks) the part of the respiratory system between the pharynx and the trachea; has walls of cartilage and muscle and contains the vocal cords (190)
laringe la parte del aparato respiratorio que se encuentra entre la faringe y la tráquea; tiene paredes de cartílago y músculo y contiene las cuerdas vocales

law of conservation of energy the law that states that energy cannot be created or destroyed but can be changed from one form to another (487)
ley de la conservación de la energía la ley que establece que la energía ni se crea ni se destruye, sólo se transforma de una forma a otra

law of conservation of mass the law that states that mass cannot be created or destroyed in ordinary chemical and physical changes (487)
ley de la conservación de la masa la ley que establece que la masa no se crea ni se destruye por cambios químicos o físicos comunes

ligament a type of tissue that holds together the bones in a joint (168)
ligamento un tipo de tejido que mantiene unidos los huesos en una articulación

limiting factor an environmental factor that prevents an organism or population from reaching its full potential of size or activity (450)
factor limitante un factor ambiental que impide que un organismo o población alcance su máximo potencial de distribución o de actividad

lipid a fat molecule or a molecule that has similar properties; examples include oils, waxes, and steroids (86)
lípido una molécula de grasa o una molécula que tiene propiedades similares; algunos ejemplos son los aceites, las ceras y los esteroides

liver the largest organ in the body; it makes bile, stores and filters blood, and stores excess sugars as glycogen (202)
hígado el órgano más grande del cuerpo; produce bilis, almacena y filtra la sangre, y almacena el exceso de azúcares en forma de glucógeno

lymph (LIMF) the clear, watery fluid that leaks from blood vessels and contains white blood cells; circulates in lymphatic system; returned to bloodstream through lymph vessels (180)
linfa el fluido claro y acuoso que se filtra de los vasos sanguíneos y contiene glóbulos blancos; circula por el sistema linfático; regresa al torrente sanguíneo a través de los vasos linfáticos

lymph node (LIMF NOHD) small, bean-shaped masses of tissue that remove pathogens and dead cells from the lymph; concentrated in the armpits, neck, and groin; high concentration of white blood cells found in lymph nodes (182)
nodo linfático masas de tejido pequeñas y con forma de frijol que eliminan los patógenos y las células muertas de la linfa; están concentrados en las axilas, el cuello y la ingle; los nodos linfáticos presentan una alta concentración de glóbulos blancos

lymphatic system (lim•FAT•ik SIS•tuhm) a network of organs and tissues that collect the fluid that leaks from blood and returns it to blood vessels; includes lymph nodes, lymph vessels, and lymph; the place where certain white blood cells mature (180)
sistema linfático una red de órganos y tejidos que recolectan el fluido que se filtra de la sangre y lo regresan a los vasos sanguíneos; incluye los nodos linfáticos, los vasos linfáticos y la linfa; el lugar donde maduran ciertos glóbulos blancos

lysosome (LY•soh•zohmz) a cell organelle that contains digestive enzymes (100)
lisosoma un organelo celular que contiene enzimas digestivas

macrophage (MAK•ruh•faj) an immune system cell that engulfs pathogens and other materials (250)
macrófago una célula del sistema inmunológico que envuelve a los patógenos y otros materiales

matter anything that has mass and takes up space (486)
materia cualquier cosa que tiene masa y ocupa un lugar en el espacio

meiosis (my•OH•sis) a process in cell division during which the number of chromosomes decreases to half the original number by two divisions of the nucleus, which results in the production of sex cells gametes or spores (327)
meiosis un proceso de división celular durante el cual el número de cromosomas disminuye a la mitad del número original por medio de dos divisiones del núcleo, lo cual resulta en la producción de células sexuales gametos o esporas

mitochondrion (my•TOH•kahn•dree•ahn) in eukaryotic cells, the organelle that is the site of cellular respiration, which releases energy for use by the cell (96)
mitocondria en las células eucarióticas, el organelo donde se lleva a cabo la respiración celular, la cual libera energía para que utilice la célula

mitosis (my•TOH•sis) in eukaryotic cells, a process of cell division that forms two new nuclei, each of which has the same number of chromosomes (121, 319)
mitosis en las células eucarióticas, un proceso de división celular que forma dos núcleos nuevos, cada uno de los cuales posee el mismo número de cromosomas

model a pattern, plan, representation, or description designed to show the structure or workings of an object, system, or concept (48)
modelo un diseño, plan, representación o descripción cuyo objetivo es mostrar la estructura o funcionamiento de un objeto, sistema o concepto

molecule (MAHL•ih•kyool) a group of atoms that are held together by chemical bonds; a molecule is the smallest unit of a substance that can exist by itself and retain all of the substance's chemical properties (85)
molécula un grupo de átomos unidos por enlaces químicos; una molécula es la unidad más pequeña de una sustancia que puede existir por sí misma y conservar todas las propiedades químicas de esa sustancia

muscular system a collection of muscles whose primary function is movement and flexibility (172)
sistema muscular un conjunto de músculos cuya función principal es permitir el movimiento y la flexibilidad

mutation a change in the structure or amount of the genetic material of an organism (385)
mutación un cambio en la estructura o cantidad del material genético de un organismo

mutualism a relationship between two species in which both species benefit (440)
mutualismo una relación entre dos especies en la que ambas se benefician

native species a species that was not introduced and that naturally occurs in a given ecosystem both in the past and now (451)
especie nativa una especie que no se ha introducido y que se encuentra de forma natural en un ecosistema dado, del pasado o actual

natural selection the process by which individuals that are better adapted to their environment survive and reproduce more successfully than less well adapted individuals do (286)

selección natural el proceso por medio del cual los individuos que están mejor adaptados a su ambiente sobreviven y se reproducen con más éxito que los individuos menos adaptados

nephron (NEF•rahnz) the unit in the kidney that filters blood (204)

nefrona la unidad del riñón que filtra la sangre

nervous system the structures that control the actions and reactions of the body in response to stimuli from the environment; it is formed by billions of specialized nerve cells, called neurons (210)

sistema nervioso las estructuras que controlan las acciones y reacciones del cuerpo en respuesta a los estímulos del ambiente; está formado por miles de millones de células nerviosas especializadas, llamadas neuronas

neuron a nerve cell that is specialized to receive and conduct electrical impulses (212)

neurona una célula nerviosa que está especializada en recibir y transmitir impulsos eléctricos

niche the role of a species in its community, including use of its habitat and its relationships with other species (418)

nicho el papel que juega una especie en su comunidad, incluidos el uso de su hábitat y su relación con otras especies

noninfectious disease a disease that cannot spread from one individual to another (260)

enfermedad no infecciosa una enfermedad que no se contagia de una persona a otra

nucleic acid a molecule made up of nucleotide subunits that carries information in cells (87)

ácido nucleico una molécula compuesta por subunidades de nucleótido que contiene la información de las células

nucleotide in a nucleic-acid chain, a subunit that consists of a sugar, a phosphate, and a nitrogenous base (383)

nucleótido en una cadena de ácidos nucleicos, una subunidad formada por un azúcar, un fosfato y una base nitrogenada

nucleus 1. in a eukaryotic cell, a membrane-bound organelle that contains the cell's DNA and that has a role in processes such as growth, metabolism, and reproduction, 2. in physical science, an atom's central region, which is made up of protons and neutrons (78)

núcleo 1. en una célula eucariótica, un organelo cubierto por una membrana, el cual contiene el ADN de la célula y participa en procesos tales como el crecimiento, metabolismo y reproducción, 2. en ciencias físicas, la región central de un átomo, la cual está constituida por protones y neutrones

observation the process of obtaining information by using the senses; the information obtained by using the senses (28)

observación el proceso de obtener información por medio de los sentidos; la información que se obtiene al usar los sentidos

omnivore an organism that eats both plants and animals (427)

omnívoro un organismo que come tanto plantas como animales

organ a collection of tissues that carry out a specialized function of the body (108)

órgano un conjunto de tejidos que desempeñan una función especializada en el cuerpo

organ system (AWR•guhn SIS•tuhm) a group of organs that work together to perform body functions (109)

aparato o sistema de órganos un grupo de órganos que trabajan en conjunto para desempeñar funciones corporales

organelle one of the small bodies in a cell's cytoplasm that are specialized to perform a specific function (78)

organelo uno de los cuerpos pequeños del citoplasma de una célula que están especializados para llevar a cabo una función específica

organism a living thing; anything that can carry out life processes independently (74, 106)

organismo un ser vivo; cualquier cosa que pueda llevar a cabo procesos vitales independientemente

osmosis the diffusion of water through a semipermeable membrane (122)

ósmosis la difusión del agua a través de una membrana semipermeable

ovary in the female reproductive system of animals, an organ that produces eggs (225)

ovario en el aparato reproductor femenino de los animales, un órgano que produce óvulos

pancreas (PANG•kree•uhz) the organ that lies behind the stomach and that makes digestive enzymes and hormones that regulate sugar levels (202)

páncreas el órgano que se encuentra detrás del estómago y que produce las enzimas digestivas y las hormonas que regulan los niveles de azúcar

parasitism (PAR•uh•sih•tiz•uhm) a relationship between two species in which one species, the parasite, benefits from the other species, the host, which is harmed (441)

parasitismo una relación entre dos especies en la que una, el parásito, se beneficia de la otra, el huésped, que resulta perjudicada

passive transport the movement of substances across a cell membrane without the use of energy by the cell (122)

transporte pasivo el movimiento de sustancias a través de una membrana celular sin que la célula tenga que usar energía

pathogen a microorganism, another organism, a virus, or a protein that causes disease (248)

patógeno un microorganismo, otro organismo, un virus o una proteína que causa enfermedades

pedigree a diagram that shows the occurrence of a genetic trait in several generations of a family (364)

pedigrí un diagrama que muestra la incidencia de un carácter genético en varias generaciones de una familia

penis the male organ that transfers sperm to a female and that carries urine out of the body (224)

pene el órgano masculino que transfiere espermatozoides a una hembra y que lleva la orina hacia el exterior del cuerpo

pharynx (FAIR•ingks) the part of the respiratory system that extends from the mouth to the larynx (190)

faringe la parte del aparato respiratorio que va de la boca a la laringe

phenotype (FEEN•uh•typ) an organism's appearance or other detectable characteristic (349)

fenotipo la apariencia de un organismo u otra característica perceptible

phospholipid (FOSS•foh•LIH•pyd) a lipid that contains phosphorus and that is a structural component in cell membranes (88)

fosfolípido un lípido que contiene fósforo y que es un componente estructural de la membrana celular

photosynthesis (foh•toh•SYN•thuh•sys) the process by which plants, algae, and some bacteria use sunlight, carbon dioxide, and water to make food (120, 474)

fotosíntesis el proceso por medio del cual las plantas, las algas y algunas bacterias utilizan la luz solar, el dióxido de carbono y el agua para producir alimento

placenta the partly fetal and partly maternal organ by which materials are exchanged between a fetus and the mother (228)

placenta el órgano parcialmente fetal y parcialmente materno por medio del cual se intercambian materiales entre el feto y la madre

Plantae a kingdom made up of complex, multicellular organisms that are usually green, have cell walls made of cellulose, cannot move around, and use the sun's energy to make sugar by photosynthesis (136)

Plantae un reino formado por organismos pluricelulares complejos que normalmente son verdes, tienen una pared celular de celulosa, no tienen capacidad de movimiento y utilizan la energía del Sol para producir azúcar mediante la fotosíntesis

population a group of organisms of the same species that live in a specific geographical area (416)

población un grupo de organismos de la misma especie que viven en un área geográfica específica

predator an organism that kills and eats all or part of another organism (438)

depredador un organismo que mata y se alimenta de otro organismo o de parte de él

prey an organism that is killed and eaten by another organism (438)

presa un organismo al que otro organismo mata para alimentarse de él

probability the likelihood that a possible future event will occur in any given instance of the event (362)

probabilidad la probabilidad de que ocurra un posible suceso futuro en cualquier caso dado del suceso

producer an organism that can make its own food by using energy from its surroundings (426)

productor un organismo que puede elaborar sus propios alimentos utilizando la energía de su entorno

prokaryote (proh•KAIR•ee•oht) a single-celled organism that does not have a nucleus or membrane-bound organelles; examples are archaea and bacteria (79)

procariote un organismo unicelular que no tiene núcleo ni organelos cubiertos por una membrana, por ejemplo, las arqueas y las bacterias

protein a molecule that is made up of amino acids and that is needed to build and repair body structures and to regulate processes in the body (86)

proteína una molécula formada por aminoácidos que es necesaria para construir y reparar estructuras corporales y para regular procesos del cuerpo

Protista a kingdom of mostly one-celled eukaryotic organisms that are different from plants, animals, and fungi (136)

Protista un reino compuesto principalmente por organismos eucarióticos unicelulares diferentes de las plantas, los animales y los hongos

pseudoscience a process of investigation that in one or more ways resembles science but deviates from the scientific methods (12)

pseudociencia un proceso de investigación que tiene semejanzas con la actividad científica, pero no cumple con los métodos científicos

Punnett square a graphic used to predict the results of a genetic cross (360)

cuadro de Punnett una gráfica que se usa para predecir los resultados de una cruza genética

R

ratio a comparison of two numbers using division (362)

razón comparacion de dos números mediante la división

recessive (rih•SES•iv) in genetics, describes an allele that is expressed only when no dominant allele is present in an individual (349)

recesivo en genética, término que describe un alelo que se expresa sólo cuando no hay un alelo dominante presente en el individuo

replication the duplication of a DNA molecule (384)
   replicación la duplicación de una molécula de ADN

respiratory system a collection of organs whose primary function is to take in oxygen and expel carbon dioxide; the organs of this system include the lungs, the throat, and the passageways that lead to the lungs (189)
   aparato respiratorio un conjunto de órganos cuya función principal es tomar oxígeno y expulsar dióxido de carbono; los órganos de este aparato incluyen a los pulmones, la garganta y las vías que llevan a los pulmones

ribosome a cell organelle composed of RNA and protein; the site of protein synthesis (96, 387)
   ribosoma un organelo celular compuesto de ARN y proteína; el sitio donde ocurre la síntesis de proteínas

RNA ribonucleic acid, a molecule that is present in all living cells and that plays a role in protein production (386)
   ARN ácido ribonucleico, una molécula que está presente en todas las células vivas y que juega un papel en la producción de proteínas

science the knowledge obtained by observing natural events and conditions in order to discover facts and formulate laws or principles that can be verified or tested (6)
   ciencia el conocimiento que se obtiene por medio de la observación natural de acontecimientos y condiciones con el fin de descubrir hechos y formular leyes o principios que puedan ser verificados o probados

sexual reproduction (SEHK•shoo•uhl ree•pruh•DUHK•shuhn) reproduction in which the sex cells from two parents unite to produce offspring that share traits from both parents (338)
   reproducción sexual reproducción en la que se unen las células sexuales de los dos progenitores para producir descendencia que comparte caracteres de ambos progenitores

skeletal system the organ system whose primary function is to support and protect the body and to allow the body to move (166)
   sistema esquelético el sistema de órganos cuya función principal es sostener y proteger el cuerpo y permitir que se mueva

small intestine the organ between the stomach and the large intestine where most of the breakdown of food happens and most of the nutrients from food are absorbed (201)
   intestino delgado el órgano que se encuentra entre el estómago y el intestino grueso en el cual se produce la mayor parte de la descomposición de los alimentos y se absorben la mayoría de los nutrientes

species (SPEE•seez) a group of organisms that are closely related and can mate to produce fertile offspring (132, 416)
   especie un grupo de organismos que tienen un parentesco cercano y que pueden aparearse para producir descendencia fértil

sperm the male sex cell (224)
   espermatozoide la célula sexual masculina

spinal cord a column of nerve tissue running from the base of the brain through the vertebral column (210)
   médula espinal una columna de tejido nervioso que se origina en la base del cerebro y corre a lo largo de la columna vertebral

stomach the saclike, digestive organ that is between the esophagus and the small intestine and that breaks down food by the action of muscles, enzymes, and acids (201)
   estómago el órgano digestivo con forma de bolsa, ubicado entre el esófago y el intestino delgado, que descompone la comida por la acción de músculos, enzimas y ácidos

structure the arrangement of parts in an organism (110)
   estructura el orden y distribución de las partes de un organismo

symbiosis (sim•bee•OH•sis) a relationship in which two different organisms live in close association with each other (440)
   simbiosis una relación en la que dos organismos diferentes viven estrechamente asociados uno con el otro

T cell an immune system cell that coordinates the immune system and attacks many infected cells (250)
   célula T una célula del sistema inmunológico que coordina dicho sistema y ataca muchas células infectadas

tendon a tough connective tissue that attaches a muscle to a bone or to another body part (173)
   tendón un tejido conectivo duro que une un músculo con un hueso o con otra parte del cuerpo

testes the primary male reproductive organs, which produce sperm cells and testosterone singular, testis (224)
   testículos los principales órganos reproductores masculinos, los cuales producen espermatozoides y testosterona

tissue a group of similar cells that perform a common function (107)
   tejido un grupo de células similares que llevan a cabo una función común

trachea (TRAY•kee•uh) thin-walled tube that extends from the larynx to the bronchi; carries air to the lungs; also called windpipe (190)
   tráquea el conducto de paredes delgadas que va de la laringe a los bronquios; lleva el aire a los pulmones

U

umbilical cord the ropelike structure through which blood vessels pass and by which a developing mammal is connected to the placenta (228)

cordón umbilical la estructura con forma de cuerda a través de la cual pasan vasos sanguíneos y por medio de la cual un mamífero en desarrollo está unido a la placenta

urine the liquid excreted by the kidneys, stored in the bladder, and passed through the urethra to the outside of the body (204)

orina el líquido que excretan los riñones, se almacena en la vejiga y pasa a través de la uretra hacia el exterior del cuerpo

uterus in female placental mammals, the hollow, muscular organ in which an embryo embeds itself and develops into a fetus (226)

útero en los mamíferos placentarios hembras, el órgano hueco y muscular en el que el embrión se incrusta y se desarrolla hasta convertirse en feto

V

vaccine a substance that is prepared from killed or weakened pathogens or from genetic material and that is introduced into a body to produce immunity (252)

vacuna una sustancia que se prepara a partir de organismos patógenos muertos o debilitados o de material genético y se introduce al cuerpo para producir inmunidad

vacuole (VAK•yoo•ohl) a fluid-filled vesicle found in the cytoplasm of plant cells or protozoans (98)

vacuola una vesícula llena de líquido que se encuentra en el citoplasma de las células vegetales o de los protozoarios

vagina the female reproductive organ that connects the outside of the body to the uterus (226)

vagina el órgano reproductivo femenino que conecta la parte exterior del cuerpo con el útero

variation (vair•ee•AY•shuhn) the occurrence of hereditary or nonhereditary differences between different invidivuals of a population (286)

variabilidad la incidencia de diferencias hereditarias o no hereditarias entre distintos individuos de una población

vein in biology, a vessel that carries blood to the heart (185)

vena en biología, un vaso que lleva sangre al corazón

W-Z

wetland an area of land that is periodically underwater or whose soil contains a great deal of moisture (455)

terreno pantanoso un área de tierra que está periódicamente bajo el agua o cuyo suelo contiene una gran cantidad de humedad

Index

Page numbers for definitions are printed in **boldface** type.
Page numbers for illustrations, maps, and charts are printed in *italics*.

dinosaur
    extinction of, 20–21
    link between birds and, 23
diploid cell, 326
disease, 161
    of cardiovascular system, 188
    of endocrine system, 218
    of immune system, 253
    infectious, 258–269
    of lymphatic system, 183
    of muscular system, 174
    of nervous system, 218
    noninfectious, **260**
    reduction and exercise, 175
    of respiratory system, 191
    of skeletal system, 171
DNA (deoxyribonucleic acid), **78**, *78*, 95, **317**, **380**
    cloning, 397
    code, 380, 383
    components of, 380
    discovery of, 381
    double-helix shape of, 382
    genes and, 348
    genetic engineering and, 396
    mutations, **385**
    nucleotides, 87, 383
    replication, 121, 384
    role of in protein building, 386–387
    structure of, 382–383
dog breed, 395
Dolly the cloned sheep, 397
domain, *133*, **134**–135
    Archaea, R4
    Bacteria, R4
    Eukarya, R4–R5
dominance, 352–353
dominant allele, **349**
Do the Math, 75, 229, 249, 362–363
double helix, 382
Down syndrome, 331
drinking water, contaminated, 264
dune, 452

E

ear, 215
eardrum, 215
Earth, 54, 285
ecology, **414**
ecosystem, **417**
    energy and matter in, 487, 488–491
    Florida's, 448–459
    freshwater, 454–455
    land, 452–453
    marine, 456–457
egg, **225**, *324*, 327, 338
    fertilization of, 227
    release of, 226
electrical message, 159
element, **84**
    Periodic Table of the Elements, *R6–R7*
embryo, **227**, 228
embryology, **299**
emphysema, **191**, *191*

empirical evidence, **7**, *9*, 12
endangered species, 365
endocrine glands, 217
endocrine system, 156, 159, 160, **216**
    disorders of, 218
    feedback mechanisms, 218
    functions of, 216
    glands of, 217
endocytosis, **124**, *124*
endoplasmic reticulum (ER), 96, **97**, *97*, *100*, 101
endoskeleton, 166
endurance exercise, 175
energy, 426, **486**
    cellular, 96, 120, 472–473
    chemical, 426, 473, 475
    in ecosystem, 488
    from food, 473, 476–477
    food webs and, 430–432
    law of conservation of, **487**
    light, 475
    in living systems, 487
    production of, 426–427
    release of, 477
    sources of, 86, 87, 486
energy pyramid, **488**, *488*
energy transfer, 428–429
Engage Your Brain, lesson opener pages, 5, 17, 27, 41, 53, 73, 83, 93, 105, 117, 129, 155, 165, 179, 197, 209, 223, 247, 259, 281, 295, 315, 325, 335, 345, 359, 379, 393, 413, 425, 437, 449, 471, 485
environment
    adaptation to, 289
    influence on traits of, 351
    levels of organization in, 416–417
    living, 415
    nonliving, 415
    response of organisms to, 125
enzyme, **199**
epithelial tissue, 107
ER. *See* endoplasmic reticulum.
esophagus, 190, **200**
estrogen, 225
estuary, **457**
euglena, *94*
Eukarya, *135*, 136, R4–R5
eukaryote, **135**, 136
eukaryotic cell, **79**, 94–95, 319, 476
European mouflon, 365
Everglades, 455
evidence
    empirical, 7, 9, 12
    supporting scientific theories, 20–22
evolution, **282**, 288
    of whales, 300–301
evolutionary theory, 280–291
    evidence supporting, 294–303
    formation of, 282–285
    natural selection and, 286–287, 288
excretory system, 157, **203**
exercise, 175. *See also* aerobic, anaerobic.

exhalation, 203
exocytosis, **124**, *124*
experiment, 19, **28**. *See also* scientific investigation.
    characteristics of, 34
    designing, R18–R22
    distinguishing, 292–293
    steps in conducting, 30–31, R20–R22
experimental group, R19
extensor, 173, *173*
extinct, **289**
eye, 214

F

fallopian tube, *225*, 226, *226*
family, *133*
farming, 55
feces, 202
feedback mechanism, **218**
feeding relationship, 438–439
female reproductive system, 225, *225*, 226, *226*
femur, *166*
fermentation, 479
fertilization, 226–227, *227*, 327, **338**, *338*
fetus, **228**
fever, 249
field investigation, 32
fieldwork, 19
filarial worm, *183*
filariasis, 183
finches, 33, *283*
fixed joint, 170
flexibility, 175
flexor, 173, *173*
Focus on Florida
    Florida ecosystems, 446-447
food, 120
    contaminated, 264
    conversion of to energy, 476–477
    energy from, 426, 473, 486
    production of by plants, 474–475
food chain, **429**
food poisoning, 262
food preservation, 266
food web, **430**–432, *431–432*
forensics, 57
forest, 452
fossil, 296-**297**
fossil fuel, *491*
fossil record, 297
fracture, **171**
fragmentation, 339
Franklin, Rosalind, *381*
fraternal siblings, 231
freshwater ecosystem, 454–455
function, **110**, 158
fungus, 261, 263, 426, 473
Fungi, **136**

G

Galápagos Islands, 282, 283
Galileo, 34
gall bladder, 202
gamete, 327
gaur, 399
gene, **348**, *348*, 383
   inheritance of, 348
   traits and, 349–350
genetic disorder, 350, 364, 365, 385
genetic diversity, 365
genetic engineering, **396**, 399
genetic material, 95, 121, 317. *See also* DNA.
genetic mutation, 385
genetics, 56
genetic variation, 286, 288
genital herpes, 230, *230*
genotype, **349**
genus, **132**, *133*
giardiasis and *Giardia lamblia*, 263, *263*
gland, **216**, 217
glial cell, 210, 212
gliding joint, *170*
glow worm, 443
glucose, 260, 475, 477
gold, 84, *85*
Golgi complex, **97**, *97*, *100*, 101
gonorrhea, 230
graph, 43–47
   bar graph, **44**, *R36*
   circle graph, **44**, 482–483, *R34*
   line graph, 46, *R35*
   making and interpreting, R34–R36
   nonlinear, 47
   showing patterns with, 46–47
   slope, R35
graphic organizers, R10–R15
green anole lizard, 419
ground tissue, 107
growth, 316
growth plate, 169
guanine (G), 380, 381, 383
guano, 443

H

habitat, **418**
hair, 248
hair cell, **215**
hammock, 455
hand washing, 267
haploid cell, 327
hearing, 215
heart, 119, 159, 173, **184**, *184*
heart attack, **188**
heat, 477
hemoglobin, 186
hemophilia, 364
hepatitis B, 230
hepatitis C, 264
herbivore, **427**

heredity, 344–355, **346**
   exceptions to complete dominance, 352–353
   Mendel's investigations of, 346–347
   patterns of, 358–367
herpes, genital, 230, *230*
Hershey, Alfred, *381*
heterozygous, 348
hibernation, 125
hinge joint, *170*
HIV, 230, 262
homeostasis, **118**, 125, 126, **160**, 203
   circulation and, 187
   problems with, 161
homologous chromosomes, **326**, 330
homozygous, 348
Hooke, Robert, 74, 76, 77
horizontal (*x-*) axis, 43
hormone, 205, **216**, **224**
   sex, 224, 225
hormone imbalance, 218
hormone levels, 218
host, 263
human immunodeficiency virus (HIV), 230, 262
human papillomavirus (HPV), 230
human skin cell, *74*
humpback whale, *106*
hydrogen fuel cell, 59
hydroponics, 55
hypertension, **188**
hypothesis, **28**
   formation of, 30, R19
   supporting, 38–39
   testing, 29, 32, R19

I

identical twins, 231
immune cells, 217
immune deficiency, **253**
immune response, 250, *251*
immune system, 157, 246–255, **249**
   disorders of, 253
   white blood cells, 250–251
immunity, **252**
immunization, 252
impact crater theory, 20–21
impulse, 212
incomplete dominance, *352*
independent variable, **29**, 31, **42**, 46
infancy, development during, 229
infection, sexually transmitted, 230
infectious disease, 230, 258–269, **261**
   causes of, 262–263
   decreasing, 266
   transmission of, 264–265
   treatment of, 266
inflammation, 249
influenza virus, 262, 264
inheritance, 347, 348–351. *See also* heredity
inherited disorder, 364, 365, 385
injuries, of muscular system, 174

insertion, 385
insulin, 218, 260
integumentary system, 157, 248
Internet source, 35
interphase, **318**
intestine
   large, **200**, 202
   small, **201**, 202, *202*
introduced species, **451**
invasive species, 419, 433
inverse relationships, 47

J

joint, **170**, *170*, 171

K

katydid, *111*
kidney, 203, **204**, *204*, 205
killer T cell, 217, 251
kingdom, *133*, 136
   Animalia, R5
   Fungi, R5
   Plantae, R5
   Protista, R4
Krysko, Kenneth, 422–423
kudzu plant, 433

L

lab safety, R16
labor, 228
lake, 454
Lamarck, Jean Baptiste, 285
land ecosystem, 452–453
large central vacuole, 98, 101
large intestine, **200**, 202
larynx, **190**
law of conservation of energy, **487**
law of conservation of mass, **487**
leaf, 108
Leeuwenhoek, Anton van, 76, 77
Levene, Phoebus, 380
lice, 230, 441
life science, 33
ligament, **168**, *168*, **170**, 171
light energy, 475
limiting factor, **450**
line graph, 46, R35
line of best fit, 43
Linnaeus, Carolus, 132, *132*
lipid, **86**
liver, 159, *161*, **202**
living conditions, 55
logic, 11
Long Horned cowfish, *111*
Look It Up! Reference Section, R1–R36
lung, 190, *191*
Lyell, Charles, 285
lymph, **180**
lymphatic system, 157, 159, **180**–181
   disorders of, 183

parts of, 182–183
lymph capillary, 181, *181*
lymph node, **182**
lymphoma, 183
lymph vessel, **182**
lysosome, **100**, *100*, 101

macrophage, *248*, **250**, *250*, 251
malaria, 263, 265
male reproductive system, 224, *224*
Malthus, Thomas, 285
mangrove, **457**
marine ecosystem, 456–457
marrow, 167, **169**, 182
mass, law of conservation of, **487**
Math Refresher, R29–R36
mathematical model, 48
matter, **486**, 487
   in ecosystem, 489–490
mean, 256–257
measuring
   graduated cylinder, R24
   metric ruler, R25
   ruler, R25
   triple beam balance, R26
mechanical digestion, 199, 201
median, 256–257
medical procedure, 266
medicine, 55, 266
medulla, 211
meiosis, 225, **327**, 338
   errors during, 331
   vs. mitosis, 330
   stages of, 328–329
memory cell, 252
Mendel, George, 56, 346–347
menstrual cycle, 226
menstruation, **226**
messenger RNA (mRNA), 386–387
metabolism, 217
metaphase, 320 *328, 329*
metric system, R27–R28
microscope, 74, *76*
   compound light, R23
   using, R23
microvilli, 202
middle age, 229
Mieschner, Friedrich, 380
mineral, 167, 169
   properties used to identify, R2–R3
mitochondria, **96**, *97, 100*, 101, 476, *478*
mitosis, 121, *121*, **319**, 327, 337, 338
   vs. meiosis, 330
   phases of, 320–321
mode, 256–257
model, 28, 48–49
   benefits and limitations of, 49
   for hypothesis testing, 32
   mathematical, 48
   physical, 48
   representing data using, 48
model car, 59

molecular biology, 299
molecule, 84, **85**
mosquito, 265
motor nerve, 210
motor neuron, 212
mouth, 200
movable joint, 170, *170*
mucous membrane, 248
multicellular organism, **77**, 94, 106
   growth of, 121
   transport systems, 119
multiple births, 231
multiple sclerosis, 218
muscle cell, *172*
muscle endurance, 175
muscle, 167, 173
muscle strain, 174
muscle strength, 175
muscle tissue, 107, 108, **172**
muscular dystrophy, **174**
muscular system, 156, 159, **172**
   function, 172
   injuries and disorders of, 174
mushroom, *426*
mutagen, **260**, 385
mutation, 287, *385*, **385**
mutualism, **440**

name, scientific, 132
native species, **451**
natural selection, **286**–287, 288
negative feedback, **218**
nematode, 183
nephron, **204**, 205
nerve, **212**
nerve bundle, *212*
nerve cell, *158*, 159
nerve damage, 218
nervous system, 157, 159, 160
   central, 210
   disorders of, 218
   functions of, 210
   peripheral, 210
   signals in, 212
nervous tissue, 107, 108
neuron, 210, **212**, 213, *213*
niche, **418**
noninfectious disease, **260**
nonlinear graph, 47
nose, 190, 215
note taking, R10–R13
nucleic acid, 86, **87**
nucleotide, 87, **383**
nucleus, **78**, *78*, 86, 94, *95*
   function, 101
   genetic material in, 95
nutrient, **86**–87, 202

objectivity, 11
observation, 10, **28**, 29

older adult, 229
Olopade, Olufunmilayo Falusi, 194–195
omnivore, **427**
order, *133*
organ, **108**, 159
organelle, **78**, *78*, 94, 95, 96, 100
organisms, 74
   classification of living, 128–141
   elements of living, 84
   interactions among, 436–445
   multicellular, **77**, 94, 106, 121
   naming of, 132
   nutrients needed by, 86–87
   organization of living, 106–109
   response to environment by, 125
   structure of, **110**
   unicellular, **77**, 106, *119*, 119
organ systems, **109**, 110, 156. *See also* body systems.
osmosis, **89**, **122**
osteoblast, 169
osteocyte, 169
osteoporosis, **171**
ovary, **225**, *225, 226*
overproduction, 286
oxygen, 84, 85, 474, 476, 478
   from photosynthesis, 120
   respiration and, 189

pancreas, **202**, *217*
pangolin, *135*
paramecium, *316*
parasite, 230, 261, 263, 441
parasitism, **441**
Parkinson's disease, 218
parthenogenesis, **339**
passive transport, **122**, *123*
pasteurization, 266
pathogen, 161, **248**, 249, 252, 261, 262–263
pedigree, 364
peer review, 22, 34
penis, *224*, **224**
People in Science
   Krysko, Kenneth, 422–423
   Olopade, Olufunmilayo Falusi, 194–195
percentage, **362**
Periodic Table of the Elements, R6–R7
peripheral nervous system (PNS), 210
peristalsis, 200
pharynx, **190**
phenotype, **349**
phloem, 119, *119*
phospholipid, **88**, *88*
photosynthesis, **99**, 120, 474–475, 478, *490*
phylum, *133*
physical characteristic, 131
physical model, 48
physical therapy, *174*
pituitary gland, 217, *217*

placenta, **228**
plant
  as producer, 426
  transport systems, 119
Plantae, **136**
plant cell, *74, 94, 94*
  parts of, 98–99
  photosynthesis and, 474–475
plant organ, 108
plant tissue, 107
plasma, **186**
plastic, 396
platelet, **186**, 249
pneumonia, **191**
pond, 454
population, **416**, 418, 439
  limits on, 450
positive feedback, 218
prairie, 452
predator, **438**, 439
prediction, making, 30, 114–115, R18
pregnancy, 228
prey, **438**, 439
primary consumer, 489
probability, **362**
problem, defining a, 30
procedure, writing, R20
producer, **426**, 473, 486, 489
progesterone, 225
prokaryote, **134**
prokaryotic cell, **79**, 94, 319, 476
prophase, 320 *328, 329*
protective tissue, 107
protein, **86**, 386–387
protist, 136, 263
Protista, **136**
pseudoscience, **12**–13
puberty, 229
pubic lice, 230
pulmonary circulation, 187
Punnett square, **360**, *360*
  patterns of heredity and, 360–361
  probability of outcomes predicted
    in, 362–363
pupil, **214**

R

rabies, 265
Radermacher, Klaus, 56
radius, *166*
ratio, **362**
Reading and Study Skills, R8–R15
receptor, 216
recessive allele, **349**
recessiveness, 352–353
rectum, 202
red blood cell, 158, 166, **186**
red marrow, 169
reference section, R1–R36
Reference Tables, R2–R7
replication, **384**, *384*
reproduction
  asexual, 316, **336**–337, 339,
    340–341
  fragmentation, 339

parthenogenesis, 339
  sexual, 326–327, **338**, 340–341
  vegetative, **337**
reproductive gland, *217*
reproductive system, 156, 159, 222–
  233
  female, 225, *225*, 226, *226*
  fertilization, 226–227
  functions of, 224–225
  male, 224, *224*
  pregnancy, 228
  sexually transmitted infection (STI),
    230
resistance exercise, 175
respiration, *490*
  cellular, **120**, 189, **476**, 477, *477*,
    478
respiratory infection, 264
respiratory system, 157, **189**
  disorders of, 191
  functions of, 189
  parts of, 190
retina, **214**
rheumatoid arthritis, 253
ribosomal RNA (rRNA), 386, 387
ribosome, **96**, 97, *97, 100*, 101, **387**
rib, *166*, 167
ringworm, 263, *263*
river, 454
RNA (ribonucleic acid), **386**–387
robot, 59
Rocky Mountain spotted fever, 265
rod, **214**
root, 108
rough endoplasmic reticulum (ER), 97
roundworm, 263

S

salamander, 443
saliva, 200, 248
salivary gland, 200
Salmonella bacteria, 264
salt balance, 205
salt marsh, **457**
saltwater ecosystem, 456–457
satellite, 55
sawgrass, 455
scapula, *166*
scatter plot, **43**
scavenger, 427
Schleiden, Matthias, 76, 77
Schwann, Theodor, 76, 77
science, **6**
  effects on society, 52–55
  characteristics, 6
  contributors to, 56–58
  vs. pseudoscience, 12–13
  skills, R16–R28
  uses of, 57
scientific explanation, 7, **8**
  evaluation of, 8–9
  evidence for, 8, 12
scientific information, evaluating
  quality of, 35
scientific investigation, 26–37

  characteristics of good, 34
  methods for, 30–31, 32
  parts of, 28–29
  planning, 30
  setting for, 32
scientific journal, 22, 34, 35
scientific knowledge, 16–25, 76
  evaluating quality of, 35
  sources of, 35
scientific method, 18–19, 30–31
  in life science, 33
  uses of, 32–33
scientific name, 132
scientific theory
  acceptance of, 20–22
scientific tool, 19
scientific work, 10–11, 19
scientist, 56
  characteristics of, 10–11
  questions asked by, 6
Scott, David, 34
secondary consumer, 489
sedimentary rock, 296, 297
selection, 287
selective breeding, 284, 395
semen, 224
senses, 214–215
sensory nerve, 210, 211
sensory neuron, 212
sensory organ, 214–215
sex cell, 326–327, 338
sex hormone, 224, 225
sex-linked disorder, 364
sexually transmitted infection (STI),
  230
sexual reproduction, 326–327, **338**,
  340–341
shivering, 125, 160
SI units, R27–R28
sickle cell anemia, 350
sight, 214
simple carbohydrate, 87
sinus infection, 262
skeletal muscle, **173**
skeletal muscle cell, *172*
skeletal system, 156, **166**, *166*. *See*
  also bone.
  bone composition, 169
  functions, 166–167
  injuries and disorders of, 171
  joints, 170
  parts of, 168
skepticism, 11
skin, 214, 248
skin cancer, 253
skin cell, *158*, 248
skin infection, 263
skull, *166*, 167
slope, determining, R35–R36. ***See also***
  graph.
small intestine, *158*, **201**, 202, *202*
smell, 215
smooth endoplasmic reticulum (ER), 97
smooth muscle, **173**
smooth muscle cell, *172*
sneezing, 261
society, impact of science on, 54–55

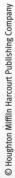